Demographic Change and Fiscal Policy

As public expenditures on health, education, and transfer programs increase, demographic change has a growing impact on public expenditures and the incentives for behavior created by public transfer programs as well. The essays in this volume discuss such timely topics as demographic change and the outlook for Social Security and Medicare in the United States; long-term decision making under uncertainty; the effect of changing family structure on government spending; how the structure of public retirement policies has encouraged early retirement in some countries and not in others; the response of local community spending to demographic change; and related topics. Contributors include many of the world's leading public finance economists and economic demographers.

Alan J. Auerbach is Robert D. Burch Professor of Economics and Law at the University of California, Berkeley, and Director of its Burch Center for Tax Policy and Public Finance. He is a member of the panel of economic advisers of the U.S. Congressional Budget Office, a research associate of the National Bureau of Economic Research, a fellow of the American Academy of Arts and Sciences, and a fellow of the Econometric Society. Professor Auerbach has served as the deputy chief of staff of the U.S. Joint Committee on Taxation and as vice president of the American Economic Association. He also has served as professor of economics and law at the University of Pennsylvania, and he has held visiting professorships at Harvard and Yale universities. The author, coauthor, editor, or coeditor of ten books, Professor Auerbach has also published dozens of scholarly articles in the profession's leading journals and has served as editor or associate editor of the *Journal of Economic Perspectives, American Economic Review, Journal of Public Economics, National Tax Journal,* and the *Review of Economics and Statistics.*

Ronald D. Lee is Professor of Demography and Economics at the University of California, Berkeley, and Director of its Center for the Economics and Demography of Aging. He is a member of the National Academy of Sciences and recently concluded a four-year term as chair of its Committee on Population. Professor Lee is a past president of the Population Association of America (PAA) and is on the Council of the International Union for the Scientific Study of Population (IUSSP). He received the Mindel C. Scheps Award for outstanding contributions to demographic methods and mathematical demography and the Irene Taeuber Award for outstanding career contributions in demographic research. He is author, editor, or coeditor of ten books and is the author of more than 100 scholarly articles and book chapters. Professor Lee's recent research examines intergenerational transfers, and he also works on methods for forecasting population, merging these interests in work on stochastic forecasts of the finances of the Social Security system and of long-term government budgets in general and studies of the fiscal consequences of immigration.

Demographic Change and Fiscal Policy

Edited by

ALAN J. AUERBACH
University of California, Berkeley

RONALD D. LEE
University of California, Berkeley

CAMBRIDGE
UNIVERSITY PRESS

PUBLISHED BY THE PRESS SYNDICATE OF THE UNIVERSITY OF CAMBRIDGE
The Pitt Building, Trumpington Street, Cambridge, United Kingdom

CAMBRIDGE UNIVERSITY PRESS
The Edinburgh Building, Cambridge CB2 2RU, UK
40 West 20th Street, New York, NY 10011-4211, USA
10 Stamford Road, Oakleigh, VIC 3166, Australia
Ruiz de Alarcón 13, 28014 Madrid, Spain
Dock House, The Waterfront, Cape Town 8001, South Africa

http://www.cambridge.org

First published 2001

Printed in the United States of America

Typeface Times New Roman 10/12 pt.   *System* QuarkXPress [BTS]

A catalog record for this book is available from the British Library.

Library of Congress Cataloging in Publication data

Demographic change and fiscal policy / edited by Alan J. Auerbach, Ronald D. Lee.
    p.   cm.
    ISBN 0-521-66244-3
      1. Population – Economic aspects – Congresses.   2. Population forecasting –
Congresses.   3. Fiscal policy – Congresses.   4. Transfer payments – Congresses.
I. Auerbach, Alan J.   II. Lee, Ronald D. (Ronald Demos)

    HB849.41.D464   2000
    339.5′2–dc21   00-037939

ISBN   0 521 66244 3   hardback

Contents

Contents

Figures

vii

Figures

Figures

Figures

Tables

Tables

Tables

Contributors

Alan J. Auerbach
University of California,
Berkeley

Axel Börsch-Supan
University of Mannheim

Steven Caldwell
Cornell University

David Card
University of California,
Berkeley

David M. Cutler
Harvard University

Peter Diamond
Massachusetts Institute of
Technology

Nada Eissa
University of California,
Berkeley

Victor R. Fuchs
Stanford University

Alla Gantman
Boston University

Jagadeesh Gokhale
Federal Reserve Bank of
Cleveland

Jonathan Gruber
Massachusetts Institute of
Technology

Kevin Hassett
American Enterprise Institute

Hilary Williamson Hoynes
University of California,
Berkeley

Thomas Johnson
Cornell University

Laurence J. Kotlikoff
Boston University

Ronald Lee
University of California,
Berkeley

Massimo Livi-Bacci
University of Florence

Thomas MaCurdy
Stanford University

Daniel McFadden
University of California,
Berkeley

Robert A. Moffitt
Johns Hopkins University

Contributors

S. Philip Morgan
Duke University

Thomas Nechyba
Duke University

Bernd Raffelhüschen
Albert-Ludwigs-University of
   Freiburg

Louise Sheiner
Federal Reserve Board

James P. Smith
RAND

Shripad Tuljapurkar
Mountain View Research

David N. Weil
Brown University

David R. Weir
University of Michigan

Robert Willis
University of Michigan

David Wise
Harvard University

Acknowledgments

This book arose from a conference of international scholars held at the University of California, Berkeley. The conference could not have occurred without funding from the Burch Center for Public Finance at Berkeley, and from the Berkeley Center on the Economics and Demography of Aging, funded by the National Institute on Aging, for which we are grateful. We also thank Denise Brauer for her efforts in planning the conference and preparing the manuscript.

CHAPTER 1

Introduction

ALAN J. AUERBACH AND RONALD D. LEE

Throughout the developed world, economies are experiencing two important trends. First, spending by governments is evolving away from the general (e.g., national defense, roads, etc.) and toward the age-specific, particularly social insurance transfer programs targeted to the elderly. Second, the combination of low birth rates and increasing longevity is inducing a marked change in the population age structure, with rapid increases in the old-age dependency ratio. Together, these trends are predicted to lead to very sharp increases in the share of GDP absorbed by government spending sometime in the next few decades, although the timing and magnitude may be expected to differ across countries.

These projections pose several interesting challenges to traditional approaches to the evaluation of fiscal policy. First, they suggest that short-run measures of fiscal balance, most notably the government budget deficit, are grossly inadequate for characterizing the true state of fiscal policy. In particular, this year's U.S. budget does not reflect the very large imbalances implicit in unfunded social insurance commitments. The same is true in Europe, the recent success in meeting the Maastricht debt targets notwithstanding. This helps explain why, in spite of current budget indicators, the United States is confronting the prospect of social security privatization and changes in the Medicare system, and why some European countries are beginning to experience labor strife as they attempt to reduce the generosity of government programs.

Second, because many of the complex demographic factors driving changes in government spending are typically omitted from economic forecasting models, these models are likely to prove inaccurate in projecting what will happen to different spending programs. Third, the

1

changing age structure, combined with the age distribution of fiscal benefits, may upset stable political environments and lead to unexpected changes in government spending patterns. Finally, with changes in fiscal burdens being projected well into the future, the question of optimal policy response requires a much longer perspective than is typical in fiscal policy analysis.

Other powerful demographic changes are also affecting public expenditures. Trends in marriage, divorce, and extramarital childbearing have created rising proportions of single-earner households with children, which are frequently in poverty. Need-based family support systems, such as those in the United States, experience budgetary pressures from these changes, although these pressures are dwarfed by those due to population aging. Immigrants and their families qualify disproportionately for need-based programs because of their often lower incomes and high fertility, while their concentration in the preretirement ages temporarily eases the consequences of population aging, with the longer-term effects open to question.

This book contains the proceedings of a conference held at the University of California, Berkeley, in October 1998, the objective of which was to develop the points raised above (except for immigration, which is not discussed in this volume). The authors and discussants who participated in the project include many of the world's leading public finance economists and economic demographers. The papers addressed theoretical, methodological, and empirical aspects of these problems. The book includes not only these writings, revised in light of issues raised at the conference, but the comments of discussants as well,[1] which have generally been paired to offer a broad economic and demographic perspective on each paper. These comments constitute an important part of the volume, for a breadth of perspective is unusually important for the topics being covered here.

The eight chapters that follow are divided into three groups. The first three focus on theory and methodology; the next two provide international comparisons; and the last three cover effects on the three main types of transfer programs in the United States, respectively, health care, social security, and poverty. Although these three chapters focus on U.S. institutions, their lessons are generalizable so that, like the other chapters, they illuminate the situation facing industrialized economies in general.

---

[1] Two of the discussants, Paul Gertler and Kenneth Wachter, chose not to submit comments for publication.

Methodology

When projecting revenues and expenditures from age-related programs, such as social security, long-range forecasts are essential to understand the impact of demographic changes. The U.S. Social Security Administration, for example, forecasts over a 75-year horizon. However, standard government methods typically provide relatively little information about the uncertainty associated with forecasts or the sources of this uncertainty. Chapter 2, by Ronald Lee and Shripad Tuljapurkar, describes and illustrates the techniques that they and other economic demographers have recently developed to provide forecasts and confidence intervals for fiscal policy variables driven by demographic factors. The authors' results suggest not only that the potential range of outcomes is extremely wide, but also that the "intermediate" forecasts currently utilized in the United States may not provide a very representative picture.

Chapter 3, by Alan Auerbach and Kevin Hassett, applies optimal control techniques to derive government decision rules for responding to long-run uncertainty about economic and demographic factors. There is a tendency in policy debates to view extreme uncertainty about the long run as a reason for inactivity, but one of the results set forth in this chapter suggests that this intuition is generally wrong. Indeed, risk aversion should encourage governments to act in a precautionary manner. The chapter goes on to consider the effects of restrictions on the ability of government continually to undertake "major" policy reforms. As numerical simulations confirm, such inflexibility provides a second reason for precautionary policy actions, although there is an asymmetry to the pattern of optimal responses to fiscal imbalances; policy should respond more forcefully when the elderly are overburdened, for it is easier to spread additional costs over many future generations.

The composition of government spending depends on the demographic makeup of the population. This is true not only because of the uses that different groups make of different government-provided goods and services, but also because demographic changes alter political outcomes. However, the impact of population structure on public spending depends on the structure of government itself. In a federal system, one dimension along which governments differ is the level of government, from national to state to local. While public spending at the federal level may be determined by centralized voting, those at the local level also depend strongly on the sorting of individuals among communities, in a process first elucidated by Tiebout (1956). In Chapter 4, Thomas

MaCurdy and Thomas Nechyba develop a positive model of government behavior. Their model predicts not only how expenditures and revenues of local governments should vary with demographic composition and spillover effects among communities, but also how higher-level governments should intervene to counteract these interjurisdictional spillovers. Using data on California counties, they find evidence in support of their model.

International Comparisons

Countries differ in the nature and timing of their demographic changes and also in the structure and generosity of their social insurance programs. International comparisons can provide insight about how serious the problems of different countries are, and perhaps they can illuminate which elements of program design would likely be most successful in dealing with the coming fiscal pressures. Comparisons can also offer evidence of the political economy of government spending, by relating differences in spending levels and patterns to differences in population structure and government organization.

Chapters 5 and 6 consider the international differences in government spending and fiscal stability associated with aging populations. The first, by Jonathan Gruber and David Wise, summarizes a recent, large-scale research project on international comparisons of old-age pension systems, focusing on the generosity and incentives for labor supply and early retirement that such systems provide. Using the United States as a benchmark, the authors discuss how the programs of other countries differ in structure and how these structural differences contribute to widely varying, and in some instances extremely powerful, incentives to leave the labor force.

Chapter 6, by Bernd Raffelhüschen, provides a European perspective on aging and fiscal health, comparing a number of countries recently analyzed in a comparison project. Using the technique of generational accounting developed by Auerbach, Gokhale, and Kotlikoff (1991), the chapter presents estimates of the fiscal imbalances of each country and decomposes these imbalances, indicating how much is due to changes in population structure and how much to preexisting national debt. Raffelhüschen finds that most of the countries in his sample face substantial fiscal imbalances and that the major part of these imbalances is attributable to demographic trends, rather than past accumulations of national debt.

Program Effects

The book's three remaining chapters all aim at providing estimates of the impact of demographic change on the costs of fiscal programs. In Chapter 7, David Cutler and Louise Sheiner evaluate the impact that demographic change has on medical care spending, currently the fastest-growing and most challenging component of the U.S. federal budget. They start with the well-known fact that medical care spending rises with age and ask what this implies about the level of medical care spending as life expectancy increases. They quickly show why the simplest intuition, that spending should rise because the older spend more, is inadequate, for it uses cross-sectional differences at a fixed point in time in predicting changes over time, when other things are changing as well. Ultimately, they argue, it is necessary to take into account the many factors, such as health, technology, and the market structure of the health care delivery system, that influence age-specific medical spending, rather than simply focus on changes in the population's age structure, to get a picture of what lies ahead.

As many have noted, the U.S. social security system has been an engine for intergenerational and intragenerational transfers, helping older generations at the expense of younger ones and, in general, lower-income individuals at the expense of higher-income ones. In Chapter 8, Steven Caldwell, Alla Gantman, Jagadeesh Gokhale, Thomas Johnson, and Laurence Kotlikoff consider these distributional issues, using a detailed microsimulation model. Their simulations present comprehensive estimates of the rates of return that social security provides, based not only on age and income, but also on race and sex. They also illustrate how the different assumptions underlying the Social Security Trustees' alternative projections translate into impacts on different groups.

In Chapter 9, Robert Moffitt considers the impact of demographic change on government spending on poverty programs. Looking first at the past, he decomposes the growth in spending on AFDC, food stamps, and Medicaid into changes attributable to demographic shifts and other factors. He finds that demographic change, notably the increase in the incidence of female-headed households, has exerted a considerable impact on the growth of AFDC spending. He then considers the evidence for the alternative direction of causality, that is, the extent to which welfare benefits influence family structure. He argues that the rising rate of female-headed households cannot be attributed primarily to changes in welfare benefits. Finally, he considers the future, asking whether demographic influence on poverty-program spending is likely to be important in the coming decades. Using current demographic projections, he suggests that these changes are likely to be modest.

Conclusion

A common theme running through the chapters in this book is the importance of projecting fiscal trends by looking at disaggregated changes in population and how these changes interact with changes in fiscal programs themselves. Another evident theme is the difficulty of doing so, since it is a challenge to make reasonably accurate, detailed projections that extend far into the future. But one will also find advances in the methodology of making such projections and the analysis of how to use them. Thus, the book exposes a vast area for future research and offers some initial steps in the indicated directions.

References

Auerbach, A., J. Gokhale, and L. Kotlikoff. 1991. Generational Accounts: A Meaningful Alternative to Deficit Accounting. In David Bradford, ed., *Tax Policy and the Economy*, vol. 5 (Cambridge, Mass.: MIT Press), 55–110.

Tiebout, C. 1956. A Pure Theory of Local Expenditures. *Journal of Political Economy* 64:416–24.

CHAPTER 2

Population Forecasting for Fiscal Planning: Issues and Innovations

RONALD LEE AND SHRIPAD TULJAPURKAR

Introduction

Is population forecasting different from other kinds of forecasting, that it should warrant its own special methods and its own special discussion? In some important respects it is; in particular, long-term demographic forecasts many decades into the future may contain more useful information than is true for other forecasts, such as turning points. There are several reasons:

1. The initial age distribution of the population provides early information about future population size, age distribution, and growth rates. For example, since their birth, we have known exactly when the baby boom generations would swell the numbers of elderly.
2. The relative slowness, smoothness, and regularity of change in fertility and mortality facilitate long-term forecasts. Compared to real productivity growth or to real interest rates, for example, the vital rates are less volatile.
3. Fertility, mortality, and nuptiality have highly distinctive age patterns, which have persisted over the several centuries for which they have been observed. These regular and distinctive age

We are grateful to Michael Anderson, Timothy Miller, Carl Boe, Ryan Edwards, and Bryan Lincoln for their research contributions to projects on which this paper draws. We have benefited from comments on an earlier draft by Dan McFadden, Jim Smith, and Peter Diamond, as well as by other conference participants. Lee's research for this paper was funded by a grant from NIA, AG11761. Tuljapurkar's research for this paper was funded by a grant from NICHD, HD32124. The authors also acknowledge support by Berkeley's NIA-funded Center for the Economics and Demography of Aging.

7

patterns make the consequences of initial age distributional irregularities more predictable.

Demographers have developed methods and models for exploiting these features of population evolution in their projections. This does not mean, of course, that demographers have built a sterling record of success in long-term forecasting. Their record, which we will review later, has been a mixture of success and failure.

Demographic forecasts have many uses. A few users, such as the manufacturers of infant formula, are interested in the numbers of births by quarter in the coming year. Educational planners are interested in the numbers of school-age children, typically in a local area, over a longer horizon, perhaps five to twenty years. Some users, such as planners for Social Security and Medicare, have a much longer horizon of seventy-five years and are particularly interested in the age distributions of workers and the elderly. Social Security planners also need information on the distribution of the future population by marital status, since benefit payments differ by marital status and by living arrangements. Environmental analysts also have long horizons, but are typically less interested in the details of age distributions. This chapter will focus on long-run forecasts of national populations, and specifically will consider forecasts over a seventy-five-year horizon, with detail on age distribution. Sometimes population projections are used for analytic purposes, to consider the effects of different future scenarios, rather than as predictions. Here, we will restrict our attention to predictions or forecasts. We believe that most, though not all, population projections fall into this category, despite any disclaimers by their authors.

We will also focus primarily on what might be called core demographic forecasts of fertility, mortality, migration, population size, and population age distribution. Many other demographic variables are of interest, but discussing them would take us far afield and dilute our effort. Thus we will not discuss forecasts of marriage, divorce, and the corresponding statuses of the population, household living arrangements, and kinship ties. We refer readers to Mason (1996), Goldstein (1997), Wachter (1997), and the Office of the Actuary of the Social Security Administration (henceforth OASSA) (1997) for work and literature review on these topics. Nor will we consider projections of the health, functional status, disability, or cause of death of members of the population. For these we refer readers to Manton, Corder, and Stallard (1997), Wilmoth (1996), and OASSA (1992). Forecasts of labor force participation, income, education, and related variables are even further outside our scope.

How Demographers Approach Forecasting

Demographers typically approach forecasting through disaggregation. Faced with apparently varying demographic rates, the demographer's instinct is to break the population down into skillfully chosen categories, each with its own corresponding rate. The hope is that by so doing, it will be found that these more disaggregated rates will be found to be constant or to vary in regular and predictable ways. If the population growth rate is varying, perhaps the variation results from constant age-specific birth and death rates applied to a distorted population age structure. If age-specific death rates are varying, perhaps the variation can be tamed by looking at these by cause of death. If age-specific birth rates are varying, perhaps these can be tamed by looking at birth rates by age, parity (number of children already born), and length of birth interval, all broken down by race/ethnic category, for example. To take an interesting specific example, the extremely low fertility in Western Europe might be due to continuing postponements of childbearing rather than a change in the more fundamental ultimate number of births per woman (Bongaarts and Feeney, 1998).[1] This change in timing might be revealed by a disaggregation of fertility by parity (number of prior births) and age. The currently low fertility would then reflect an atypical structure of parity by age in Europe. This strategy of proceeding by disaggregation can be illuminating. However, it is limited by its inability to cope with genuine change in the underlying rates. It is through such genuine change in underlying rates that the population compositions and structures became distorted in the first place, and such changes can be expected to continue in the future.

Certain kinds of disaggregation inevitably raise the projected totals relative to more aggregated projections. This happens because any subgroups of the population that have growth rates above the initial average will grow relative to the other subgroups, and so will receive a

---

[1] If every woman in the population postponed any planned birth for a year during some calendar year, then in that year, the total fertility rate (TFR) would be zero (except for accidental births). From this we can see that if 10% of women postponed their births in a year, the TFR would drop by 10%. We might suspect, then, that if the cross-sectional mean age at childbearing rises 0.1 years in a year, the TFR might be artificially reduced by 10%. If each generation is actually planning on having two children, then such a change in timing could depress the TFR by 0.2 births, making fertility appear far lower than its true underlying trend. Timing changes of this sort can continue for many years, so that the distortions in observed fertility can be persistent. In France, the TFR has been below replacement level since the mid-1970s, although women have been having 2.1 children on average by the end of their reproductive years (Bongaarts, 1998).

greater weight in the average of future growth rates, leading to an increase in the projected average growth rates. The level of the population projections and fertility forecasts of the U.S. Bureau of the Census rose substantially when it began to disaggregate the forecasts by race/ethnic categories a few years ago (although there other causes as well). Disaggregation of mortality by cause of death has a similar effect, when death rates by cause are extrapolated at their historical exponential rates of change. The most slowly declining cause-specific death rate, or the most rapidly rising one, then comes to dominate the total death rate in the long run, so mortality is projected to decline more slowly than is the case without disaggregation (Wilmoth, 1995). Pointing out that this is a necessary consequence of certain kinds of disaggregation does not necessarily help us understand whether the higher or lower projection is more correct.

Demographic Approaches to Predicting Future Change in Fertility

Economic theories of fertility are highly developed, and various models have been estimated and tested. In our view, however, they do not yet provide a useful basis for forecasting fertility. In any event, in order to use any of them, we would first have to develop forecasts of men's and women's potential real wages and nonlabor income, of interest rates, and of some key prices, at a minimum.

Nonetheless, there are some basic theoretical (or commonsensical) ideas that do influence fertility forecasts. The first of these is the idea that fertility is a means to achieve some desired number of surviving children, at least after the demographic transition is under way. Therefore, declining mortality or reductions in the perceived level of mortality are expected to cause a corresponding reduction in fertility. Secondly, avoiding births is costly, either in terms of forgone sexual relations or in terms of the steps needed to avoid conception or to abort a conceptus. Consequently, some portion of actual births to the population is unwanted, in the sense that if avoiding births were costless and perfectly efficient, these births would not have occurred. (Correctly accounting for the effects of mistimed pregnancies is a complicated separate issue.) If technological progress brings us closer to costless and perfectly effective contraception, we would expect a decline in the flow of births and in the number of children ultimately born to the average woman. With these two simple and uncontroversial ideas, we have reason to expect a long-term downward trend in fertility, without applying more interesting but also more questionable behavioral theories of fertility. Of course, both of these effects have a natural limit, which has already nearly been reached in the case of mortality (about 98.5% of all children born survive to age 20 in the United States under current mortality). Unwanted birth rates have also declined greatly in the past forty years.

How about forecasting change in the desired number of surviving births (completed family size)? One approach is simply to ask women, through surveys, how many children they expect to have ultimately and when they expect to have them.[2] Analysis has shown that responses are not highly predictive for individuals, but do much better when averaged for age groups. Because childbearing mostly takes place fairly early in a woman's adult life and because plans change as years pass, data from such surveys are not very informative about fertility more than a few years into the future. Furthermore, if fertility closely follows these plans and expectations, then observing current fertility may provide the same information as the surveys. However, when timing patterns are changing, leading to distortions in the current fertility rate, survey data of this sort may give a truer indication of long-run tendencies. Thus survey data for European populations typically show that women want around two children, although the European Total Fertility Rate (TFR) currently averages only 1.4 children per woman (Bongaarts, 1998).

Demographic Approaches to Predicting Future Change in Mortality

There are also behavioral, biological, evolutionary, mechanical, and statistical models of functional status and survival (see Manton, Stallard, and Tolley, 1991; Lee and Skinner, 1996; Wachter and Finch, 1997; Wilmoth, 1998; and Tuljapurkar and Boe, 1998). With a few exceptions, none is currently a useful basis for forecasting, although they influence the general range of possibilities that must be entertained as possible. The work of Manton and colleagues estimates nonlinear models relating risk factors and lifestyle behaviors to mortality and functional status such that mortality forecasts can be derived if forecasts of the driving forces are available. In our view, the advantage of this approach lies in its ability to link functional status, disease states, and cause of death in a dynamic structural model and to use this model to analyze the consequences of certain kinds of policy-relevant changes. We do not believe it

---

[2] This kind of question has been asked in many different ways: expected, ideal, wanted, desired, desired if life could be lived over, desired given your actual economic circumstances, and so on. Originally only married women were sampled, but more recently the surveys have been broadened to include all women.

will provide more accurate long-term forecasts of mortality, because of the complexity of the approach, the shortness of the available time series that must be used to forecast lifestyle behaviors, the large number of parameters that must be estimated, and the nonlinear way that parameters and forecasted lifestyle behaviors or risk factors interact to generate the mortality forecast.

There are also many empirical studies of mortality change over time, and these make a very useful contribution to the forecasting problem by revealing the pace and pattern of change in death rates by age and sex. For example, it is useful to know that although U.S. female old age mortality has been stagnating for the past fifteen years, elsewhere in the industrial world it has continued to decline rapidly or even accelerated (Kannisto et al., 1994; Horiuchi and Wilmoth, 1995), so there is good reason to expect the mortality decline for older U.S. women to accelerate in the future. The recent stagnation is not a consequence of approaching an upper limit.

Historical and International Analogy

Demographic transition theory is a combination of empirical generalization based on the earlier experience of countries that have already achieved low fertility (until recently, largely European) and some generalizations about the influence of socioeconomic change on fertility levels. Suffice it to say that this theory is of no use for predicting the future fertility of industrial nations. Some projection procedures for countries earlier in the transition have used curves fitted to the fertility and mortality trajectories of countries that are farther along in the transition or have completed it. These procedures have been surprisingly successful, but they are not useful for posttransitional populations.

Implicit Assumptions

Population projections are based on a set of assumptions that are only occasionally stated explicitly. Projections assume there will be no catastrophic event, such as nuclear war or a collision with a large comet. They usually also make no provision for more predictable changes, such as global warming. More generally, projections assume that there will be no deep structural change, in the sense that they extrapolate history and expect the future to be like the past in certain respects.

Most projections assume that vital rates vary independently of the distribution of the population across the categories to which they apply. Put differently, it is usually assumed that there is no kind of feedback in the demographic system. Such an assumption rules out the theory advanced by Richard Easterlin (1968, 1978) that larger generations tend to experience economic and social adversity, leading them to have lower fertility and perhaps causing them to produce fewer births than would a smaller generation. Conventional methods would have predicted a baby bust in the 1950s and early 1960s instead of the actual baby boom, because the parental generations born in the 1930s were small. Similarly, conventional methods would have predicted more births in the late 1960s and 1970s as the baby boom children began to reproduce, rather than the actual baby bust. Easterlin did in fact predict the baby bust, but he also predicted a new baby boom in the later 1980s and 1990s, which never materialized. The dynamic behavior and forecast methods derived from populations subject to Easterlin-type feedback have been studied (e.g., Lee, 1974; Lee, 1976; Wachter, 1991). The U.S. Bureau of the Census actually incorporated feedback in experimental population forecasts published in 1975. On balance, although the feedback models are very interesting, there is not sufficient empirical evidence to justify using them for practical forecasts.

Those who believe that the world population is already unsustainably large argue that the environment will bite back in response to further population growth, leading to higher mortality and lower fertility. Sanderson (1995) has modeled and discussed the projection issues raised by this view. Others suggest that if fertility continues for much longer at below replacement levels (as in Europe or Canada), there will be a public policy response in the form of powerful pronatalist policies. Econometric and demographic studies suggest, however, that the ability of governments to affect fertility in industrial nations is quite weak. Romania achieved spectacular increases in fertility when it suddenly outlawed abortion and contraception, but these gains were short-lived, as fertility quickly returned to its earlier levels. Sweden for a time appeared to have substantially raised its fertility through a combination of policies making it easier for parents to rear children without financial or career sacrifice. However, these policies turn out to have affected only the timing of births, and fertility has now fallen back to its earlier levels.

It is, perhaps, surprising that projections of mortality take no account of forecasts of public expenditures on health care or on medical research, even when both are discussed together (as in Lee and Skinner, 1996).

While many of these assumptions may seem extreme, it is really not clear how one could proceed without making them. Generally, we think it reasonable to proceed in this way.

Assessing Performance of Past Projections

Census Projections of U.S. Fertility

Traditionally, the Bureau of the Census (BC) has focused its best efforts on the fertility forecasts, while the Office of the Actuary of the Social Security Administration (OASSA) has focused on the mortality forecast. For this reason, we will examine the past record of BC for fertility projections and of OASSA for mortality projections.

Figure 2.1 plots all the forecasts made by the U.S. Bureau of the Census since 1949. Where a middle forecast was given, we have plotted that. Where no middle forecast was given, we plotted the average of the two middle-range forecasts. We also plotted the actual TFR for each year over this period. The methods used to make these forecasts have relied to varying degrees on extrapolation, professional judgment, survey data on birth expectations, and basic insights from sociological and economic theory. In our view, the fertility forecasts not only correspond to the view of this official agency, but also reflect the prevailing opinions of professional demographers. The forecasters are competent, and we do not mean to suggest that any of these forecasts was a bad guess in its historical context. The figure shows clearly the severe limits on demographers' ability to forecast fertility. Every turning point is missed, and by and large the projections simply mimic the level of fertility in the years immediately preceding the forecast. Indeed, the ultimate level of the fertility forecast is correlated +0.96 with the average TFR in the five years preceding the published forecast. It is particularly striking that the forecasters do not have in mind a central value toward which the forecasts converge over time. The ultimate forecast levels range from 1.8 to 3.4 births per woman.

Recent fertility forecasts by BC foresee an ultimate TFR of 2.245 (Day, 1996: 2, middle series). In our view, this forecast is unrealistically high. It follows from the assumption that there will be no change or convergence in the fertility of any race/ethnic group between 1995 and 2050 (Day, 1996: 2). The projected increase in the TFR from the current 2.055 to the future 2.245 is due entirely to projected changes in the race/ethnic composition of the population. However, research has shown that when fertility is examined by immigrant generation, there is strong convergence to the level of non-Latino whites after two generations (Smith and Edmonston, 1997). The persistence of high fertility of immigrant groups will therefore depend on first- and second-generation immigrants remaining a constant share of the total membership of the Asian and Latino race/ethnic groups, which is consistent with forecasts (Smith and

14

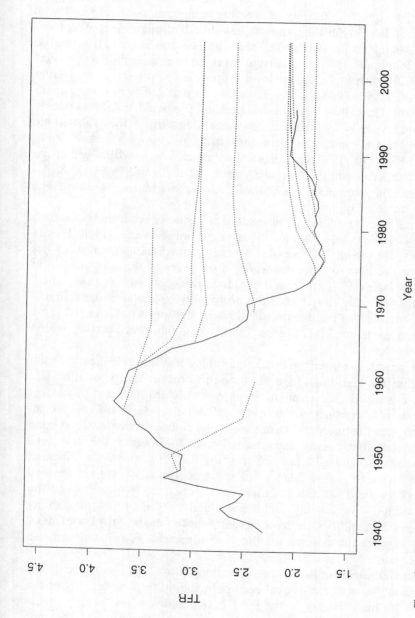

Figure 2.1. TFR: Actual and Middle Series Projections, All Forecasts, 1940–2005. *Note:* Middle series is calculated as the simple average of moderate high and moderate low series when no middle series is forecast. *Source:* U.S. Bureau of the Census, *Current Population Reports*, Series P-25.

15

Edmonston, 1997). However, as fertility drops in countries sending immigrants to the United States, which has been occurring in recent decades, we would expect the fertility of entering immigrant women to be lower on arrival. Fertility in Eastern Asia has already dropped below replacement level in many countries. The Mexican TFR has dropped from a high near 7 in the late 1960s to a current level below 3, with the UN predicting it will reach replacement level around 2015. Yet BC is projecting that the TFR for Hispanic women will remain at 2.98 births per woman until 2050 (Day, 1996: A7). These actual and predicted changes seriously undermine the BC projection of constant fertility within race/ethnic groups. The BC's low assumption for fertility also appears unrealistically high at 1.91 (Day, 1996: 4), in light of the much lower fertility in Europe and lower fertility in the United States in the 1970s and 1980s. OASSA's intermediate assumption is a TFR of 1.9, which we believe is reasonable, with a range of 1.6 to 2.2.

Figure 2.2 is based on the same set of projections, but it shows the high and low brackets for each forecast and does not show the middle. Eleven brackets are shown. For five of these eleven brackets, actual fertility has escaped the high-low bounds *within three years of the base year*; in at least one case (1972), this was before the projection was even published. It is not generally stated what the probability coverage of these brackets is intended to be, but presumably the authors would regard these brackets as having failed, since more than half were wrong within three years.

But what is the intent of brackets of this sort? Because they are used to define the high-low range for long-run brackets on population size and other variables, one might argue that they are intended to bracket the long-run averages for fertility, but not necessarily to capture all year-to-year fluctuations. On this view, one could not say they had been unsuccessful until many decades had passed. However, the violations of bounds in Figure 2.2 are not typically the result of minor blips, but rather seem to reflect longer-run changes. Have forecasters learned from this record? It appears that forecasters quickly forgot about the past volatility of fertility and were lulled by the period of stability between 1975 and 1987, narrowing their brackets as the baby boom faded into the past. The bracket for the 1985 forecast was violated within a single year.

Some indication of the uncertainty about future fertility may be drawn from analysis of the historical record, including the low fertility of the 1930s, the high fertility of the baby boom, and the low fertility of the baby bust. This record suggests that the small variation of the past two decades should not lull forecasters into complacency. Until we

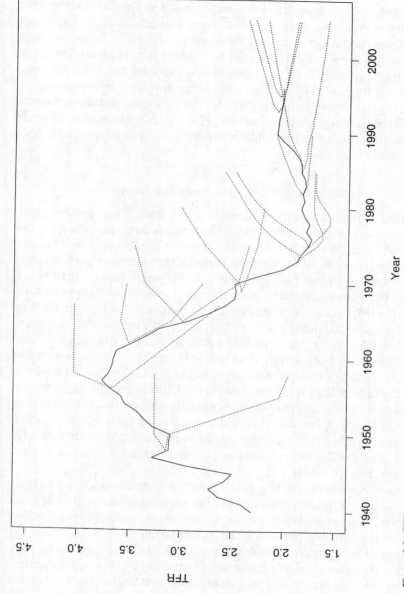

Figure 2.2. TFR: Actual and High and Low Projections, 1940–2005. *Source*: U.S. Bureau of the Census, *Current Population Reports*, Series P-25.

17

understand the causes of the baby boom, we should not dismiss it as a one-time anomaly. Comparison with other industrial and industrializing countries also indicates that caution is called for. The average TFR in Europe is only 1.4 births per woman, and for all the industrialized country populations, including that of the United States, it is still only 1.6. Some populations have TFRs around 1.2 or 1.3 (Spain, Italy, Germany, Hong Kong). It is still too early to say whether these low levels of fertility primarily reflect timing distortions of the sort discussed earlier, or whether they indicate a long-term low level or even a continuing trend toward still lower fertility. Under these circumstances, it would be prudent to consider the possibility that U.S. fertility may be lower in the long run than the 1.6 children per woman assumed in the OASSA "high cost" projection.

Social Security Projections of U.S. Mortality

Figure 2.3 plots the average of male and female life expectancy projections (intermediate, when more than one is available) done by the OASSA from 1945 to the present. Forecasts made between 1945 and 1965 were quite accurate until the early 1970s, when mortality began to drop more rapidly, and life expectancy to rise more rapidly, than anticipated. The period of rapidly rising life expectancy left all the earlier forecasts in error by two or three years, a discrepancy that has persisted up to the present for those earlier projections. Not surprisingly, projections made just before or just at turning points in the rate of change of mortality have fared the worst. Thus the 1974 projection most thoroughly reflects the belief that the slow gains from 1955 to 1968 would continue into the future. The projection done in 1983, just at the end of the period of rapid mortality decline, most thoroughly reflects the belief that the period of rapid gains would continue, leading to early errors of about one year in life expectancy. Examination of the separate forecasts for males and females reveals similar patterns, but with larger errors for females than for males.

This review of the entire past record of OASSA does not suggest any systematic tendency to project life expectancy gains that are too large or too small. But in more recent years, in our view, OASSA has been predicting gains that are substantially too low. This point is supported by comparison with international mortality trends. The population of Japan currently has a life expectancy of 80.3 years. According to OASSA projections in recent years, the United States will not reach 80.3 until just before 2050 (for example, see Trustees, 1998: 60), which seems unduly pessimistic. According to the BC Middle Series, life

18

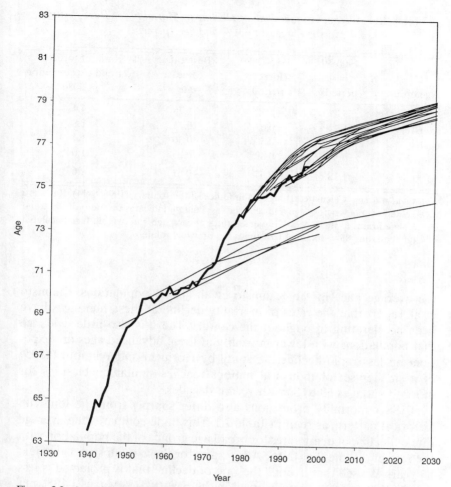

Figure 2.3. Actual and Middle Series Projections of Life Expectancies for the United States, 1930–2030. *Source*: Social Security Administration, Actuarial Studies.

expectancy will reach 80.25 in the United States in 2035. This also seems to us to be too pessimistic. A careful study of mortality trends at ages 80 to 100 in 19 countries with reliable data concludes that "In most developed countries outside of Eastern Europe, average death rates at ages above 80 have declined at a rate of 1 to 2% per year for females and 0.5 to 1.5% per year for males since the 1960s." (Kannisto et al., 1994: 794). OASSA, however, projects a future rate of decline at ages above 85 of only 0.5% per year (see Table 2.1), which is less than half

19

Table 2.1. *Average Annual Rate of Decline in Mortality for Base Period versus Forecast by Age and Sex (percent)*

Age group	1900–91 (base period)	1995–2080 (forecast period)	Base rate – forecast rate	Ratio of forecast to trend extrapolation in 2080
0–14	3.27	1.52	1.75	4.4
15–64	1.39	0.68	0.71	1.8
65–84	0.86	0.50	0.36	1.4
85+	0.54	0.49	0.05	1.0
TOTAL	1.18	0.57	−0.61	1.67

Notes and sources: Calculated from data in Office of the Actuary (1996: 8–14). Rates are unweighted averages across age and sex. The last column indicates the ratio of the trend extrapolated rates to the OASSA projected rates at each age and overall. It is calculated by exponentiating 85 years times 0.01 times the previous column.

the average pace in the Kannisto et al. (1994) populations. Kannisto et al. report that the rates of mortality decline at these high ages have been accelerating throughout the century. There is also little evidence that populations with lower mortality at these advanced ages are experiencing less rapid declines. A study by Horiuchi and Wilmoth (1995) of a smaller set of industrial nations reaches similar conclusions for mortality at ages 60 to 80 over recent decades.

OASSA mortality projections also differ sharply from the long run historical pattern, as seen in Table 2.1. This table compares the average rate of decline of death rates for broad age groups of the population with the rate of decline that OASSA forecasts for these groups over the next 85 years. We see that overall, the rate of decline that is projected is less than half as rapid as that observed in the past (0.57% versus 1.18% per year). This is further evidence that OASSA may be under-projecting future gains in life expectancy.

When we look at the age pattern of the discrepancies, we see that they are greatest at the younger ages, and decline to near zero for the 85+ category. The overall death rate would be 67% higher in 2080 under the OASSA projection than under trend extrapolation. The death rate for children would be 4.4 times as high, for working ages would be 1.8 times as high, for the younger elderly would be 1.4 times as high, and for the oldest old would be nearly the same. There is mounting evidence in U.S. mortality experience in recent decades, as well as in the age pattern of recent international mortality trends, to suggest that OASSA is correct in this regard. Unfortunately, this apparent change in the age pattern of mortality decline means that the improvements in the survival of working age people will be slower relative to past trends, which will adversely affect the finances of Social Security.

Dealing with Uncertainty

Long-term demographic forecasts are obviously highly uncertain, as are most other kinds of long-term forecasts.

Scenarios

The most common means of assessing and communicating uncertainty, in demographic forecasting as in other kinds of forecasting, is to formulate high and low trajectories for the key inputs to the forecast, to combine these into collections of input trajectories called "scenarios," and then to prepare and present the results of at least two such scenarios in addition to the preferred forecast. Often these alternate scenarios are identified as "high" and "low" in some sense. As examples of this procedure, the BC bundles high fertility, low mortality, and high net immigration into a "high" scenario, because all the trajectories are conducive to a high future population size or growth rate. OASSA, by contrast, bundles low fertility, low mortality, and low immigration into a "high cost" scenario, because these choices are all conducive to a higher old-age dependency ratio and higher costs per taxpayer for the system.

The scenario approach does not attach any probability coverage to the forecast bands, and for good reason. Any probabilistic interpretation of the scenarios would founder immediately on inconsistencies. To provide probability bounds for fertility or births in each year, the brackets would have to be wide enough to contain annual blips and drops, but most of this high-frequency variation would cancel out and be irrelevant for the longer-run evolution of the population. This kind of problem infects the brackets for almost all demographic variables that are forecast. Age groups involve summing over births and deaths in individual years, so brackets should be proportionally smaller. Births result from applying birth rates across a broad range of age groups, and again there should be averaging of errors and brackets should be proportionately smaller.

21

Table 2.2. *High-Low Ranges for Forecasts of Selected Items to 2050 as Percentage of Middle Forecast (calculated as 100(H − L)/2*M)*

	BC (1992 forecast, to 2050)	OASSA (1992 forecast, to 2050)	Lee-Tuljapurkar (1994 forecast, to 2050)
Children	±44	±31	±49
Working age	±26	±13	—
Elderly	±27	±9	±10
Old-age dependency ratio:			
65+ / 20–64	±3	±21	±35
Total dependency ratio:			
(<20 + 65+) / 20–64	±10	±0	±24

Notes: Calculated as (High − Low) / (2*Middle). For BC, High minus Low; for OASSA, High Cost minus Low Cost; for Lee-Tuljapurkar, upper 95% bound minus lower 95% bound. The date of publication of the forecast is indicated; all are for the year 2050, which is the latest published by the BC. For BC, "Children" are <18; for OASSA and Lee-Tuljapurkar, <20. "Elderly" are always 65+. Lee and Tuljapurkar did not publish a probability bound for the working-age population, so none is shown.

A related kind of problem comes from the need to bundle alternative trajectories into scenarios, with choices made about how to bundle them, as illustrated by the description of BC and OASSA procedures earlier. Table 2.2 shows the range of uncertainty for BC and OASSA projections published in 1992, with a time horizon of 2050. The numbers in the table are the difference between the high and the low projection, divided by twice the middle projection, expressed in percentages. The BC column indicates a high degree of uncertainty for the number of children, the number in the working ages, and the number of elderly. However, near certainty is indicated for the old-age dependency ratio (OADR), because high fertility leads to more workers and low mortality leads to more elderly, so bundling the two together in a scenario yields very little variation in the OADR. The total dependency ratio (TDR) has larger variation, because it is additionally affected by variations in the number of children, which are not offset. However, even for the TDR, the range appears to be inappropriately small, given the uncertainty about its constituent parts.

The OASSA column shows less uncertainty about each of the population elements forecast, but the OADR has a range seven times as great as that of the BC. The reason is clear: OASSA bundles low fertility with low mortality, and so the uncertainties in the two reinforce, rather than offset, each other. But now the TDR has uncertainty near zero! These kinds of internal inconsistencies are an intrinsic feature of attempts to represent uncertainty through scenarios. The problem is that BC assumes a perfect negative correlation of errors in forecasting fertility and mortality ($\rho = -1.0$), while OASSA assumes a perfect positive correlation ($\rho = +1.0$). In truth, there is little basis for assuming any correlation between the two at all. The last column shows the 95% intervals from stochastic population forecasts (to be discussed later), in which the correlation is assumed to be zero.

Random Scenarios Based on Expert Opinion

A new approach developed by Lutz, Sanderson, and Scherbov (1996, 1997) and Lutz and Scherbov (1998) seeks to avoid these difficulties through a "random scenario" approach. In this approach, the high, medium, and low trajectories for fertility, mortality, and migration are mixed by randomly choosing trajectories independently within the high-low range. The trajectories for each variable maintain their shape across time, but are multiplied up or down by $(1 + \varepsilon_{i,j})$, where i varies over fertility, mortality, and migration and j indicates the particular random scenario to be simulated. Note that $\varepsilon_{i,j}$ does not vary with t, that is, over the forecast horizon. Fertility, for example, will always be somewhat high, or somewhat low, over any particular random scenario. Through random simulation, a set of many random scenarios is generated. Then the appropriate summary statistics (mean, median, probability distributions) can be calculated from this set. Note that the initial high, medium, and low trajectories for the rates are taken as given by this method. In actual applications, they have either been developed through consultations with panels of experts or taken from the ranges provided by government statistical agencies responsible for preparing projections (the various counterparts to BC or OASSA).

This approach does, indeed, seem preferable to the traditional scenario approach, since it avoids the false assumption that fertility and mortality forecasting errors are correlated either +1.0 or −1.0. However, it still assumes that errors in fertility (and mortality) are perfectly correlated over time. If fertility is higher than expected in the first few years of some random scenario, it will be higher than expected for all future years ($\varepsilon_{i,j}$ does not vary with t). In real life, however, fertility rises and falls in unpredictable ways, and mortality declines sometimes rapidly and sometimes slowly. Random scenario forecast sets generated in this way will never allow for the possibility of a baby boom or a baby bust, as episodes occurring along an otherwise medium trajectory. They cannot possibly represent correctly the variance-covariance structure of population forecasts. Whether their deficiencies lead to important quantitative distortions, or to negligible ones, has not yet been established.

Pflaumer (1988) proposed a different approach, which avoids assuming perfect correlation of vital rates in a given year and also avoids assuming perfect intertemporal correlation of errors in each vital rate. He used Monte Carlo methods to draw random values for each vital rate in each time period, assuming some probability distribution for the vital rates within the high-low range that was taken from official forecasts. Pflaumer assumed there was no autocorrelation of forecast errors in the vital rates, which is inconsistent with very high empirical estimates of autocorrelation in fertility and in rates of change in mortality. With zero autocorrelation, most of the year-to-year variance in the vital rates averages out over time, and consequently probability bands from this method appear to be far too narrow.

These difficulties in converting expert views on middle trajectories and high-low ranges into probabilistic projections raise troubling questions about the expert opinions themselves. What question does the expert try to answer, when asked for a 90% probability range for fertility in 2030? Does the expert seek a range that will contain 90% of annual values for 2030 or one that will contain 90% of the long-run average fertility trajectories? This apparently minor distinction alone makes a difference of 40 or 50% in the width of the interval, based on a fitted statistical model for U.S. fertility (Lee, 1993). Does the expert have in mind an autocorrelation structure for the errors? Aside from these questions of interpretation, one might wonder whether an expert would be capable of sensibly guessing at probability bounds with coverage of 90% versus 95 or 99%. We would have great difficulty doing this ourselves.

Analysis of ex Post Errors

Another approach is to use ex post evaluations of the sort produced by Keyfitz (1981) and Stoto (1983) to develop probability bounds for the growth rate and size of the projected population. Stoto concluded that an optimistic standard error for the annual growth rate forecast by the BC would be 0.3%, on the basis of UN projections for developed countries and a pessimistic standard error (based solely on US BC forecast performance) would be 0.5%. The BC itself estimates a mean square error of 0.31% for a ten-year horizon, consistent with Stoto's optimistic interval, and 0.45% for a twenty-year horizon, consistent with Stoto's pessimistic interval (Day, 1996: 30). BC does not report standard errors analogous to Stoto's, so direct comparison may be misleading.

The Time Series Approach to Forecasting Vital Rates and Population

A small literature has developed a different treatment of uncertainty in population forecasting, based on the analysis of historical time series of fertility and mortality. This literature is discussed and evaluated in Lee (1999). Besides the present authors and their collaborators, whose work is discussed below, the main contributors have been Alho (1990) and Alho and Spencer (1985, 1990), Cohen (1986), and McNown and Rogers (1989, 1992).

Over the past decade, Lee, Carter, and Tuljapurkar have developed the time series approach to population forecasting in a series of articles. Lee and Carter (1992) developed a statistical time series model of mortality, and Lee (1993) developed a related model for fertility. These were subsequently used to produce stochastic population forecasts by Lee and Tuljapurkar (1994), which will be discussed at length below. Here, we will briefly discuss the time series models of fertility and mortality.

Mortality

Let $m(x,t)$ be the death rate for age x in year t. Let $a(x)$ and $b(x)$ be age-specific but time-invariant parameters, and let $k(t)$ be a parameter that varies over time but is independent of age. The model used by Lee and Carter was:

$$\ln(m(x,t)) = a(x) + b(x)k(t) + \varepsilon(x,t).$$

None of the variables on the right is directly observable, but the model has a least squares solution, which can be found, for example, by using elements of the singular value decomposition (SVD).[3] The model in fact

---

[3] Lee and Carter then used a second stage, in which the SVD estimates of $a(x)$ and $b(x)$ were taken as given from the first stage, but $k(t)$ was reestimated so as to yield the observed total number of deaths in conjunction with the observed population age distribution. This second step also made it possible to extend the time series estimate of $k(t)$ to years in which only the total number of deaths, but not its breakdown by age, was available. This is useful for countries such as the United States, where there is a substantial lag before age-specific mortality data are published. The estimation can be achieved in a single step by using weighted SVD, where the weights are the numbers of deaths at each age; this method has been developed and applied by Wilmoth (1993), but

has given a very good fit for the time series of age-specific death rates to which it has been applied. For example, it accounts for 97.5% of the variance over time in the age-specific death rates in the United States for 1933 to 1987, excluding the rate for the open interval, 85+.[4] Gomez de Leon (1990) selected this same model in an independent exploratory data analysis of the long historical Norwegian mortality data set. It is important to model the log of the death rates, because otherwise projection leads to negative death rates.

When $k(t)$ declines linearly, each $m(x,t)$ declines at its own exponential rate, $b(x)dk/dt$. The strategy is to model the time series $k(t)$ using standard statistical time series methods. When this is done for the United States, a random walk with drift works quite well, and this is also true for some other countries. The fitted model can then be used to forecast $k(t)$.

Figure 2.4 plots the fitted values for $k(t)$ for the United States, 1900 to 1996.[5] The basic linearity of the decline in k is striking, despite some fluctuations about the downward trend. Surprisingly, the decline in k in the first half of the period is almost exactly equal to the decline in the second half of the period. By contrast, life expectancy declined twice as much in the first part of the period as in the second, but lives saved by falling mortality shift increasingly to older ages, where the increment to life expectancy is smaller because there are fewer remaining years in any case. The figure also shows the 95% probability bounds for the forecast of k. The uncertainty in the forecast of k includes three components: the innovation term in the fitted random walk process of k; uncertainty of the estimated rate of drift in the random walk process; and a 1/97 chance

in this case, the range of $k(t)$ cannot be extended. The second step is necessary to achieve a good fit to the number of deaths or to life expectancy, since fitting the log of the death rates gives extremely low death rates in youth the same weight as extremely high death rates in old age. Lee and Carter took $a(x)$ to be the sample mean of $\ln(m(x,t))$ for each x, arguing that this would best capture the underlying age profile of mortality. However, in this case, the model will not give the best possible fit to $\ln(m(x,t))$ for the jump-off period of the forecast. One can alternatively take $a(x)$ to equal the log of the death rates for the last period observed, which guarantees a perfect fit to the age structure of mortality at that point. Bell (1997) has shown that this gives better forecast performance, at least over the short run.

[4] That is, it accounts for 97.5% of the variance that remains after subtracting the age-specific means $a(x)$. The $a(x)$ factors by themselves would account for a very high fraction of the variance in the $\ln(m(x,t))$ matrix, because average death rates vary by a factor of 500 or 1,000 across age groups in a given year.

[5] Indirect methods were used to fit the mortality model for years 1900 to 1932, before all states belonged to the death registration area. Because of uncertainty about the quality of the age-specific data that has been produced for these years, the use of the indirect method, choosing k to match the number of deaths observed in each year, given the population age distribution, seems preferable.

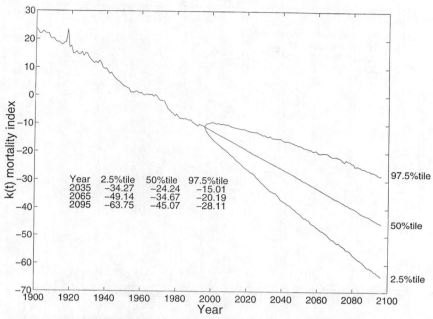

Figure 2.4. Lee-Carter Mortality Index, $k(t)$, Fitted (1900–96) and Forecasted (1997–2096).

each year that an epidemic similar to the flu epidemic of 1918 (a 6-unit increase in k) will occur.[6] In future work, we plan to take into account the fitting errors in the basic model as well. Using the equation given above, the death rates for each age in each future year can be calculated, and from them, any desired life table functions can be found.

Figure 2.5 plots the resulting forecast for life expectancy for each year, with its 95% interval. Life expectancy is forecast to rise roughly twice as fast as under the OASSA projection, which has it rising only to 81.5 by 2070, versus 86.0 here, from a current level of just over 76. The high OASSA forecast is slightly below the mean Lee-Carter forecast. Recall, however, that the Lee-Carter age pattern of decline projects higher survival in the working years relative to OASSA, so that implications for Social Security finances are less severe than one might expect.

Figure 2.6 compares the Lee-Carter (1992) and OASSA (1992) forecasts of life expectancy at birth to the actual data for 1990 through 1997;

[6] In 1918, the epidemic reduced life expectancy by 7 years, but the same increase in k in 1996 would reduce e0 by only 2.4 years.

27

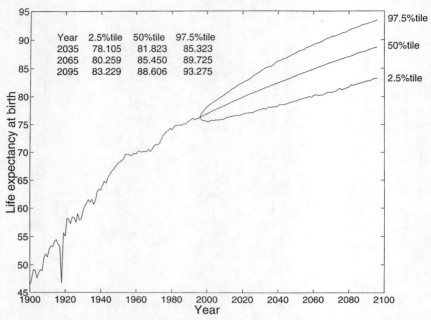

Figure 2.5. Life Expectancy at Birth, Fitted (1900–96) and Forecasted (1997–2096).

both forecasts used data through 1989.[7] The OASSA forecasts are indicated by triangles and can be seen to be on the low side in most years. The Lee-Carter published forecasts are marked by diamonds, and they are all too high. There is, however, an important difference in the source of these errors in the Lee-Carter and OASSA forecasts. The OASSA errors result from a rate of increase that is lower than the actual rate. The Lee-Carter errors result from an error in estimating life expectancy in the jump-off years 1988 and 1989, for which Lee and Carter did not have access to the actual age-specific mortality data and instead inferred mortality in those years indirectly from the published numbers of deaths. This led to an overestimate of life expectancy for 1989 by about 0.3 years, and this error persists in their forecasts. Although wrong in their baseline data, Lee and Carter do appear to have gotten the rate of increase correct. The dashed line, and its bounds, is the fore-

---

[7] The 1997 value is not yet available. The value used here for 1997 was estimated by a regression of e0 on the age-adjusted death rate in recent years, together with the observed age-adjusted death rate for 1997, which is available.

28

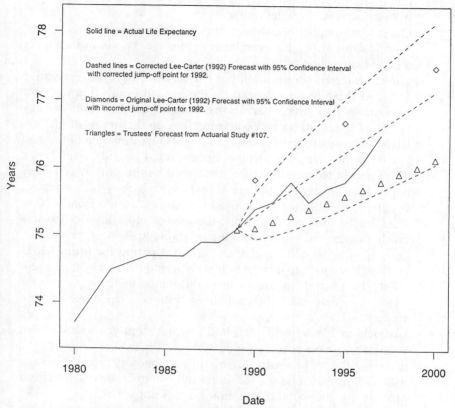

Figure 2.6. Projections of Life Expectancy at Birth, 1990–2000.

cast that Lee and Carter should have made had their baseline data been accurate.[8]

We should note the following features of this approach to forecasting mortality:

- Statistical time series models in the Box-Jenkins tradition were never intended for long-term forecasting. They rely on simple, low-order linear approximations to processes that may be much more complicated. The approximations may work well for forecasting a

---

[8] Accurate forecasts would have been generated had $a(x)$ been estimated at the most recently observed values of $\ln(m(x,t))$, instead of at the sample means (see Bell, 1997). Lee-Carter preferred to use sample means for $a(x)$ on the grounds that they might better reflect long-run age patterns in the future.

29

few periods ahead, but there is no good reason to expect them to perform well far into the future.

- Our model implicitly assumes that variations over time in age-specific rates are highly correlated across age. This is, in fact, quite a good assumption.
- Forecasting errors for mortality will arise from errors in forecasting $k(t)$, and these in turn depend on the explicit innovation term for the random walk process, errors in estimating the drift term, and any errors of specification and conceptualization. Errors from $k(t)$ are likely to dominate errors from $\varepsilon(x,t)$ and from estimation of the $a(x)$ and $b(x)$, after a few decades (see appendix to Lee and Carter, 1992).
- The trend fit to mortality (here described by the drift in $k(t)$) may depend sensitively on the time period over which $k(t)$ is estimated. For the United States, it was most recently estimated from 1900 to 1996. In the nineteenth century, the rate of mortality decline was much slower; indeed, sometimes mortality rose over fairly long periods. How should we pick the relevant period for fitting? It is, perhaps, deceptive to lean heavily on a period defined by data availability. Fortunately, it makes little difference to the U.S. forecast which start date after 1900 is chosen, until one has moved all the way up to 1960.
- Horiuchi and Wilmoth (1995) find that in recent years death rates at older ages have been declining more rapidly than at younger ages, reversing the earlier pattern. Switches of this sort are inconsistent with the simple model used here, but whether this is a serious problem for the method or a minor one is not yet clear.
- McNown and Rogers (1989, 1992) have taken a different approach in a series of articles in which they fit a multiparameter nonlinear curve successively to each cross-sectional set of death rates and then model and forecast the time series of parameters to generate mortality forecasts. Recent reviews and evaluations by HCFA (Foster, 1997), by a NIA/NAS workshop (Stoto and Durch, 1993), and by Bell (1997) have favored the Lee-Carter approach; also see Tuljapurkar and Boe (1998).

Fertility

Building on earlier work (Lee, 1974), Lee (1993) developed a time series model for U.S. fertility. It is conceptually similar to the mortality model just discussed, although the birth rates are not logged. Fertility trends are somewhat different at the older and younger ages, and modeling the log of the birth rates gives too much weight to the very low rates for older ages, making the estimated fertility index (analogous to $k(t)$) behave quite differently from the TFR.

There are two special problems in modeling fertility. First, an ordinary time series analysis leads to long-run forecasts of fertility that converge to its sample period mean, at a TFR of 2.65 children per woman. However, the actual TFR has been at or below 2.0 for the past twenty-five years, and the rest of the industrial world has far lower fertility, so 2.65 seems unrealistically high. Lee (1993) argued that there had been structural change in fertility, due to mortality decline during the twentieth century, improved contraception, and perhaps other changes, such as rising female educational attainment and male-female wage convergence. Because of these structural changes, it made sense to impose a lower ultimate fertility level on the time series process than had been observed in the past, based on extraneous information. For this reason, constrained mean models were used to fit and forecast U.S. fertility.[9] Lee (1993) took a mean midway between the BC and OASSA middle assumptions. In recent work, Lee and Tuljapurkar (1998a, 1998b) have taken the long-run mean to equal the middle assumption of OASSA, or 1.9 children per woman. Tuljapurkar and Boe (1997) have examined the sensitivity of the forecasts to variations in the assumed means, as well as to prior and empirical distributions for the level of the constrained mean. In many cases, the results appear relatively insensitive to such variations. They also found in a retrospective validation test that stochastic fertility intervals perform well in the sense of containing realized future fertility, unlike official fertility forecasts.

Standard diagnostic methods indicate that the fertility series should be differenced before modeling. When this is done, probability bounds on the forecasts widen rapidly with forecast horizon to include impossibly high levels of the TFR and negative ones. Lee (1993) argued that for long-term forecasts it makes sense to use the point estimate of the first-order autoregressive coefficient, which here was slightly below unity, rather than first differencing. When this is done, both the forecasts and their probability bounds appear reasonable.

---

[9] Another special feature is that the TFR cannot be negative, nor can it exceed sixteen or so children per woman, for biological reasons. In practice, it appears highly unlikely that the TFR could again rise above a level of, say, four births per woman in the United States. Lee (1993) imposed limits like these on the model through logistic transformations of the data series and retransformations of the forecast. This approach appeared successful, but subsequent analysis by Tuljapurkar found that the probability distribution of the fertility forecasts was rectangularized, raising the variance. In subsequent work, the constrained mean alone was used. In the forecasts discussed in this chapter, the occasional simulated age-specific fertility values below zero were set at zero, and runs with any TFR >4 or <0 were discarded. Only about 1.5% of runs were affected.

Figure 2.7 plots the historical series together with the forecast and the probability bounds, based on a constrained mean of 1.9, with limits of 0 and 4.0, and an ARMA(1,1) process. Note that the width of the 95% probability bounds widens to 0.8 to 3.0 children per woman by 2040. This 2.2 range is much wider than the OASSA range of 1.6 to 2.2, or 0.6. The figure also plots the probability bounds for the cumulative average of fertility along each sample path up to each date, which is arguably a better basis of comparison to OASSA's intervals. The 95% bounds for this by 2040 are 1.4 to 2.6, for an interval of only 1.2. But these intervals are still not comparable to those for OASSA's scenario method. If OASSA were aiming for a 95% probability coverage by its combined intervals of the eight inputs that vary, that probability coverage would have to apply to the joint variation of the eight, of which fertility is just one. The fertility interval would therefore need to have much less than 95% coverage and therefore would need to be considerably narrower than its 95% range. Taking these considerations into account, the stochastic fertility range does not seem unreasonably wide. Some may think that a TFR of 3 is out of the question for the future. It is important to keep in mind the message of Figure 2.1, however: reality often violates our prior notions of what is plausible.

Without doctoring, time series forecasting methods do not perform well for fertility. After doctoring, one might wonder what useful information is provided by the forecast that was not extraneously imposed on it. In our view, the autocovariance structure of the fertility process is the key information that is derived from the time series analysis.

Migration

Modeling and forecasting net immigration would encounter many of the same difficulties as for fertility, and similar methods could be used to circumvent them. However, because immigration is so subject to policy decisions, we prefer to take the immigration trajectory as given rather than to forecast it stochastically. Lee and Tuljapurkar (1994) assumed that immigration follows the level and age pattern of the middle OASSA projection.

Comment on Time Series Models for Long-Run Vital Rate Forecasts

We do not believe that fitting time series models to indices of fertility and mortality is a panacea for demographic forecasting. Mechanical approaches can produce absurd results, and judgment must enter the

32

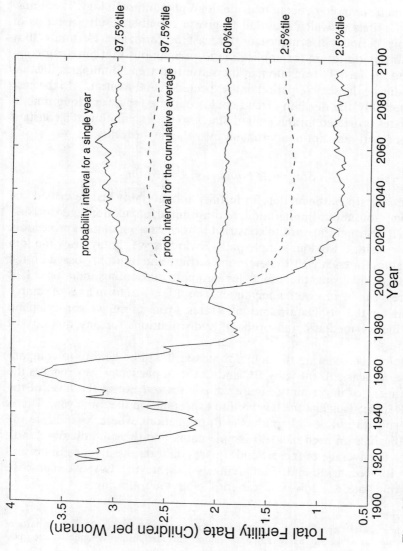

Figure 2.7. Total Fertility Rate, Historical (1917–96) and Forecasted (1997–2096), with 95% Probability Intervals for Annual Values for the Cumulative Average up to Each Horizon.

33

process at many points. The long horizons for which we apply time series forecasting methods violate common rules of thumb, such as not to forecast over horizons longer than one-third the length of the sample period. The time series forecasts must be assessed in the context of other information from biology, economics, demography, and sociology. There may be situations in which they fail to give acceptable results in terms of sample period performance or forecast performance. Certainly they require modification for application to populations that have not completed the fertility transition, in the sense that trend dominates fluctuation during the sample period or is expected to in the future.[10] In the case of mortality, the declining trend could continue for a very long time at the rates projected for the United States, so the assumption of a constant rate of drift may not be a problem over the next century.

Stochastic Population Forecasting

Given the stochastic models for fertility and mortality just described, the assumption about immigration, and an initial population age distribution, it is straightforward to construct a stochastic population projection, that is a single random sample path. To do this, we simply draw random variables for each year to determine fertility and mortality based on the models, and using the usual demographic accounting identities. This process can be repeated many times – say, 1,000 – to form a set of sample paths for the population and vital rates. From these, we can calculate the means, medians, and probability distributions for any quantity of interest.[11]

Before considering the actual forecasts, it will be helpful to compare these forecasts to those by BC and OASSA, particularly as regards the treatment of uncertainty. Figure 2.8 is a scatter plot of the level of the TFR in 2050 against the level of life expectancy in the same year. This is shown for the Lee-Tuljapurkar (LT) projections, where Xs indicate the 2050 values on each of 1,000 sample paths, and the solid diamond indicates the average of these. Solid squares indicate the high, medium, and low BC scenarios, and solid triangles indicate the OASSA high-cost, intermediate, and low-cost scenarios. Note the following:

---

[10] Some analysts speak of the current very low levels of fertility observed in parts of Europe as a "second demographic transition." This idea further complicates the question of whether stationary time series models are appropriate.

[11] Note that the forecasts (expected values and probability bounds) of fertility and mortality from the time series models are not themselves used in the simulations. Instead, many random sample paths are generated, describing a large number of possible trajectories.

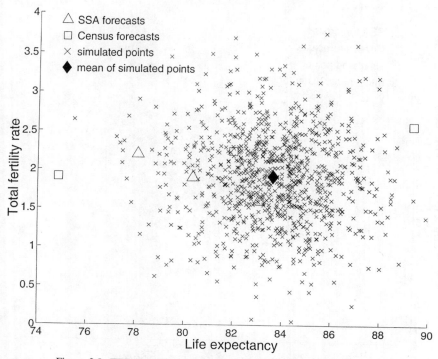

Figure 2.8. TFR by Life Expectancy in 2050 (1,000 simulated points).

1. The 1,000 points from LT sample paths form a circular cloud, while the three points representing the scenarios for BC and OASSA each fall on a straight line, reflecting the assumed correlation of +1.0 for BC and −1.0 for OASSA.

2. The LT range for the TFR (vertical distance) is very much greater than the fertility range for either BC or OASSA. LT assign some small probability to TFR values near 0 and near 4, although TFRs outside that range are assigned probability zero.[12]

3. The LT range for e0 is narrower than is BC's, but it is wider than that for OASSA. The LT e0 distribution is centered higher than that of BC or OASSA.

4. The lines joining the BC and the OASSA scenarios are not orthogonal, because the e0 range for BC is so much wider, which flattens the slope of the connecting line relative to OASSA.

---

[12] When the TFR falls below 0.7, negative fertility rates occur at some older ages. These are set equal to zero.

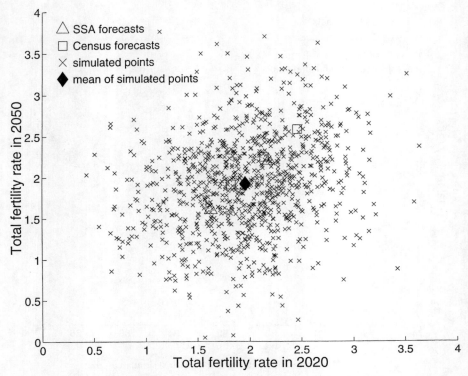

Figure 2.9. TFR in 2050 by TFR in 2020 (1,000 simulated points).

5. The random scenario method, described earlier, could be based on OASSA scenarios. Its randomly simulated points would then all lie within a circle with center on the intermediate-cost scenario and radius equal to the distance from that point to the high- or low-cost scenario (assuming these are symmetrically spaced). Alternatively, the random scenario method could be based on the BC scenarios in the same way.

Figure 2.9 is a scatter plot of the TFR in 2050 against the TFR in 2020. Again, this is shown for each LT sample path, as well as for the BC and OASSA scenarios. The LT Xs are now contained in a large circle, roughly speaking.[13] As expected, fertility is perfectly correlated at these two years in the BC and OASSA scenarios, which highlights one of their major weaknesses. The random scenario method would merely fill in the

[13] Evidently, the strong autocorrelation in the fertility series is quite attenuated after thirty years.

line between the markers for BC or OASSA as the case may be; here, there is no circle. When a similar plot is done for e0 in 2050 by e0 in 2020 (not shown), the general features of the chart are the same, but now the LT scatter forms an oblong with a positive slope, twice as long as high. This shape reflects the greater persistence of random shocks in the mortality model, because it is a random walk.

Forecasts of Population Aging and Total Dependency Ratios in the United States

Figure 2.10 plots the LT forecasts of the old-age dependency ratio (OADR) with 95% probability intervals, together with the BC and OASSA projections for comparison. Focusing on the central forecasts, we note that all agree about the sharp upswing in the OADR from 2010 to 2030, when the baby boom generations born 1946 to 1965 are turning 65. After 2030, the lower mortality projected by LT leads to higher ratios than those predicted by the other forecasts. (Note that the BC ratio is defined over a denominator of 18- to 64-year-olds, compared to 20- to 64-year-olds for OASSA and LT.) For OASSA and LT, the OADR continues to rise after 2040, when all the baby boom generations have already turned 65 and have begun to die out. In the BC forecast, the ratio begins to fall again after 2040, because of the higher fertility assumed by BC. It is important to realize that population aging in the United States and elsewhere is not a transitory event due to the baby boom, but rather a permanent and probably continuing change that is punctuated by the baby boom's retirement. The median LT forecast has the OADR rising to 0.45 in 2072, more than twice the initial level of 0.21. This exceeds the OASSA forecast of 0.41.

Now consider the range of the forecasts. Here, we note that LT has the widest interval (0.29 to 0.79 in 2072), but it is not so much wider than that of OASSA. The shocker is the BC interval, which is less than one-third the width of the OASSA interval and less than one-quarter the width of the LT interval. The reason is that BC bundles high fertility and low mortality together, as discussed earlier, in contrast to OASSA. BC is well aware of the problem and provides a separate scenario to give a more reasonable indication of uncertainty for the OADR, but this discrepancy reflects the deep problems with scenarios.

Figure 2.11 shows the total dependency ratio (TDR) in a similar way. (Note again that BC uses a different definition of working ages, which accounts for the lower level.) LT forecasts a TDR rising to 0.88 by 2070, higher than OASSA's 0.83. The differences in central forecasts are not large, but the differences in intervals are striking. First, note the much

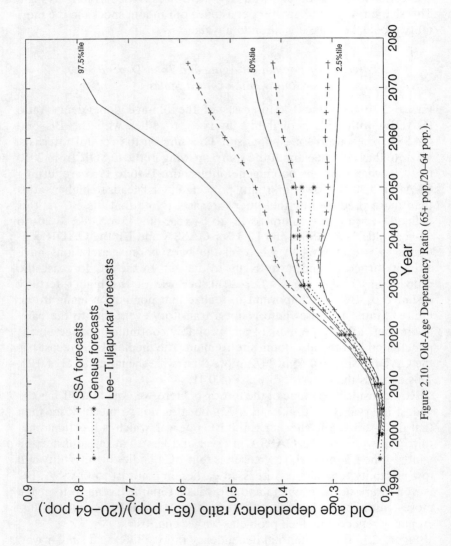

Figure 2.10. Old-Age Dependency Ratio (65+ pop./20-64 pop.).

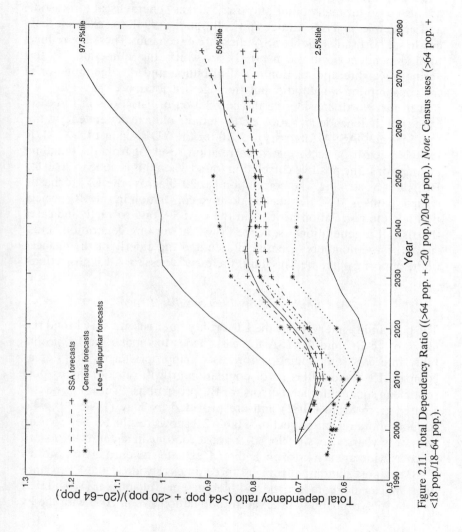

Figure 2.11. Total Dependency Ratio ((>64 pop. + <20 pop.)/20–64 pop.). *Note:* Census uses (>64 pop. + <18 pop./18–64 pop.).

wider intervals for the LT forecast (0.66 to 1.18 in 2072), due to the effect of the wide fertility range on the child dependency ratio. Second, note that the OASSA range is extremely narrow, with practically no range at all in 2050. Again, this is due to the bundling strategy. Although the OASSA projections are focused on the old-age dependency ratio, they are also used for many other purposes, such as general fiscal forecasting and academic analyses. Cutler and colleagues (1990), for example, calculate support ratios for OASSA alternative scenarios. These are refined total dependency ratios (inverted), in which the numerator is the earnings-weighted population age distribution and the denominator is the consumption-weighted population age distribution.

It is also worth considering the correlation of variations in forecasts of the youth dependency ratio (YDR) and the old-age dependency ratio. Plotting the OASSA forecasts to 2070 for the YDR against the OADR reveals a nearly perfect negative correlation, resulting from the bundling assumptions. The positive correlation found when this is done to 2050 for BC is not as striking. The correlation for 2070 across the LT stochastic sample paths is –0.4. Neither the positive correlation in the BC projection nor the correlation near –1 in the OASSA one correctly indicates the risk of a generational squeeze in which working generations must support large numbers of both children and the elderly or the chances of the opposite outcome. This limits their usefulness for fiscal projections.

Are the Probability Intervals Too Broad?

The probability intervals for the LT fertility forecasts are very broad relative to the BC and OASSA forecasts. Does this make the LT probability intervals for population forecasts inappropriately wide? Let us compare LT standard errors of population growth rates to the ex post root mean squared forecast errors for BC projections.[14] These can be calculated from Stoto (1983) and are provided by Day (1996: 30), who includes more recent projections. Table 2.3 shows results for horizons up to twenty years. Day's (1996: 30) ex post root mean squared errors are twice as wide at each horizon as the LT ex ante standard errors. Stoto's (1983) ex post standard errors are three times as wide as the LT ex ante ones. We can also compare the width of the Lee-Tuljapurkar (1994: 1185) ex ante 95% probability interval for population size in 2050 with the ex

---

[14] By construction, the LT forecasts have the correct long-term mean, whereas this is not true of the BC or OASSA forecasts. For this and other reasons, we should expect narrower intervals for the LT forecasts than would be estimated from ex post analysis of BC or OASSA forecast performance.

Table 2.3. *Standard Errors for Forecasts of Annual Population Growth Rate by Horizon (percent)*

Forecast Horizon (Years)	BC, by Day (1996)	BC, by Stoto (1983)	Lee-Tuljapurkar (stoch. sim.)
5	0.17	0.38	0.13
10	0.31	0.48	0.17
15	0.40	0.61	0.18
20	0.45	0.65	0.19

Notes and sources: Calculations by Day (1996: 30) and Stoto (1983) are ex post analyses of the difference between the projected and the actual average population growth rate for each horizon, based on forecasts from 1945 to 1970 (Stoto) or 1950 to 1992 (Day). The Lee-Tuljapurkar figures are based on the standard error of projected growth rates on individual sample paths around the mean forecast.

ante high-low population size forecast of BC (Day, 1993); they match almost exactly. Since the Lee-Tuljapurkar method for generating the median or mean forecast is very different from that of BC, there is no reason why the stochastic ex ante standard errors should match the ex post or ex ante uncertainty of BC forecasts. However, these comparisons do make it clear that the LT probability intervals for population size or growth rate are not wider than either the ex post or the ex ante BC intervals, despite the much greater ranges for fertility that are incorporated in the stochastic forecasts. The stochastic intervals are, quite appropriately, wider for other demographic quantities, such as the total dependency ratio, which involves less averaging and cancellation across errors than do population size or growth rate.

Stochastic Demographic Forecasts Applied to Government Budgets

General Approach

These stochastic population projections can be used as a basis for stochastic projections of government budgets. The Congressional Budget Office (CBO) has drawn on the Lee-Tuljapurkar set of stochastic simulations to construct long-term probabilistic projections of the federal budget (CBO, 1996, 1997, 1998). Over the past few years, Lee and Tuljapurkar have developed their own set of stochastic budget projections, with a special emphasis on social security (Lee and Tuljapurkar, 1998a, 1998b), but more recently including forecasts for government budgets in general (Lee, Tuljapurkar, and Edwards, 1998). Here, we will give a few illustrations and sketch the general approach.

In addition to the stochastic demography, which has already been described, we develop simple time series models for real productivity growth (purged of age composition effects), real interest rates (return on treasury bills held by the Social Security Administration), and, in some applications, the return on stock market equity. In all cases, we use constrained-mean models. For most of the work, productivity growth rates and interest rates are modeled as independent time series, but when the return on equity is included, a Vector Autoregressive (VAR) model is used. Future work will seek to treat inflation and unemployment in similar ways. We do not incorporate any feedback from the outcomes of our budget projections to these economic variables. It may seem odd to treat only four or five variables as stochastic, while treating many other important and uncertain variables, such as health care costs per enrollee, future disability rates, or defense expenditures as if their future trajectories were known with certainty. The structure of transfer programs is constantly changing, yet we take these as frozen for the next seventy-five years by current legislation. We do not have a good response to this objection. Perhaps these stochastic forecasts should be taken as indicating a lower bound on uncertainty about the future. Perhaps they should be viewed as forecasts conditional on some assumptions known to be unrealistic, yet capable of shedding light on the long-term viability of those assumptions.

Using the *Current Population Survey* and published Social Security Administration data, we have estimated average cross-sectional age profiles of tax payments (for seven kinds of federal, state, and local taxes) and costs of program use (for twenty-eight kinds of federal, state, and local services, including some that are quasi-public goods). In most cases, age schedules for both tax payments and costs of benefits are shifted each year with productivity growth, while debt or trust fund projections are based on government deficits or surpluses and the interest rate (or, in some experiments for Social Security, the rate of return on equities for a portion of the trust fund). We have generally tried to follow the approach and assumptions of the long-run projections by the CBO, except in a few respects. We do forecasts under a variety of assumptions about budget balancing; for example, we assume that payroll tax rates are varied so as to keep the Social Security trust fund equal to 100% of the following year's expenditures and that all other tax rates are varied so as to prevent the federal debt-to-GDP ratio from exceeding 0.8.

We modify our estimated age profiles for Social Security to reflect legislated changes in the normal retirement age (NRA) and experiment with further variations in the NRA. We follow the health care cost assumptions of the Medicare Trustees (Board of Trustees, 1996), which imply that the rate of increase in per enrollee costs will decline gradually to the rate of productivity growth over the next few decades (see also Lee and Skinner, 1999). We depart from the Medicare Trustees' procedures in explicitly distinguishing among the health costs at each age of those dying within a year, those dying within one to three years, and all others (Lubitz, Beebe, and Baker, 1995; Miller, 1998). This leads to lower cost projections, because declining mortality now has little effect on total health care costs, since increases in the elderly population at each age are offset by decreases in the proportion of elderly who are within three years of death at each age. As a consequence, uncertainty about the future course of mortality is largely filtered out, and the health cost projections therefore have narrower intervals than they would otherwise.

Fiscal Implications of Demographic Change

Figure 2.12, drawn from Lee, Tuljapurkar, and Edwards (1998), show the forecasts and probability intervals for government expenditures (under currently legislated benefit structures) separately for programs that are primarily directed toward the elderly, primarily directed toward children, or primarily age neutral.[15] Panel D of Figure 2.12 shows overall expenditures, the aggregate of these other three. Focusing on central values, we see that old-age expenditures will rise dramatically from 8.5% of GDP to 22.5%, reflecting both population aging and rising health costs per enrollee. Expenditures on children remain flat, as do age-neutral expenditures. Total government expenditures rise in line with the expenditures for the elderly.

The shapes of the probability fans are very different. The fan for children is very narrow for the first five years before the uncertain births reach school age, but after this the fan opens up very rapidly because of uncertain fertility and then levels off. For the elderly, the beginning of the fan is quite narrow, since only uncertain mortality is affecting the numbers of elderly. The aging of the baby boom is predictable with only moderate uncertainty, but the number of workers who will generate GDP becomes increasingly uncertain, widening the fan on expenditures as a share of GDP. Finally, once the uncertain births begin to retire, sixty

---

[15] The programs have been grouped by age according to the average dollar-weighted age of program beneficiaries. Lee, Tuljapurkar, and Edwards (1998) carried out a similar analysis, but strictly separated out expenditures at each age, rather than treating whole programs as the unit. The results are very similar.

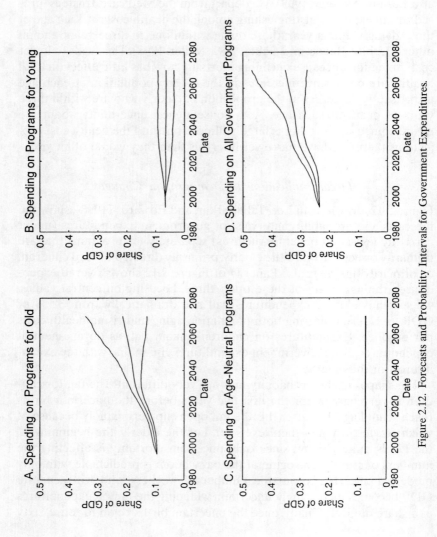

Figure 2.12. Forecasts and Probability Intervals for Government Expenditures.

or so years into the forecast, the fan widens rapidly. The age-neutral forecasts are highly certain, since many are a constant share of GDP by assumption, and only the Earned Income Tax Credit is age dependent. The shape of the overall fan reflects these three components and the covariations among them.

The analysis in Lee, Tuljapurkar, and Edwards (1998) indicates that the OASDI program accounts for less than 30% of the increase in expenditures on the elderly, with combined health care programs accounting for 57% of the increase. Fixing Social Security will not by itself solve the long-run budgetary problems, although it obviously must be an important part of any solution.

Social Security

According to the most recent Trustees' Report (Board of Trustees, 1998: 23), long-run actuarial balance could be restored through 2072 if the payroll tax rate were raised by 2.19%. We have examined this policy option using our stochastic simulations and found that with a 2% increase, there would still be a 75% probability of exhaustion before 2070. Policies that appear to work well in the mean often turn out to fail in the majority of cases in our simulations.

Here we will show results of three different kinds of stochastic forecasts, each conditional on a different assumption about policy. First, consider the tax rate necessary each year to provide a reserve fund equal to 100% of the next year's expenditures on benefits, where the tax rate is left fixed at the current 12.4% until it needs to be raised to meet this condition. The resulting probability distributions for the payroll tax rate are shown in Figure 2.13. The median tax would remain at 12.4% until 2022, rise rapidly as the baby boom retires, and then rise more slowly to 21% in 2070, doubling from its initial value. The lower 0.025 probability bound remains at 12.4% until 2043 and then rises modestly to 15% in 2070. The upper 97.5% bound rises roughly linearly from 2003 to 34% in 2070. These projected payroll tax rates are conceptually similar to the Social Security Administration (SSA) cost rate projections, for expenditures as a percent of payroll. Their high-medium-low cost rates for 2070 are 29%, 20%, and 14% (Board of Trustees, 1998: 109), which may be compared to our 34%, 21%, and 15%.

We next consider the effects of investing part of the trust fund in equities, with a stochastic return constrained to have a long-run mean of 7% (real). Figure 2.14 plots histograms for the date of trust fund exhaustion. Panel A shows that under the current policy of investing 100% in treasury bills there is only a 2.5% chance of nonexhaustion before 2071, with

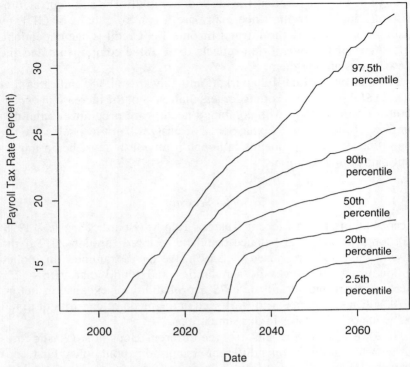

Figure 2.13. Tax Rate for Year-Ahead Balance (*distribution by selected probability percentiles*).

a median date of exhaustion around 2031, consistent with SSA projections. Panel B shows that if 50% of the fund were invested in equities by 2010, the median date of exhaustion would move back slightly to 2037 and the chance of nonexhaustion by 2071 would rise to 16.7%. Panel C considers what would happen if 90% of the fund were invested in equities in 2000. In a deterministic simulation of this policy, the fund balance would still be positive after a century, in 2097, so this approach appears very promising. However, the stochastic simulation shows that the median date of exhaustion would be pushed back only to 2045, and there would still be a two-thirds chance of fund exhaustion by 2072.[16]

---

[16] The fund balance implied by the deterministic scenario with 90% of the trust fund invested in equities rises to 40% of GDP by 2050. The distributions of fund balances are highly skewed in stochastic simulations, with means far exceeding medians. For example, in 2050 the mean fund-to-GDP ratio is 85%, while the median is −8%.

46

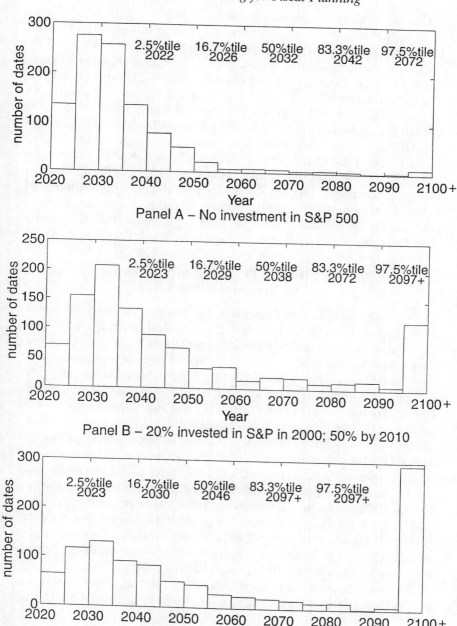

Figure 2.14. Histograms of 1,000 Dates of Exhaustion for Three Investment Scenarios.

Our last example considers the effects of increasing the NRA. Panel A of Figure 2.15 shows a histogram for the long-run actuarial balance (1998–2072) under current legislation (which raises the NRA to 67 by 2022). The median actuarial balance is –2.4%, not much different from the intermediate Trustees' (Board of Trustees, 1998: 23) value of –2.19%. The 95% interval is –6.26% to –0.01%, which is quite similar to the Trustees' range of –5.4% to +0.25%. Panel B shows the distribution if the NRA is increased to age 70 by 2033. The median has now moved up to –1.37%, and the 95% interval has moved up to –4.4% to +0.63%. Panel C shows the distribution if the NRA is increased to 71 years by 2022. The median actuarial balance is now +0.24%, and the 95% range is –1.79% to +1.61%. There is still a 34% probability of fund exhaustion before 2070 under this scenario, but there is also a 15% chance that the trust fund in 2072 would exceed $20 trillion (of course, with this large a trust fund, the assumption of no economic feedback is unacceptable).

The Past Record of Projections of Social Security Finances by the Trustees

The OASSA has occasionally published evaluations of the performance of their projections, but these have been of limited scope. The most comprehensive we could find was that of Bayo (1990), which examines projections made from 1980 to 1989. Bayo (1990: 1) argues convincingly that the cost rate (i.e., program costs as a proportion of taxable payroll) is the most suitable item for ex post analysis, because it is less subject to policy changes than the others. Bayo (1990: 12) concluded that projections of cost rates done in 1983 to 1990 were generally pessimistic relative to subsequent reality, which he attributes to the economic recovery during this period. We present a more comprehensive analysis of the performance of projections done between 1950 and 1989. Before 1972, the projections used a "level earnings, level benefits" method, which made no attempt to take into account the effect on benefits of future productivity growth. The projections properly made no attempt to project the sporadic changes in legislated benefit. We have adjusted these projections ex post to reflect the actual benefit changes that subsequently occurred, providing a more comparable series (Lee and Miller, 1998).

The first column of Table 2.4 gives average forecast errors by forecast horizon, where errors are measured as (Actual – Projected)/Actual.[17] The

---

[17] Bayo (1990) estimates errors as (Actual – Projected)/(Taxable Earnings) and concludes the projections have been successful because the errors were generally less than 0.8%. However, since costs were around 11% over this period, an error of 0.8% is better viewed as a 7% error (0.07 = 0.8/11), which is less satisfactory.

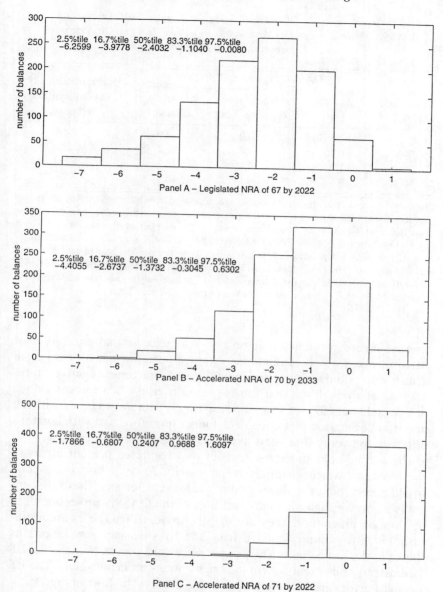

Figure 2.15. Histograms of 1,000 Actuarial Balances in 2072 for Three Retirement Age Scenarios. *Note*: Balances were calculated as percentages.

Table 2.4. *Errors of Cost Rate Forecasts from ex Post Analysis of OASSA Projections and ex Ante Analysis of Lee-Tuljapurkar Stochastic Forecasts by Horizon (percent)*

Years since Forecast	OASSA Forecasts, 1950–1989			Standard Error of Lee-Tuljapurkar Forecast
	Average Error	Root Mean Squared Error	Forecast Range	
1–4	–2.6 (7)	3.0	2.9	2.4
5–14	+0.2 (25)	7.0	11.2	5.5
15–24	–1.2 (26)	11.1	13.3	6.8
25–34	+3.6 (16)	9.1	16.9	7.9

Notes and sources: The first three columns are calculated from all available Reports of the Trustees from 1950 through 1989, with the average error calculated as (Actual – Projected)/Actual. Numbers in parentheses represent the number of observations on which the average is based. The OASSA forecasts have been adjusted to reflect subsequent unanticipated changes in legislated benefit levels, modifying the pre-1972 "level earnings, level benefit" forecasts. The OASSA Forecast Range is calculated from Board of Trustees (1998: 169–170) as 100 * (High – Low)/(2 * Intermediate). The Lee-Tuljapurkar standard errors are calculated from the stochastic simulations as (Actual – Forecast)/Actual.

average errors in the first column reveal an excellent adjusted forecast performance, with no evident bias. Average percentage errors are small at all horizons and are sometimes positive and sometimes negative. More-detailed analysis shows that this is generally true when forecasts done before and after 1972 are examined separately (not shown here), with the important exception that after 1972, longer-term forecasts with horizons of fifteen to twenty-four years averaged a negative error of 12.0%.

The second column shows the root mean squared percent errors of the forecasts, which generally increase with forecast horizon, as one would expect, but drop down a bit at the longest horizon. These are generally narrower than the high-low range of the OASSA projections, but of a similar magnitude. They are slightly broader than the ex ante forecast standard errors calculated from the LT stochastic simulations, as shown in the last column. This is what we would expect, because the LT forecasts by construction have the "right" long-run mean values. The LT standard errors are half the width of the Trustees' high-low range.

Conclusion

We begin by summarizing our main points and then conclude with thoughts about the uses to which stochastic forecasts might be put.

Summary

Assessing Recent Official U.S. Vital Rate Forecasts

- In retrospect, it appears that over the last fifty years, both the BC and OASSA forecasters attached too much importance to the most recently observed levels or rates of change of fertility and mortality.
- Recent BC projections of U.S. fertility, based on race/ethnic disaggregation, appear to be too high. Recent OASSA fertility projections appear reasonable, although the range may be too narrow in light of international experience.
- Recent projections of life expectancy gains by both the BC and OASSA appear to be substantially too low, in light of past U.S. experience and international levels and trends in low-mortality countries.

Uncertainty in Population Forecasts

- The standard method for dealing with uncertainty in demographic (and many other) forecasts is the use of high, medium, and low scenarios. This approach is deeply flawed, because it is based on very strong and implausible assumptions about the correlation of forecast errors over time and between fertility and mortality. The random scenario method is an improvement, but it retains some of the same flaws.
- Stochastic population forecasts based on time series models of vital rates (Lee-Tuljapurkar, 1994) appear to offer some important advantages, although long forecast horizons in demography far exceed the intended use of these models, and it is necessary to impose external constraints on the models in some cases to obtain plausible forecast behavior. One should not rely on mechanical time series forecasts, in any case; they should be assessed in relation to external information.
- A parsimonious time series model for mortality appears to perform well within sample in applications in various countries and suggests future life expectancy gains in the United States at roughly twice the rate projected by the BC and OASSA.

Results of Population Forecasts

- Middle forecasts by the BC, OASSA, and Lee-Tuljapurkar (LT) agree closely on the timing and extent of increase in old-age dependency ratios as the baby boom ages (although the LT projections are somewhat higher because of lower mortality), but the BC forecasts show some amelioration after 2040, due to higher fertility. After 2040, the LT forecasts continue to increase, doubling to 0.45 by 2070, while the OASSA forecasts increase to 0.41. The OASSA range is three times as wide as that of the BC, reflecting inherent flaws in the scenario method.

- Middle forecasts of the total dependency ratio by the BC and LT agree fairly closely, but are somewhat higher than the OASSA forecast (the LT prediction is 0.88 in 2070; the OASSA one is 0.83). The OASSA range is extremely narrow, reflecting inherent flaws in the scenario method, but the BC range is far too narrow as well.
- In BC forecasts, the correlation between errors in forecasting youth dependency ratios and old-age dependency ratios is close to –1.0. In BC forecasts, it is moderately positive. These correlations result from the bundling of assumptions in scenarios. LT forecasts show a correlation of –0.6 to –0.4, indicating partially offsetting variations in the proportions of children and elderly, as one would expect.

Stochastic Fiscal Projections
- We did an analysis of the performance of OASSA projections of cost rates since 1950, for forecast horizons of up to thirty-five years. Performance was generally very good, with no systematic bias, small average errors, and root mean squared errors smaller than the published high-low ranges. Projections done from the mid-1970s to the mid-1980s have underprojected costs by 12%, however.
- Middle forecasts by Lee, Tuljapurkar, and Edwards (1998) suggest that government expenditures on the elderly will increase by over 150% in relation to GDP by 2070, while expenditures on children and age-neutral expenditures will remain flat. Taxes rise from 24% as of 1997 to 38% of GDP in the median forecast to 2070 (if debt/GDP is constrained), while the 95% probability range for taxes in 2070 goes from 25% to 53% of GDP.
- Increased costs of Social Security excluding Medicare account for nearly 30% of the increase in expenditures on the elderly, but a larger share, 57%, is due to health costs in the median forecast. Fixing Social Security will not take care of the long-term budget problem.
- Investing 90% of the Social Security reserve fund in equities yielding 7% (real) would fix the system according to a deterministic simulation, but in a stochastic forecast, there is still a two-thirds chance of exhaustion, with a median exhaustion date of 2044 and a negative median (but strongly positive mean) fund balance in 2050.
- Raising the payroll tax rate by 2% immediately should nearly put the system in long-term actuarial balance according to OASSA

projections, but still leaves a 75% chance of fund exhaustion before 2070 in LT stochastic forecasts.

- Raising the normal retirement age to 71 by 2023 raises the median long-term actuarial balance above zero in LT stochastic forecasts, but still leaves a 43% chance of fund exhaustion before 2070.

Some Possible Uses for Stochastic Population Forecasts and Demographically Based Stochastic Fiscal Forecasts

Once our research project had progressed to the point of producing stochastic population projections, we found that people were not sure how they differed from conventional scenario-based forecasts, nor was it clear how and why they might be used. We decided that we should develop some applications ourselves, or otherwise the projections would most likely languish in academic journals. This decision led to the stochastic projections of government budgets that we have described and illustrated in this paper. Now the question arises, What use are these stochastic fiscal forecasts? How might they be put to use?

We suggest that policies be viewed as filters that attenuate or amplify the consequences of variance and uncertainty. Any calculation that can be done recursively along a deterministic economic-demographic trajectory can also be done along each of the thousand sample paths in a stochastic simulation set. Proceeding in this way, it should be straightforward to evaluate the success of different policies in dealing with uncertainty. One of the most basic questions is the following: In the face of uncertainty about the future finances of the Social Security system, should we accumulate a large reserve fund to buffer the system against likely future adversity, or should we tailor our policy to future realities as they unfold? Of course, we would like to achieve a high expected rate of return, by keeping taxes low and benefits high. But there are also specific concerns with variability. Given the nonlinearity of the deadweight loss function for taxes, there is an advantage to avoiding unnecessary changes in tax rates. Considerations of intergenerational equity argue for equalizing cohort rates of return, in the context of changing tax and benefit regimes and increasing survival in old age. Given an appropriate loss function, the success of alternative policies in handling uncertainty could be assessed. Alternatively, more-formal methods might be used to calculate the optimal tax rate trajectory. Issues of this sort are considered by Auerbach and Hassett in Chapter 3.

The stochastic simulations could also be used as a testing ground for theoretical ideas developed using simpler but unrealistic models.

Smetters (1998) finds that in a stochastic overlapping-generations economy with two population age groups, prefunding a public defined-benefit pension system like our Social Security would reduce ex ante unfunded liabilities much more than would replacing it with a system of private accounts, when in both cases funds are invested in equities. The older literature debated whether in an unfunded system intergenerational inequities would be better smoothed by a defined-contribution or a defined-benefit system. Stochastic fiscal and demographic forecasts could readily be used to examine issues of this sort.

We hope that the availability of the stochastic simulations/forecasts will stimulate others to think about potential uses and to put them to use in new ways.

References

Alho, Juha M. 1990. Stochastic Methods in Population Forecasting. *International Journal of Forecasting* 6:521–30.

Alho, Juha M., and Bruce D. Spencer. 1985. Uncertain Population Forecasting. *Journal of the American Statistical Association* 80:306–14.

———. 1990. Error Models for Official Mortality Forecasts. *Journal of the American Statistical Association* 85:609–16.

Bayo, Francisco R. 1990. *A Simple Evaluation of Projections in OASDI Trustees Reports*. Actuarial Note 132 of the Social Security Administration, U.S. Department of Health and Human Services.

Bell, William. 1997. Comparing and Assessing Time Series Methods for Forecasting Age-Specific Demographic Rates. *Journal of Official Statistics* 13:279–303.

Board of Trustees, The Federal Hospital Insurance Trust Fund. 1996. *The 1996 Annual Report of the Board of Trustees of the Federal Hospital Insurance Trust Fund*. 104th Congress, 2d session, Report No. 104-227. Washington, DC: U.S. Government Printing Office.

Board of Trustees, Federal Old-Age and Survivors Insurance and Disability Insurance Trust Funds. 1998. *The 1998 Annual Report*. Washington DC: U.S. Government Printing Office.

Bongaarts, John. 1998. Global Population Growth: Demographic Consequences of Declining Fertility. *Science* 282:419–20.

Bongaarts, John, and Griffith Feeney. 1998. On the Quantum and Tempo of Fertility. *Population and Development Review* 24:271–92.

Cohen, Joel. 1986. Population Forecasts and Confidence Intervals for Sweden: A Comparison of Model-Based and Empirical Approaches. *Demography* 23:105–26.

Congressional Budget Office of the United States. 1996. *The Economic and Budget Outlook: Fiscal Years 1997–2006*. Washington, DC: U.S. Government Printing Office.

———. 1997. *Long-Term Budgetary Pressures and Policy Options*. Washington, DC: U.S. Government Printing Office.

1998. *Long-Term Budgetary Pressures and Policy Options.* Washington, DC: U.S. Government Printing Office.

Cutler, David, James Poterba, Louise Sheiner, and Lawrence Summers. 1990. An Aging Society: Opportunity or Challenge? *Brookings Papers on Economic Activity* 1:1–56, 71–3.

Day, Jennifer Cheeseman. 1993. *Population Projections of the United States, by Age, Sex, Race, and Hispanic Origin: 1992 to 2050.* U.S. Bureau of the Census, *Current Population Reports,* P25-1092. Washington, DC: U.S. Government Printing Office.

1996. *Population Projections of the United States, by Age, Sex, Race, and Hispanic Origin: 1995 to 2050.* U.S. Bureau of the Census, *Current Population Reports,* P25-1130. Washington, DC: U.S. Government Printing Office.

Easterlin, Richard A. 1968. *Population, Labor Force, and Long Swings in Economic Growth: The American Experience.* New York: National Bureau of Economic Research.

1978. What Will 1984 Be Like? Socioeconomic Implications of Recent Twists in Age Structure. *Demography* 15:397–432.

Foster, R. 1997. Evaluation of Mortality Assumptions in the Trustees' Report. HCFA Memorandum. Office of the Chief Actuary, Health Care Financing Administration, Baltimore, MD.

Goldstein, Joshua. 1997. Forecasting the Future of U.S. Divorce Rates. Paper presented at the 1997 Annual Meetings of the Population Association of America, Washington, DC.

Gomez de Leon, José. 1990. Empirical DEA Models to Fit and Project Time Series of Age-Specific Mortality Rates. Unpublished manuscript, Central Bureau of Statistics, Norway.

Horiuchi, Shiro, and John Wilmoth. 1995. Aging of Mortality Decline. Paper presented at the 1995 Annual Meetings of the Population Association of America, San Francisco.

Kannisto, Vaino, Jens Lauritsen, A. Roger Thatcher, and James Vaupel. 1994. Reductions in Mortality at Advanced Ages: Several Decades of Evidence from 27 Countries. *Population and Development Review* 20:793–810.

Keyfitz, Nathan. 1981. The Limits of Population Forecasting. *Population and Development Review* 7:579–93.

Lee, Ronald. 1974. Forecasting Births in Post-Transitional Populations: Stochastic Renewal with Serially Correlated Fertility. *Journal of the American Statistical Association* 69:607–17.

1976. Demographic Forecasting and the Easterlin Hypothesis. *Population and Development Review* 2:459–68.

1993. Modeling and Forecasting the Time Series of U.S. Fertility: Age Patterns, Range, and Ultimate Level. *International Journal of Forecasting* 9:187–202.

1999. Probabilistic Approaches to Population Forecasting. In Wolfgang Lutz, James Vaupel, and Dennis Ahlburg, eds. *Rethinking Population Projections.* Supplement to *Population and Development Review* 24:156–90 (1999).

Lee, Ronald, and Lawrence Carter. 1992. Modeling and Forecasting the Time

Series of U.S. Mortality. *Journal of the American Statistical Association* 87:659–71.

Lee, Ronald, and Timothy Miller. 1998. A Research Note on the Performance of Actuarial Projections of the Cost Rate: An ex-Post Analysis. Working Paper of the Project on the Economic Demography of Interage Transfers, Department of Demography, University of California at Berkeley.

Lee, Ronald, and Jonathan Skinner. 1996. Assessing Forecasts of Mortality, Health Status, and Health Costs during Baby-Boomers' Retirement. In C. Citro, ed., *Modeling the Impact of Public and Private Policies on Retirement Behavior and Income.* Washington, DC: National Academy of Sciences.

1999. Will Aging Baby Boomers Bust the Federal Budget? Longevity, Health Status, and Medical Costs in the Next Century. *Journal of Economic Perspectives* 13, no. 1 (Winter):117–40.

Lee, Ronald, and Shripad Tuljapurkar. 1994. Stochastic Population Projections for the United States: Beyond High, Medium and Low. *Journal of the American Statistical Association* 89:1175–89.

1998a. Uncertain Demographic Futures and Social Security Finances. *American Economic Review* 88:237–41.

1998b. Stochastic Forecasts for Social Security. In David Wise, ed., *Frontiers in the Economics of Aging.* Chicago: University of Chicago Press.

Lee, Ronald, Shripad Tuljapurkar, and Ryan Edwards. 1998. Uncertain Demographic Futures and Government Budgets in the US. Unpublished manuscript, Department of Demography, University of California at Berkeley; presented at the 1998 Annual Meetings of the Population Association of America, Chicago.

Lubitz, James, James Beebe, and Colin Baker. 1995. Longevity and Medicare Expenditures. *New England Journal of Medicine* 332:999–1003.

Lutz, Wolfgang, Warren Sanderson, and Sergei Scherbov. 1996. Probabilistic Population Projections Based on Expert Opinion. In Wolfgang Lutz, ed., *The Future Population of the World: What Can We Assume Today?*, rev. ed. London: Earthscan Publications.

Lutz, Wolfgang, Warren Sanderson, and Sergei Scherbov. 1997. Doubling of World Population Unlikely. *Nature* 387:803–5.

Lutz, Wolfgang, and Sergei Scherbov. 1998. An Expert-Based Framework for Probabilistic National Population Projections: The Example of Austria. *European Journal of Population* 14:1–17.

Manton, Kenneth, Larry S. Corder, and Eric Stallard. 1997. Chronic Disability Trends in Elderly United States Populations: 1982–94. *Proceedings of the National Academy of Science* 94:2593–8.

Manton, Kenneth, Eric Stallard, and H. Dennis Tolley. 1991. Limits to Human Life Expectancy: Evidence, Prospects, and Implications. *Population and Development Review* 17:603–38.

Mason, Andrew. 1996. Population and Housing. *Population Research and Policy Review* 15:419–35.

McNown, Robert, and Andrei Rogers. 1989. Forecasting Mortality: A Parameterized Time Series Approach. *Demography* 26:645–60.

1992. Forecasting Cause-Specific Mortality Using Time Series Methods. *International Journal of Forecasting* 8:413–32.

Miller, Timothy. 1998. Longevity and Medicare. Working Paper, Project on the Economic Demography of Interage Transfers, Department of Demography, University of California at Berkeley.

Office of the Actuary, Social Security Administration (OASSA). 1992. *Life Tables for the United States Social Security Area, 1990–2080.* Actuarial Study no. 107, SSA Pub. No. 11-11536. Baltimore: Social Security Administration.

1997. *Social Security Area Population Projections: 1997.* SSA Pub. No. 12-11553. Baltimore: Social Security Administration.

Pflaumer, Peter. 1988. Confidence Intervals for Population Projections Based on Monte Carlo Methods. *International Journal of Forecasting* 4:135–42.

Sanderson, Warren. 1995. Predictability, Complexity, and Catastrophe in a Collapsible Model of Population, Development, and Environmental Interactions. *Mathematical Population Studies* 5:259–80. Special issue.

Smetters, Kent. 1998. Privatizing versus Prefunding Social Security in a Stochastic Economy. Unpublished manuscript, University of Pennsylvania, Department of Economics.

Smith, James, and Barry Edmonston, eds. 1997. *The New Americans.* Report of the National Academy of Sciences Panel on Economic and Demographic Consequences of Immigration. Washington, DC: National Academy Press.

Stoto, Michael. 1983. The Accuracy of Population Projections. *Journal of the American Statistical Association* 78:13–20.

Tuljapurkar, Shripad, and Carl Boe. 1997. Validation, Probability-Weighted Priors, and Information in Stochastic Forecasts. Unpublished manuscript, Mountain View Research, Mountain View, CA.

1998. Mortality Change and Forecasting: How Much and How Little Do We Know? *North American Actuarial Journal* 2:3–47.

Wachter, Kenneth W. 1991. Elusive Cycles: Are There Dynamically Possible Lee-Easterlin Models for U.S. Births? *Population Studies* 45:109–35.

1997. Kinship Resources for the Elderly. *Philosophical Transactions of the Royal Society of London,* ser. B, 352:1811–17.

Wachter, Kenneth W., and Caleb E. Finch, eds. 1997. *Between Zeus and the Salmon: The Biodemography of Longevity.* Washington, DC: National Academy of Sciences Press.

Wilmoth, John R. 1993. Computational Methods for Fitting and Extrapolating the Lee-Carter Model of Mortality Change. Technical Report, Department of Demography, University of California, Berkeley.

1995. Are Mortality Projections Always More Pessimistic When Disaggregated by Cause of Death? *Mathematical Population Studies* 5:293–319.

1996. Mortality Projections for Japan: A Comparison of Four Methods. In Graziella Caselli and Alan Lopez, eds., *Health and Mortality among Elderly Populations.* New York: Oxford University Press, pp. 266–89.

1998. The Future of Human Longevity: A Demographer's Perspective. *Science* 280:395–7.

Comment

DANIEL McFADDEN

Demographic Forecasting

The authors have given an excellent statement of the current state of demographic forecasting. The main points of their paper are as follows:

- A key element in demographic forecasts is projection of fertility rates. Volatility in rates, partly induced by timing choices, makes fertility projections uncertain. Over a horizon of two or three generations, this has a major impact on the reliability of projections of total population and age distribution.
- Another key element in demographic forecasts is projection of survival curves. Life expectancies are projected to continue to rise, but it is uncertain whether trends over the past century will be sustained.
- Current Census projection methods are flawed because (1) too much attention is paid to *recent* fertility and mortality rates, (2) current fertility projections appear to be too high, (3) current mortality rate projections appear to be too high, and (4) the high/medium/low scenarios do a poor job of representing uncertainty in the forecasts.
- The elderly dependency ratio (65+ population/20–64 population) will peak around 41% to 45% in the decade 2030 to 2040, depending on the forecast. (Census projections made in 1966 were more optimistic, predicting a maximum elderly dependency ratio around 35% to 36%.)

Forecasting Methodology and Stochastic Simulation

The engine that drives most demographic forecasts is a cohort-component accounting relationship (see Figure 2-1.1). Once a cohort is

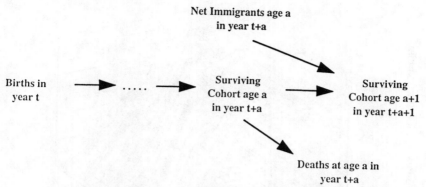

Figure 2-1.1. Cohort-Component Accounting Relationship.

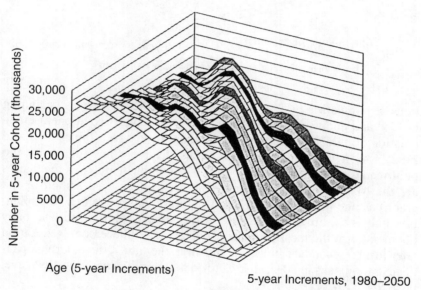

Figure 2-1.2. Census Midlevel Population Projections.

born, it marches through the years, reduced by deaths and possibly augmented by net immigration. Variations in fertility and in mortality alter the age distribution and total population as time passes. Traditional demographic forecasting deals with cohorts broken down by sex and race, but usually not disaggregated further, and employs scenarios to fix vital rates and provide some information on forecast uncertainty. For example, Figures 2-1.2 and 2-1.3 show Census midlevel and low projec-

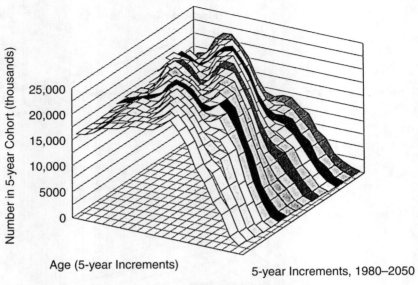

Figure 2-1.3. Census Low Population Projections.

tions of population by five-year cohort, at five-year intervals beginning in 1980 and ending in 2050. I have done some cohort-component interpolation of published tables to obtain these results (see Tables 2-1.1 and 2-1.2)[1]. As a consequence, these totals diverge somewhat from the published Census numbers after 2020. The notable features of the figures are the total population increase (the area under each ribbon of the graph) as one moves forward into the future and the march of population bulges toward the southeast as the largest cohorts age. The baby boomers form the most prominent bulge; their children one generation later form a secondary bulge. As shown in the tables, the elderly dependency ratio peaks in 2035, at 35% to 36%, compared with the 1995 level of 19.9%.

Lee and Tuljapurkar point out that the scenario method does not provide *statistical* confidence bounds, primarily because the coincidences of positive or negative effects assumed in scenarios are inconsistent with empirical correlations between rates, and because the scenarios fail to account for the actual patterns of autocorrelation and innovation and the compounding of disturbances over time. A major innovation of the

---

[1] The sources for this discussion are U.S. Bureau of the Census (1997), U.S. Immigration and Naturalization Service (1997), and U.S. National Center for Health Statistics (1996).

Table 2-1.1. *Resident Population by Age, U.S. Census Middle Series, with Cohort-Component Interpolations (thousands)*

Year	Age									Total	Elderly Dep. Rat. (%)
	0–14	15–24	25–34	35–44	45–54	55–64	65–74	75–84	85+		
1980	51,290	42,487	37,082	25,634	22,800	21,703	15,581	7,729	2,239	226,545	19.9
1985	51,534	39,992	41,696	31,691	22,460	22,135	16,858	8,890	2,668	236,924	20.4
1990	53,852	37,021	43,159	37,435	25,057	21,112	18,048	10,012	3,022	248,718	21.3
1995	57,468	36,224	40,835	42,570	31,109	21,141	18,743	11,149	3,652	262,891	21.8
2000	58,832	38,390	37,351	45,116	37,452	24,009	17,930	12,110	4,609	275,799	21.4
2005	59,241	41,481	36,536	42,681	42,583	29,822	18,009	12,463	4,983	287,799	20.6
2010	59,685	43,565	38,709	39,042	45,093	35,872	20,524	11,906	5,583	299,980	21.1
2015	61,898	43,834	41,832	38,194	42,625	40,777	25,528	12,037	5,665	312,389	23.3
2020	64,828	43,366	43,936	40,469	39,006	43,136	30,627	13,823	5,539	324,730	26.6
2025	67,402	44,528	44,219	43,731	38,178	40,732	34,793	17,243	5,614	336,441	30.5
2030	69,355	46,856	43,741	45,931	40,475	37,294	36,692	21,807	6,721	348,871	34.3
2035	71,442	49,096	44,907	46,223	43,726	36,526	34,536	25,295	8,750	360,501	35.1
2040	73,978	50,604	47,252	45,725	45,920	38,752	31,671	26,539	10,991	371,432	34.1
2045	77,034	51,840	49,515	46,945	46,190	41,850	31,081	25,344	13,149	382,948	33.1
2050	80,197	53,573	51,039	49,398	45,704	43,942	33,049	23,505	14,232	394,639	32.7
Official immigration, 1991–96	851	898	863	671	414	179	57	75	62	4,069	7.5
Implicit net immigration, 1991–95	1,365	1,393	1,338	1,041	641	277	88	117	95	6,356	7.5
Pct. of Cohort	2.4%	3.8%	3.3%	2.4%	2.1%	1.3%	0.5%	1.0%	2.6%	2.4%	
Exchange students, 1991–95	0	726	908	182	0	0	0	0	0	1,815	

Table 2-1.2. Resident Population by Age, U.S. Census Low Series, with Cohort-Component Interpolations (thousands)

Year	Age									Total	Elderly Dep. Rat. (%)
	0–14	15–24	25–34	35–44	45–54	55–64	65–74	75–84	85+		
1980	51,290	42,487	37,082	25,634	22,759	21,703	15,581	11,607	2,239	230,382	19.9
1985	51,534	39,992	41,696	31,691	25,693	22,135	16,858	13,070	2,668	245,337	20.4
1990	53,852	37,021	43,159	37,435	31,333	21,112	18,048	14,371	3,022	259,353	21.3
1995	57,468	36,224	40,835	42,570	37,722	21,141	18,743	15,516	3,652	273,871	21.8
2000	57,788	38,390	37,351	45,116	42,889	24,009	17,930	16,114	4,609	284,196	21.4
2005	55,946	41,481	36,536	42,681	45,418	29,822	18,009	15,415	4,983	290,291	20.6
2010	52,854	43,565	38,709	39,042	42,931	35,872	20,524	15,483	5,583	294,563	21.1
2015	51,779	42,651	41,832	38,194	39,287	40,777	25,528	17,645	5,665	303,359	23.3
2020	52,037	39,646	43,936	40,469	38,453	43,136	30,627	21,947	5,539	315,791	26.7
2025	52,403	38,072	43,036	43,731	40,767	40,732	34,793	26,331	5,614	325,479	31.2
2030	51,922	38,119	39,999	45,931	44,041	37,294	36,692	29,912	6,340	330,250	34.8
2035	51,053	38,808	38,405	44,983	46,250	36,526	34,536	31,545	7,787	329,895	35.9
2040	50,322	38,765	38,447	41,810	45,257	38,752	31,671	29,691	9,228	323,944	35.4
2045	50,126	37,950	39,143	40,146	42,072	41,850	31,081	27,228	10,589	320,185	34.8
2050	50,125	37,292	39,105	40,191	40,408	43,942	33,049	26,721	11,122	321,955	35.5
Official immigration, 1991–96	851	898	863	671	414	179	57	75	62	4,069	7.5
Implicit net immigration, 1991–95	1,365	1,393	1,338	1,041	641	277	88	117	95	6,356	7.5
Pct. of Cohort	2.4%	3.8%	3.3%	2.4%	1.7%	1.3%	0.5%	0.8%	2.6%	2.3%	
Exchange students, 1991–95	0	726	908	182	0	0	0	0	0	1,815	

authors is the use of stochastic simulation to estimate the *distribution* of future population features and establish realistic confidence bounds. They use the cohort-component accounting relationship for aggregate cohorts, but draw vital rates from a joint distribution that reflects their empirical correlation and time series structure. Using repeated simulations, they provide year-by-year confidence bounds for the forecasts. Their analysis shows that there are substantial probabilities that Social Security and Medicare trust fund accounts will be exhausted in the next fifty years even if their funding is designed to maintain positive *expected* balances.

Some care should be taken in interpreting these results. First, one must distinguish between year-by-year confidence bounds and a confidence region that contains a specified percentage of the forecast sample paths. The latter could be set by constructing barrier curves for which the probability of a crossing is a specified percentage. A confidence fan of the latter type will open more rapidly than the fan for year-by-year confidence bounds. Put another way, the probability that sample paths will make excursions outside year-by-year confidence bounds is high. From the standpoint of economic policy, bounds on the sample paths, such as the probability of crossing the exhaustion barrier curve, seem particularly relevant. On the other hand, if policy permits bailouts or borrowing from general funds, then exhaustion of some time averages of the sample paths may be more important and less likely than a crossing of the nonsmoothed paths. Second, the authors have done pioneering work on the time series properties of vital rates; but more research is needed before the dynamic structure of these rates is firmly established. In particular, fertility rates and birth timing appear quite volatile over generations. Third, the authors allow for the possibility of a major future event, such as the 1919 influenza epidemic, but it is intrinsically difficult to attach probabilities to rare, catastrophic events, such as war, major epidemics, and economic depressions.

Lee and Tuljapurkar make the observation that heterogeneities in vital rates across the population may be important for long-range forecasts, as selection enriches the proportions of more fertile or more robust groups. Heterogeneity may also matter for fiscal policy. For example, to forecast the impact of means testing or taxation of Social Security benefits, it is important to articulate the relationship between wealth and mortality. Use of simulation methods makes it easy to capture these effects by analyzing more disaggregated cohorts. One modeling extreme, not usually taken by demographers but popular with population biologists, is to disaggregate to the level of individual agents and simulate the entire process of mating, reproduction, and survival.

Fertility

The authors have done an admirable job of marshaling domestic and international evidence on fertility and identifying some of the sources of uncertainty in projections. A stylized account of their findings is that while there are important economic determinants of fertility, particularly real wages and nonlabor income and some prices, there are major swings in fertility across time, often correlated across countries, that remain unexplained. Time series analysis of fertility rates suggests that they may have a unit root. Birth timing appears to be a major source of volatility. Underlying these observations are the biological limits on fertility. Taken together, these facts suggest a chaotic nonlinear dynamics for births. If this is a correct characterization, then the implications for population forecasts are sobering: highly volatile and unpredictable fertility rates make population forecasts more than a generation or two ahead very problematic.

Net Immigration

Lee and Tuljapurkar utilize Census scenarios on immigration. Their simulations do not model uncertainty in the immigration rate, and they do not consider immigration policy as part of their policy analysis. In fact, immigration and the subsequent fertility of immigrants will have a significant impact on total population and on the age distribution of population. Over the half-decade 1991–95, total population growth was 5.8%, composed of 7.9% growth through resident births and 2.6% growth through net immigration, less 4.6% decline through death. Thus, immigration accounted for almost half of the net population increase. Legal immigration is currently about 800,000 persons per year. Census projections assume that this level will remain the same for the next fifty years. However, Census population projections can be used to extract implicit immigration levels, using the cohort-component accounting identity, and indicate net immigration levels around 1.2 million per year. In addition, there are crude estimates of the number of illegal immigrants (about 5 million in 1996) and the net rate of illegal immigration (about 500,000 to 750,000 per year between 1994 and 1996). Many undocumented immigrants are not counted by the Census.

About two-thirds of legal immigrants (and presumably also undocumented immigrants) are between 15 and 54 years of age, with the highest concentration in ages 20–44. The elderly dependency ratio among legal immigrants is only 7.5%. Thus, the immediate impact of immigration is to reduce the elderly dependency ratio for the overall population. Continued immigration in the current pattern will cause an economically significant reduction in this ratio over the next forty years, despite the fact that immigrants eventually end up in the numerator.

Immigration policy is a direct instrument that potentially can be used to shift the burden of Social Security and Medicare programs. Increasing immigration quotas, particularly liberalizing conversion of potentially high-wage foreign students to immigrant status and converting undocumented workers into taxpaying immigrants, directly expands the worker base that finances these programs with an age profile that is favorable to the management of these programs over the next three decades. A careful look at the fiscal impacts of immigration requires an analysis of its impact on the employment and wages of domestic workers and on the gross domestic product, as well as net flows through taxes, transfers, and services. Smith and Edmonston (1997) conclude that immigrants have a net positive fiscal impact. Studies by Altonji and Card (1991), Butcher and Card (1991), and Card (1990) have found that immigrants mostly add to total product, rather than redistributing total product away from comparable domestic workers.

An inhumane policy alternative, which is popular in California, is to restrict the entitlements of immigrants. If this were to take the form of denying Social Security or Medicare to new immigrants, this would be particularly beneficial to the management of these entitlements for the current resident population. On one hand, the argument can be made that if there is an announced policy of "taxation without entitlements" for new immigrants and immigrants come with full knowledge of this policy, then this is a Pareto-improving allocation. On the other hand, I am unaware of any country with a "guest worker" program that has been able to sustain its program in the face of humanitarian and political pressure from the disadvantaged groups.

Morbidity and Mortality

The morbidity and mortality of elderly cohorts in the future will strongly influence the viability of Social Security and Medicare programs and the demand for sectors of the economy that service the elderly subpopulation, particularly health services, housing, and leisure services. Over the past century, life expectancies have been increasing, partly because of more effective medical procedures and partly because of improved life conditions, such as reduced smoking and better nutrition. Demographic projections that matter for Social Security and Medicare, particularly the size and health status of the elderly, are highly sensitive to the prospects for continuation of these trends.

Two major issues regarding morbidity and mortality were raised in the past decade and are now at least partially answered. The first, called squaring the survival distribution, was the proposition that modern medical intervention appeared to be increasingly effective in overcoming health problems that could cause "premature" death, but that humans had a natural biological ceiling, so that survival curves would increasingly remain high until the biological ceiling was reached and then drop precipitously. The accumulated evidence appears to be that to the contrary, if individuals survive specific diseases that have a high incidence between ages 60 and 80, then the rate of increase of mortality rates diminishes, and no biological maximum is evident.

The second issue was a concern that improved medical procedures might increase morbidity by permitting individuals to survive health problems that leave them frail and unable to care for themselves. The evidence now is that in net this is not a problem: increasing survival probabilities are usually accompanied by increasing probabilities of remaining in good health without major medical interventions (see Hurd, McFadden, and Merrill, 1998). An exception may be increasing reliance on drug maintenance programs for the elderly, and any policy to cap drug costs may have substantial demographic implications.

Figure 2-1.4, taken from McFadden (1994), gives the historical drift of survival curves and time series projections into the future. These curves are obtained by fitting Gompertz approximations to male and female mortality rates, using the actuarial approach of Spencer (1989) and Palmer (1989), for census years between 1900 and 1990; extrapolating the Gompertz coefficients, using a linear trend; and then aggregating across sexes. This is similar but not identical to the time series analysis of mortality of Lee and Carter. These survival curves are higher than Census projections, supporting Lee and Tuljapurkar's judgment that Census mortality rate projections are too high.

Conclusions

Even more striking than the rapid rise in the elderly dependency ratio and shift in economic resources to the elderly that are implied by expected patterns of fertility and mortality in the next fifty years is the uncertainty with which any of these forecasts can be made. A major contribution of Lee and Tuljapurkar is to provide machinery that quantifies this uncertainty and makes it clear that public policy on Social Security

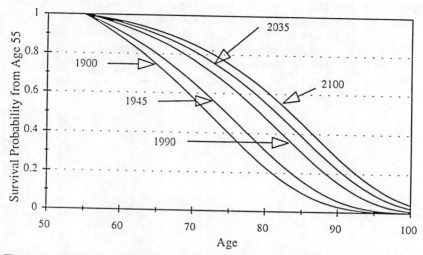

Figure 2-1.4. Survival Curves from Age 55, Total Population, from Trended Gompertz Estimates. *Source*: Reproduced with permission from McFadden (1994).

and Medicare must do more than just achieve positive expected balances. Their redesign must be sufficiently flexible and adaptive to ensure feasibility under a broad range of demographic outcomes.

References

Altonji, J., and D. Card. 1991. The Effects of Immigration on the Labor Market Opportunities of Less-Skilled Workers. In J. Abowd and R. Freeman, eds., *Immigration, Trade, and the Labor Market*. Chicago: University of Chicago Press.

Butcher, K., and D. Card. 1991. Immigration and Wages: Evidence from the 1980's. Princeton Industrial Relations Section Working Paper 281.

Card, D. 1990. The Impact of the Mariel Boatlift on the Miami Labor Market. *Industrial and Labor Relations Review* 43:245–57.

Hurd, M., D. McFadden, and A. Merrill. 1998. Healthy, Wealthy, and Wise? Socioeconomic Status, Morbidity, and Mortality among the Elderly. University of California Working Paper.

McFadden, D. 1994. Demographics, the Housing Market, and the Welfare of the Elderly. In D. Wise, ed., *Studies in the Economics of Aging*. Chicago: University of Chicago Press.

Palmer, B. 1989. Implications of Changing Elderly Male Mortality. Ph.D. thesis, MIT.

Smith, J., and B. Edmonston. 1997. *The New Americans: Economic, Demographic, and Fiscal Effects of Immigration*. Washington, DC: National Academy Press.

Spencer, G. 1989. *Projections of the Population of the United States by Age, Sex, and Race.* U. S. Bureau of the Census, Series P-25.

U.S. Bureau of the Census (1997). *Current Population Reports*, P25–1095.

U.S. Immigration and Naturalization Service (1997). *Statistical Yearbook.*

U.S. National Center for Health Statistics (1996). *Vital Statistics of the United States.*

CHAPTER 2-2

Comment

JAMES P. SMITH

This is an excellent chapter by two of the best. In a field where expedient compromise is the rule rather than the exception, for some time now, Lee and Tuljapurkar have been doing the most thoughtful basic work on population forecasting. While forecasting practitioners in government agencies are sometimes constrained by what are viewed as politically acceptable ranges, the more basic constraint is that they rarely have the time or resources to conduct inquiries challenging the theoretical and statistical pillars upon which population forecasting rests. That job has been given to the likes of Ron Lee and Shripad Tuljapurkar, and it is in good hands indeed.

Demographic forecasting is an extremely useful analytical tool. Instead of relying on summary aggregate statistics, such as the total size or growth rate of the population, the value of the demographic approach is that it builds up its projections from demographically disaggregated vital rates. We know with reasonable certainty that the size of the population will not continue to grow (as aggregate growth rates might suggest), but rather will soon begin to decline and in fact will do so in a narrowly specified time span. We also know a good deal about the future age and sex structure of populations far into the future. The "no change status quo" scenario built up from disaggregated vital rates is often quite at odds with projections based on population aggregates.

The most useful aspect of demographic forecasting involves obtaining the best estimate of the baseline projection. Regarding baseline projections, I believe that Ron and Tulja are on very solid ground and are quite persuasive in their arguments that the baseline assumptions in the Social Security Administration and Census projections should be revised. For example, they argue, and I agree, that the Census baseline fertility projection is probably too high (2.2). They point out that the Census

69

fertility rate depends in part on future immigrants to the United States having the same numbers of children as current immigrants do. That is not a plausible assumption, since fertility rates in the main sending countries (Mexico, China, The Philippines) have been declining rapidly during the last decade and are already less than Census immigrant assumptions. Simply by correcting that assumption, Ron and Tulja show that the baseline fertility rate would be 2.0. Similarly, because the Social Security Administration ignores recent declines in mortality and the higher life expectancies in Western Europe than in the United States, it has too pessimistic an assumption about future mortality built into its projections. Based on Ron and Tulja's sound arguments, I would join them in recommending immediate changes in the baseline demographic models of both the Social Security Administration and the Census.

The rest of the chapter deals with uncertainty in demographic projections, and here there is more controversy. The authors do offer a more coherent discussion about what demographic uncertainty means, and their criticisms of the high/low/medium approach are on the mark. No explicit probabilities are ever attached to these thresholds, so it is difficult to quantify the meaning of uncertainty. Moreover, extreme assumptions that appear to allow for uncertainty imply almost no uncertainty at all for certain policy-relevant outcomes. As Lee and Tuljapurkar correctly point out, the combined high fertility–low mortality assumptions allow for almost no variation in the dependency ratio. The high-fertility assumption predicts a lot of future workers, while the low-mortality one predicts a lot of older dependents.

With that said, I still have reservations about the stochastic approach to uncertainty outlined by Ron and Tulja. My problems can best be illustrated with their fertility projections. Their projections are based, of course, on the past, and this past is dominated by the postwar baby boom and baby bust. In fact, they show that any Census projection made during the baby bust years was always too high. It had to be over before you could believe it. But their projection model for the baseline scenario faced the same problem: It would not generate sensible baseline numbers, so they simply imposed an answer by constraining the mean to 1.85. But then they proceed to use the same time series data to calculate an uncertainty forecast. The uncertainty displayed in their Figure 2.7, not surprisingly, is quite high – unbelievably high, I would claim. For example, by the year 2000, their 95% bounds are about a year (1.5 to 2.5), and their steady state bounds by the year 2020 are 3 to less than 1.

I think these are unrealistically wide bands, especially over such a short horizon. The reason they arise is easy to understand. The years that

70

encompass both the baby boom and baby bust periods are years of high and unprecedented variance in fertility. In this case, the past may not be prologue. My view is the baby boom should be downweighted in projections, because it is historically unique and may be quite unlikely to happen again, at least in this magnitude. There is a basic asymmetry to their "loved the variance, hated the mean" approach to the fertility time series data. They impose an answer for the mean projection, since they do not like what the data say, but accept what the data say about variance. It is, after all, the same data sending both messages.

One of the reasons I find the variances in their fertility projections unreasonable is that I am implicitly using some structure, while they seem to be unwilling to introduce any. I do not think fertility rates will rise to anywhere near 3, because I believe the fundamental changes in women's labor market role over the last few decades will continue. These changes – higher labor force participation rates and higher wages – should keep fertility down. While their skepticism about structure is understandable, some ideas about the structural determinants of these demographic outcomes should be a companion, not a substitute, for these demographic projections.

In another dimension, Ron and Tulja probably understate demographic uncertainty. In their projections, they use current immigration rates in their forecasts without any variation at all. Immigration policy is by no means certain, and it can have a dramatic effect on these outcomes. In a recent National Academy volume (to which both Ron Lee and I were contributors), future populations were projected with net immigration rates 50% higher and 50% lower than current rates.[1] These bands produced U.S. populations that ranged as low as 349,000 and as high as 426,000 in the year 2050. This range is about the same as what is produced by the fertility uncertainty in their models. I would suggest that uncertainty about immigration policy be added to the model.

The final part of the chapter is quite innovative in combining demographic uncertainty and public finance. The implied future variation in public finance parameters, such as the payroll tax, is computed in light of the substantial demographic uncertainty that exists. The implied variation is enormous – for example, payroll taxes vary between 0.15 and 0.33. Here, the projection has a different meaning, as it is not really a forecast at all, since we know it will not ever happen. In the worst-case scenarios, some other adaptations will be made (raising taxes or cutting benefits) that will probably smooth out the impact.

---

[1] See *The New Americans: Economic, Demographic and Fiscal Effects of Immigration*, ed. James P. Smith and Barry Edmonston (Washington, DC: National Academy Press, 1997).

How should we react to the types of fiscal uncertainty demonstrated so well by Ron and Tulja? Should we adapt risk-averting policies right now to avoid the really bad outcomes? Or should we wait until some of the uncertainty is resolved? Good papers make you ask important questions at the end, and this mark is easily reached by Ron and Tulja.

CHAPTER 3

Uncertainty and the Design of Long-Run Fiscal Policy

ALAN J. AUERBACH AND KEVIN HASSETT

Introduction

Over time, the share of federal government expenditures tied to age-related programs, particularly those focusing on the elderly, has grown rapidly. For example, U.S. spending on Social Security (OASDI) and Medicare alone has risen from 15 percent of the federal budget in fiscal year 1966 (the year of Medicare's introduction) to 35 percent in fiscal year 1998 and is projected to grow to 44 percent of the federal budget during the next decade (Congressional Budget Office 1998). Combined with the changing composition of the U.S. population, this change in spending composition has led to serious questions about the viability of current fiscal policy, both in the United States and abroad (e.g., Auerbach et al. 1999).

Dealing with the apparent fiscal imbalances associated with aging populations raises difficult questions about how and when to change policy. Projected long-term cash-flow imbalances are so large that significant immediate adjustments appear necessary to avert serious economic problems. However, with considerable uncertainty about how serious future cash-flow imbalances will be, there is also a natural tendency to put off dealing with problems that might not materialize. This tendency is magnified by the perception that old-age transfer programs, particularly Social Security, are a "third rail" of American politics, and a sense that a change today may make it harder to alter the system tomorrow. As a result, policy changes have been relatively infrequent, suggesting that a key feature of the current system is that it does not allow policy

We are grateful to our discussants, Peter Diamond and Shripad Tuljapurkar, and other conference participants for helpful comments on an earlier draft.

makers to adjust taxes and transfers very frequently; that is, Social Security policy is "sticky."

The fundamental question addressed in this chapter is how and when to deal with long-term fiscal imbalances that are at once very significant and very uncertain, given that political constraints may make frequent changes to the system impossible. Unlike much current discussion, which focuses on the institutional features of specific reforms, such as whether to scale back and/or privatize the Social Security system, our approach is to use simpler and more stylized models in search of more general conclusions regarding the nature of optimal policy responses. We consider policy under different assumptions regarding the flexibility of government decisions. To account for the various types of important economic shocks, we consider three sources of uncertainty: depreciation (which affects the productivity of capital), technological progress (which affects the productivity of both capital and labor), and life span, which affects the consumption needs of different generations.

We proceed in two steps. First, we explore the impact of uncertainty on optimal policy when policy is free to change each period. Second, we construct a simulation model to help us examine the impact of policy stickiness on social welfare and the choice of optimal policy.

Government Policy in an
Overlapping-Generations Model

Throughout the chapter, we analyze policy design using the familiar two-period overlapping-generations model. For the sake of simplicity, we assume that there are no bequests, no heterogeneity within each generation, and no capital market imperfections. Thus, we abstract from many of the important issues that arise, for example, in discussions of optimal Social Security design, because we wish to focus on issues of timing and intergenerational redistribution.

Consider an economy in which each generation lives for two periods. There are three sources of uncertainty: general productivity, the rate of capital depreciation, and life span, as represented by the length of life during the second period. Each generation has a single, representative individual.

Initially, we assume that production and preferences are Cobb-Douglas. Production of output is

$$Y_t = K_t^\alpha A_t^{1-\alpha}, \tag{1}$$

where K_t is the capital stock and A_t is the level of labor productivity at date t. In efficiency units, the wage rate at t is

$$w_t = (1-\alpha)\left(\frac{K_t}{A_t}\right)^\alpha, \tag{2}$$

while the gross return to capital is

$$r_t = \alpha\left(\frac{K_t}{A_t}\right)^{\alpha-1}. \tag{3}$$

Preferences obey

$$U_t = \ln C_{1t} + E_t\beta_{t+1}\ln\left(\frac{C_{2t+1}}{\beta_{t+1}}\right), \tag{4}$$

where U_t is the expected utility of the generation born in period t, $C_{1t}(C_{2t})$ is the consumption of the younger (older) generation in period t, and β_t is the length of second-period life for the older generation in period t. The form of second-period utility is based on the notion that the period is really divided into β subperiods, each with equal weight and consumption.

Consider first the economy's equilibrium without government. Utility maximization (which with homothetic preferences can be considered in terms of efficiency units) yields the expression for first-period consumption:

$$C_{1t} = \frac{w_t}{1 + E_t\beta_{t+1}}. \tag{5}$$

Letting δ_t be the rate of capital depreciation at date t, we know that

$$C_{2t} = K_t(1 + r_t - \delta_t). \tag{6}$$

Thus, from (1), (2), (3), (5), and (6), the capital transition equation is

$$K_{t+1} = Y_t + (1-\delta_t)K_t - C_{1t}A_t - C_{2t} = K_t^\alpha A_t^{1-\alpha}(1-\alpha)\left(1 - \frac{1}{1+E_t\beta_{t+1}}\right). \tag{7}$$

This provides a complete solution for the economy's evolution with no government. Now, consider the impact of having safe government debt, B_t, and taxes on each generation, T_{1t} and T_{2t}, such that

$$B_{t+1} = (1+v_t)B_t - T_{1t}A_t - T_{2t}. \tag{8}$$

where v_t is the market-determined safe rate of return.

There are various possible interpretations of the terms T_{1t} and T_{2t}. One may think of them as representing the tax and benefit components, respectively, of a public pension scheme. However, for convenience, we assume that the second-period tax, T_{2t}, is imposed as a proportional tax on second-period capital income. Although this appears to impose a distortion, the government's optimal policy will turn out to be one that eschews distortionary taxation.

Letting θ_t be the amount of savings put into government bonds in period t, we may write the household's optimization problem at time t as

$$\max_{C_{1t}, \theta_t} \ln C_{1t} + E_{t+1}\beta_{t+1} \ln\left[\frac{(W_t - T_{1t} - C_{1t} - \theta_t)(1 + r_{t+1}^n - \delta) + \theta_t(1 + v_{t+1}^n)}{\beta_{t+1}}\right], \quad (9)$$

where the superscript n signifies an after-tax return. The household now chooses how much to invest in government bonds, θ, as well as how much to consume in the first period, C_1. Combining the two first-order conditions corresponding to these choices yields

$$C_{1t} = \frac{W_t - T_{1t}}{1 + E_t\beta_{t+1}}, \quad (10)$$

which corresponds to (5) for the no-government case. The expression for second-period consumption corresponding to (6) is

$$C_{2t} = K_t(1 + r_t - \delta_t) + B_t(1 + v_t) - T_{2t} = K_t(1 + r_t - \delta_t) + B_{t+1} + T_{1t}A_t, \quad (11)$$

where the last substitution follows from (8). Substituting (10) and (11) into (7) yields the modified transition equation for capital:

$$K_{t+1} = K_t^\alpha A_t^{1-\alpha}(1-\alpha)\left(1 - \frac{1}{1 + E_t\beta_{t+1}}\right) - T_{1t}A_t\left(1 - \frac{1}{1 + E_t\beta_{t+1}}\right) - B_{t+1}. \quad (12)$$

Optimal Policy without Constraints

We are now in a position to maximize social welfare through the choice of $\{T_{1t}, T_{2t}, B_{t+1}\}$ at date t, subject to expectations at date t. We assume an additively separable social welfare function with weight ω_t assigned to generation t. Our objective, therefore, is to maximize

$$V_t = \omega_{t-1}\beta_t \ln C_{2t} + \omega_t \ln(C_{1t}A_t) + E_t V_{t+1}, \quad (13)$$

76

subject to the transition equation in (12).[1] To do so, we form the Hamiltonian with costate variable λ_t associated with (12).

Note that for the government's problem of maximizing (13), based on (10) and (11) and subject to the resource constraint described in (12), the initial stock of government debt, B_t, is absent: the stock of debt is irrelevant to the optimal solution. This makes sense, because national debt is simply an accounting construct in this model (see, e.g., Auerbach and Kotlikoff, 1987, for further elaboration). It is possible to increase the initial stock of debt and reduce the transfers to the elderly in the initial period of optimization without affecting the welfare of the young or the old or the opportunity set available for the future. This shift would occur, for example, if we relabeled some of the taxes and transfers of a Social Security system as purchases of debt and payments of interest and principal on that debt.

After some algebra, the first-order conditions with respect to T_{1t}, B_{t+1}, and K_t yield the following expressions for the optimal values of C_{1t} and C_{2t} and the optimal evolution of λ_t:

$$C_{1t}A_t = \frac{\omega_t}{\lambda_t};\tag{14a}$$

$$C_{2t} = \frac{\omega_{t-1}\beta_t}{\lambda_t};\tag{14b}$$

and

$$\lambda_{t-1} = E_{t-1}[\lambda_t(1+r_t-\delta_t)].\tag{15}$$

These conditions would also follow if we had maximized (13) through the direct choice of $\{C_{1t}, C_{2t}\}$. This result confirms that, through the choice of taxes and debt, the government can achieve its first-best solution in a decentralized context. This equivalence hinges on the government's ability to set these instruments freely; that is, there is one free instrument for each agent at each time. We reconsider this assumption below. For now, though, we maintain the assumption that government has the instrument flexibility needed to implement its optimal policy.

Indeed, as this equivalence does not depend on the Cobb-Douglas assumptions, we can consider the direct choice of $\{C_{1t}, C_{2t}\}$ for other assumptions regarding preferences and production. Expression (15) remains the same, although the definition of r_t is dependent on the

---

[1] There is an additional term in the objective function, $-\omega_{t-1}\ln\beta_t$, but this does not vary with government policy.

production function. For general Constant Elasticity of Substitution preferences,

$$U_t = \frac{1}{1-\gamma_1}C_{1t}^{1-\gamma_1} + \frac{1}{1-\gamma_2}E_t\left[\beta_{t+1}\left(\frac{C_{2t+1}}{\beta_{t+1}}\right)^{1-\gamma_2}\right],$$ (16)

expressions (14a) and (14b) are replaced by

$$C_{1t}A_t = \left(\frac{\omega_t}{\lambda_t}\right)^{\frac{1}{\gamma_1}};$$ (17a)

and

$$C_{2t} = \left(\frac{\omega_{t-1}\beta_t}{\lambda_t}\right)^{\frac{1}{\gamma_2}}.$$ (17b)

There are a number of interesting points to make concerning the optimal conditions laid out in (15) and either (14) or (17). First, the optimal degree of risk sharing depends on the relative risk aversion of the young and elderly. In (16), γ_1 and γ_2 equal the coefficients of relative risk aversion of the young and old, respectively. If $\gamma_1 = \gamma_2$, then (17) (or (14), for the special case of $\gamma_1 = \gamma_2 = 1$) calls for complete risk sharing.[2] As discussed by Diamond (1997) and Bohn (1998), this will generally require government instruments to transfer risk between generations. As these authors have noted, the desired degree of risk sharing can be accomplished by adjusting the portfolio of the public pension scheme, for example, the share of the Social Security trust fund that is placed in equity rather than debt. But there are many alternative ways to achieve the same allocation, and there need be no connection whatsoever between trust fund investment policy and intergenerational risk sharing.

This risk-sharing result holds not only for productivity risks – $C_{1t}A_t/C_{2t}$ should be independent of A_t and δ_t when $\gamma_1 = \gamma_2$ – but also for life-span risk as well: consumption *per unit time* of the elderly, C_{2t}/β_t, should also bear a fixed ratio to $C_{1t}A_t$, independent of β_t.

A second result may be observed by comparing conditions (17a) and (17b) for successive periods, using (15):

$$(C_{1t}A_t)^{-\gamma_1} = E_t\left[\beta_{t+1}C_{2t+1}^{-\gamma_2}(1+r_{t+1}-\delta_{t+1})\right].$$ (18)

---

[2] Recall that C_{1t} is measured in efficiency units, so $C_{1t}A_t$ is per capita consumption by the young.

Uncertainty and the Design of Long-Run Fiscal Policy

This is precisely the standard Euler equation that prevails in the absence of the capital income tax, T_{2t+1}, which implies that capital income taxes should be used to spread risk, but not to distort saving, a familiar result from the dynamic optimal tax literature (e.g., Judd, 1989; Chari et al., 1994). This is accomplished by taxing only the excess return to capital.

Another point to make regarding the optimal policy involves the evolution of λ_t, the marginal social value of a unit of investment at date t. The first-order conditions (17a) and (17b) call for the marginal social value of consumption of young and old to be set equal to this value. Expression (15) also may be viewed as an Euler equation, relating to the shadow price of capital, λ_t. Using (17a) to rewrite (15) in terms of first-period consumption in successive periods (a similar expression holds for second-period consumption), we obtain

$$\left(C_{1t}A_t\right)^{-\gamma_1} = E_t\left[\left(C_{1t+1}A_{t+1}\right)^{-\gamma_1}\left(1+r_{t+1}-\delta_{t+1}\right)\cdot\frac{\omega_{t+1}}{\omega_t}\right], \tag{19}$$

which relates the marginal utility of successive generations' consumption. To understand this result, it is helpful to consider the special case in which $r_{t+1} - \delta_{t+1}$ is known at date t. This will be true if A_{t+1} and δ_{t+1} are known at date t. In this case, (19) calls for the marginal utility of first-period consumption to follow a random walk, with drift $(1 + r_{t+1} - \delta_{t+1})$ $(\omega_{t+1}/\omega_t) \approx r_{t+1} - \delta_{t+1} - \eta_{t+1}$, where $\eta_{t+1} = 1 - (\omega_{t+1}/\omega_t)$ is the government's pure rate of time preference. This finding is reminiscent of Barro's (1979) tax-smoothing result, although here the smoothing of tax burdens associated with the smoothing of consumption derives from the objective of intergenerational equity, not the minimization of deadweight loss for an infinite-horizon household.

Even for this special case of a zero-risk return, $r_{t+1} - \delta_{t+1}$, consumption itself is not projected to follow a random walk with drift. To see why this is so, consider the simple case in which the drift factor equals zero, so that the optimal policy sets $(C_{1t}A_t)^{-\gamma_1} = E_t[(C_{1t+1}A_{t+1})^{-\gamma_1}]$. By Jensen's inequality, it follows that $C_{1t}A_t < E_t(C_{1t+1}A_{t+1})$. The logic is straightforward: if we wish to set the expected value of the next period's marginal utility to equal a particular level, risk aversion implies that, on average, consumption must exceed its level at this specified marginal utility – the consumption level in the absence of uncertainty. Indeed, the greater the fluctuations in consumption or the degree of relative risk aversion, γ_1, the greater this precautionary saving should be.

This result deserves emphasis: uncertainty about the future should reduce consumption today, and increased uncertainty or risk aversion should reduce consumption more. Greater uncertainty increases the chance of a favorable outcome, in which case the extra saving will prove to have been unnecessary. But it will also increase the chance of an unfavorable outcome, and risk aversion will lead us to weight the latter effect more heavily than the former. It does not matter that it is the risk aversion of future generations, because the government's social welfare criterion links the welfare of present generations with those yet unborn. The result also does not hinge on whether future generations are expected to be better off than current generations, which should influence the optimal level of saving but not the impact of added risk on that saving.

The equilibrium path of the economy can be described by the solution to two equations in K and λ, which we obtain using the optimum conditions (15) and (17). For the case of Cobb-Douglas production, we have

$$\lambda_{t-1} = E_{t-1}[\lambda_t(1+\alpha K_t^{\alpha-1}Z_t - \delta_t)], \tag{20a}$$

and

$$K_{t+1} = K_t^\alpha Z_t + (1-\delta_t)K_t - \left(\frac{\omega_t}{\lambda_t}\right)^{\frac{1}{\gamma_1}} - \left(\frac{\omega_{t-1}\beta_t}{\lambda_t}\right)^{\frac{1}{\gamma_2}}, \tag{20b}$$

where we define $Z_t = A_t^{1-\alpha}$ as the level of total factor productivity. In general, this nonlinear system has no analytical solution. However, we may obtain explicit results for small deviations from a long-run, deterministic steady state by solving a linearized version of (20). In this steady state, the government's pure rate of time preference, $\eta = (\omega_t/\omega_{t+1}) - 1$, must be constant, with the rate of return $r^* - \delta^*$ equal to it. One important limitation of this analysis is that linearization removes elements of risk and risk aversion from consideration. Thus, for simplicity, we set $\gamma_1 = \gamma_2 = \gamma$, for which case γ equals the inverse of the intertemporal elasticity of substitution. Another apparent limitation is that we implicitly are ruling out permanent trends in the stochastic variables A, δ, and β, although one can envision deviations of very long duration.

This linear version of the model has two characteristic roots, one of which is stable ($\mu_1 < 1$) and the other of which is unstable ($\mu_2 > 1$). We obtain the exact solution by imposing two terminal conditions, the fixed value of the initial capital stock and the requirement that the capital stock not explode over time. The result is

$$K_t = \mu_1 K_{t-1} + (1-\mu_1)K^* + \sum_{s=t}^{\infty} \mu_2^{-(s-t+1)}E_{t-1}(\Gamma_s), \tag{21}$$

where

$$\Gamma_s = Y^* \left[\frac{K^{*\alpha}(Z_{s-1} - Z_s) - K^*(\delta_{s-1} - \delta_s)}{Y^*} - \frac{\dfrac{1}{\gamma}\omega_{s-1}^{\frac{1}{\gamma}}\beta^{*\frac{1}{\gamma}-1}(\beta_{s-1} - \beta_s)}{\omega_s^{\frac{1}{\gamma}} + (\omega_{s-1}\beta^*)^{\frac{1}{\gamma}}} \right.$$

$$\left. + \frac{1}{\gamma} \cdot \frac{\alpha K^{*\alpha-1}(Z_s - Z^*) - (\delta_s - \delta^*)}{1 + r^* - \delta^*} \right], \qquad (22)$$

and

$$Y^* = K^{*\alpha} - \delta^* K^* \qquad (23)$$

is steady-state output.

Each of the terms in brackets in (22) has a straightforward interpretation. The first equals the percentage change in the output shock between periods $s - 1$ and s. The second equals the percentage change in "consumption need" induced by the life-span shock between periods $s - 1$ and s. The last term measures the impact on desired consumption (through the intertemporal elasticity parameter, γ) of the percentage deviation of the discount factor, $1 + r - \delta$, from its long-run value.

The first two factors call for more resources to be carried into periods when resources are expected to fall or consumption needs increase, while the last factor calls for more saving when the rate of return to capital is higher. However, given that the weighted average of all future expected values of Γ_s matter, the policy to be followed at date t depends on the anticipated evolution of these shocks.

For example, suppose that total factor productivity follows the first-order process $Z_t = \rho Z_{t-1} + (1 - \rho)Z^* + \varepsilon_t$. Then the contribution of productivity shocks to the last term in (21) is

$$\left[\frac{1-\rho}{\mu_2 - (1-\rho)} K^{*\alpha} + \frac{\rho}{\mu_2 - \rho} \cdot \frac{\alpha K^{*\alpha-1} Y^*}{\gamma(1 + r^* - \delta^*)} \right] (Z_{t-1} - Z^*). \qquad (24)$$

Where ρ is small (strong mean reversion), the first term matters more; where ρ is large (persistent shocks), the second term is more important. However, both terms work in the same direction and the net effect of an increase in ρ is ambiguous. The derivative of the term in (24) with respect to ρ is positive if and only if

$$\sqrt{\frac{r^*}{\gamma(1+r^*-\delta^*)}} > \frac{\mu_2-\rho}{\mu_2-(1-\rho)}, \tag{25}$$

which, for $\rho \in [0,1]$, is most likely to hold for $\rho = 1$ and least likely to hold for $\rho = 0$. Indeed, if $\sqrt{\frac{r^*}{\gamma(1+r^*-\delta^*)}} \in \left(\frac{\mu_2-1}{\mu_2}, \frac{\mu_2}{\mu_2-1}\right)$, then there is some critical value of ρ, $\hat{\rho}$, below which the term in (24) decreases with ρ and above which it increases. As $\mu_2 \to 1$ (which occurs, for example, as $\alpha \to 1$), this interval $\to (0,\infty)$ and the existence of $\hat{\rho}$ is more likely.

This ambiguity is present because an increase in the duration of a productivity shock makes it more valuable to save more, but also less necessary. The relative importance of these efforts depends not only on parameters such as γ (a higher value weakening the effect of an increase in ρ), but also on the value of ρ itself. A similar ambiguity holds with respect to shocks to the rate of depreciation, δ.

On the other hand, the impact of life-span shocks is clear: a positive shock to life span should reduce current capital accumulation. With more consumption needed in the near term, less capital should be accumulated. This result may seem counterintuitive, if one thinks of longer life span as making individuals better off and more able to make transfers to other generations. But the key here is the impact on the *marginal* value of consumption; with longer life span, a generation must spread its resources over a longer period. We also observe that the more durable this positive shock, the smaller the reduction in capital accumulation – and the greater the decline in consumption – that should occur. This is because future generations are expected to be less able to provide resources for current ones. It seems clear that similar results would hold if the additional value of consumption came from a larger cohort, that is, by an extensive rather than intensive population shock.

How fast and how much investment should respond to these shocks also depends on the values taken by the roots (μ_1, μ_2). The general expression for these roots is

$$\mu_i = 1 + \frac{r^*-\delta^*+x}{2} \pm \frac{1}{2}\sqrt{(r^*-\delta^*+x)^2 + 4x}, \tag{26}$$

where

$$x = \frac{Y^*\alpha(1-\alpha)K^{*\alpha-2}Z^*}{\gamma(1+r^*-\delta^*)} = \frac{Y^*(1-\alpha)r^*}{K^*\gamma(1+r^*-\delta^*)}. \tag{27}$$

82

Clearly, μ_1 is decreasing in x and μ_2 is increasing. Thus, where x is large (see (21)), investment adjusts quickly (μ_1 is small) and does not depend as much on distant future values of the shock term, Γ_s (μ_2 is large). This will be true, for example, for a low value of the risk aversion coefficient, γ. At the other extreme, as $\gamma \rightarrow \infty$, $\mu_1 \rightarrow 1$ and $\mu_2 \rightarrow (1 + r^* - \delta^*)$. Higher risk aversion makes adjustment more costly. The same effect occurs as $\alpha \rightarrow 1$, as the marginal product of capital becomes independent of the level of the capital stock. The same effect, it can be shown, also occurs as the elasticity of substitution between capital and labor rises. The intuition is that there is less importance in being at the "wrong" capital stock value if deviations in the level of capital have a minimal impact on its marginal productivity.

It is useful to summarize the results thus far. First, as others have noted, government policy should allocate policy risks across each pair of overlapping generations in accordance with their tolerance for risk. This can be accomplished in a variety of ways. Second, policy should adjust at each date to eliminate expected changes in the marginal value of consumption, suitably discounted. Third, with risk aversion and uncertainty, this will generally imply precautionary fiscal policy that sets aside more than what government *expects* it will need in the future. Fourth, policy should respond differently to productivity shocks and demographic shocks. Like increases in life expectancy, negative productivity shocks require a reduction in investment and a reduction in current consumption, with the latter growing with the expected duration of the shock. However, negative productivity shocks also discourage capital accumulation by making that accumulation less productive, and the net impact on investment of a shock's persistence is no longer clear. Finally, the speed of adjustment should rise with a fall in the degree of risk aversion or with a decline in the capital share of output or a fall in the elasticity of substitution between capital and labor.

Limits on Policy Changes

Thus far, we have considered government policy when there is sufficient instrument flexibility for the government to control consumption directly. In a more realistic setting, this is unlikely to be the case, both because there are more targets (such as the consumption levels of different groups within each generation) and fewer instruments. Once one considers these more realistic cases, it is again necessary to analyze the effects of fiscal instruments explicitly, as consumption levels now must be chosen from a constrained set.

One complication that may arise is that it may not be possible to change government's instruments in every period. This may reflect political difficulties or, implicitly, the large fixed costs associated with major policy changes. To be concrete, let us suppose that the tax rates T_1 and T_2 cannot be changed in successive periods. Given that each period in an overlapping-generations model corresponds to roughly thirty years, this restriction corresponds to the notion that major changes in, say, the Social Security or Medicare system may be possible only once every few decades.

With this restriction, the government's problem now has an additional state variable, say, d_t, which equals 0 if $T_{1t-1} = T_{1t-2}$ and $T_{2t-1} = T_{2t-2}$ and 1 otherwise. Letting $V_t^0(V_t^1)$ be the government's objective function in period t if $d_t = 0$ (1), we may express these functions (for the case of Cobb-Douglas preferences) as

$$
\begin{aligned}
V_t^0 &= \max[\omega_{t-1}\beta_t \ln C_{2t} + \omega_t \ln(C_{1t}A_t) + E_t(V_{t+1}^1), \ V_t^1]; \\
V_t^1 &= \omega_{t-1}\beta_t \ln \overline{C}_{2t} + \omega_t \ln(\overline{C}_{1t}A_t) + E_t(V_{t+1}^0),
\end{aligned}
\tag{28}
$$

where $\overline{C}_{it}$ is the value of C_{it} chosen when $\{T_{1t}, T_{2t}\}$ equals $\{T_{1t-1}, T_{2t-1}\}$. Note that with this restriction the initial level of debt will generally matter. This is evident from inspection of expression (11), for with T_{2t} fixed, the level of consumption by the elderly, C_{2t}, varies with B_t.

This problem can only be solved numerically. We use the following approach, starting with some assumed terminal period, say M. In period M, the world ends, and the government must pay off its debt. To do so, it must be able to choose $\{T_{1M}, T_{2M}\}$, which means that it cannot have chosen $\{T_{1M-1}, T_{2M-1}\}$. The choice of $\{T_{1M}, T_{2M}\}$ is made by maximizing the welfare of that period's consumption by young and old, for there is no future. As $\{T_{1M-1}, T_{2M-1}\}$ may not be chosen, this tax vector is set equal to $\{T_{1M-2}, T_{2M-2}\}$. Knowing that it will not choose to vary taxes in period $M - 1$, the government faces no cost in varying taxes in period $M - 2$ from their previous values; it will vary taxes in period $M - 2$ if it can – that is, if it has not varied them in period $M - 3$. Thus, for each of periods $M, M - 1$ and $M - 2$, the government's decision of whether to vary taxes is a trivial one. For periods $M - 3$ and earlier, though, the decision must be evaluated using expression (28) comparing the option value of waiting to adjust taxes, $E_t(V_{t+1}^0 - V_{t+1}^1)$, with the current-period cost of doing so, $\omega_{t-1}\beta_t[\ln C_{2t} - \ln \overline{C}_{2t}] + \omega_t[\ln(C_{1t}A_t) - \ln(\overline{C}_{1t}A_t)]$. As we go back to earlier and earlier periods, we derive the optimal values $\{T_{1t}, T_{2t}\}$ as functions of the state variables, which include the capital stock, K_t, and all relevant information regarding the stochastic variables, A_t, δ_t, and β_t. To obtain

Table 3.1. *Optimal Policy Rules under Government Discount Rate = 2, Four-Period Horizon*

	$\rho = 0.9$ $\beta = 0.7$	$\rho = 0.9$ $\beta = 1.0$	$\rho = 0.9$ $\beta = 1.3$	$\rho = 0.1$ $\beta = 0.7$	$\rho = 0.1$ $\beta = 1.0$	$\rho = 0.1$ $\beta = 1.3$
Unconstrained						
V	−2.136	−2.570	−3.188	−2.467	−2.815	−3.180
C_1	0.149	0.118	0.078	0.140	0.113	0.096
C_2	0.304	0.320	0.319	0.280	0.324	0.348
K	0.058	0.073	0.112	0.091	0.073	0.066
T_1	0.060	0.080	0.136	0.036	0.084	0.116
T_2	−0.104	−0.120	−0.120	−0.080	−0.124	−0.148
Debt	0.044	0.040	−0.016	0.044	0.040	0.032
Constrained						
V	−2.343	−3.330	−4.187	−2.570	−2.941	−3.291
C_1	0.111	0.054	0.039	0.089	0.072	0.059
C_2	0.287	0.275	0.258	0.280	0.315	0.338
K	0.116	0.182	0.213	0.141	0.124	0.113
T_1	0.113	**0.200**	0.220	0.133	**0.167**	0.190
T_2	−0.088	**−0.075**	−0.058	−0.080	**−0.115**	−0.138
Debt	−0.025	−0.125	−0.162	−0.053	−0.052	−0.052
Inaction range						
T_1		(0.03, 0.24)			(0.16, 0.17)	
T_2		(−0.20, −0.04)			(−0.12, −0.11)	

infinite-horizon policy rules, we would need to keep going back in time, lengthening the government's planning horizon until these functions converged (i.e., ceased to depend on t).

To keep the state space manageable, we limit our analysis to cases in which the production terms A_t and δ_t are deterministic and constant, normalized to 1 and 0 respectively, and life span, β_t, is governed by a first-order process, $\beta_t = \rho\beta_{t-1} + (1 - \rho)\beta^* + \varepsilon_t$, with $\beta^* = 1$. This means that only the current value of β enters as a state variable at date t. Also, because there is no productivity risk, the before-tax return to capital in period t is known at the beginning of period t. Hence, capital and government debt are perfect substitutes and the return to debt, v_t (which is needed to calculate B_{t+1} when taxes are fixed in period t) equals the return to capital, r_t.

Table 3.1 presents the results of simulations of this model for different initial values of second-period life span, β, and the serial correlation of the process governing life span, ρ. The innovations of this process, ε, are assumed to be drawn from a uniform distribution over the interval $[-0.1, 0.1]$. Also, the government's discount rate, r^*, is set equal to 2, and the initial capital stock is set to its steady-state value in the linearized model.[3] The initial stock of debt is set to zero. Taxes on young and old, T_1 and T_2, from the "previous" period, which are state variables because of the government's policy constraints, are both set equal to 0.1. We assume that policy was not adjusted in the previous period, so that government does have the option of moving in the initial period.

Because the amount of time required for each simulation rises explosively as the government's horizon lengthens, we present results for a four-period horizon, that is, for period $M - 3$ as defined above. As discussed above, this is the first horizon (from the end) for which the government's decision regarding whether to adjust policy is not a trivial one. Also, given the size of the discount factor and the implicit length of each period, this horizon should be sufficiently long to provide a general picture of the results. We solve the model by using a grid search technique.[4] For each simulation, Table 3.1 presents the value achieved by the value function at the optimal policy and the corresponding values of consumption and taxes for young and old and debt and capital carried into the next period.

For the sake of comparison, we also present simulations for the case in which there are no restrictions on policy changes. The top panel of the table, labeled "unconstrained," presents the results of these simulations, while the simulations for the model with constraints appear in the table's lower panel.

Let us first consider the results for the unconstrained model. As discussed earlier, the government's decision in this case simplifies to a two-step problem: it allocates consumption to each generation in a given period to satisfy the ratio implied by combining expressions (14a) and (14b) and then chooses the capital stock to spread resources over time to satisfy expression (15). This implies that $C_2/C_1 = (1 + r^*)\beta$, which equals 3β for our assumption that $r^* = 2$, as the simulations in the top panel

---

[3] Remember that each period in this life-cycle model represents a generation of perhaps thirty years, so a discount factor of 2 corresponds to a compounded annual discount factor of around 3.7%.
[4] We chose this technique after attempts at using derivative-based methods failed to converge.

confirm approximately.[5] The unconstrained results are also consistent with the prediction from the linearized model regarding the impact of ρ on the response of consumption to a shock to current life span, β. Recall that as the shock to β is expected to be more permanent (ρ is large), we can less afford an increase in the current consumption of the elderly. Thus, consumption of the elderly should increase less and saving should be higher, when ρ is high. Indeed, this is quite evident when we compare the changes in C_2 as β increases for $\rho = 0.1$ and $\rho = 0.9$. In fact, saving actually rises with β for the $\rho = 0.9$ case, which may reflect either the additional complications of the model over its linearized version or the fact that our earlier results held for the infinite-horizon case.

Another result worth noting is that, for $\beta = 1$, the capital stock is the same when $\rho = 0.9$ and when $\rho = 0.1$. To analyze this result, note first that when $\beta_t = 1$, $\beta_{t+1} = 1 + \varepsilon_{t+1}$, so that the distribution of β_{t+1} is independent of ρ. The distribution of subsequent values of β will also have a mean of 1, but will have greater variance when $\rho = 0.9$, because shocks will persist. Thus, our finding is that increased future variance has no impact on capital accumulation, a result that might seem counterintuitive. It can be shown, however, at least in the two-period version of this model with logarithmic utility, that a simple increase in the variance of β is neutral with respect to capital accumulation. In our simulations, the outcome is more complicated because factor prices are also changing with β, as a result of variations in capital accumulation. Our result suggests that these variations have essentially no net impact.

Turning now to the simulations for the constrained model, we find that in all cases the government chooses to adjust tax policy in the initial period, given the assumed values of T_1 and T_2, 0.1, from the "previous" period. Because it then cannot adjust policy in the next period and must adjust policy in the final period, this means that the government's initial policy must stay in place for three periods.

As one would expect, anticipating so little flexibility leads the government to sacrifice current consumption to provide for the future. In percentage terms, the reduction in C_1 is larger than that in C_2, perhaps reflecting the fact that the young may be expected to "recover" part of the government's precautionary saving when they are old. The reduction in C_2 is stronger for higher values of ρ and higher values of β. We conjecture that the first result derives from the higher variance of future

---

[5] This relationship holds exactly when we use a high number of potential policy variables in the grid search, but in this case, the computer program can take several days to find the optimal policy.

shocks, to which policy may not be able to respond. The second result may be attributable in part to the fact that future generations are, in general, expected to be worse off when the current value of β is high. Thus, in each case, the welfare cost of having the "wrong" fiscal policy will be greater (because the errors are greater or their costs are higher), and this leads the government to exact a greater sacrifice from the current elderly.

There may also be a more subtle reason why there is less of a reduction in C_2 when β is small. When β is less than 1, it is expected to rise in the future. With policy set each period, we would then expect to have to raise the consumption of the elderly in the future, presumably by reducing their taxes. However, with policy variables constrained at their current values, this adjustment will not be possible. It may be necessary, then, to reduce the taxes on the elderly today, forcing more of the precautionary saving adjustment onto the young. This effect would be most important for low values of ρ, when we are more certain that life expectancy will revert to "normal" and rise in the near future. Indeed, it is most observable in the table for the case of $\rho = 0.1$ and $\beta = 0.7$. For this case, the consumption of the elderly does not drop at all between the unconstrained and constrained case – all of the precautionary saving is being forced on the young. This additional effect would be absent, of course, if our transfer to the elderly were fixed not in total value but per unit of time spent in old age, as, indeed, old-age pension annuities are.

This factor helps explain why the pattern of changes in C_1 is not monotonic with respect to increases in ρ and β. Still, taking the changes in C_1 and C_2 together, the impact on precautionary saving – the difference in capital between the unconstrained and constrained policy scenarios – is higher and rises more quickly with β when $\rho = 0.9$ than when $\rho = 0.1$, consistent with the initial intuition given when discussing C_2.

At the bottom of Table 3.1, we present estimates of the range of inaction in the policy-constrained version of the model, for the cases of $\beta = 1$ and $\rho = 0.9$ and 0.1. In parentheses are the values of T_1 and T_2 that define the boundary of the set over which the government would choose inaction, if the other tax happened to be set equal to its optimal current-period value.

For example, for $\rho = 0.9$, if the lagged value of T_2 happened to equal -0.075, its optimal value in the current decision period (in bold in the table), then government would choose inaction for $T_1 \in [0.03, 0.24]$, bracketing the optimal value (also in bold) of 0.200. Setting T_1 at its optimal value of 0.200, we find an inaction range for T_2 of $[-0.20,-0.04]$. These ranges are quite broad relative to those for $\rho = 0.1$.[6] This difference suggests that there is much greater value in waiting to adjust policy if the next period's information is more "permanent." That is, when $\rho = 0.9$, the shock in the next period, $M - 2$, will also have an important impact on life span in periods $M - 1$ and M. Thus, being able to adjust policy in period $M - 2$ has greater value than it would if the shock in period $M - 2$ were more temporary, as it is when $\rho = 0.1$.

Another interesting pattern in these results is that the optimal values of T_1 and T_2 each lie much closer to the upper boundary of their respective inaction ranges than to the lower boundary. We may infer from this that suboptimal current tax rates are much more costly if they are too high than if they are too low. The logic is straightforward: mistakes in the first direction lead to taxes being too high, and consumption too low, for only one set of generations (those currently alive), while mistakes in the other direction lead to taxes being too high, and consumption too low, for a larger number of generations. Being able to spread a given burden over more generations reduces its overall cost, given the concavity of utility and hence the social welfare criterion.

This suggests an apparent paradox: that through its decisions of whether to act, the government will tend to sustain taxes that are too low and cut taxes that are too high, leading to a bias toward taxes that are too low. However, it is important to recall that, if it acts, the government tends to choose taxes that are higher than in the unconstrained case. Thus, taking into account both periods of action and periods of inaction, it does not follow that taxes will be lower, on average, in the constrained world than in the unconstrained world. While our intuition is that taxes will be higher, on average, this is an open question that we hope to resolve in future work. We also hope to explore other questions involving inaction and uncertainty, such as the impact of an expectation that uncertainty will be resolved (i.e., an expected decline in the variance of the innovations, ε.) In addition, we are exploring how much of the large gap in social welfare between the constrained and unconstrained models can be closed through the use of devices that make political action less necessary, such as indexing of policy variables to the expected lifetime of the elderly.

---

[6] Indeed, the grid size of 0.01 being used to estimate the inaction range is really too large for this problem, for the boundaries of the two inaction ranges are at successive points on the grid.

Table 3.2. *Optimal Policy Rules under Government Discount Rate = 1, Four-Period Horizon*

	$\rho = 0.9$ $\beta = 0.7$	$\rho = 0.9$ $\beta = 1.0$	$\rho = 0.9$ $\beta = 1.3$	$\rho = 0.1$ $\beta = 0.7$	$\rho = 0.1$ $\beta = 1.0$	$\rho = 0.1$ $\beta = 1.3$
Unconstrained						
V	−2.491	−2.652	−2.791	−2.865	−3.147	−3.457
C_1	0.258	0.220	0.189	0.235	0.199	0.177
C_2	0.358	0.434	0.486	0.330	0.402	0.450
K	0.160	0.122	0.101	0.211	0.175	0.149
T_1	−0.016	−0.012	−0.004	−0.044	0.020	0.060
T_2	0.000	−0.076	−0.128	0.028	−0.044	−0.092
Debt	0.016	0.088	0.132	0.016	0.024	0.032
Constrained						
V	−2.721	−3.230	−3.691	−2.887	−3.200	−3.480
C_1	0.244	0.187	0.156	0.219	0.191	0.164
C_2	0.351	0.401	0.423	0.354	0.401	0.443
K	0.181	0.188	0.197	0.203	0.185	0.169
T_1	−0.015	0.035	0.056	−0.015	0.035	0.085
T_2	0.008	−0.043	−0.065	0.004	−0.043	−0.085
Debt	0.008	0.008	0.008	0.011	0.008	0.000

Table 3.2 presents the results of the same set of simulations for the case in which the discount factor, r^*, is set equal to 1. For the unconstrained policy simulations, the use of a lower discount rate makes higher capital accumulation optimal. In this case, the effects of imposing policy constraints are qualitatively similar to those shown in Table 3.1. In particular, the capital stocks under the constrained runs are generally higher than for the comparable unconstrained simulations. However, the increases are much smaller for this lower value of r^*, presumably because the higher rate of initial capital accumulation leaves greater margin for error. Indeed, for $\beta = 0.7$ and $\rho = 0.1$, the capital stock actually falls when the constraint is imposed. The reason appears to be the one discussed above: that the only way to provide a reasonable level of consumption for the longer-lived future elderly is to "overfeed" today's short-lived elderly. Thus, today's young have to bear all (in fact, more than all) of the reduction in consumption induced by policy constraints. As discussed above, this phenomenon would be absent if the policy constraint applied to an old-age annuity rate rather than the total old-age payment.

Conclusions

One cannot draw universal conclusions from a model as simple as the one used in this paper. However, our results illustrate a number of points relevant to current discussion of long-run policy making. We emphasize two of these points here.

First, it is important to concentrate on fundamental economic effects. The impact of policies ultimately occurs through their impact on distribution and incentives. Thus, we learn more by focusing on how policy changes alter distribution and incentives and not being diverted by superficial distinctions, such as whether the policy change takes the form of public pension reform or a shift to a private pension program or whether the policy change occurs within the pension area or some other part of the government budget.

Second, in itself, the presence of uncertainty about the future offers little apparent justification for waiting to act in response to an anticipated fiscal imbalance. With a risk-averse population, the costs of future outcomes even worse than those expected outweigh the benefits of outcomes better than expected. This suggests not only that action should not be delayed, but that action should actually be accelerated – that some precautionary saving may be called for, in addition to whatever changes are needed to respond to an expected fiscal imbalance. The added realism of restrictions on the frequency of policy changes alters this result in two offsetting ways. The prospect of being unable to set policy in the future occasions even more precautionary saving today, *if the government acts*. However, the government may also choose not to exercise its valuable option to set policy and, because the impact of its policies on the elderly cannot be reversed in the future, it is more likely to choose inaction when fiscal tightening is called for. Thus, the optimal policy response over time might best be characterized by great caution in general, but punctuated by occasional periods of apparent irresponsibility. Much research remains to be done on this issue.

References

Auerbach, Alan J., and Laurence J. Kotlikoff. 1987. *Dynamic Fiscal Policy*. Cambridge: Cambridge University Press.

Auerbach, Alan J., Laurence J. Kotlikoff, and Willi Leibfritz. 1999. *Generational Accounting around the World*. Chicago: University of Chicago Press.

Barro, Robert J. 1979. On the Determination of the Public Debt. *Journal of Political Economy*, October, 940–71.

Bohn, Henning. 1998. *Risk Sharing in a Stochastic Overlapping Generations Economy*. University of California, Santa Barbara.

Chari, V. V., Lawrence J. Christiano, and Patrick J. Kehoe. 1994. Optimal Fiscal Policy in a Business Cycle Model. *Journal of Political Economy*, August, 617–52.

Congressional Budget Office. 1998. *The Economic and Budget Outlook: Fiscal Years 1999–2008*. Washington, DC: U.S. Government Printing Office.

Diamond, Peter A. 1997. Macroeconomic Aspects of Social Security Reform. *Brookings Papers on Economic Activity*, Fall, 1–66.

Judd, Kenneth. 1989. *Optimal Taxation in Dynamic Stochastic Economies*. Hoover Institution.

Comment

PETER DIAMOND

This chapter explores two questions: (1) whether increased uncertainty implies that an optimal consumption plan should have less current consumption, and (2) how adding a constraint that tax variables cannot be adjusted in two consecutive periods changes optimal consumption. The authors use a two-period overlapping generations (OLG) model, not the fifty-five-period model one might have anticipated. I am grateful for this simplification, but I wish they had gone even further. Two-period models are even simpler than two-period OLG models. I will use a two-period model to discuss the first of their two questions. Then I will consider the issue of a decision process that deviates from full optimality as a further element shaping how we should react to increased uncertainty. I will discuss these issues without a formal model, a sort of background discussion for their chapter.

Risk and Savings

In a one-agent, two-period, one-good model, we have a utility function $u(a, b, x)$, where a is first-period consumption, b is second-period consumption, and x is a random element of preferences. In addition, we have a production relation,

$$b = f(a, y); \qquad f_a < 0, \; f_y > 0, \tag{1}$$

where y is a random element of production.

The random variables x and y are jointly distributed, $G(x, y; z)$, where z is a shift variable, with increases in z representing increases in risk. We have the first-order condition for optimal consumption:

$$u_a = E\{u_b f_a | z\}. \tag{2}$$

The response of optimal consumption to increased risk is derived by calculating da/dz in (2) and looking for sufficient conditions to sign this expression. Of course, this is not a new question (see, e. g., Leland, 1968). And we know that there is not an unambiguously signed answer that is true for all utility functions and all production functions for all reasonable definitions of increased risk. So we could explore the combinations of assumptions on u, f, and G that do give a sign. (This exploration would plausibly start with the theorems in Athey [1998a, 1998b].)

This chapter has started with intertemporally additive preferences. This is an important assumption, one that can affect conclusions and one that appears empirically false for individual intertemporal preferences. Alternatively, we could interpret the model as referring to different cohorts, converting the additivity assumption from an empirical one about preferences into a normative one about social welfare functions. Here, too, it seems to me to be unsatisfactory. Particularly in an OLG setting, the distribution of consumption at a particular point of time is an important ingredient in evaluations of the social gain from increased consumption by a single agent at that time. Is the assumption of additivity important? Answering that question depends on theorems on the robustness of the findings in this chapter, findings that are a start on this issue whatever the degree of robustness.

In considering risks, it seems important to recognize that the risks in this model are not independent. For example, life expectancy risk is not independent of productivity and rate of return risks. Particularly for the elderly, I think that mortality depends on resources devoted to the elderly, which in turn depends on productivity. Moreover, research successes that affect productivity may well be correlated with research successes that enhance life expectancy. Correlations may change the importance of risks – in this case, we are more likely to have more resources when we are more likely to value them more.

Political Solutions

The chapter recognizes that the process generating legislation to respond to realizations of stochastic variables and to changes in risk differs from a single optimization problem with only technological constraints. The chapter focuses on a single element of difference – considering a single optimization, but with government control variables that can only be adjusted from time to time, with time-specific rather than state-specific change possibilities. To explore this issue, we need to think about what we mean by government control variables.

Comment

Nominal Social Security benefits used to change only when there was a legislated change. Then, in 1972, benefits were indexed to the consumer price index (CPI). So we had more frequent adjustments in nominal benefits, but with adjustments subject to limited response to the economic and demographic environment, as given by a particular indexing formula that was not a function of any other variables. In other words, we converted decisions about benefits taken from time to time into limits on the relationship between benefits and the state of nature plus an expectation of less frequent legislation.

At one extreme, we could consider legislating a complete strategy as a function of a complete description of the states of nature. In this case, there is no need for future legislation, and the infrequency of the ability to change is irrelevant. To move toward reality from this abstract starting place, we would think about limits on the complexity allowed in the strategy and, perhaps more important, our inability to list all the states of nature. Recognizing this inability is where the rules/discretion debate needs to start. (For a discussion of legislation in an incomplete contracts frame, see Diamond [1996].)

But I suspect that this approach would still miss the most important elements of how the political process differs from a single optimization. The political process is a preset process for reaching a decision (legislation or inaction), in which different people have different objectives and different evaluations of the trade-offs available. Thus I disagree with the authors that this issue is best analyzed in an abstract formulation without detailed institutional details. The details of the institutional design seem to me very important. Let us consider a historical example.

In the 1970s there were two candidates for reform of the overindexed Social Security system – the one that was adopted and one that used price indexing everywhere. Because of anticipated real wage growth and progressivity of the benefit formula, the latter approach would have generated a better financial position for Social Security over time. Congress would respond differently to the financial positions of the two different institutions over time. A price-indexed system would be less likely to have the current financial and political status. If a price-indexed system accrued large reserves, it would be easier for Congress to solve that problem by raising benefits or cutting taxes than doing the reverse. Ease of legislation is not symmetric.

Similarly, we can ask how a standard defined-benefit Social Security system would be different from one with automatic indexing of benefits to life expectancy at retirement. Such indexing could be done as in Sweden, with proportional cuts in benefits for everyone in a cohort, based on life expectancy when they reach age 60. Alternatively, it could

95

be done (far worse in my opinion) by indexing the normal retirement age. These two approaches differ in that increasing the normal retirement age gives larger percentage cuts in benefits to those retiring early than to those retiring late. Without some such indexing, the financial problems that arise with continuing improved mortality would require a congressional response. With either of these approaches to automatic adjustment, adaptation to the increased cost is solely by benefit cuts, not by tax increases. It seems to me unlikely that an optimal system would adapt completely on the benefit side and not at all on the tax side. One also needs to think about how one might want to change the early entitlement age, but that depends on more than just life expectancy, since both morbidity and job opportunities and interest in working need not be changing in lock step with mortality. So choosing an automatic adjustment makes it less likely that other factors will be adjusted. But the indexing selected will be a function of a very incomplete list of the considerations that would go into a congressional decision to spread the cost of adjusting to financial difficulty around the system.

There are similar issues in considering introduction of a defined-contribution portion in order to construct a mixed defined-benefit defined-contribution system. For example, a defined-contribution system that uses the market to relate benefits to life expectancy reduces benefits for increased life expectancy. And, adapting a defined-benefit system to changing circumstances is likely to differ from adapting the sum of changes in the two portions of a mixed system. For example, a sense of entitlement affects political pressures. Would a plan such as the Personal Security Accounts (Advisory Council on Social Security, 1997), which has individual accounts and a flat benefit, react differently to payroll tax shortfalls than would a fully defined benefit system? Almost surely – preserving a flat benefit is cutting all benefits by the same dollar amount, an unlikely outcome when adapting an earnings-related benefit system to the same revenue problem. (For discussions of Social Security policy that incorporate such political considerations, see Diamond, 1997, 1998, and Panel on Privitzation of Social Security, 1998.)

It is also the case that the legislative process reflects political pressures that are themselves strongly influenced by expectations and by previous legislation. So legislation can set in train political pressures that strongly affect later legislation (see, e. g., Heclo, 1998, Panel on Privatization of Social Security, 1998). For example, setting up individual accounts is likely to come with restrictions on access to the accounts at retirement that will affect how much widows end up with compared with what the couple had. Will the sense of private ownership inherent in individual accounts change such rules over time?

Comment

But exploring such issues would be a very different chapter from the one I am discussing here.

I did not ask whether we indeed have increased uncertainty today or are just concerned about uncertainty because we are discussing some reforms to address long-run problems, problems that we have been aware of for a long time. I suspect it is the latter, suggesting that less abstract, more concrete models are needed to examine how Social Security policy today should reflect the uncertainty.

References

Advisory Council on Social Security. 1997. Report of the 1994–1996 Advisory Council on Social Security. Washington, DC.

Athey, Susan. 1998a. Comparative Statics under Uncertainty: Single Crossing Properties and Log-Supermodularity. Unpublished, MIT.

———. 1998b. Characterizing Properties of Stochastic Objective Functions. Unpublished, MIT.

Diamond, Peter. 1996. Insulation of Pensions from Political Risk. In S. Valdes, ed., *The Economics of Pensions: Principles, Policies, and International Experience.* Cambridge: Cambridge University Press.

———. 1997. Macroeconomic Aspects of Social Security Reform. *Brookings Papers on Economic Activity* 2:1–87.

———. 1998. The Economics of Social Security Reform. In R. Douglas Arnold, Michael Graetz, and Alicia Munnell, eds., *Framing the Social Security Debate: Values, Politics and Economics.* Washington, DC: Brookings Institution Press, pp. 38–64.

Heclo, Hugh. 1998. A Political Science Perspective on Social Security Reform. In R. Douglas Arnold, Michael Graetz, and Alicia Munnell, eds., *Framing the Social Security Debate: Values, Politics and Economics.* Washington, DC: Brookings Institution Press, pp. 65–89.

Leland, Hayne E. 1968. Savings and Uncertainty: The Precautionary Demand for Saving. *Quarterly Journal of Economics* 82:465–73.

Panel on Privatization of Social Security. 1998. *Evaluating Issues in Privatizing Social Security.* Washington, DC: National Academy of Social Insurance. Also available from MIT Press.

Comment

SHRIPAD TULJAPURKAR

The chapter by Auerbach and Hassett (henceforth referred to as AH) is an interesting and instructive analysis of economic decisions taken under conditions of demographic change and economic uncertainty. As I am a demographer, my comments focus on demographic facts relevant to the analysis they present and insights from their paper that might inform the analysis of interactions between demographic and economic factors. I consider four questions.

Persistent Trends in Life Expectancy

The key demographic ingredient in the analysis is a life-span variable that represents what demographers call the expectation of life. Demographic analysis indicates (as discussed, for example, by Lee and Tuljapurkar in Chapter 2) that the expectation of life is increasing in a persistent, even approximately linear, fashion. Thus, it is probably realistic to model life-span changes by

$$\beta_t = \beta_{t-1} + h + \varepsilon_t,$$

or

$$\beta_t = \beta_{t-1} + h\exp(-\theta\beta_t) + \varepsilon_t,$$

rather than by the autoregressive process that AH employ in their numerical analysis.

The main features of these two equations are that serial correlation is high and a trend is persistent. What might be the impact of such persistence on the equilibria and dynamics of the AH model?

Comment

Stickiness of Policy

AH make an illuminating analysis of the degree to which policy is "sticky," meaning that there is a broad range of conditions under which inaction is acceptable. Two questions arise.

First, AH report that this range of inaction is particularly broad when the autocorrelation of life-span shocks is high. This seems counterintuitive – if autocorrelation is, indeed, high, a positive shock now, say, makes a positive shock more likely in the future. In other words, there is a lot of information in the current shock, so why wait? It is not obvious, at least to me, that the information trade-off relevant to stickiness goes in the direction that AH's results imply.

Second, if we ignore the above quibble, AH find that a sticky adaptive policy is likely to be optimal. In other words, a wait-and-see approach may pay dividends. A direct lesson for analysts working on, say, Social Security policy options, is to explore adaptive, "sticky" policies as potentially more efficient than long-term, forward-looking policy.

Replacement Rates and Transfers

Much current interest focuses on PAYGO (i.e., pay-as-you-go) retirement systems and their variants. A central dynamic driver in any PAYGO system is the relationship between benefit outflows and tax inflows over time. In rough terms, the difference between these flows depends on the product

$$(\text{replacement ratio}) \times (\text{dependency ratio}),$$

where the replacement ratio is the ratio of average benefits to average taxes, measured per capita, and the dependency ratio is the ratio of the number of beneficiaries to the number of taxpayers.

In the AH model, the effect of changes in the dependency ratio is captured schematically by changes in the life expectancy parameter. But there is no equivalent in the AH analysis for the replacement ratio. Might the replacement ratio be captured in the AH model by a relationship between the flows T_1 and T_2, or between these flows and economic variables? For example, for the study of pension plans one can imagine relevant variants of the AH model in which T_2 is determined by the wage level or the ratio (T_2/T_1) is determined by productivity. The risk-sharing results in the AH analysis may well change significantly in the presence of such a coupling.

The point of introducing such a relationship would be to make contact with the literature that explores risk sharing in PAYGO systems. This literature (e.g., Thogersen, 1998) is rather more simplistic than AH in treating economic dynamics. I believe it would be most instructive to examine PAYGO risk sharing in the AH framework.

Risk Aversion

In their analysis of a linearized version of their model, AH note that the linearization cannot capture effects of risk aversion. In problems involving nonlinear stochastic dynamics in other fields, it is often true that a second-order analysis (through quadratic nonlinearities) allows one to examine the response of dynamics to variance. Might this approach work here? Or, are there reasons why one would not expect such an analysis to work?

In relation to the simulation results shown here, it may be useful to explore the effects of differences between the risk-aversion parameters γ_1 and γ_2. Returning again to the context of pensions, it is conventional to view older people as being more risk averse than younger people; but it is also known that risk aversion is something that can be changed by education about risks (as witnessed by the successful campaign waged by mutual funds to get people to invest in equities). Can one use risk aversion as a modifiable behavioral trait that could function as a long-run policy tool? How do the dynamics of the AH analysis change if risk aversion is not fixed over time?

Overall, I found the chapter by Auerbach and Hassett to be illuminating and thought provoking. I hope that we will see further exploration of some of the richer questions that remain a challenge.

Reference

Thogersen, Oystein. 1998. A Note on Intergenerational Risk-Sharing and the Design of Pay-as-You-Go Pension Programs. *Journal of Population Economics* 11:373–78.

CHAPTER 4

How Does a Community's Demographic Composition Alter Its Fiscal Burdens?

THOMAS MaCURDY AND THOMAS NECHYBA

Introduction

With local communities providing such diverse services as education, public safety, infrastructure, and public health care, the demographic characteristics of a locality's population (e.g., age composition) surely play a fundamental role in determining both a community's fiscal needs and its fiscal capacity. Furthermore, a community's ability to efficiently fund services through the rents individuals derive from them is sharply curtailed by a variety of critical intercommunity spillovers that lead to benefits being enjoyed outside the jurisdiction of the community. These spillovers not only arise from the familiar routes associated with public goods being consumed by nonresidents, but also come into play for community investments in people who leave jurisdictions before realizing returns from such investments. The presence of these intercommunity spillovers constitutes a primary force generating what we call "fiscal burdens," which govern the fiscal federalism that relates policies of local and central governments. Throughout, we will define the fiscal burden of a local government as the excess of its expenditures valued by "outsiders" over the tax revenues it receives from them. This chapter investigates the relatively unexplored questions of the extent to which a community's age composition impacts its fiscal

MaCurdy gratefully acknowledges research support from NIH grant HD32055-02, and Nechyba acknowledges support from the Center of Economic Policy Research (CEPR) at Stanford. Opinions expressed in this paper are those of the authors and do not represent the official position or policy of any agency funding this research. The authors thank Jed Devaro, Katie Carman, and Gregory Besharov for many useful comments and expert research assistance and Antonio Rangel for helpful discussions. Some of this research was conducted while Nechyba was on leave as a National Fellow at the Hoover Institution, whose support is gratefully acknowledged.

burden and the extent to which intergovernmental transfers from central governments can and do compensate the localities for these burdens.

The analysis develops a simple theoretical model that clarifies the role of demographics and the associated spillovers in local government finance, that highlights the funding problems arising in this context, and that explores the potential remedies through central government transfers. To explore the practical applicability of this model, this study conducts an empirical analysis of county budgets in California, examining the impact of a county's age composition on its local government's expenditures and revenues. This analysis sheds light on the net impact of marginal shifts in demographic compositions on county budgets and allows us to ask whether state and federal transfers compensate for these shifts. This empirical analysis, which focuses on overall flows of intergovernmental transfers and therefore avoids the usual fungibility issues that arise in a narrower analysis of specific transfer and expenditure categories, suggests that the observed flows of intergovernmental transfers are broadly consistent with the predictions of our economic model.

Demographic Characteristics and Community Budgets

The simple theoretical framework presented in the section "Demographic Groups, the Cost of Public Goods, and Local Fiscal Burdens" incorporates the demographic composition of a community as an important element in the cost function a local government faces for providing different levels of public services. The fraction of the local population composed of school-age children within a jurisdiction, for example, clearly has implications for the total (or per resident) cost of providing a given level of school quality to all students. In a simple world where local public spending simply represents consumption to current residents, where the taxes they pay are simply payments for benefits received, and where local governments do not attempt to strategically influence local demographic characteristics, no local fiscal burdens arise. There is thus no role for a central government, and fiscal federalism is an uninteresting issue. However, this simple world does not exist, and, instead, a variety of consequential spillovers interfere with a community's provision of many public goods and generate local fiscal burdens. In the case of public education, for example, a community is unable to fund investments in current schoolchildren if the rents from such investments cannot be taxed in the future as a result of the mobility of those students when they reach adulthood. It is only when various kinds of spillovers are explicitly introduced into the model that local fiscal burdens (as defined at the beginning of the chapter) arise, and it is under those circumstances that central transfers to local governments emerge and improve upon decentralized outcomes. Differences in local demographic compositions combined with the existence of spillover benefits into other jurisdictions therefore generate variable fiscal burdens for different communities.

In light of this, it is perhaps surprising that there exist (to our knowledge) few prior attempts aimed at linking local fiscal burdens to local demographic characteristics, and those that do exist are generally concerned with issues quite unrelated to the issues we raise here.[1] A substantial empirical literature arising from Bergstrom and Goodman (1973), for example, has focused on estimating demands for local public goods ranging from public education to public safety and municipal services, and in the process demographic characteristics have often been included as explanatory variables.[2] The focus of these studies, however, has been the estimation of income and price elasticities, and little attention or interpretation has been given to coefficients on demographic variables. This has resulted in relatively little consensus regarding the role of local demographic characteristics in determining local public-good demands. More recently, Cutler, Elmendorf, and Zeckhauser (1993) have attempted to unravel the politics that gives rise to state and local public-goods bundles, and Poterba (1997) has provided evidence of political competition between generations in determining state support of public education. However, while these papers have attempted to discover something about local demand for public goods, none has taken the broader approach of linking demographic characteristics to overall fiscal burdens, nor have they asked to what extent spillovers that depend in part on demographic characteristics are internalized through present intergovernmental grants. It is in these dimensions that this chapter attempts to fill a void, and it is to this end that we now turn to a brief review of the literature on fiscal federalism and intergovernmental grants.

---

[1] A notable exception is offered by Echevarria (1995), who uses a model that is somewhat similar to ours to theoretically investigate the consequences of population growth on the relative needs of different governments in a federal system.

[2] Bergstrom and Goodman's (1973) original work focused on estimating local political equilibria and included fractions of demographic groups in the local population but neglected to take into account the now well-recognized presence of Tiebout bias (Goldstein and Pauly, 1981; Rubinfeld, Shapiro, and Roberts, 1987). Other notable papers attempting to estimate local public-good demand in various contexts include those of Gramlich and Rubinfeld (1982), Denzau and Grier (1984), Megdal (1984), and Bogart (1991).

A Brief Look at the Literature on Fiscal Federalism

The notion that intergovernmental transfers can potentially improve on purely decentralized government finance in the presence of spillovers is, of course, not new.[3] Furthermore, the idea of "spillovers" itself has evolved considerably. The earlier literature focused mainly on consumption spillovers across communities at a given time, while the more recent literature has paid more attention to interjurisdictional tax externalities (arising from local non-benefit taxation of mobile bases)[4] and externalities arising from strategic community competition.[5] The basic underlying message from the economics literature, however, has remained relatively constant: appropriately designed central grants can, in most cases, internalize interjurisdictional externalities regardless of their source.[6] In the section "Local Spillovers and the Emergence of Fiscal Burdens and Fiscal Federalism," we attempt to capture all these types of spillovers in a simple local public finance model and demonstrate conditions under which grants by central governments originate to alleviate the fiscal burdens from spillovers.

While the economic merits of this analysis are relatively unchallenged, some recent empirical work suggests that this model (often known as fiscal federalism) fails to provide a convincing explanation of the grant

[3] The basic ideas have been presented in many contexts over the past three decades (see Breton, 1965; Williams, 1966; Pauly, 1970; Bradford and Oates, 1971; Wilde, 1971; Oates, 1972; Gramlich, 1977; Inman and Rubinfeld, 1979; Arnott and Grieson, 1981; Gordon, 1983; Inman and Rubinfeld, 1996), although empirical documentation of spillover effects remains relatively scarce (Weisbrod, 1965; Greene, Neenan, and Scott, 1974). Spillovers, however, are often not thought of in the way we model them. Wyckoff (1984), for example, estimates the degree of education spillover *within* communities from parents to nonparents, while we are concerned mainly with education investment spillovers *across* jurisdictions due to mobility considerations.
[4] This idea owes much of its prominence to the "New View" of property taxation as largely a tax on all forms of capital, first explored by Mieszkowsi (1972) and since elaborated by Mieszkowski and Zodrow (1989) and Zodrow and Mieszkowski (1986). A general approach to internalizing such externalities through fiscal federalism can be found in Gordon (1983) and Inman and Rubinfeld (1996). A recent caveat to this literature is offered by Lee (1998), who argues that if individuals hold diversified portfolios that include fixed factors in other jurisdictions, then local governments will take into account the benefit to other jurisdictions when capital migrates.
[5] Tax competition in a strategic setting is explored in Wilson (1986) and Wildasin (1989), and expenditure competition is most often discussed in terms of a hypothesized "race to the bottom" when communities consider the impact on local community composition when setting local welfare policy. Besharov and Zweiman (1998) further point out that strategic policy considerations also arise in regulatory rather than tax/expenditure dimensions.
[6] Some special cases have been identified in which this is not the case (Krelove, 1992; Myers, 1994), but these cases are of relatively narrow empirical interest given the special assumptions required (Inman and Rubinfeld, 1996).

systems we observe in the United States. Inman (1988) and Inman and Rubinfeld (1996), for example, suggest that a model of distributive and party politics dominates the economic model of fiscal federalism as an explanation for federal grant policy, and Hulten and Schwab (1997) similarly find federal infrastructure policy to be inconsistent with predictions from the economic framework.[7] It has thus become clear from such works that political barriers to the implementation of efficiency-enhancing central government grants may, at least in some cases, interfere with the potential economic benefit from intergovernmental fiscal interaction.[8] In light of this new conventional wisdom, our empirical findings that grant flows to communities in California broadly support the implications of the economic model of fiscal federalism are thus somewhat surprising (see the section "Empirical Analysis of California Counties").

The empirical strategy employed to arrive at this conclusion is new in that it analyzes the impact of demographic factors and intergovernmental transfers on the entire local government's budget, rather than focusing on individual budget categories and their corresponding federal or state grant programs. Our approach, then, examines the overall impact of intergovernmental grants on local budgets and thus surmounts issues of fungibility that would be neglected were we to follow the more conventional empirical approach. In particular, local governments can often nominally use state or federal aid for some stated purpose, but then reduce local contributions for that purpose and either cut local taxes or raise spending in an entirely different category. A grant for school lunch programs, for instance, may allow local governments to devote fewer of their own resources to school budgets and raise expenditures for public parks. As a result, it may appear that school lunches are funded through government transfers when in fact they are funded locally, with grants intended for school lunches but diverted to other uses. Our approach differs from previous approaches in that it asks, How does a marginal change in the population affect the revenues (from both taxes and grants) as well as expenditures by local governments, and how effectively do state and federal transfers respond to changes in fiscal burdens

---

[7] Del Rossi and Inman (1994) argue that federal infrastructure investment is, in fact, in part a political payment to special interests.

[8] For a more detailed illustration of some of these political barriers, see Inman and Rubinfeld (1996) and McKinnon and Nechyba (1997). It should be noted, however, that public-choice economists disagree about the extent to which such political barriers are important. While Tullock (1983) emphasizes the role of imperfect information in providing politicians with the means to engage in inefficient special interest redistribution, Becker (1983) and Wittman (1989) argue that political competition ensures efficient redistribution.

associated with demographic changes? This allows us to investigate more directly whether the whole system of intergovernmental grants operates to compensate localities for the different fiscal burdens they incur from different demographic compositions.

Outline of Chapter

This chapter develops a conceptual model of government finance in which fiscal relationships between two levels of government emerge as the result of interjurisdictional spillovers arising from the local provision of a public good. In contrast to previous discussions of fiscal federalism, however, the local cost of providing this good is modeled as depending critically on the demographic makeup of local jurisdictions, which then causes fiscal relationships between different levels of government to depend in part on the geographic distribution of demographic groups. The section "Demographic Groups, the Cost of Public Goods, and Local Fiscal Burdens" assumes away all forms of interjurisdictional externalities and demonstrates that in such a world local fiscal burdens (as defined above) *do not arise*, despite the fact that differences in local demographic characteristics will certainly cause different local governments to face very different expenditures. The section "Local Spillovers and the Emergence of Fiscal Burdens and Fiscal Federalism" then introduces various types of spillovers that generate fiscal transfers from central governments. Because the size of local government expenditures and taxes depends crucially on local demographic characteristics, the presence of spillovers and the resulting emergence of central government grants implies that these transfers will also depend critically on demographic compositions. The goal of these sections is to present as succinctly as possible both the importance of local demographic characteristics in determining local public expenditures and the role of the existence of spillovers in generating fiscal interactions between different levels of government. For expositional simplicity and to highlight issues of concern, our analysis deliberately excludes political economy considerations raised elsewhere in the literature.[9] The section "Implications of a Community's Age Composition for Fiscal Policy" operationalizes the relatively abstract notions discussed in the two preceding sections by projecting how these factors would influence the spending and revenue patterns of the local governments making up counties. The section "Empirical Analysis of California Counties" empirically tests whether the flows of grants to counties in California are broadly consistent with these

---

[9] See, for example, Inman and Rubinfeld (1996) and Weingast (1995).

predictions. The final section concludes the paper with a brief summary of our findings, along with some final remarks and qualifications.

Demographic Groups, the Cost of Public Goods, and Local Fiscal Burdens

We begin by introducing a precise way in which demographic groups matter in determining local public expenditures. We then consider an idealized setting in which the fact that different communities are composed of different demographic groups does not impose any differences in fiscal burdens on these communities. In fact, under this idealized setting, *no* community experiences *any* fiscal burdens – for example, expenditures on public services financed locally but valued by "outsiders" – and all residents simply pay lump sum taxes related to the benefits they derive from these expenditures.

Demographic Groups and Public-Good Costs

Suppose that jurisdiction i is one of many jurisdictions in a state and that the demographic makeup of the population in this jurisdiction at time t can be summarized by the vector $x_t^i = (N_t^i, \mathbf{n}_t^i)$, where N_t^i is the population size and $\mathbf{n}_t^i = (n_{1,t}, \ldots, n_{K,t})$ represents a vector of population shares for K different types of agents. While individuals may in principle differ in many respects, such as race, sex, cultural background, etc., most of our analysis will focus on age differences. In particular, we assume in our empirical work that types can be grouped into three age categories denoted J (young), M (middle-aged) and E (elderly). In the absence of demographic differences other than age, the vector x_t^i can therefore simply be written as $(N_t^i, J_t^i, M_t^i, E_t^i)$, where J_t^i, M_t^i, and E_t^i represent the shares of the population falling into the three age categories, respectively. Throughout, we will assume that each generation is of equal size at all times (and thus that the total population in the economy remains constant across time), but individuals are able to choose among jurisdictions at each point in time.[10] Given this mobility assumption, the vector x_t^i of local population size and composition is therefore determined endogenously through the location choices of individuals, while the overall demographic characteristics of the entire population are exogenous.

---

[10] Whenever the local age distribution is assumed to characterize demographic differences across jurisdictions, the model becomes an overlapping-generations model. At time $t + 1$, each age group advances, with the oldest exiting the model and a new young generation entering.

Suppose a local government i in period t produces a local public good g_t^i and faces a cost function $c(\mathbf{x}_t^i, g_t^i)$.[11] Note carefully that g_t^i is an argument that enters individual utility functions and thus represents the total level and quality of a particular local public good consumed by local residents, not the expenditure required to achieve it (which is given by the cost function). For example, g_t^i may be "public safety," which is achieved through some level of spending $c(\mathbf{x}_t^i, g_t^i)$ that depends on the demographic composition of the community. Similarly, "lack of poverty" is a public good that may be achieved through welfare spending, and the levels of spending required will depend critically on local demographics. Likewise, "quality public education" is a public good whose per capita expenditure is zero if no school-age children are present in the community. Whether we view g_t^i as a specific public good or a composite of a variety of public goods produced locally, the demographic composition of the community will determine how much a given level of the good will cost (in total and per resident) for a given community, and communities with different demographic characteristics will face different expenditures for providing the same level of g.

More precisely, the size and composition of the local jurisdiction providing a public good g can enter the cost function in three distinct ways (which are outlined in Table 4.1), depending on the type of public good g represents: First, unless g is a pure public good exhibiting no rivalry within the local jurisdiction, the cost of providing a given level of g depends on the population size, N_t^i, in the jurisdiction. Most public expenditures by local governments are in fact devoted to goods that are at least somewhat rivalrous and thus involve some crowding through N_t^i in the cost function.[12] Second, to the extent that public expenditures other than those representing pure public goods are targeted at specific demographic groups, the share of the local population representing such groups determines the total cost of providing any particular level of the public service g. If g represents public education of a certain quality, for example, the number of children in the locality is directly related to the total level of spending required. Third, local population externalities may cause some public services to be more or less expensive than they would be in the absence of such externalities. In the case of education, for example, peer effects may cause education of a particular quality to be

---

[11] A more general version of the model might include past public-good spending as one of the arguments in this cost function. This would give rise to a public investment channel separate from that described below. For expositional convenience, we forgo such a generalization here.

[12] See Ladd (1998) for a survey of the empirical evidence regarding the relationship between population size and fiscal burdens of local communities.

Community Demographics and Fiscal Burdens

Table 4.1. *Impact of Demographic Characteristics on Cost Function*

Nature of the Public Expenditure (g)	Relevant Demographic Characteristics	Examples
Rivalry of g (i.e., degree of population crowding)	Population size	Total cost of local fireworks is independent of population size (pure public good), while cost of local crime prevention rises with population size (public service)
Degree of targeting to population segments	Size of targeted groups (age distribution)	Young: Welfare, child nutrition, education, Head Start, tuition subsidies Middle-aged: Some welfare programs, job training, unemployment insurance Elderly: Social Security, health care (hospitals, Medicare), retirement benefits
Population externalities	Family characteristics; culture/gender; socioeconomic status	Education: Peer effects in classrooms Crime Prevention: Male/female

substantially more expensive in the presence of some demographic characteristics than in the presence of others. As already mentioned, much of our empirical discussion will focus on the second of these factors, more particularly on the impact of the age distribution.

Absence of Fiscal Burdens in an Idealized Setting

In the next section, we will incorporate this model of demographics and public-goods costs into a general framework of fiscal federalism in which different types of public goods give rise to different kinds of spillovers. Before doing so, however, we note that in the absence of interjurisdictional spillovers, central governments will have no role whatever in alleviating fiscal burdens in such a model, either through grants or otherwise.

109

More precisely, suppose that many jurisdictions coexist and that individuals sort themselves into communities based in part on their tastes for public services (as suggested by Tiebout, 1956). As we will point out more formally in the next section, the assumption of no interjurisdictional spillovers in this model implies the exclusive use of benefit taxes by all local governments, the absence of any expenditure spillovers for any of the public goods and services provided by local governments, and the absence of attempts by local governments through their tax/expenditure policies to encourage or discourage any demographic group from residing within the jurisdiction. Under these conditions, individuals within jurisdictions pay benefit taxes (i.e., taxes proportional to the benefits from public services they receive), and local governments can fully use such taxes as all the benefits are strictly contained within jurisdictions.[13]

A priori, there is no reason, however, to believe that a Tiebout equilibrium of this kind will result in communities that mirror one another's demographic characteristics.[14] Given that these characteristics fundamentally determine the cost of providing particular kinds of public goods (as modeled above), it follows that both total and per-resident public expenditures will differ across jurisdictions *even if* all jurisdictions end up providing precisely the same level of public goods. In terms of the model introduced in the subsection "Demographic Groups and Public Good Costs," even if all public-good levels g are the same across all jurisdictions, the expenditures incurred by these jurisdictions to produce g are given by $c(\mathbf{x},g)$ and will therefore differ, assuming that $\mathbf{x}$ differs across jurisdictions. Nevertheless, in the absence of spillovers, each individual will pay only in proportion to benefits received, and no benefits will be consumed outside the jurisdiction that spends its resources on producing these benefits. Thus, despite different per-resident public expenditures resulting from differences in demographic characteristics, no community will experience any fiscal burdens.

Local Spillovers and the Emergence of Fiscal Burdens and Fiscal Federalism

We now consider more precisely the strength of the assumption that there exist no interjurisdictional spillovers by describing in some detail

---

[13] Under certain additional conditions, the absence of spillovers further implies efficient provision of public goods. For an accessible elaboration of the precise conditions under which efficiency obtains, see, for example, Scotchmer (1994).

[14] While such an equilibrium generally exists, it is easy to demonstrate it would not be stable.

the channels through which this assumption may be violated. In the process, the analysis presents a model of fiscal federalism and local public finance in which central governments engage in fiscal transfers, and where in the absence of such transfers, local governments would, indeed, experience fiscal burdens, and where this generates inefficiencies, which can be corrected centrally.

As suggested earlier, we remain relatively agnostic about the precise political process at work, assuming only that both local and central decisions are based on an objective function that incorporates individual utility levels of residents of different types within the relevant jurisdiction. Note that we do not necessarily insist on purely benevolent government processes but only require that both local and central processes take individual utilities of different demographic types as their arguments in some particular welfare function. In the absence of some implicit constraints on the central government, however, there would be no economic justification for the existence of local jurisdictions because the center could always do at least as well as a decentralized system by simply mimicking decentralized outcomes. Thus, all our analysis implicitly assumes that central governments are constrained to providing more-uniform levels of public goods across jurisdictions than those jurisdictions otherwise would, which then gives rise to an economic justification for local political jurisdictions that are, unlike the central government, able to match local public-good bundles to local tastes.[15]

In the remainder of this section, we elaborate the precise conditions under which fiscal transfers from the central government emerge in equilibrium given that local governments are charged with providing a particular public good or service *g*. These conditions all involve interjurisdictional spillovers of some kind. We begin by defining and outlining interjurisdictional expenditure links that generate three different types of expenditure spillovers, which lie at the core of our empirical analysis. We then discuss the equilibrium properties of this model, with particular focus on the conditions under which central governments will provide transfers to local governments in equilibrium, assuming two restrictive conditions hold: (i) all governments are constrained to use

---

[15] This constraint is implicit, for example, in Oates's (1972) well-known Decentralization Theorem. The idea of local matching of tastes to public-good bundles is, of course, reinforced by Tiebout's (1956) notion that individuals will tend to sort into jurisdictions according to their tastes for public goods. Other constraints on the central government that have been cited as justifications for lower-level governments include the less efficient use of policy-relevant local information by central governments (Hayek, 1966) and the inability of central governments to conduct policy experiments.

benefit taxes, which implies that no additional spillovers are generated through the local tax system; and (ii) local governments are assumed to view population characteristics as exogenous when setting local public expenditure and tax policy. Finally, we generalize the model by relaxing the two restrictive assumptions and providing an overall framework into which our results can be fit and then conclude our theoretical exposition with some caveats.

Spillovers from the Expenditure Side

Suppose jurisdiction i is one of J different local jurisdictions and each jurisdiction produces a single public good in each time period. Important spillovers from these local expenditures on public goods can then enter in three distinct ways: (i) across communities within the current time period; (ii) within the community but across time; and (iii) across communities and across time. In this section, we present a simple mechanism that capture these three kinds of spillover effects, which we will call (i) interjurisdictional *consumption* spillovers and (ii) intra- and (iii) interjurisdictional *investment* spillovers, respectively. These spillovers are central to our empirical analysis in that they will determine the extent to which a central government can improve on decentralized financing of public goods through intergovernmental transfers.

The Formal Model of Fiscal Federalism with Expenditure Spillovers

Suppose income at time t in jurisdiction i is denoted Y_t^i. While this will clearly depend on the demographic composition $\mathbf{x}_t^i$ of the community, it may also depend on past investments the jurisdiction has made (such as investments in infrastructure). Thus current public expenditures by jurisdiction i may result in future income for residents of that jurisdiction. Similarly, investments made by communities neighboring jurisdiction i may raise income in jurisdiction i in the future. If community j invests in public education at time t, for example, and if the beneficiaries of that education migrate to community i when they reach middle age at time $t+1$, then community i's income in $t+1$ rises as a direct consequence of the investment by jurisdiction j in time t. We therefore model income in jurisdiction i at time t as a function of the community's demographic composition as well as past public-good levels both within and outside community i; for example,

$$y_t^i = y(\mathbf{x}_t^i) + a(g_{t-1}^i) + \beta\left(\sum_{j \neq i} g_{t-1}^j\right), \tag{1}$$

where $\alpha(0) = \beta(0) = 0$, $\alpha'' < 0$, and $\beta'' < 0$, and α' and β' depend on the type of public expenditure.[16]

Two expenditure spillovers are introduced through this community income equation. First, when $\alpha' \neq 0$, public-good spending in jurisdiction i today leads to either higher or lower total income in that jurisdiction tomorrow.[17] We will call such effects *intrajurisdictional investment spillovers*. This kind of spillover, while it is fully contained within the community, occurs from one time period to the next and may therefore be intergenerational when viewed in the context of an overlapping-generations model. Second, when $\beta' \neq 0$, public-good spending in jurisdiction i today causes per capita income in jurisdiction j to either rise or fall tomorrow. This may occur through two distinct channels, depending on the degree of interjurisdictional mobility we assume. If populations are not mobile, then investments in local roads, for instance, may cause neighboring communities to experience some spillover benefits from increased economic activity in the future. On the other hand, if populations are mobile, then greater spending on such activities as local public education in jurisdiction i may lead to greater income in jurisdiction j in the future as the beneficiaries of education in jurisdiction i move to jurisdiction j. As we will mention shortly, such migrations are possible even in a steady-state equilibrium in which the overall demographic composition within communities remains the same but symmetric relocation of individuals for reasons other than local public goods occurs. We will refer to such effects as *interjurisdictional investment spillovers*.

Denoting private consumption in community i as q_t^i, the community then faces a budget constraint,

$$q_t^i = y_t^i - c(\mathbf{x}_t^i, g_t^i).^{18}$$

$$(2)$$

[16] Note that for expositional convenience we are restricting investment spillovers to be the same among all jurisdictions. This could easily be remedied by specifying a β function for each jurisdiction, but the central idea would remain the same. Further, whenever we use derivative notation, such as $\beta' > 0$, we will implicitly be making statements about the derivative at every argument (i.e., $\beta' > 0$ will be taken to mean $\beta'(x)$ for all $x > 0$).

[17] This may occur whether populations are mobile or not. In the absence of mobility, local public investments, such as those in local infrastructure, may directly raise the future per capita incomes of individuals currently residing in that community. In the presence of mobility, such increases in per capita incomes would decrease because of immigration from other jurisdictions unless those jurisdictions also engaged in similar public investments. Given that in equilibrium other jurisdictions must invest sufficiently for no net migrations to take place, however, benefits from such investments would in fact remain in the locality.

[18] As we point out in the subsection "Non-Benefit Taxation," this specification of the community budget implicitly assumes away tax externalities and thus assumes the exclusive use of benefit taxation.

THOMAS MaCURDY AND THOMAS NECHYBA

Individuals care about their private- and public-good consumption in each period, where type k's private-good consumption $q_{k,t}^i$ is simply that type's income minus the individual's tax payment, which the local government sets (in a lump sum way, for now) at $\tau_{k,t}^i$.[19] Furthermore, the consumption value of public goods produced in jurisdiction j at time t may, for some types of public expenditures, "spill over" into the utility functions of individuals in community i. The utility of resident k in jurisdiction i at time t is then assumed to be given by the function

$$u_{k,t}^i = \phi(q_{k,t}^i, g_t^i) + \gamma\left(\sum_{j \neq i} g_t^j\right), \tag{3}$$

where $\gamma(0) = 0$, $\gamma'' < 0$, and γ' depends on the type of public expenditure.[20] Note that this specification of individual utilities gives rise to a third expenditure spillover through the function γ; for example, whenever $\gamma' \neq 0$, current public-good production in community j generates current consumption benefits in community i. This may occur, for example, when local governments are charged with regulating CO_2 emissions, a reduction of which would benefit neighboring jurisdictions as well. We will call such spillovers *interjurisdictional consumption spillovers*.

Examples of Different Types of Local Public Goods
Table 4.2 provides some additional illustrative examples of how the first derivatives of the α, β, and γ functions uniquely capture all relevant expenditure externalities. Local parks, for example, are unlikely to bring about any increases in future community income (thus $\alpha' = \beta' = 0$), nor are they likely to generate consumption spillovers for residents in other communities (thus $\gamma' = 0$). Consequently, expenditures on local parks represent pure consumption value for local residents, and the local government is thus able to fully finance these through local benefit taxes. Public education, on the other hand, while representing consumption for current parents, is also an investment that raises future incomes. If residents are locationally fixed, then all future income generated from this investment remains within the jurisdiction that is undertaking the investment ($\alpha' > 0$, $\beta' = 0$) and can therefore be taxed locally (so long as local governments have access to credit markets). If, on the other hand, chil-

---

[19] We will place restrictions on this tax function, which maps individuals onto tax payments, shortly.

[20] As for the case of investment spillovers, we are restricting consumption spillovers to be the same among all jurisdictions, which could again be remedied by specifying a γ function for each jurisdiction. Furthermore, additional notation could be used to allow the γ function to differ across types of agents, but this yields no additional insights for the present purposes.

114

Table 4.2. *Typical Expenditure Externalities*

Public Expenditure	α'	β'	γ'
Local park, local library	0	0	0
Police/fire protection	0	0	0
Education without mobility	+	0	0
Local road	+	0	0
Education with mobility	(+)	+	0
Pollution control of CO_2 emissions	0	0	+
Road connecting communities	+	+	0
Welfare/health	0	0	(+)

dren that benefit from the investment are able to leave the jurisdiction once they enter the labor force, the increased income will benefit a different community ($\beta' > 0$), and the benefits from this investment cannot be taxed by the local jurisdiction.[21] At the same time, regardless of mobility assumptions, residents of jurisdiction i are unlikely to benefit today from current education spending in other jurisdictions ($\gamma' = 0$). In contrast, control of carbon dioxide pollution, while it certainly has local consumption value, also directly generates consumption benefits for residents of other jurisdictions ($\gamma' > 0$) but is unlikely to bring about substantial changes in future community incomes ($\alpha' = \beta' = 0$). Welfare spending intended to produce reductions in poverty may be more controversial because views differ on whether the reduction in poverty is a local or a state public good. If it is a state public good – for example, if individuals care not only about poverty within their community – an interjurisdictional consumption externality arises ($\gamma' > 0$). If, on the other hand, the reduction in poverty is a local public good, then benefits are fully contained within the spending jurisdiction ($\gamma' = 0$).[22]

---

[21] This assumes that parental utility functions do not fully take into account the future gains in the children's income (i.e., parents cannot be modeled as infinitely lived individuals), and to the extent that they do, parents do not control the local political process. As modeled, education brings some current consumption value to parents and nonparents, but this consumption value is not modeled as necessarily relating to the future income of children.

[22] An additional issue arises in the case of welfare when the reduction in poverty is viewed as a local public good and when the poor are mobile. In particular, a jurisdiction might reduce welfare benefits in an attempt to cause the poor to migrate out of the community (thus leading to the often cited "race to the bottom"). This case is excluded here because we assume that the local public-choice process takes demographic characteristics as fixed, an assumption that will be relaxed in the subsection "Strategic Manipulation of Local Demographic Characteristics."

Steady-State Equilibrium under Special Assumptions

In equilibrium, local governments are assumed to choose a public-good level g and a tax system τ (which specifies a lump sum tax payment for each demographic group k) to maximize their objective function subject to the budget constraint (2), subject to the actions taken by other jurisdictions, and subject to the system of transfers the central government designs. Again, while we will not specify a precise local political process that governs local public choices, we assume that the objective function of each local government takes as its arguments the utilities of the different demographic groups present in its jurisdiction. Individual agents choose locations in each time period, taking as given the public good/tax packages offered by different jurisdictions. Thus, individual actions in each period endogenously determine the demographic composition of communities. Furthermore, the central government, taking local objectives as given, employs an objective function identical to that of local governments (but considering residents of the entire state rather than any particular community) to determine a tax/grant system. A full equilibrium can therefore be defined as follows:

Definition: A *steady-state equilibrium* is a set of population characteristics $\{x^i\}_{i=1,...,J}$, a set of local public-good levels $\{g^i\}_{i=1,...,J}$, a set of local tax systems $\{\tau^i\}_{i=1,...,J}$, and a state tax/transfer system such that

1. each individual in any given time period – taking as given public good/tax packages in different communities – cannot improve his or her utility by moving;
2. each local government – taking as given the community budget constraint, the actions of other local governments, and the central government's transfer system – has maximized its objective in determining its local public-good level and its local tax system; and
3. the central government – taking as given the objectives of local governments – has maximized its objective in designing its tax/grant system.

Population Migrations and Demographic Compositions in the Steady-State Equilibrium

Given that the overall distribution of demographic groups in the state does not change between time periods, it is important to note that the population size and the population composition within communities

116

must, in the steady-state equilibrium, also remain constant across time even if individuals migrate between time periods; that is, while it is possible, for example, that individuals move between jurisdictions in their life cycle, it has to be the case that $\mathbf{x}_t^i = \mathbf{x}_{t+1}^i$ for all t and all i in any steady state.[23] Thus, it may be that some workers in jurisdiction i move to community j at some time t for reasons exogenous to the model as long as they are replaced by workers from outside jurisdiction i. This is, of course, true only in the steady-state equilibrium, and out-of-equilibrium net migrations are certainly possible.

Implications of Expenditure Spillovers for Equilibrium Central Transfers

In order to focus explicitly on expenditure externalities, we will begin our analysis by assuming that governments face two further constraints: (i) only benefit taxes can be used to raise revenues;[24] and (ii) demographic features of communities $(\mathbf{x}_t^i)$ are taken as fixed when policies are determined in jurisdiction i. The first of these assumptions excludes from the analysis tax-generated interjurisdictional externalities (which we will introduce in the subsection "Non-Benefit Taxation"), while the second prohibits strategic tax or spending policies aimed at altering the demographic composition of the community (which will be added to the model in the subsection "Strategic Manipulation of Local Demographic Characteristics").

A local public good g's spillover characteristics can then be fully characterized by the vector of functions (α, β, γ) associated with the type of good g represents, and the nature of this vector determines the extent to which the rents generated from public expenditures can be captured locally and thus financed through benefit taxes. If local public expenditures give rise to interjurisdictional consumption externalities $(\gamma' > 0)$,

---

[23] Technically, some other types of equilibria in which population characteristics rotate between jurisdictions are also plausible but are of little empirical interest. We will therefore restrict ourselves to steady-state equilibria in which such rotations do not occur.

[24] This is a restriction that is implicitly already assumed in the community budget constraint we have specified (see equation (2)), and it goes beyond lump sum taxation in that it requires taxes to be both lump sum *and* in some sense proportional to the benefits received by a particular agent. The extent to which local governments employ benefit taxes is the subject of much academic controversy. Hamilton (1975, 1976) and Fischel (1992), for instance, argue that residential property taxes approximate local benefit taxes, while Mieszkowski (1972), Zodrow and Mieszkowski (1986), and Mieszkowski and Zodrow (1989) argue that such taxes are borne to a large extent by all forms of capital and thus do not represent benefit taxes. As we will point out in the subsection "Non-Benefit Taxation," additional tax externalities arise when local governments do not use benefit taxes to fund expenditures.

for example, at least some of the rents from the jurisdiction's activity are consumed outside the jurisdiction and can therefore not be taxed under benefit taxation. This is the classic example of positive interjurisdictional spillovers (Oates, 1972). If, on the other hand, local public expenditures represent investments that generate future income, the extent to which benefit taxation can be employed to finance such expenditures depends crucially on whether the future income is realized within the local jurisdiction ($\alpha' > 0$) or outside it ($\beta' > 0$). To the extent that such future income remains in the local jurisdiction, current bonds can be financed through future benefit taxes from those agents whose income was affected, and no additional central government intervention is called for. But if incomes rise in jurisdiction j as a result of public investments in jurisdiction i, these rents cannot be captured through benefit taxation in jurisdiction i.

Whenever a public good g is characterized by $\beta' > 0$ and/or $\gamma' > 0$, benefit taxation at the local level is therefore not sufficient to finance levels of the good g that are optimal from the perspective of the central government. Furthermore, the central government is able to employ matching grants that cause lower-level governments to internalize spillover externalities, which thus improves (from the center's perspective) on the decentralized outcome. Note that the transfers themselves can be directed either at local governments directly or at residents of local jurisdictions in the form of deductions or credits for local taxes on central government tax forms.[25] The important feature of such grants to the central authority is that they change relative prices of local public goods to local governments and can thus cause local governments that maximize their own objectives to implicitly take into account the spillover externalities their policies cause. Furthermore, in equilibrium, the taxes collected by the central authority would in fact represent benefit taxes in that local residents would simply be paying for the benefits received from policies enacted in other jurisdictions. So in the presence of local public goods that exhibit either interjurisdictional consumption or investment spillovers ($\beta' \neq 0$ and/or $\gamma' \neq 0$), a central government that maximizes its objective subject to the constraints outlined above will therefore initiate a tax/transfer

---

[25] For a detailed analysis of the equivalence between these schemes, see Nechyba (1996). It should be noted, however, that much of the literature on intergovernmental grants has been devoted to the empirical documentation of quite different local public finance responses, depending on whether the grant is given to local governments or local voters. This effect has become known as the "flypaper effect" and has been discussed in detail by, among others, Gramlich (1977), Romer and Rosenthal (1980), Wyckoff (1991), and Hines and Thaler (1996).

system.[26] In the absence of either $\beta' \neq 0$ and/or $\gamma' \neq 0$, however, no such central government tax/transfer systems can improve (from the center's perspective) on decentralized outcomes.[27]

Non-Benefit Taxation and Competition for Demographic Groups

Our exclusive focus on expenditure externalities thus far is convenient given the empirical analysis we will stipulate in the section "Implications of a Community's Age Composition for Fiscal Policy" and report in the section "Empirical Analysis of California Counties," but it is made possible only because of the two special assumptions of exclusive use of benefit taxation and no strategic manipulations of demographic characteristics by local governments. Both for the sake of completeness and in order to point out the limits of the results in this paper, we now relax each of these assumptions in turn.

Non-Benefit Taxation

The assumption of benefit taxation at the local level has allowed us to focus exclusively on the ability of local governments to finance public goods of different types from the rents produced from these public goods, and it has allowed central government tax/transfers to arise only when expenditure spillovers are present. As is well known, however, additional externalities from competitive interactions between local governments arise when such governments employ non-benefit taxation, and these externalities can also be addressed through higher-level government interventions.[28] The discussion above, therefore, implicitly assumes that the tax assignment problem has been solved and that local governments are constrained in the space of tax policies they can utilize to meet their fiscal obligations. In the absence of such constraints, local tax distortions may generate further channels through

---

[26] In most cases, such central government grants would in fact cause a Pareto improvement from the local governments' perspective and could therefore be viewed as a collusive agreement between local governments in which the center acts as an enforcer. For a formal example in which federal grants emerge as a result of such collusion, see Nechyba (1997).

[27] While the public finance literature therefore recommends matching grants for the internalization of externalities, other problems may arise from such grants. For our purposes, we are concerned about the local fiscal burden, which could also be addressed, though perhaps not as easily, through block grants.

[28] See Starrett (1980), Gordon (1983), Inman and Rubinfeld (1996), and McKinnon and Nechyba (1997) for more detailed discussion of these tax-induced externalities than we are able to offer here.

which central government transfers can improve on decentralized outcomes.

By far the most cited such externality is described in the tax competition literature, which demonstrates that local non-benefit taxation of mobile tax bases causes underutilization of these bases because local governments do not consider the benefits from the movement of the tax base to other jurisdictions when setting their tax rates. The most common example of this is taxation of mobile capital.[29] The opposite effect of overutilization of tax bases, on the other hand, may arise when local governments are able to export tax burdens to other jurisdictions by using non-benefit, source-based (rather than residence-based) taxes on locally concentrated goods, such as tourist attractions.[30] Finally, whenever local governments are charged with taxing activities that themselves have interjurisdictional spillovers, additional tax externalities arise.[31]

While we will not explicitly focus on these effects in our later analysis, we note that they are conceptually quite similar to the types of effects we have modeled. Tax competition and tax exporting can be incorporated into our model by changing the budget constraint for jurisdiction i to

$$q_t^i = y_t^i - \delta\big(c(\mathbf{x}_t^i, g_t^i)\big) + \lambda\bigg(\sum_{j \neq i} c(\mathbf{x}_t^j, g_t^j)\bigg). \tag{4}$$

Under strict benefit taxation (as described in the previous section), $\delta = 1$ and $\lambda = 0$. In the presence of tax competition, $\delta > 1$ and $\lambda > 0$; that is, if local expenditures are funded through a non-benefit tax on mobile

---

[29] For a more detailed analysis of tax competition for capital, see Mieszkowski (1972), Wilson (1986), Zodrow and Mieszkowski (1986), Wildasin (1989), and Gordon (1992).

[30] Consumption taxes can be exported whenever a good is scarce outside a jurisdiction (e.g., Disney World) and consumers are thus forced to purchase that good in a particular location. Exporting of factor taxes, on the other hand, can occur whenever a factor is relatively immobile (e.g., land) and is used in the production of an export commodity. Given the relatively high mobility of most factors – in particular, labor and capital (see Grieson, 1980; Feldstein and Vaillant, 1994; Papke, 1991) – lower-tier governments are limited in their ability to export taxes on these factors. Similar types of issues arise when localities tax exports that are produced by noncompetitive industries. See also McLure (1967), Arnott and Grieson (1981), McLure and Mieszkowski (1983), and Mintz and Tulkens (1996) for various applications, and see Pindyck (1978) and Kolstad and Wolak (1983, 1985) for empirical illustrations.

[31] In particular, taxes on activities with locally concentrated benefits but geographically diffuse costs (smokestack industries) will tend to be underutilized, while taxes on activities with locally concentrated costs but geographically diffuse benefits (landfills) well tend to be overutilized. The former is often referred to as a "beggar thy neighbor" distortion (and often leads to inefficient negative taxes [Oates and Schwab, 1988], while the latter is sometimes referred to as a NIMBY ("not in my backyard") policy [Gordon, 1983; Inman and Rubinfeld, 1996; Nechyba and McKinnon, 1997].

Table 4.3. *Components of Tax and*
Spending Externalities

Expenditure externalities	
Consumption	$\gamma' \neq 0$
Investment	$\beta' \neq 0$
Non-benefit taxation externalities	
Tax competition	$\delta > 1, \lambda > 0$
Tax exporting	$\delta < 1, \lambda < 0$
Taxation of spillover activities	$\gamma' \neq 0$

capital, an increase in the local tax rate causes capital to leave and thus local income to decline ($\delta > 1$), but if other jurisdictions also use similar taxes, capital from those jurisdictions flows to jurisdiction i, thus causing local income to rise ($\delta > 0$). Similarly, in the presence of tax exporting, $\delta < 1$ as some of the local fiscal expenditures are shifted outside the jurisdiction, while $\lambda < 0$, as other jurisdictions shift their burdens as well. In the absence of central government transfers, tax competition over non-benefit taxes therefore leads to underprovision of local public goods (from the central government perspective), as some of the benefits from the public good/tax system in jurisdiction i (i.e., the increase in consumption elsewhere) are ignored by that jurisdiction's local government. Tax exporting, on the other hand, leads to overprovision of local public goods (from the center's perspective), as local jurisdictions do not take into account the cost of their public good/tax system incurred outside the jurisdiction. Finally, if local public goods are funded through taxes on activities that themselves cause consumption spillovers, then the public-good/tax system causes γ' (in the utility function) to deviate from 0.[32]

This discussion suggests that unless local public expenditures are financed through benefit taxation, local expenditure and tax programs should ideally be studied jointly. Henceforth, we will therefore sometimes speak of the local public-good/tax system. Table 4.3 summarizes the tax and spending externalities that give rise to central transfers in our model.

---

[32] For example, if jurisdiction i raises taxes from smokestack industries in community i, $\gamma' > 0$, as such a tax causes lower pollution outside jurisdiction i and thus generates a positive consumption externality. Similarly, if jurisdiction i raises tax revenues from local landfills, $\gamma' < 0$, because the local jurisdiction does not take into account the positive benefits to residents outside jurisdiction i from having the landfill in jurisdiction i.

121

Strategic Manipulation of Local Demographic Characteristics

Our second simplifying assumption was that local governments take the vector of demographic characteristics x_t^i as fixed when setting tax and spending policies. While we have argued that although it is true that in equilibrium this vector does not change across time (even if migrations take place), the equilibrium itself will differ depending on whether local governments attempt to strategically manipulate local population size or the local demographic composition. Suppose, for example, that the reduction of poverty is a local public good and that poor individuals are mobile. If local governments are assumed to take x_t^i as fixed when setting welfare spending, a local government will choose some level of transfers to the poor that maximizes its objective. When local governments perceive that a reduction in welfare spending will cause poor individuals to leave the community, however, the local government can achieve a reduction in poverty by lowering or eliminating its welfare programs. In an environment where all local governments attempt to manipulate x_t^i in this manner, the often hypothesized "race to the bottom," leading to equilibrium underfunding of local welfare programs (from the center's perspective), may occur. More generally, given that the cost function for public goods has x_t^i as one of its arguments, strategic setting of local tax/spending policies with an aim of affecting x_t^i may lead to either more or less funding than would occur under nonstrategic setting of such policies, depending on how various demographic characteristics enter the cost function. In the case of education, for example, high-income jurisdictions may spend artificially large amounts on public schools in order to price low-income individuals (whose peer characteristics may be worse) out of the local school system and thus control local demographic characteristics (Hoyt and Lee, 1997). As before, similar central government tax/transfer programs will therefore arise to address the implicit externalities that result when local governments act strategically to influence local demographic variables.

Summary and Additional Caveats

Before considering additional caveats, the basic conclusions thus far can be summarized as follows within the context of our model: In general, local tax and expenditure policies must be viewed jointly, and unless the local public-good/tax system in all communities is such that $\beta' = \gamma' = \lambda = 0$ and $\delta = 1$, and/or if local governments attempt to strategically influence x_t^i, our model predicts (generically) that central government transfers will arise and improve (from the central government's perspective) on decentralized financing of public goods.[33]

Some additional caveats arising from the absence of an explicit underlying political model may be in order. First, we have assumed that the public-choice process within jurisdictions is able to credibly issue bonds today to finance public investments to be realized in the future. As suggested in Rangel (1998), it is not clear that such credible commitment is always possible. However, if the state government has an objective function similar to that of the local governments, it would be similarly unable to solve such intergenerational problems and state grants would be unable to address this concern. Second, by assuming that the state political process mirrors that of local governments in taking into consideration the individual utilities of its residents in the same way, we argue that state transfers are capable of internalizing the externalities we point to. While this possibility certainly exists to the extent that the spillovers do not cross state boundaries, a different political model of the state public-choice process might suggest that such internalization of externalities is an unlikely outcome of state transfer policies. Inman and Rubinfeld (1996), for instance, suggest that a model of distributive politics in which localities are represented by representatives in the state legislature may yield state grant systems that do not reflect the externality-internalizing structure that is in principle possible. Other concerns arising from different types of political-economy models include loss of political accountability and local control when complex state grants govern local public decision-making.[34] Thus, the extent to which real-world political systems can effectively utilize intergovernmental grants to remedy the types of problems arising under decentralized public finance we have outlined is an empirical issue calling for careful analysis of how state and federal grants actually operate. We now attempt such an analysis for the case of California.

---

[33] This statement includes the word "generically" because there exist circumstances when the conditions in the first part of the statement are violated, thus giving rise to the presence of interjurisdictional externalities, but where the existing spillovers exactly offset one another. For example, one could have positive spillovers (consumption externalities) on the expenditure side that are exactly offset by negative spillovers (tax exporting) on the tax side. Such events, of course, do not occur generically.

[34] See McKinnon and Nechyba (1997) for a review of some of these political-economy arguments. A further issue raised by McKinnon and Nechyba involves concerns over monetary policy and a softening of local budget constraints, concerns that arise only in regard to federal transfers and do not arise in state and local fiscal interactions. Given that we focus in later sections on counties within California and the state of California, there is no need here to raise such issues.

Implications of a Community's Age Composition for Fiscal Policy

This section considers an important application of the above framework designed to explore the ways in which the age composition of a local community's population alters the intergovernmental transfers that its local government receives to fund expenditures. We assume here that the demographic composition of community i at time t is fully described by the vector $\mathbf{x}_t^i = (N_t^i, J_t^i, M_t^i, E_t^i)$, representing the size of the local population and the fractions of the population that are young, middle-aged, and elderly. Further, local governments take their demographic composition as given (i.e., we assume away the externalities from strategic manipulation of local demographic characteristics), and spillover externalities arise solely through expenditures (i.e., $\lambda = 0$ and $\delta = 1$ for all public goods). Finally, public-good cost functions for different types of public goods all take the form

$$c(\mathbf{x}_t^i, g) = \eta_J * (N_t^i J_t^i)g + \eta_M * (N_t^i M_t^i)g + \eta_E * (N_t^i E_t^i)g, \qquad (5)$$

where $(N_t^i J_t^i)$ is the number of young, $(N_t^i M_t^i)$ is the number of middle-aged, and $(N_t^i E_t^i)$ is the number of elderly in the population of community i at time t, and η_J, η_M, and η_E represent the relative crowding characteristics of the different age groups in the production of the local public good. For education, for example, η_M and η_E would equal zero, while η_J would be positive. Note that this cost function incorporates no fixed costs and specifies the marginal cost of extending the service g to an additional individual as constant but differing across age groups. Thus the function contains no scale effects from population growth, which implies that it could equivalently be written in per capita terms, where all N_t^i arguments drop out of the right-hand side of (5).

Age Composition Alters a Locality's Public Goods and Funding Sources

Given this setup, public goods can differ only along two dimensions: first, their spillover functions (α, β, γ), and second, their cost function parameters (η_J, η_M, η_E). Tables 4.4 and 4.5 give examples of extreme types of public goods in both these dimensions. Table 4.4 defines four stylized public goods along the spillover dimension: g_1 represents a pure local consumption good with no interregional or intergenerational spillovers; g_2 is a pure local investment good with intergenerational but no interregional spillovers; g_3 represents an investment with interjurisdictional spillovers; and g_4 constitutes a good with only interjurisdictional con-

Table 4.4. *Spillover Parameters for Four Stylized Public-Good Types*

	Spillover Parameter					
Public Good Type	α'	β'	γ'	δ	λ	Example
g_1 (pure local consumption)	0	0	0	1	0	Local park
g_2 (pure local investment)	+	0	0	1	0	Local infrastructure
g_3 (interjurisdictional investment spillover)	0	+	0	1	0	Education
g_4 (interjurisdictional consumption spillover)	0	0	+	1	0	Pollution control

Table 4.5. *Cost Function Parameters for Three Stylized Public-Good Types*

	Cost Parameter			
Cost Function Type	η_J	η_M	η_E	Example
c_1 (targeted to the young)	+	0	0	Education
c_2 (targeted to the middle-aged)	0	+	0	Job training
c_3 (targeted to the elderly)	0	0	+	Community nursing home

sumption spillovers. Table 4.5 categorizes public goods along the cost dimension where goods of type c_1, c_2, and c_3 are targeted solely at the young, middle-aged, and elderly, respectively.

Our model predicts no sharing between different levels of government of goods of type g_1 and g_2 and the emergence of central government grants for the financing of public goods of type g_3 and g_4. Furthermore, a community whose public good is of spillover type g_3 and cost type c_1 will receive central government grants only proportional to the fraction of its population that is young. Thus, the level of central government funding received by a given community depends on both the spillover type of its public good and the demographic composition of its population.

While both the spillover parameters in Table 4.4 and the cost function parameters in Table 4.5 are extreme, note that any real public good is some combination of these stylized entities. For example, investment by local communities in roads typically contains some local investment value (g_2) to the extent that it is spent on local roads and some spillover investment value (g_3) to the extent that it is spent on connecting roads.

On the cost side, such spending may benefit all age groups to some (although not necessarily an equal) extent. Infrastructure spending is therefore likely to be a convex combination of g_2 and g_3 on the spillover dimension (Table 4.4) and some convex combination of all three cost functions (Table 4.5). The size of the weight in these combinations given to g_3 on the spillover dimension then determines the fraction of total road spending by the local government that is funded through central government transfers in our model. Furthermore, the relative weight given to each of the three stylized public goods in the cost dimension (Table 4.5) links the total size of local spending on a given level of infrastructure to the local demographic characteristics of the community and thus indirectly links the size of the central government infrastructure funding within the community to local demographics.

Application to Spending in Counties

The fact that local governments supply services for residents within counties provides an interesting context for considering practical implications of our analysis. Interpreting a county as having a single local government, one can generally classify the spending by these governments into five broad categories: education, health, welfare, police/fire protection, and infrastructure. The central governments here include both the state and federal governments.

Table 4.6 categorizes each of these spending classifications in terms of the simplified spillover and cost dimensions introduced above and derives (last column) the resulting predictions given by the model. Education, for example, is largely a public good of type g_3 in the spillover dimension, and its per-resident costs for a community depend solely on the fraction of the community that is of school age (i.e., education is a public good of type c_1 on the cost dimension). Our model therefore implies that much of the funding for education will come from the state level (to internalize interjurisdictional investment spillovers), and the per capita level of funding will be directly related to the fraction of the local population that is young.

The remaining predictions in the table are similarly and straightforwardly derived from the stylized model above. Health expenditures are assumed to be somewhat more targeted to the young and the elderly (c_1, c_3), while welfare spending, given its emphasis on spending on children, is assumed to be relatively more targeted to the young (c_1). Safety (i.e., police and fire protection) expenditures, on the other hand, are likely to be more pronounced (for any level of public safety) the greater the fraction of M (given that most in the J generation are children under

126

Table 4.6. *California County Spending Categories as Convex Combinations of Stylized Public Goods*

Spending Category	Spillover Dimension[a]	Cost Dimension[a]	Implication from Model
Education	(g_1), g_3	c_1	Central grants targeted at communities with large J
Health	g_1, (g_3)	c_1, (c_2), c_3	Local funding, limited central grants
Welfare	g_1, (g_3), (g_4)[b]	c_1, (c_2), (c_3)	Mainly local funding if local public good; some central funding targeted somewhat to J otherwise
Police and fire protection	g_1, (g_4)	(c_1), c_2, (c_3)	Some central funding, somewhat targeted to communities with M
Infrastructure	g_1, g_2, g_3	(c_1), c_2, (c_3)	Split between local and central funding, somewhat targeted to communities with large M

[a] In this column, we enclose an item in parentheses to indicate that it is of secondary importance as a component in the expenditure category under consideration and thus receives relatively smaller weight in the perceived combination of stylized goods making up the category.

[b] Depends on whether reductions in poverty are local or state public goods.

the age at which they commit crimes and given that the elderly are statistically less likely to be involved in crime). Finally, infrastructure, such as roads, is likely to be used somewhat more by the working population and is therefore also assumed to be somewhat more targeted to the M generation (c_2).

On the spillover side, education is denoted largely as an interjurisdictional investment good, while we interpret health, welfare, and safety as largely current local-consumption goods (although spending on health and welfare in part involves investments in children that contain elements of intergenerational spillovers, and public safety may spill over into neighboring jurisdictions). Finally, infrastructure expenditures, to the extent that they mix local projects with projects of wider regional investment potential, are denoted both a local and an interjurisdictional investment good.

Empirical Analysis of California Counties

To explore the empirical applicability of our model of fiscal federalism, we analyze data on fifty-eight California counties – their expenditures, their tax and grant revenues, and the age composition of their populations – to test the predictions of the model. The spending categories analyzed correspond to those presented in Table 4.6. Our data integrate the fiscal activities of all local governments within a county, so our measures of county expenditures represent totals spent on all residents within a county. Our data combine all transfers from state or federal governments to local governments in a county into a single net "intergovernmental transfer." Finally, our tax revenue variable reflects the portion of county expenditures paid for directly by local residents.

We begin with a brief description of our data and then present a set of elementary empirical specifications capturing the key relationships linking expenditure categories and funding sources. After presenting our regression results, the discussion explores the implications of our results for the issues identified in our theoretical analysis.

Data Description

Data on revenues and expenditures for the fifty-eight California counties in fiscal years 1986–87 and 1991–92 are drawn from the Census of Governments, a survey conducted every five years by the U.S. Bureau of the Census. Each observation represents the total expenditures (or revenues) in a given county, including transactions not just for the county level of government but also for all municipalities, townships, school districts, and special districts within that county. The broad expenditure categories include education (K–12 and community colleges), health (including hospitals), public welfare, and police and fire protection. The residual category is "infrastructure," which includes all expenditures not classified in the other groups. We refer to this category as "infrastructure" rather than "other expenditures" because the bulk of these expenditures are infrastructure related. Our data also provide direct measures of intergovernmental transfers to counties (from the federal and state levels of government) and the amount of total local taxes used to fund expenditures within the county. All demographic variables are from the 1990 Census STF3A files for the California counties.

The appendix at the end of this chapter offers detailed descriptions of these data.

Table 4.7 reports descriptive statistics (the mean, minimum, and maximum and the lower, median, and upper quartiles) summarizing our data for both 1987 and 1992. The top three rows present findings for county population, total expenditures, and total revenues. The remaining rows report statistics for variables appearing in our regressions: rows 4–10 are the share variables for expenditures and revenues, rows 11–18 are the corresponding per capita variables, and the last five rows are demographic variables from the 1990 Census summary tape files (STF3A). All pecuniary values are measured in 1990 dollars, using the CPI (all items) for all urban consumers in the western region of the United States as the deflator. All revenue and expenditure variables, apart from the totals, are shown in thousands of dollars. Median income is shown in ten thousands of dollars.

Empirical Specification

The purpose of our empirical analysis is to discover the systematic relationship linking the five expenditure categories (i.e., education, health, welfare, police and fire protection, and infrastructure) to the two revenue categories (intergovernmental transfers and local taxes). We do this by introducing separate empirical specifications for each of the measures treated as dependent variables. Our analysis considers two forms of dependent variables: measures expressed as budget shares, and measures formed by calculating per capita (i.e., per resident) expenditures and revenues.

We estimate models of the form

$$y = X\beta + \varepsilon, \tag{6}$$

where y is a 58×1 vector of expenditure or revenue variables for the fifty-eight California counties, X is a 58×5 matrix of regressors, β is a 5×1 parameter vector, and ε is a 58×1 vector of mean-zero disturbances. The matrix X is the same across all specifications. It includes the fraction of persons in a county aged 0 to 20 (termed here the "young proportion"), the fraction of persons in a county aged 65 or older (termed the "elderly proportion"), median income for households in the county, the fraction of households in the county living in rural (farm or nonfarm) areas, and an intercept. With the fraction of persons aged 21–64 (middle-aged) excluded from regression relations, coefficients on the young proportion show how much the fitted component of y in (6) responds to a

129

Table 4.7. Summary Statistics, California Counties

Variable	Mean		Minimum		Lower Quartile		Median		Upper Quartile		Maximum	
	1987	1992	1987	1992	1987	1992	1987	1992	1987	1992	1987	1992
County expenditure and revenue variables												
Population (1,000s)	465.2	513.1	1.3	1.1	31.8	36.7	120.1	133.5	432.7	480.6	8295.9	8863.2
Total expenditures ($millions)	1.124	1.389	0.007	0.007	0.078	0.099	0.272	0.333	1.114	1.428	20.798	24.304
Total revenue ($millions)	1.182	1.427	0.006	0.008	0.078	0.096	0.291	0.338	1.129	1.387	21.363	26.227
Education share (%)	0.383	0.383	0.198	0.199	0.339	0.344	0.381	0.381	0.426	0.429	0.565	0.563
Health share (%)	0.101	0.114	0.017	0.022	0.045	0.058	0.095	0.094	0.146	0.162	0.283	0.335
Welfare share (%)	0.110	0.113	0.036	0.047	0.079	0.083	0.104	0.104	0.139	0.141	0.217	0.204
Police and fire protection share (%)	0.073	0.072	0.032	0.031	0.059	0.059	0.071	0.067	0.086	0.085	0.124	0.141
Infrastructure share (%)	0.333	0.318	0.177	0.169	0.277	0.266	0.340	0.313	0.371	0.363	0.581	0.478
Intergovernmental transfers share (%)	0.502	0.479	0.307	0.257	0.418	0.404	0.496	0.487	0.570	0.551	0.732	0.686
Taxes share (%)	0.498	0.521	0.268	0.314	0.430	0.449	0.504	0.513	0.582	0.596	0.693	0.743
Education per capita ($1,000s)	0.944	1.076	0.573	0.646	0.820	0.886	0.904	1.025	1.057	1.258	1.799	2.144
Health per capita ($1,000s)	0.254	0.333	0.041	0.057	0.114	0.150	0.233	0.265	0.357	0.432	0.927	1.293
Welfare per capita ($1,000s)	0.270	0.316	0.108	0.119	0.198	0.234	0.270	0.310	0.320	0.394	0.480	0.600

Police and fire protection per capita ($1,000s)	0.182	0.204	0.078	0.095	0.136	0.148	0.172	0.189	0.208	0.228	0.476	0.800
Infrastructure per capita ($1,000s)	0.845	0.908	0.414	0.463	0.662	0.702	0.773	0.849	0.873	1.017	2.936	2.986
Total expenditures per capita ($1,000s)	2.493	2.838	1.822	2.128	2.164	2.395	2.377	2.680	2.645	2.962	5.051	6.493
Taxes per capita ($1,000s)	1.298	1.485	0.723	0.783	1.076	1.214	1.259	1.419	1.472	1.593	2.729	3.161
Intergov. transfers per capita ($1,000s)	1.303	1.371	0.651	0.657	1.065	1.073	1.281	1.330	1.444	1.544	3.091	3.665
Demographic variables (as of 1990)												
Fraction of households in rural areas	0.365		0.000		0.109		0.296		0.632		1.000	
Median household income ($10,000s)	3.056		2.049		2.457		2.875		3.505		4.854	
Fraction of population aged 0–20	0.304		0.194		0.283		0.298		0.330		0.393	
Fraction of population aged 21–64	0.568		0.506		0.543		0.563		0.590		0.661	
Fraction of population aged 65 and up	0.128		0.061		0.102		0.122		0.149		0.264	

Note: All monetary values are 1990 dollars, deflated by the CPI for all urban consumers (western region of the country).

131

shift in the population from the middle-aged group to the young group; and coefficients on the elderly proportion reveals the effects on y of increasing the share of the elderly population, with a corresponding decline in the middle-aged group. Differences in the young and elderly coefficients indicate how shifts in the population between these two groups influence fitted values of y.

Regression Results

For each specification of the **y** and **X** variables, we report two sets of estimates of model (6), least squares and least absolute deviations. We implement bootstrap procedures to compute all reported coefficient estimates and standard errors, drawing 1,000 replications for each estimation. Furthermore, we report these results for different ways of measuring the **y** variables: as shares of total expenditures or revenues and in per capita terms. In both cases, the **y** variables are averages of the 1987 and 1992 data, expressed in 1990 dollars.[35]

Results for Expenditure and Revenue Shares

In Table 4.8, all of the **y** variables are measured as shares of total expenditure or shares of total revenue. The first column of the table lists the dependent variables. For example, the first pair of rows of the "Expenditure Shares" part of the table gives the results for which **y** = 0.5 (1987 education expenditure / 1987 total expenditure) + 0.5 (1992 education expenditure / 1992 total expenditure), and the first pair of rows under "Revenue Shares" gives the results for which **y** = 0.5 (1987 intergovernmental transfers / 1987 total revenue) + 0.5 (1992 intergovernmental transfers / 1992 total revenue). Two results are reported in each main row of the table. The first and uppermost result appearing in each main row is the bootstrapped least squares coefficient, with its bootstrapped standard error immediately below it in parentheses. Immediately below this standard error is another bootstrapped coefficient, but for least absolute deviations (LAD) estimation (or median regression) rather than ordinary least squares (OLS). Immediately below this coefficient is its bootstrapped standard error. For example, consider the first main row of the table, for **y** = Education Share. The average bootstrap OLS coefficient based on 1,000 draws is 1.001, and its standard deviation is 0.369. The average bootstrap LAD coefficient based on 1,000 draws is

---

[35] We combine years simply to summarize our empirical findings more succinctly. We obtain similar estimates for all specifications whether we use only one year of data or a seemingly unrelated framework that combines years.

Table 4.8. *Effects of Population Age Composition on Expenditure and Revenue Shares for California Counties*

Budget Measure	Proportion in Age Group		Median Income ($10,000s)	Rural	Intercept
	20 and Below	65 and Above			
Expenditure shares					
Education share	1.001**	0.493	0.003	0.049	−0.009
	(0.369)	(0.535)	(0.017)	(0.052)	(0.209)
	0.896**	0.688	0.005	0.036	−0.006
	(0.479)	(0.647)	(0.024)	(0.060)	(0.276)
Health share	0.062	0.553*	0.009	0.011	−0.014
	(0.334)	(0.405)	(0.019)	(0.048)	(0.186)
	−0.027	0.510	0.008	−0.012	0.025
	(0.569)	(0.541)	(0.032)	(0.070)	(0.311)
Welfare share	0.183*	0.005	−0.041**	−0.061**	0.202**
	(0.161)	(0.206)	(0.008)	(0.017)	(0.090)
	0.211*	0.001	−0.041**	−0.061**	0.195**
	(0.164)	(0.230)	(0.008)	(0.024)	(0.086)
Police and fire protection share	−0.253**	−0.131	0.007**	−0.025**	0.153**
	(0.094)	(0.147)	(0.004)	(0.013)	(0.053)
	−0.179*	−0.031	0.009**	−0.030**	0.111**
	(0.119)	(0.180)	(0.005)	(0.014)	(0.066)
Infrastructure share	−1.021**	−0.967**	0.020*	0.026	0.688**
	(0.321)	(0.449)	(0.013)	(0.042)	(0.173)
	−1.223**	−1.024**	0.015	−0.004	0.778**
	(0.382)	(0.536)	(0.016)	(0.049)	(0.198)
Revenue shares					
Intergovernmental transfer share	0.663**	−0.139	−0.085**	−0.018	0.571**
	(0.389)	(0.646)	(0.021)	(0.048)	(0.239)
	0.541	−0.290	−0.091**	−0.051	0.662**
	(0.553)	(0.825)	(0.031)	(0.067)	(0.331)
Taxes share	−0.696**	0.126	0.083**	0.014	0.448**
	(0.397)	(0.636)	(0.020)	(0.047)	(0.240)
	−0.571	0.271	0.089**	0.048	0.356
	(0.529)	(0.817)	(0.029)	(0.066)	(0.317)

Notes: All estimates and standard errors were computed with bootstrap procedures (with 1,000 sample draws). For each budget measure, the first row shows the least squares coefficients, and the second row shows the least absolute deviations coefficients. Numbers in parentheses are standard errors.

* Statistically significant at the 75% confidence level.   ** Statistically significant at the 90% confidence level.

0.896, and its standard deviation is 0.479. The five columns of the table correspond to the five columns (one intercept and four independent variables) of **X**.

The estimates of Table 4.8 indicate that increasing the proportion of young in a community raises the share of expenditures devoted to education and decreases the shares going to safety (i.e., police and fire protection) and infrastructure. There is slight evidence that more young also leads to higher welfare spending, but significance levels for these coefficients are very marginal. On the revenue side, more young leads to a greater proportion of local funding coming from intergovernmental transfer revenues, with a correspondingly lower share paid for by a county's own taxes.

More elderly in a community increases the allocation of expenditures on infrastructure. While none of the elderly coefficients associated with revenues are statistically significant, their pattern suggests that more elderly results in lower proportions of revenues from intergovernmental transfers and less from local taxes.

Three sets of differences between the young and elderly coefficients in Table 4.8 are statistically significant. Shifting population from old to young increases the share of spending going to education. On the revenue side, the share from intergovernmental transfers falls, and the share from local taxes rises.

Results for per Capita Measures
Table 4.9 reports the second main set of results. All dependent variables here – listed in the first column – are now in per capita terms, rather than shares of total expenditures or revenues. We construct **y** in (6) by averaging the per capita measures for 1987 and 1992; for example, education per capita is 0.5 (1987 education expenditures / 1987 population) + 0.5 (1992 education expenditures / 1992 population), with all monetary values expressed in 1990 dollars. All other **y** variables in Table 4.9 are defined analogously.

The results in Table 4.9 broadly confirm the conclusions reached from Table 4.8. Increasing the proportion of young in a community raises per capita education expenditures and lowers safety and infrastructure per capita spending. From a revenue perspective, more young leads to less local government tax revenue per capita.

More elderly in a community also leads to less spent on infrastructure per capita. While only marginally significant, the elderly coefficients associated with per capita revenues indicate that a higher fraction of elderly leads to lower amounts of funding coming from both intergovernmental transfers and local government taxes.

Table 4.9. *Effects of Population Age Composition on per Capita Expenditures and Revenues for California Counties*

Per Capita Measure	Proportion in Age Group		Median Income ($10,000s)	Rural	Intercept
	20 and Below	65 and Above			
Expenditure per capita					
Education per capita	2.143**	0.052	−0.046	0.352**	0.360
	(0.921)	(2.018)	(0.052)	(0.131)	(0.629)
	1.813**	−0.884	−0.056	0.325**	0.613
	(0.980)	(1.700)	(0.052)	(0.161)	(0.583)
Health per capita	−0.155	1.052	−0.016	0.037	0.241
	(1.130)	(1.264)	(0.061)	(0.142)	(0.618)
	−0.235	0.514	0.013	0.047	0.208
	(1.889)	(1.627)	(0.104)	(0.208)	(1.042)
Welfare per capita	0.312	−0.467	−0.116**	−0.094**	0.646**
	(0.467)	(0.649)	(0.021)	(0.056)	(0.261)
	0.107	−0.647	−0.122**	−0.093*	0.742**
	(0.713)	(0.947)	(0.030)	(0.078)	(0.388)
Police and fire protection per capita	−1.157**	−1.214	−0.004	0.015	0.705**
	(0.577)	(1.095)	(0.019)	(0.085)	(0.341)
	−0.746*	−0.529	−0.0002	−0.082*	0.505**
	(0.479)	(0.721)	(0.017)	(0.057)	(0.273)
Infrastructure per capita	−4.864**	−6.152*	−0.047	0.409*	3.129**
	(2.408)	(4.339)	(0.086)	(0.350)	(1.413)
	−3.651*	−4.103*	−0.029	0.074	2.514**
	(2.316)	(3.493)	(0.093)	(0.248)	(1.360)
Total per capita	−3.846	−7.156	−0.230*	0.757*	5.162**
	(4.117)	(7.176)	(0.163)	(0.577)	(2.427)
	−0.226	−5.503	−0.163	0.440	3.689
	(5.693)	(7.624)	(0.252)	(0.501)	(3.334)
Revenue per capita					
Intergovernmental transfer per capita	−0.418	−3.343	−0.326**	0.328	2.761**
	(2.068)	(4.161)	(0.095)	(0.318)	(1.314)
	0.107	−4.427*	−0.351**	0.039	2.872**
	(2.225)	(2.897)	(0.104)	(0.234)	(1.331)
Taxes per capita	−5.353**	−4.804*	0.019	0.335	3.443**
	(2.912)	(4.124)	(0.120)	(0.340)	(1.631)
	−2.682	−2.402	0.125	0.314	1.976
	(4.918)	(6.323)	(0.195)	(0.410)	(2.771)

Notes: All estimates and standard errors were computed with bootstrap procedures (with 1,000 sample draws). For each per capita measure, the first row shows the least squares coefficients, and the second row shows the least absolute deviations coefficients. Numbers in parentheses are standard errors.

* Statistically significant at the 75% confidence level.   ** Statistically significant at the 90% confidence level.

Table 4.10. *Budgetary Consequences of Changing the Age Composition of a County's Population in California, Least Squares Estimates*

Shift in Age Composition of Population	Effects on Expenditures	Effects on Revenues
Old ⟹ middle-aged	Infrastructure + $6,152	IG Transfers + $3,343
		Own Taxes + 4,804
	Total + $6,152	Total + $8,147
Young ⟹ middle-aged	Education − $2,143	IG Transfers + $418
	Safety + 1,157	Own Taxes + 5,353
	Infrastructure + 4,864	
	Total + $3,878	Total + $5,771
Young ⟹ old	Education − $2,138	IG Transfers − $2,925
		Own Taxes + 549
	Total − $2,138	Total − $2,376

The differences between the young and elderly coefficients in Table 4.9 affirm the insights revealed in Table 4.8. Shifting population from old to young increases per capita expenditures on education and per capita intergovernmental transfers.

Implications of Findings

Tables 4.10 and 4.11 explore the budgetary consequences of changing the age composition of a California county's population. The tables are designed to answer the question, How does a change in the age composition of a county's population alter a local government's spending on public goods and on its sources for funding these expenditures? All information in these tables is derived from the two sets of regression results (LS and LAD) of Table 4.9, in which all dependent variables are measured per capita. Table 4.10 presents the budgetary implications calculated using the least squares coefficients of Table 4.9, and Table 4.11 gives the corresponding computations using the median coefficients.

The first column of each table signifies the nature of the demographic change under consideration. Thus, the first row considers the consequences of increasing the fraction of middle-aged people by decreasing the fraction of elderly people by the same magnitude, with the fraction of young people held constant. The other two rows are defined analo-

Table 4.11. *Budgetary Consequences of Changing the Age Composition of a County's Population in California, Least Absolute Deviation Estimates*

Shift in Age Composition of Population	Effects on Expenditures	Effects on Revenues
Old ⇒ middle-aged	Infrastructure + $4,103	IG Transfers + $4,427
		Own Taxes + 2,402
	Total + $4,103	Total + $6,829
Young ⇒ middle-aged	Education − $1,813	IG Transfers − $107
	Safety + 746	Own Taxes + 2,682
	Infrastructure + 3,651	
	Total + $2,584	Total + $2,575
Young ⇒ old	Education − $2,694	IG Transfers − $4,534
		Own Taxes + 280
	Total − $2,694	Total − $4,254

gously. The second column of each table projects the effect of the specified demographic change on per capita expenditures, while the third column predicts the effects on per capita revenues. The values in both columns are simply the responses implied by the point estimates reported in Table 4.9. For the last rows, describing the effects associated with shifting population from the young to the elderly group, the listed values reflect differences in the estimated young and elderly coefficients reported in Table 4.9. However, not all expenditure categories from Table 4.9 appear in the second column of Tables 4.10 and 4.11. We included only those categories where at least one of the estimated coefficients in Table 4.8 or 4.9 is statistically significant at the 90% confidence level for either the LS or the LAD estimates. So if an estimated coefficient from the median regression is significant at the 0.10 level but the corresponding coefficient from least squares estimation is not significant, then the variable is still included in the second column in both tables. In the third column, we include predicted responses of both per capita intergovernmental transfers and local government taxes to the demographic shift under consideration.

Tables 4.10 and 4.11 largely confirm the predictions of Table 4.6. While the totals for the changes in expenditures and revenues associated with each demographic shift may appear to produce budgetary imbalance, conventional hypotheses tests indicate that total changes in expenditures and revenues are never significantly different from one another for any of the shifts considered, using either LS or LAD estimates. Inspection of the individual findings in Tables 4.10 and 4.11 reveals a variety of systematic patterns. A demographic change from young to either middle-aged or elderly brings about a marginal decline in education spending and, as evidenced in the last rows of the tables, a corresponding marginal decline in intergovernmental grants. Marginal infrastructure spending rises with demographic changes toward the middle-aged (from either the young or the elderly), thus confirming our intuition that those of working age are disproportionately crowded in the cost function for infrastructure. Furthermore, the budgetary numbers are consistent with the view that marginal spending on infrastructure is in fact shared between the central and local governments, a finding that is again consistent with Table 4.6. In the case of marginal changes in public safety expenditures, the findings do indicate a rise expected from a demographic shift from the young to the middle-aged, but they show no such marginal increase (as was hypothesized in Table 4.6) when the shift is from the old to the middle-aged. The middle rows of Table 4.10 further suggest that public safety expenditures are largely funded locally, again a prediction consistent with Table 4.6.[36]

Simplified to their essence, the findings shown in Tables 4.10 and 4.11 are consistent with the following view of fiscal relationships linking county governments with state/federal governments. Marginal changes in education are fully funded by intergovernmental transfers from state/federal governments. Public safety expenditures are primarily funded by local taxes. Infrastructure expenditures are jointly funded by intergovernmental transfers and local taxes, with an even split approximating the contributions.

Conclusion

This chapter has developed a model of fiscal federalism that links levels of local government expenditures to local demographic characteristics,

---

[36] This conclusion, while somewhat tentative, can be reached as follows. From the top row of Table 4.10, we can infer that slightly more than half of marginal infrastructure expenditures are covered by the state, and from the last row we can infer that roughly all of the marginal education expenditures are funded by the state. When focusing on the middle row, we can therefore infer that state grants fall by roughly $2,100 due to less education spending and rise by roughly $2,500 due to higher infrastructure spending. The changes in education and infrastructure spending alone therefore account for a $400 increase in intergovernmental grants as a shift from the young to the middle-aged occurs, which is precisely the predicted increase in state funding. Thus we conclude that the increase in funding for safety is paid for locally. Similar calculations from Table 4.11, however, are not as conclusive.

highlights interjurisdictional spillovers (rather than demographic differences) as the culprit that creates local fiscal burdens, and suggests a role for a central government to alleviate these burdens. The analysis focuses on three types of spillovers interfering with fully decentralized funding of public goods: interjurisdictional consumption spillovers (wherein benefits occur across communities within the current time period), and intra- and interjurisdictional investment spillovers (wherein benefits occur across time and within and across communities). Central governments can mitigate interjurisdictional spillovers by making transfers to local governments based on the demographic composition of each locality's population, with age being a vital distinguishing characteristic. According to our model of fiscal federalism, the fraction of local public expenditures financed through intergovernmental transfers depends on the particular combination of expenditures for public goods provided in a locality, a combination that arises because different public goods are subject to the different spillovers. Since the age composition of the population significantly alters both local tax revenues and expenditures on different types of public goods, this composition is thus predicted to change the fraction of local goods funded by central government transfers.

Using data on California counties for the years 1987 and 1992, we find intriguing evidence supporting the implications of our model. Our analysis considers levels of spending in counties on five broad expenditure categories: education, health, welfare, police and fire protection, and infrastructure. Not surprisingly, the age makeup of a county's residents strongly influences its allocations across these expenditure categories. Given the differing characteristics of these goods, such shifts in allocations signify distinctive alterations in the types and sizes of spillovers encountered. In response to this, our fiscal federalism model predicts particular adjustments in intergovernmental transfers from central governments (state and federal) for each of these spending categories. Our empirical results indicate that central governments act to fund marginal changes in education expenditures fully through intergovernmental transfers, while public safety expenditures are primarily funded by local taxes. Infrastructure expenditures are jointly funded by intergovernmental transfers and local taxes. By itself, finding that central government funding fully pays for marginal changes in educational expenses in California seems hardly surprising, since the state operates under the *Serrano* judicial decision, which requires equal per-pupil spending across districts. However, our results do not merely indicate that a K–12 budget allocation adjusts to compensate for the number of youth in school – we do not examine such individual budget items – instead our estimates show that net transfers adjust to compensate. This net transfer measure totals all categories of revenues received from central government sources and thus accounts for fungibility achieved through adjustments of local funding. Moreover, our findings for other reallocations of expenditures and corresponding shifts in total net transfers are broadly consistent with the fiscal relationships hypothesized by our model. Of course, analyzing data from a single state sharply limits what can be learned about the applicability of our model. To develop more-convincing evidence, we must replicate our findings with data from states in which nominal funding rules for education and other services are quite different. This exercise is left to future research.

A few qualifications are in order. While the empirical analysis suggests that gross flows in central transfers correspond qualitatively to the predictions of our simplified model and thus compensate jurisdictions for local fiscal burdens from spillovers, we can say little in regard to whether the size and nature of these flows is optimal without both gathering more information on the magnitude of expenditure and tax spillovers and exploring the particular incentives contained within grant programs.[37] We also emphasize briefly that in interpreting our results, the reader should keep in mind that there is much distinction between the optimal division of government financing of public goods and the optimal degree of local control over the funds that are spent. Our suggestion throughout this chapter, for example, that state financing of education may be appropriate given the potentially large interjurisdictional investment components of education funding, is a suggestion only about the funding side. Neither our theoretical model nor our empirical results shed any light on how financial resources, once transferred, should be further directed and controlled.

Appendix

Two sources of data were used in our empirical analysis: data on county finances obtained from the Census of Governments[38] and data on demographics extracted from the 1980 U.S. Census. All expenditure and

---

[37] More precisely, much of the literature on fiscal federalism has focused on issues of optimal grant design, with price and income effects, fungibility, and various principle agent problems arising as concerns. Clearly, a simple look at gross flows of government resources across broad spending categories is not sufficient to come to a conclusion about issues of this kind.

[38] U.S. Bureau of the Census, *1987 Census of Governments*, vol. 4, *Government Finances*, no. 5, *Compendium of Government Finances*, and the corresponding volume for 1992. Hereafter, we refer to these simply as *Compendiums*.

revenue variables are in thousands of dollars, with the exception of total expenditures and total revenue, which are in millions of dollars. All pecuniary variables used in this chapter are measured in 1990 dollars, adjusted by the CPI (all items) for all urban consumers in the western region of the United States. For more detail about the variables, consult the 1987 and 1992 *Compendiums*.

Revenue and Expenditure Data for California Counties

Our revenue and expenditure data for all California counties in fiscal years 1986–87 and 1991–92 are from the Census of Governments, a survey conducted every five years by the U.S. Bureau of the Census. For each revenue and expenditure category, our data represent the sum of the totals for each local government in a given county. That is, a total for a particular county includes data not only for the county government but also for all municipalities, townships, school districts, and special districts within that county.[39]

All of our revenue and expenditure data are from the Local Government Finances portion of the Census, which contains information for the 3,042 county, 19,221 municipal, and 16,695 township governments existing in the United States in fiscal years 1986–87 and 1991–92. The initial data collection phase used three methods: mail canvass, field compilation, and centralized collection from state sources. Detailed Census schedules with reporting instructions were used in the mail canvass. Census examiners then reviewed these and conducted extensive correspondence, when necessary, to verify incomplete and questionable responses. In some cases, Census enumerators visited local government offices to obtain this information.

The field compilations had two components. Initial plans required Census representatives to compile data for the largest county and municipal governments, typically those counties with populations exceeding 500,000 and municipalities with populations exceeding 300,000, by accessing records on site. The second component of field compilation

---

[39] Not all geographic areas known as counties have county governments. When municipal and county governments have been consolidated, or substantially merged, the composite units are classed as municipalities for the Census reporting of governmental statistics. In California, the only county without a county government is the city and county of San Francisco. As defined for Census statistics on governments, a municipal government is a political subdivision within which a municipal corporation has been established to provide general local government for a specific population concentration in a defined area. This includes all active governmental units officially designated as cities, boroughs, towns, and villages.

endeavored to resolve questions that arose during the survey by having the Census agents review source material in the local government offices. Finally, in California, a central data collection system existed for the county and municipal levels of government. When needed, the Census staff obtained supplementary data from special tabulations in other state offices, printed reports, secondary sources, or supplemental mailings directly to the local governments.[40]

The revenue and expenditure data include all net receipts and expenditures for all local governments within each county (net of correcting within-county intergovernmental transfers and transactions, such as recoveries of refunds), excluding debt issuance and retirement, loan and investment, agency, and private transactions. Internal transfers among the agencies of a particular government are excluded from these data. Therefore a government's contribution to a retirement fund that it administers is not considered an expenditure, nor is the receipt of this contribution by the retirement fund considered revenue.

In our data, the relationship between the totals of revenue and expenditure for a given county do not provide a direct measure of budgetary balance. Government expenditure includes all capital outlay, including a significant fraction that is financed by borrowing, while revenue does not include receipts from borrowing. In addition, the relationship between the totals of revenue and expenditure may be distorted further by changes in cash and security holdings and contributions to retirement systems.

Taxes and intergovernmental transfers are the two broad revenue categories that we consider. We further partition taxes into property taxes and other taxes and intergovernmental transfers into transfers from the federal government and transfers from the state government. Our broad expenditure categories include education, health and hospitals, public welfare, police and fire protection, and infrastructure. The following is a complete list of all expenditure and revenue variables discussed in this paper, with precise definitions provided when needed.

Direct General Expenditures
> *Total.* Includes all expenditures of the local governments, excluding utility, liquor stores, employee-retirement or other insurance-trust expenditures, and any intergovernmental payments.
> *Education.* Includes expenditures for provision or support of schools and other educational facilities and services, including those for educational institutions beyond the high school level operated by local

---

[40] For more detail on data collection procedures and methodology, consult the introductory chapters of the *Compendium*s.

governments (e.g., community colleges). Covers such related services as pupil transportation, school milk and lunch programs and other cafeterias, health and recreational programs, and the like.

Health and hospitals. Includes outpatient health services, including public health administration, research and education, treatment and immunization clinics, nursing, etc.; financing, construction, and operation of nursing homes; financing, construction, acquisition, maintenance, and operation of hospital facilities; provision of hospital care; and support of public or private hospitals.

Public welfare. Covers support of and assistance to needy persons contingent upon their needs. Includes Cash Assistance paid directly to needy persons under categorical (Old Age Assistance, Aid to Families with Dependent Children, Aid to the Blind, and Aid to the Disabled) and other welfare programs; vendor payments made directly to private purveyors for medical care, burials, and other commodities and services provided under welfare programs; welfare institutions; and any intergovernmental or other direct expenditure for welfare purposes. Pensions to former employees and other benefits not contingent on need are excluded.

Police and fire protection. Includes expenditures for preservation of law and order and traffic safety. Covers police patrols and communications, crime prevention activities, detention and custody of persons awaiting trial, traffic safety, and vehicular inspection. Also covers firefighting organizations and auxiliary services, fire inspection and investigation, support of volunteer fire forces, and other fire prevention activities, including cost of fire-fighting facilities, such as fire hydrants and water, furnished by other agencies of the government.

Infrastructure. This is a residual category representing expenditures that do not fall under the other four subcategories. This category covers expenditures on the general functions of government (legislative, as well as management and support); transportation (streets, highways, storm drains, street trees and landscaping, public transit, airports, ports and harbors); community development (planning, construction and engineering regulation enforcement, redevelopment, housing, employment, and community promotion); culture and leisure (parks and recreation, marinas and wharfs, libraries, museums, golf courses, sports arenas and stadiums, community centers and auditoriums).[41]

---

[41] For more details on the categories of expenditure and revenue in the California cities and counties, see Office of the Controller, *Financial Transactions Concerning the Cities of California: Annual Report 1991–1992* and the corresponding volume for counties.

General Revenue

Total. Includes all revenue except utility, liquor stores, and employee-retirement or other insurance-trust revenue. All tax revenue and all intergovernmental revenue, even if designated for employee-retirement or local utility purposes, is classified as general revenue.

Intergovernmental. transfers. Covers amounts received from the federal or state government as fiscal aid, as reimbursements for performance of general government functions and specific services for the paying government, or in lieu of taxes. Excludes amounts received from other governments for sale of property, commodities, and utility services. All intergovernmental revenue is classified as general revenue.

Total taxes. Defined as all compulsory contributions exacted by a government for public purposes, except employee and employer assessments for retirement and social insurance purposes, which are classified as insurance trust revenue. Total taxes include amounts received from all taxes imposed by a government.

Demographic Data for California Counties

The explanatory variables in our regressions are constructed using demographic data from the 1990 Census of Population STF3A files for California counties. We consider three age categories: age 0 to 20, 21 to 64, and 65 and older. So, for example, the age 0 to 20 regressor is simply the fraction of people in a given county falling into this age category. The regressor called "rural" is the fraction of households in a given county that are in rural (farm or nonfarm) areas. The median income regressor is the median household income for the each county, in ten thousands of 1990 dollars.

References

Arnott, R., and R. Grieson. 1981. "Optimal Fiscal Policy for a State or Local Government." *Journal of Urban Economics* 9:23–48.

Becker, G. 1983. "A Theory of Competition among Pressure Groups for Political Influence." *Quarterly Journal of Economics* 98:371–400.

Bergstrom, T., and R. Goodman. 1973. "Private Demands for Public Goods." *American Economic Review* 63:280–96.

Besharov, G., and A. Zweiman. 1998. "Increasing Returns in Production and Spill-over Effects of Regulation." Mimeo, Stanford University.

Bogart, W. 1991. "Observable Heterogeneity and the Demand for Local Public Spending." *National Tax Journal* 44(2):213–23.

Bradford, D., and W. Oates. 1971. "Towards a Predictive Theory of Intergovernmental Grants." *American Economic Review* 61:440–48.

Breton, A. 1965. "A Theory of Government Grants." *Canadian Journal of Economics and Political Science* 31:175–87.

Cutler, D., D. Elmendorf, and R. Zeckhauser. 1993. "Demographic Characteristics and the Public Bundle." In *Proceedings of the 48th Congress of the International Institute of Public Finance/Institut International de Finances*, 178–98.

Del Rossi, A., and R. Inman. 1994. "Changing the Price of Pork: The Impact of Increased Local Cost Sharing on the Demand for Core of Engineers Water Resource Projects." Mimeo, University of Pennsylvania.

Denzau, A., and K. Grier. 1984. "Determinants of Local Spending: Some Consistent Estimates." *Public Choice* 44(2):375–83.

Echevarria, C. 1995. "On Age Distribution of Population, Government Expenditures and Fiscal Federalism." *Journal of Population Economics* 8:301–13.

Feldstein, M., and M. Vaillant. 1994. "Can State Taxes Redistribute Income?" NBER Working Paper 4785.

Fischel, W. 1992. "Property Taxation and the Tiebout Model: Evidence for the Benefit View versus the New View." *Journal of Economic Literature* 30:171–77.

Gordon, R. 1992. "Can Capital Income Taxes Survive in Open Economies?" *Journal of Finance* 47:1159–80.

1983. "An Optimal Taxation Approach to Fiscal Federalism." *Quarterly Journal of Economics* 98:567–86.

Gramlich, E. 1977. "Intergovernmental Grants: A Review of the Empirical Literature." In *The Political Economy of Fiscal Federalism*, ed. W. Oates. Lexington, MA: Lexington Books.

Gramlich, E., and D. Rubinfeld. 1982. "Micro Estimates of Public Spending Demand Functions and Tests of the Tiebout and Median-Voter Hypotheses." *Journal of Political Economy* 90:536–60.

Greene, K., W. Neenan, and C. Scott. 1974. "Fiscal Incidence in the Washington Metropolitan Area." *Land Economics* 52:13–31.

Grieson, R. 1980. "Theoretical Analysis and Empirical Measurement of the Effects of the Philadelphia Income Tax." *Journal of Urban Economics* 8:123–37.

Hamilton, B. 1975. "Zoning and Property Taxes in a System of Local Governments." *Urban Studies* 12:205–11.

1976. "Capitalization of Interjurisdictional Differences in Local Tax Prices." *American Economic Review* 66:743–53.

Hayek, F. A. 1996. "The Economic Conditions of Interstate Federalism." In *Individualism and Economic Order*. Chicago: University of Chicago Press.

Hines, J., and R. Thaler. 1996. "The Flypaper Effect." *Journal of Economic Perspectives* 9:217–26.

Hoyt, W., and K. Lee. 1997. "Subsidies as Sorting Devices." Mimeo, University of Kentucky.

Hulten, C., and R. Schwab. 1997. "A Fiscal Federalism Approach to Infrastructure Policy." *Regional Science and Urban Economics* 27:139–59.

Inman, R. 1988. "Federal Assistance and Local Services in the United States: The Evolution of a New Federalist Order." In *Fiscal Federalism*, ed. H. Rosen. Chicago: University of Chicago Press.

Inman, R., and D. Rubinfeld. 1979. "The Judicial Pursuit of Local Fiscal Equity." *Harvard Law Review* 92:1662–750.

——— 1996. "Designing Tax Policy in Federalist Economies: An Overview." *Journal of Public Economics* 60:307–34.

Kolstad, C., and F. Wolak. 1983. "Competition in Interregional Taxation: The Case of Western Coal." *Journal of Political Economy* 91:443–60.

——— 1985. "Strategy and Market Structure in Western Coal Taxation." *Review of Economics and Statistics* 67:239–49.

Krelove, R. 1992. "Efficient Tax Exporting." *Canadian Journal of Economics* 25:145–55.

Ladd, H. 1998. *Local Government Tax and Land Use Policies in the United States*. Northampton, MA: Edward Elgar.

Lee, K. 1998. "Individual Actions and Governmental Strategic Interactions: An Efficient Nash Equilibrium." Mimeo, Towson State University.

McKinnon, R., and T. Nechyba. 1997. "Competition in Federal Systems: The Role of Political and Financial Constraints." In *The New Federalism: Can the States Be Trusted?* ed. J. Ferejohn and B. Weingast. Stanford, CA: Hoover Institution Press.

McLure, C. 1967. "The Interstate Exporting of State and Local Taxes." *National Tax Journal* 20:49–77.

McLure, C., and P. Mieszkowski. 1983. *Fiscal Federalism and the Taxation of Natural Resources.* Lexington, MA: Lexington Books.

Megdal, S. 1984. "A Model of Local Demand for Education." *Journal of Urban Economics* 16(1):13–30.

Mieszkowski, P. 1972. "The Property Tax: An Excise Tax or a Profits Tax?" *Journal of Public Economics* 1:73–96.

Mieszkowski, P., and G. Zodrow. 1989. "Taxation and the Tiebout Model." *Journal of Economic Literature* 27:1098–146.

Mintz, J., and H. Tulkens. 1996. "Optimality Properties of Alternative Systems of Taxation of Foreign Capital Income." *Journal of Public Economics* 60:373–400.

Myers, G. 1990. "Optimality, Free Mobility, and the Regional Authority in a Federation." *Journal of Public Economics* 43:107–21.

Nechyba, T. 1996. "A Computable General Equilibrium Model of Intergovernmental Aid." *Journal of Public Economics* 62:363–99.

——— "Local Property and State Income Taxes: The Role of Interjurisdictional Competition and Collusion." *Journal of Political Economy* 105:351–84.

Nechyba, T., and R. McKinnon. 1997. "Tax Competition in Federal Systems:

Political Accountability and Fiscal Constraints." In *The New Federalism: Can the States be Trusted?* ed. J. Ferejohn and B. Weingast. Stanford, CA: Hoover Institution Press, pp. 3–61.

Oates, W. 1972. *Fiscal Federalism*. New York: Harcourt, Brace, Jovanovich.

Oates, W., and R. Schwab. 1988. "Economic Competition among Jurisdictions: Efficiency Enhancing or Distortion Inducing?" *Journal of Public Economics* 35:333–53.

Papke, L. 1991. "Interstate Business Tax Differential and New Firm Location: Evidence from Panel Data." *Journal of Public Economics* 45:47–68.

Pindyck, R. 1978. "Gains to Producers from the Cartelization of Exhaustible Resources." *Review of Economics and Statistics* 60:238–51.

Poterba, J. 1997. "Demographic Structure and the Political Economy of Public Education." *Journal of Public Policy Analysis and Management* 16:48–66.

Rangel, A. 1998. "Forward Intergenerational Goods." Mimeo, Stanford University.

Romer, T., and H. Rosenthal. 1980. "An Institutional Theory of the Effect of Intergovernmental Grants." *National Tax Journal* 33:451–58.

Rubinfeld, D., P. Shapiro, and J. Roberts. 1987. "Tiebout Bias and the Demand for Local Public Schooling." *Review of Economics and Statistics* 69(3):426–37.

Scotchmer, S. 1994. "Public Goods and the Invisible Hand." In *Modern Public Finance*, ed. J. Quigley and E. Smolenski. Cambridge, MA: Harvard University Press.

Starrett, D. 1980. "Measuring Externalities and Second Best Distortions in the Theory of Local Public Goods." *Econometrica* 48:627–42.

Tiebout, C. 1956. "A Pure Theory of Local Expenditures." *Journal of Political Economy* 64:416–24.

Tullock, G. 1983. *The Economics of Income Redistribution*. Boston: Kluwer-Nijhoff.

Weingast, B. 1995. "The Economic Role of Political Institutions: Market-Preserving Federalism and Economic Development." *Journal of Law, Economics, and Organization* 11:1–31.

Weisbrod, B. 1965. "Geographic Spillover Effects and the Allocation of Resources to Education." In *The Public Economy of Urban Communities*, ed. J. Margolis. Washington, DC: Resources of the Future.

Wildasin, D. 1989. "Interjurisdictional Capital Mobility: Fiscal Externality and Corrective Subsidy." *Journal of Urban Economics* 25:193–212.

Wilde, J. 1971. "Grants-in-Aid: The Analytics of Design and Response." *National Tax Journal* 24:134–55.

Williams, A. 1966. "The Optimal Provision of Public Goods in a System of Local Governments." *Journal of Political Economy* 74:18–33.

Wilson, J. 1986. "A Theory of Inter-Regional Tax Competition." *Journal of Urban Economics* 19:296–315.

Wittman, D. 1989. "Why Democracies Produce Efficient Results." *Journal of Political Economy* 97:1395–1424.

Wyckoff, P. 1984. "The Nonexcludable Publicness of Primary and Secondary Public Education." *Journal of Public Economics* 24:331–51.

———. 1991. "The Elusive Flypaper Effect." *Journal of Urban Economics* 30:310–28.

Zodrow, G., and P. Mieszkowski. 1986. "Pigou, Tiebout Property Taxation and the Underprovision of Local Public Goods." *Journal of Urban Economics* 19:356–70.

Comment

HILARY WILLIAMSON HOYNES

A simple examination of local government expenditures shows that there is significant variability in the level and composition of expenditures across localities. In this chapter, Thomas MaCurdy and Thomas Nechyba examine how demographics affect the fiscal burden of communities and what role central governments can play in compensating local areas for fiscal burdens. To examine this question, the chapter develops a model of fiscal federalism and explores the implications of the model in an empirical analysis of the expenditures and finances of California counties.

This model of fiscal federalism has three components. Local areas engage in providing public goods, such as education, safety, and infrastructure. Each area chooses allocations for public goods by maximizing a social welfare function subject to its budget constraint, which incorporates the links between demographics and the costs of providing local public goods. Individuals, who have preferences for public and private goods, decide where to locate, taking into account the package of taxes and local public goods across areas. If there are no spillovers (over time or space), then a local government can reach the social optimum by using benefit taxes. The authors then discuss how the presence of expenditure spillovers can lead to underprovision of the public good. They define the fiscal burden of a community as the total valuation of the public good (for both residents and nonresidents of the community) over and above the current populations' willingness to pay for the local public good. A central government is then introduced, which chooses a tax and intergovernmental transfer scheme to maximize social welfare. A primary concern of the chapter is to explore when and to what extent central governments can compensate local governments for fiscal burdens, thereby correcting the underprovision.

149

The innovation in the theory lies in the attention paid to the role of demographics. How do demographics fit in? First, preferences for and utilization of local public goods may vary across demographic groups. Second, demographics affect the nature of the externality or spillover and hence the amount of the intergovernmental transfer. Consequently, the ability to efficiently fund services depends on the demographic composition of the community. In other words, demographics affect the degree to which the central government can provide transfers to local areas and thereby correct for the market failure.

I like the model and think that it has important policy applications. In particular, I like the attention paid to modeling the source of the externality. The authors consider current-period interjurisdictional spillovers (e.g., interjurisdictional consumption spillovers) and future-period interjurisdictional spillovers (e.g., interjurisdictional investment spillovers). They also allow for spillovers across time within a community (e.g., intrajurisdictional investment spillovers). They discuss the range of possible local public goods and the extent to which they exhibit these different types of externalities. The authors choose, throughout most of the chapter, to use the age composition of the community as the demographic dimension of interest. This is an obvious choice, as age alone surely explains a significant portion of the variation in expenditures on local public goods due to demographics. However, I think that the potentially most important application of this model is in discussions of the fiscal impact of immigration.

I have three sets of comments. First, I explore the channels through which demographics matter for local public goods. Second, I discuss the model's implications for local and central government tax instruments. In particular, I am interested in the feasibility of using taxes to correct the market imperfections that arise here. Third, I discuss what we have learned in the empirical exercise and how it relates to the theory.

Demographics and Local Public Goods

The main conclusion of this chapter is that demographics affect the fiscal burden of a community. I would like to elaborate on the discussion in the chapter by outlining some possible routes through which demographics may matter. First, suppose that a local community has chosen a particular level or intensity for a public good. Given that decision, demographics can affect the fiscal burden for (at least) two reasons. First, different groups may have different utilization rates. For example, the young may disproportionately consume education, while the elderly disproportionately consume health services. Second, the demographic com-

150

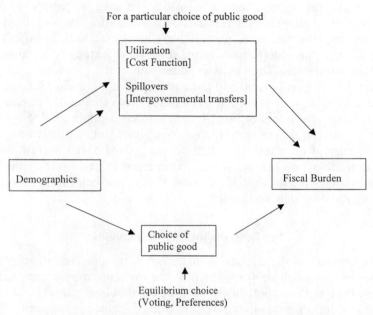

Figure 4-1.1. Links between Demographics and Fiscal Burden.

position of the community also has implications for the importance of spillovers and the ability to raise money to fund programs locally. For example, different demographic groups may have different mobility rates. Also, demographic groups consume goods with differing degrees of spillovers. Both of these mechanisms take the level of the public good as fixed. However, the demographics of the area will also determine (through voting processes) the level or quality of the public good. The local public good is a choice variable and is determined, in part, by the demographic mix. Different groups may have different tastes for the level or quality of the public good.

These points are illustrated in Figure 4-1.1. The figure presents a simple flow chart of these three channels through which demographics may affect local expenditures. The chart relates "demographics" on the left to the "fiscal burden" on the right. The upper panel of the flow chart illustrates that utilization and spillovers may be linked to demographics, given a level for (or quality of) the public good. The lower panel illustrates that demographics may affect the equilibrium choice for the public good.

151

To make this more concrete, consider the case of public libraries. Suppose that all groups have the same utilization rate of libraries. Further, suppose there are no spillovers associated with libraries. But suppose that the elderly have tastes for a more extensive library with more costly services. Then as more elderly enter the community, higher-quality libraries will result, and the cost of providing library service will increase. I think it is important to consider these channels separately.

The chapter's model of fiscal federalism has a public choice component, as local areas are making decisions about public goods using the preferences of their residents. If different groups have different utility functions, then this feature is indeed captured in the model. I think it would be useful to make this clearer. This is also important for interpreting the empirical results.

Implications for Tax Instruments

A major result of the analysis is that, even in the presence of spillovers across space and time, it may be possible for intergovernmental transfers to correct the underprovision of the local public good. The authors point out that transfers may take the form of a block grant or matching grant to the local government or a tax credit or deduction to the relevant individuals. In theory, with full information, one might be able to design a transfer that could correct most market failures. But in practice, the spillovers may be very extensive and complicated, and I wonder if such transfer schemes are feasible. In MaCurdy and Nechyba's Table 4.2, examples of the local public goods range from pollution control to roads to education to health and welfare. Each of these goods exhibits different spillovers. This implies different grant payments for different programs, which we in fact see in practice. My concern is less with implications of the variation across *goods*, but in the variation across *areas* in the degree of the externality. For example, take education. Some areas may have high rates of out-migration while others may have much lower rates. Or consider pollution control. Some areas, because of local geography or density, may generate greater spillovers than other communities. It is not clear that one could design a transfer that would correct the externality while also satisfying horizontal equity.

I have a second, more speculative comment about tax instruments. The model assumes that the localities take the characteristics of the population as given. But they may be able to influence the demographic mix of the population by the choice and structure of taxes. Examples include property tax rates, limitations on size of lots, and regulations discouraging renting.

Comment

Lessons in Empirical Analysis

The chapter investigates the implications of the model with an empirical analysis of California counties. Specifically, the authors run regressions that relate expenditure and revenue shares (or per capita expenditures and revenues) to demographic variables, such as the fraction of young or old, median income, and percent age rural. They run a cross-sectional regression for the fifty-eight counties in California. The results suggest that demographics have an important impact on expenditure and revenue outcomes. For example, a shift in the population from the young to the old reduces expenditures on education, but it also reduces the size of intergovernmental transfers, resulting in little change to the fiscal burden.

An important caveat exists in interpreting these results. The identification of the demographic variables comes from variation across counties. So to the extent that there are any omitted variables at the county level that are correlated with the demographics, the estimates will be biased. Examples of important omitted variables might be differences in costs of living or labor costs.

One possible solution may be to extend the analysis to include more time periods and control for fixed county effects. However, the demographic composition of local areas may change very slowly, making it difficult to estimate the parameters using variation across areas in trends in demographics. Table 4-1.1 presents some estimates of the age and racial/ethnic composition of four California counties to illustrate this point. Specifically, the table presents data from the 1970, 1980, and 1990 Decennial Censuses for Alameda (which contains Oakland), Fresno (an important rural, agricultural county), Los Angeles, and San Diego counties. These figures suggest that the counties do not change quickly and that there is a great deal more cross-sectional variation than over time-variation. For example, between 1970 and 1990 the percent age of the population that is over 65 increased from 9.3% to 9.7% in Los Angeles and from 8.7% to 10.9% in San Diego.[1]

On a related but more minor point, the conclusion that a shift in population toward the young does not increase fiscal burdens strikes me as being not very surprising in this particular application. The explanation is that expenditures and intergovernmental transfers both increase, so

---

[1] This is not inconsistent with the model. In fact, if we remained in the steady state, then, by definition, the demographic composition would be constant. The point is essentially an empirical one. If the variation is primarily cross-sectional, then fixed-effects approaches will not be appropriate.

Table 4-1.1. *Demographic Characteristics of Selected California Counties,*
1970–90 (percent)

	Year	Alameda	Fresno	Los Angeles	San Diego
Black	1970	20.2	9.8	14.6	7.8
	1980	18.4	4.9	12.6	5.6
	1990	17.9	5.0	11.2	6.4
Hispanic	1970	—	—	—	—
	1980	11.2	29.3	27.6	14.8
	1990	14.2	35.5	37.8	20.4
Age <18	1970	31.2	36.1	32.1	32.0
	1980	25.1	29.8	27.2	25.6
	1990	23.7	31.4	26.2	24.4
Age ≥65	1970	9.2	9.0	9.3	8.7
	1980	10.3	10.1	9.9	10.3
	1990	10.6	10.4	9.7	10.3

Source: Published data from the 1970, 1980, and 1990 Decennial Censuses.

fiscal burden does not change. This is explained by the fact that California's system of educational finance is completely centralized. Virtually all locally raised funds are transferred to the state and then redistributed to the school districts. I am not claiming that this educational finance structure does not fit within the model. It may have resulted in part to address the spillovers raised in the paper. But empirically, I am not sure that the regressions tell us anything beyond what we already knew by studying the educational finance system directly.

CHAPTER 4-2

Comment

ROBERT J. WILLIS

MaCurdy and Nechyba (MN) have written a very interesting chapter that is likely to provide a point of departure for significant future work on fiscal federalism and, especially, for incorporation of demographic factors in empirical applications of theories of local public goods. As an extra benefit, they provide the reader with a thorough and wide-ranging review of the theoretical literature in this area, which this reader at least found to be worth the price of admission. The chapter develops a model of local public goods in which the benefits and costs of goods may vary with the demographic composition of the community, especially age. For example, the benefits and costs of publicly supported education or nursing homes clearly depend on how many school-age children or elderly there are in the community. Other expenditures, such as local infrastructure, are less sensitive to the age composition of the community.

There are several classic questions within the local public finance and fiscal federalism literatures that they address within this framework. The one on which they focus most attention is whether individual jurisdictions will choose optimal levels of local public goods and, if not, whether departures from optimality can be offset by the actions of higher levels of government. They begin by considering a case in which neither local public goods nor local taxes create any spillover effects across jurisdictional boundaries. In this case, a Tiebout equilibrium will exist, in which households are sorted across communities according to their tastes and benefit taxes may be used to finance optimal levels of local public goods. While taxes and levels of public-good provision may vary across jurisdictions because of differences in demographic composition, in equilibrium, no household has an incentive to change its location, no locality can do better in terms of its objective function by altering its

155

policies, and there is no role for a central government to improve on its allocation.

Conversely, the potential exists for central government policies to improve on the decisions of localities when there are significant spillovers of benefits or costs across jurisdictions, when localities do not impose benefit taxes, or when jurisdictions behave strategically through tax competition and tax exporting. For example, if there are spillover benefits to other jurisdictions from the provision of a given type of public good in a given locality, the state or federal government can improve welfare by providing tied transfers to localities to induce them to increase supplies of that good. MN sidestep the political economy question of whether or why a higher level of government would engage in such transfers and, for much of their analysis, set aside strategic responses that local governments might undertake in order to game the system. Rather, they ask whether observed patterns of local expenditures on age-targeted public goods, local tax revenues, and intergovernmental transfers in California conform to those that would be expected on the hypothesis that the state and federal governments maximize an objective function that respects individual preferences and that localities do not behave strategically. Given the emphasis in the fiscal federalism literature on strategic behavior, MN find it surprising that their empirical results conform quite closely to their theory.

Even if it were not successful in explaining the data, there is much to commend the modeling approach that MN take. Their theory is very straightforward, it permits them to incorporate specific hypotheses about different age-targeted public goods, and it leads to fairly clear-cut hypotheses. From a normative point of view, failure of the data to conform to theoretical predictions might indicate a "failure" of government organization that merits further investigation, while positive empirical results might suggest that a system of fiscal federalism can operate with reasonable efficiency.

I will elaborate on these points, using the example of public education. The MN model goes substantially further than most of the literature in considering how spillovers might occur. In addition to the usual interjurisdictional spillovers involving current benefits (e.g., residents of locality B benefit from nice parks in locality A), the MN model allows for spillovers that might occur over time for public investment goods. In particular, they suggest that past educational expenditures may raise the incomes of current residents of a jurisdiction who stay in the same locality in which they were reared (an intrajurisdictional investment spillover) or raise incomes in other jurisdictions to which children move when they reach adulthood (an interjurisdictional investment spillover). As they

Comment

point out in footnote 24, this need not cause a spillover if parents who pay taxes to educate their children in period $t - 1$ care about the children's adult earnings in period t and take the effect of education on future earnings into account in their voting decisions in period $t - 1$. MN assume that parents do not fully take the effect of education on future earnings into account and thus hypothesize that education has a spillover effect. Their empirical findings, which show that an increase in the proportion of children increases both the share and level of intergovernmental transfers, are consistent with such spillovers.

Going back at least to Becker's Woytinsky Lecture (Becker, 1967), human capital theorists have emphasized the importance of parental motivations for educating children in determining the distribution of income and the returns to investment in human capital. Given that public schools are the primary vehicle through which these investments take place, I wish that MN had devoted more attention to a consideration of what their work might imply for the American public schooling system, which, alone among the world's school systems, relies primarily on local finance. In particular, would they be willing to argue that their empirical findings showing a positive effect of the share of children on intergovernmental transfers imply that parents do not fully incorporate the pecuniary returns to education into their decisions about investing in their children? If so, their model provides both a rationale for public intervention in parental schooling decisions and evidence that government action operates in the "right direction." I rather doubt that they (or I) would be willing to push the model or findings that far, but I do think that further exploration along these lines might be fruitful.

In this regard, a useful next step would be to replicate their analysis in other states. California ranks relatively high (fourteenth) among states in the importance of state aid to education, with only about 34% of spending originating at the local level, while 56% is provided by the state (U.S. Dept. of Education 1996). There is very substantial variation in the fraction of educational expenditures provided by states, ranging from a high of 90% in Hawaii to a low of 8% in New Hampshire. While there is no theoretical reason to suppose that the magnitude of the share of state aid to education is necessarily related to the degree to which the state offsets spillovers with intergovernmental transfers, this wide degree of variation suggests that it would be hazardous to assume that the results in this chapter for California hold true generally. Fortunately, it seems likely that this excellent chapter will provoke researchers to explore the issues it raises in a number of ways, including exploring data from other states.

References

Becker, Gary S. 1967. *Human Capital and the Personal Distribution of Income.* Ann Arbor: University of Michigan Press.

U.S. Department of Education, National Center for Education Statistics. 1996. *Common Core of Data Survey*, table 156.

CHAPTER 5

Social Security, Retirement Incentives, and Retirement Behavior: An International Perspective

JONATHAN GRUBER AND DAVID WISE

The largest entitlement program in the United States today is the Social Security (SS) program. Social Security benefits payments in 1997 amounted to over $316 billion, which is almost 18% of the federal budget and about 4% of U.S. GDP for that year; this represents a doubling as share of GDP in the past thirty years. Social Security in the United States is also a system in fiscal imbalance. The convergence of three trends in the early twenty-first century will cause problems with the long-run solvency of the program. Two of these trends are the aging of the "baby boom" cohort and the drop in the fertility rate of U.S. families. As a result, the ratio of persons over age 65 to those aged 20–64 has risen from 0.14 in 1950 to 0.21 today and is projected to rise to 0.36 by 2030 and to 0.41 by 2070. The third trend is the reduction in the rate of growth in real wages in the United States, which has lowered the base of earnings on which SS benefits commitments can be financed. As a result, current estimates imply that if the structure of the program remains unchanged, payroll taxes to finance this program, currently at 12.4% of payroll, would have to rise to over 18%.

This type of fiscal imbalance is reflected not only in the Social Security system in the United States, but in social security systems throughout the industrialized world. Indeed, the projected actuarial deficits in social security systems in other nations dwarf those of the United States. Figure 5.1 shows the ratio of the number of persons age 65 and over to the number age 20–64 for a sample of eleven countries. In six of the countries, this ratio will exceed 0.5 by 2050; in Spain, it will exceed 0.6.

These demographic trends have placed enormous pressure on the financial viability of the social security systems in these countries. The financial pressure is compounded by another trend. In virtually every

159

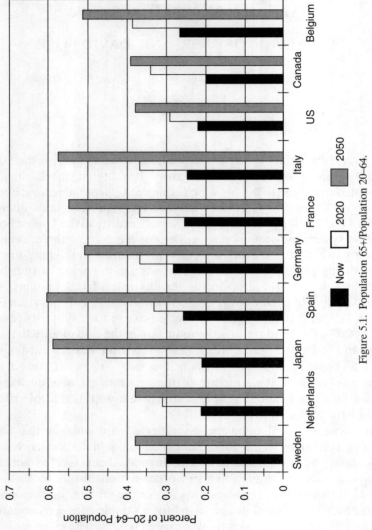

Figure 5.1. Population 65+/Population 20-64.

country, employees are leaving the labor force at younger and younger ages. In some countries, the labor force participation rates of 60- to 64-year-old men have fallen by 75% over the past three decades.

What accounts for the striking decline in labor force participation? One explanation is that social security provisions themselves provide an enormous incentive to leave the labor force early, thus by their very structure exacerbating the financial problems that they face. The purpose of this chapter is to summarize the financial incentives for retirement faced by older workers in the United States and around the world and the correspondence between these financial incentives and the actual retirement decisions that are made. The work that is summarized here is part of an ongoing National Bureau of Economic Research project on international social security comparisons. This project is organized by Jonathan Gruber and David Wise, and the results of the first round of analysis are presented in Gruber and Wise (1999). The participating countries are as follows:

- Belgium (Pestieau and Stijns, 1999)
- Canada (Gruber, 1999)
- France (Blanchet and Péle, 1999)
- Germany (Börsch-Supan and Schnabel, 1999)
- Italy (Brugiavini, 1999)
- Japan (Oshio and Yashiro, 1999)
- Netherlands (Kapteyn and de Vos, 1999)
- Spain (Boldrin, Jimenez, and Peracchi, 1999)
- Sweden (Palme and Svensson, 1999)
- United Kingdom (Blundell and Johnson, 1999)
- United States (Diamond and Gruber, 1999)

We begin with a review of the trends in labor force participation, in the United States and around the world, highlighting the remarkable reduction in the participation of older workers in the labor force, and then document the current patterns of labor force participation by older workers in the United States and in these other countries. We then use data from several individual countries to illustrate the relationship between social security provisions and withdrawal from the labor force, first discussing the relationship between the age of benefits entitlement and retirement patterns across several nations and then summarizing across the full sample of nations the retirement incentives inherent in their different systems. Finally, we compare these incentives to actual patterns of retirement across this sample of nations, finding a striking correlation between countries that tax work heavily at older ages and countries that have little labor supplied at those ages.

161

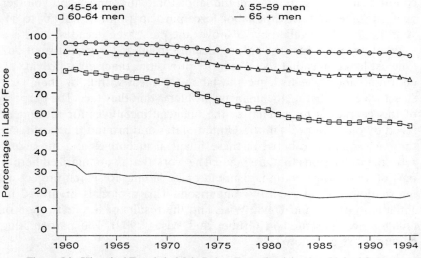

Figure 5.2. Historical Trends in Male Labor Force Participation, United States.

Labor Force Participation

The Decline since 1960

The decline in the labor force participation of older persons is one of the most dramatic features of labor force change over the past several decades. The decline for the United States is illustrated in Figures 5.2 and 5.3, which graph the labor force participation rates of men and women in different age groups since 1960. We focus on four age groups: 45–54; 55–59; 60–64; and 65 plus. For men (Figure 5.2), there is a decline in the labor force participation of all of these groups. The decline for the youngest group is slight, while the decline for the 60–64 group is much more precipitous; for the latter group, labor force participation has fallen from above 80% in 1960 to 52% in 1994. There is also a large percentage decline, albeit from a smaller base, for the oldest group, where participation rates have been halved, from 35% to 17%.

For women (Figure 5.3), the pattern is quite different: any trend toward earlier retirement is dominated by increased labor force participation across cohorts. Even for those age 60–64, participation is rising; for the oldest group, participation declines slightly.

This dramatic decline in labor force participation for older men in the United States is well known and has been the subject of much commentary, particularly in terms of the role that Social Security might

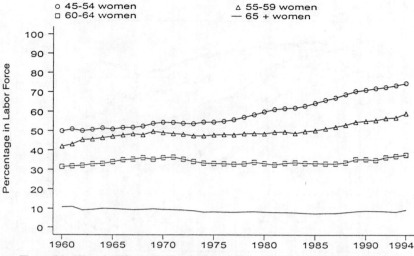

Figure 5.3. Historical Trends in Female Labor Force Participation, United States.

have played in this trend. What is less well known, however, is that the decline is much more striking in other industrialized nations. The labor force participation rates of men age 60 to 64 for the years 1960 to 1996 are shown for ten of the eleven countries in the sample (data for Canada were not available) in Figure 5.4. The decline was substantial in each of the countries, but was much greater in some countries than in others. In the early 1960s, the participation rates were above 70% in each of the countries and above 80% in several countries. By the mid-1990s, the rate had fallen to below 20% in Belgium, Italy, France, and the Netherlands. It had fallen to about 35% in Germany and 40% in Spain.

The U.S. decline from 82% to 53% was modest in comparison to the much more precipitous decline in these European countries. The decline to 57% in Sweden was also large, but modest when compared to the fall in other countries. Japan stands out with the smallest decline of all the countries, from about 83% to 75%. Labor force participation rates of 45- to 59-year-old men, as well as those of men age 60 and older, have also declined substantially.

The individual country analyses summarized here also present parallel information for women. While labor force participation is increasing for women throughout the industrialized world, most other countries differ from the United States in that for older women (60–64) labor

163

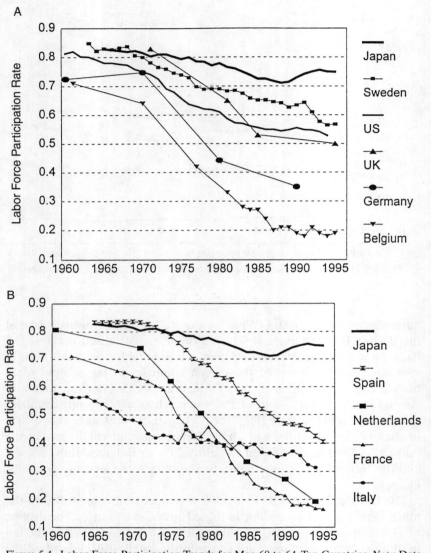

Figure 5.4. Labor Force Participation Trends for Men 60 to 64, Ten Countries. *Note*: Data for Canada were not available. Japan is shown in both panels for reference.

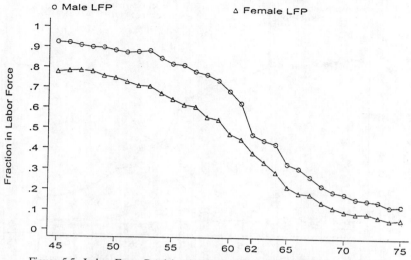

Figure 5.5. Labor Force Participation Rates by Age and Sex, United States.

force participation is still falling, albeit less precipitously than male participation.

The Decline with Age and "Non-Work"

Of particular interest for the analysis in this paper is the current relationship between labor force participation and age. The age pattern of labor force participation for men and women for the U.S. case is depicted in Figure 5.5. At age 45, the participation of men is significantly higher than that of women, although almost 80% of 45-year-old women were working in 1994–95. There is then a gradual parallel decline for men and women until around age 55, at which point the pace of the decline steepens; this is particularly true for men, so that the participation gap closes substantially by age 62. By age 75, participation has dropped quite low, with less than 20% of men and 10% of women participating in the labor force.

Figure 5.6 considers in more detail the allocation of time among men as they age, by dividing activities at each age into employment, unemployment, disability, and retirement. The top line, showing the share of men employed, mirrors the age trend in Figure 5.5. There is very little age trend in either unemployment or disability, although both categories do shrink over time. The dominating trend here is increased retirement with age.

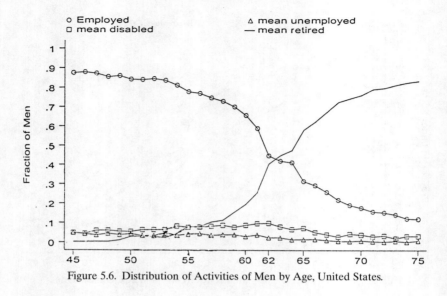

Figure 5.6. Distribution of Activities of Men by Age, United States.

This same relationship between labor force participation and age for men is shown for each of the eleven countries in the sample in Figure 5.7. The countries are ordered by labor force participation at age 65. At age 50, approximately 90% of men are in the labor force in all of the countries. The decline after age 50 varies greatly among countries. By age 65, virtually no men in Belgium are working; in Japan about 60% are still in the labor force. Indeed, only about 25% of men in Belgium are working at age 60. In Japan, on the other hand, 75% are working at age 60.

One simple means of comparing the extent of labor withdrawal of older men across countries is to compare the average proportion of men not participating in the labor market. Consider the proportion of men not working at a given age (1 – LFP, where LFP is the labor force participation rate); this is about 0.95 for Belgium and about 0.40 for Japan at age 65, for example. Loosely speaking, we can refer to this as "non-work" at that age. If non-work is added up over all ages and divided by the number of ages, we measure total non-work for a given age range as a percentage of total work capacity in that age range.

The non-work measures for all of the countries are shown in Figure 5.8. The non-work measure ranges from 67% in Belgium to 22% in Japan. The United States is toward the bottom of the range, with a non-work measure of 37%. Of course, these are only relative measures; there is no reason to assume that all men who are not working

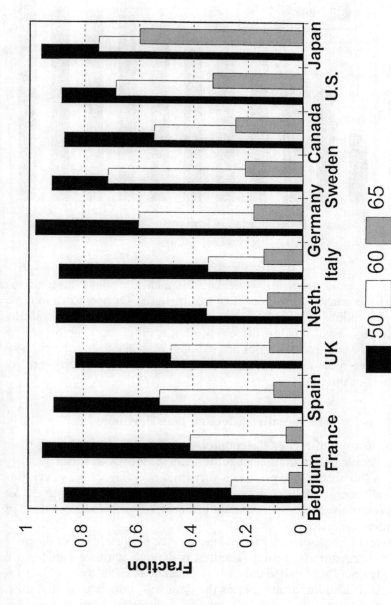

Figure 5.7. Labor Force Participation by Country and Age.

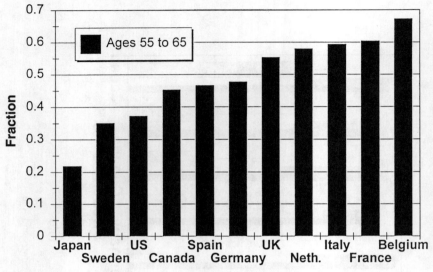

Figure 5.8. Nonwork, Ages 55 to 65.

should, or could, work. In particular, this measure might differ across countries because of differences in health status. Or non-work may be higher in countries in which a larger proportion of jobs are physically demanding. Nevertheless, these enormous differences across fairly similar industrialized countries are striking. We will consider below how this relative measure is related to the provisions of the social security programs in the countries.

The Incentive Effects of Plan Provisions

The key feature of each of the country analyses summarized here is their highly detailed computation of retirement incentives in social security plans. In this section, we provide a very brief overview of the provisions of social security plans that can create large retirement incentives. We then present evidence on how these incentives appear to be reflected in retirement behavior.

Two features of social security plans have an important effect on labor force participation incentives. The first is the age at which benefits are first available. This is called the early retirement age. The "normal" retirement age is also important, but as the data will show, is typically much less important than the early retirement age. It may once have been that the normal retirement age was when most people were expected to retire; now, in most countries, few people work until the "normal" retirement age.

The extent to which people continue to work after the early retirement age is closely related to the second important feature of plan provisions, the pattern of benefit accrual. Suppose that at a given age a person has acquired entitlement to future benefits upon retirement. The sum of this future stream of benefits, expressed in terms of today's dollars, is that person's social security wealth at that age (SSW_a).[1] The key consideration for retirement decisions is how this wealth will evolve with continued work. If a person is 59, for example, what is the change in SSW if he or she retires at age 60 instead of age 59? The difference between SSW if retirement is at age a and SSW if retirement is at age $a + 1$, $SSW_{a+1} - SSW_a$, is called *SSW accrual.*

We compare the SSW accrual to net wage earnings over the year. If the accrual is positive, it adds to total compensation from working the additional year; if the accrual is negative, it reduces total compensation. The ratio of the accrual to net wage earnings is an implicit tax on earnings if the accrual is negative and an implicit subsidy to earnings if the accrual is positive. Thus a negative accrual discourages continuation in the labor force, and a positive accrual encourages continued labor force participation. This accrual rate, and the associated tax rate, is a key calculation, which is made in the same way for each of the countries considered here. As it turns out, the pension accrual is typically negative at older ages: continuation in the labor force means a loss in pension benefits, which imposes an implicit tax on work and provides an incentive to leave the labor force.

The magnitude of the SSW accrual and that of the corresponding tax or subsidy differ greatly from country to country and are determined by several provisions. The most important is, of course, the magnitude of the benefits to which the worker and his or her family, are entitled; any taxes or subsidies are multiples of the generosity of the benefits structure. These benefit effects can even be multiplied if, as in the U.S. case, there is tax subsidization of benefits relative to earnings. The second is the adjustment to benefits if a person works for another year. An additional year of work means a delay in receiving benefits, which thus will be received for one year less. In some countries, there is an "actuarial" adjustment, such that benefits are increased to offset the fact that they are received for fewer years. But in other countries, there is no such adjustment. The greater the adjustment, the greater the inducement to continue working.

---

[1] Technically, the future stream of benefits is discounted to today's dollars by both the rate of interest and the likelihood that the individual will live to each future age.

If the adjustment is not large enough to offset the fewer years of benefit receipt, however, there is an incentive to leave the labor force. Third, a person who continues to work must pay social security taxes on earnings, lowering net social security accrual. These tax payments make retirement more attractive. Fourth, the additional year of earnings is often used in the recomputation of social security benefits, which are typically based on some measure of lifetime average earnings. Since earnings are often higher later in life than earlier, this may raise net accrual, making retirement less attractive. This effect may be especially important for the younger old who are not fully "vested" in their social security system until they have paid in for some minimal number of years. Finally, a delay in receiving benefits raises the odds that the worker might die without being able to collect any benefits. This lowers net social security accrual and may be an important consideration for the oldest workers.

In addition to social security plan provisions, other government and private programs may also affect the relationship between social security plan provisions and observed retirement patterns. One is the availability of employer-provided pension plans. For example, about half of all employees in the United States are covered by employer-provided plans, and about half of these are defined-benefit plans, which have substantial retirement incentive effects, as has been emphasized by Stock and Wise (1990a, 1990b) and Lumsdaine, Stock, and Wise (1991, 1992, 1994). In most European countries, employer-provided plans are much less prevalent; the most important exceptions are the United Kingdom and the Netherlands. The other programs that may have an important effect on retirement are unemployment and disability insurance. In many European countries, these programs essentially provide early retirement benefits before the official social security early retirement age. While these other programs affect the comparisons that are made here, the basic relationship between social security plan provisions and retirement is typically quite clear. In some cases where these plans are especially important, the country analyses have incorporated them into the "social security" incentive calculations.

The remainder of this chapter discusses the role of these two important features of social security systems: the age of benefits entitlement and the implicit tax on work through the structure of social security benefits.

Age of Benefits Entitlement:
Country-Specific Examples

To illustrate the relationship between social security plan provisions and retirement behavior, we begin with evidence from the United States and then turn to two other countries that have seen substantial changes in the structure of their social security systems: Germany and France. Data from these three countries allow a simple within-country comparison of change in plan provisions over time and the corresponding change in the labor force participation of older people. The experience of these countries also highlights a feature of retirement that is common to all countries: the concentration of retirement at social security early and normal retirement ages. In the final section we discuss overall evidence based on all of the eleven countries and draw general conclusions based on between-country comparisons.

The U.S. Case

Key Institutional Features

For understanding the retirement implications of the structure of SS in the United States and the corresponding implications of systems in other countries, it is useful to quickly review the institutional structure of our SS system. The "normal retirement age" (NRA) for receipt of SS benefits is 65, although since 1956 for women and 1961 for men, persons have been able to claim their SS benefits at age 62 if they wish to do so. The system is financed by a payroll tax of 5.3% on both the employer and employee, up to a taxable maximum earnings per year of $68,400. The amount that a worker receives upon claiming SS benefits is a function of his or her average indexed monthly earnings (AIME), which is the real monthly earnings averaged over the highest thirty-five years of earnings. A key feature of this process is that additional higher-earnings years can replace earlier lower-earnings years, since only thirty-five years are used in the calculation. This function is progressive; a dollar of contributions yields a higher benefit for a low-income than for a higher-income worker.

Adjustments to the benefit level are based on the age at which benefits are first claimed. For workers claiming benefits before the normal retirement age (currently 65, but legislated to slowly increase to 67), benefits are decreased by 5/9 of one percent per month, so that for those claiming benefits on their 62nd birthday, the benefits are 80% of what they would have been if they had waited until their normal retirement age. The reduction is called the actuarial reduction factor. Individuals can also delay the receipt of benefits beyond age 65 and receive a delayed retirement credit (DRC). For workers reaching age 65 in 1996, an additional 5% is paid for each year of delayed receipt of benefits. Under current legislation, this amount will steadily increase until it reaches 8% per year in 2009. There are also important additional benefits provisions

171

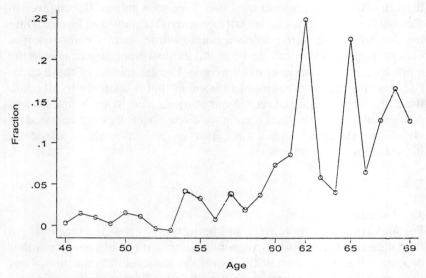

Figure 5.9. Hazard Rate of Leaving the Labor Force for Men, United States.

based on family structure: spouses of SS beneficiaries receive an additional benefit, which is 50% of the primary earner's benefit, if their SS entitlement based on their own earnings is lower than this level; dependent children are also eligible for 50% of the earner's benefit; and surviving spouses receive 100% of that benefit.

Correspondence with Retirement Decisions
The clear correspondence between the structural features of SS and individual retirement decisions in the United States can be seen clearly by examining the hazard of retirement, defined as the rate of departure from the labor force, by age (hereafter "hazard rate"): the proportion of workers who are employed at a given age who retire at that age. Figure 5.9 shows the hazard rate for men in the United States. The striking fact about this figure is the dramatic increase in labor force leaving at age 62, which is precisely the age of eligibility for early retirement under Social Security, and at age 65, which is the normal retirement age. That is, of those working at age 60, fewer than 10% retire when they turn 61; but of those working at age 61, 25% retire when they turn 62. These "spikes" are very suggestive of a role for SS in explaining the retirement behavior of men. There is also a small spike around age 55, which may reflect the early retirement provisions at that age under many pension plans. There is also another spike around age 68; the cause here is not clear,

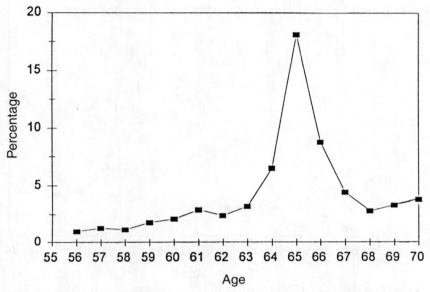

Figure 5.10a. Hazard Rates for Men in the United States, 1960. *Source*: Burtless and Moffit, 1994.

although the small denominator of the hazard after age 65 makes it hard to interpret this finding.[2]

Moreover, changes in the age of eligibility for Social Security benefits in the United States have had a large effect on retirement behavior. This pattern is illustrated in Figures 5.10a–5.10c, which show the hazard rates for men in 1960, 1970, and 1980.[3] In 1960, the normal retirement age was 65, and there was no opportunity for early retirement under Social Security. In that year, the hazard rate was low until age 65, when the departure rate jumped precipitously, reflecting the availability of Social Security benefits.

In 1961, early eligibility for retirement benefits for men at age 62 was introduced.[4] The effect of the introduction of early retirement on labor force departure rates is striking. Starting in 1970, and visible most clearly in 1980, there was a dramatic increase in the departure rate at age 62,

---

[2] That is, the spike at age 65 represents a 9.5 percentage point change in labor force participation, while the spike at age 68 represents only a 4.5 percentage point change; the latter appears almost as large as the former because the denominator is so much smaller.
[3] Taken from Burtless and Moffitt (1986).
[4] It had been introduced for women in 1956.

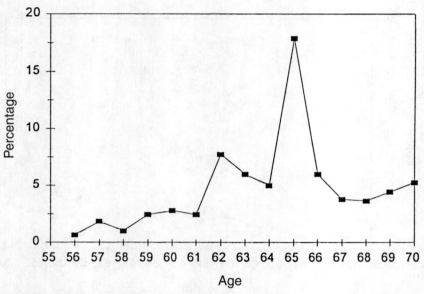

Figure 5.10b. Hazard Rates for Men in the United States, 1970. *Source*: Burtless and Moffit, 1984.

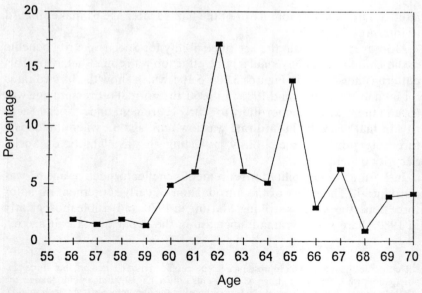

Figure 5.10c. Hazard Rates for Men in the United States, 1980. *Source*: Burtless and Moffit, 1984.

and a corresponding decrease at age 65. As a result, since 1980 the highest rate of labor force leaving has been at age 62.[5] Thus, the U.S. data suggest a very strong influence of Social Security incentives on retirement: not only are current retirement ages congruent with the ages of benefits entitlement under the SS system; there was a distinct shift toward retirement at age 62 in the wake of the introduction of that early retirement age.

The German Case

The German experience provides another striking example of the role of social security institutions in driving retirement decisions. Before 1972, the social security retirement age in Germany was 65, except for disability, and there was no social security early retirement age. But legislation in 1972 provided for early retirement at age 60 for women and at age 63 for men (given the accumulation of required social security work years). In addition, liberal use of disability and unemployment benefits effectively expanded the early retirement option. In a large fraction of cases, social security early retirement benefits were made available with no reduction in benefits; benefits taken at the early retirement age had been the same as if they had been taken at the normal retirement age. This greatly increased the net tax on work, since delaying retirement simply reduced the number of years that one could receive benefits, without increasing the annual benefit.

In fact, there was a dramatic response to this increase in retirement incentives. Over the next few years, the mean retirement age of white-collar workers was reduced by 5.5 years, as shown in Figure 5.11.[6]

The correspondence between plan provisions and retirement can also be demonstrated by considering the relationship between retirement and social security provisions at a particular point in time. The detailed provisions of the 1972 legislation are mirrored in the retirement rates by age, as illustrated by the hazard rates in Figure 5.12.

The ages of eligibility for key plan provisions are also shown in the figure so that the correspondence between plan provisions and retirement is easily seen. Men who are "disabled" or "unemployed" at age 60 and have a certain number of years of employment under the social security system are eligible for early retirement (ER) at that age. There is a

---

[5] This evolution was fairly slow. A similar pattern is seen in Canada, as documented by Baker and Benjamin (1996): early retirement at age 60 was introduced in 1987, but not until the early 1990s was it reflected in a limited way in retirement behavior.

[6] The mean retirement age is the average age of persons retiring in a given year.

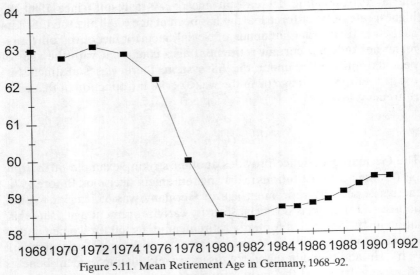

Figure 5.11. Mean Retirement Age in Germany, 1968–92.

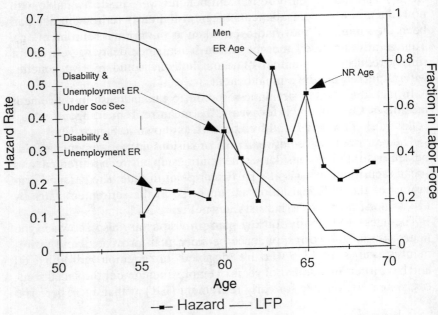

Figure 5.12. Hazard and Labor Force Participation Rates for Germany.

corresponding large jump in the retirement rate at that age. Men who have been employed for thirty-five years are eligible for early retirement at age 63, and there is a corresponding jump in the retirement rate at that age. The normal retirement (NR) age is 65, and there is a corresponding spike at that age as well.

The French Case

The experience in France provides another illustration of the effect of changes in plan provisions. Prior to 1972, the French normal social security retirement age was 65 and early retirement provisions were uncommon. In the early 1970s, "early retirement provisions" were introduced by way of guaranteed income for persons age 60 and over who lost their jobs. In 1983, age 60 became the *normal* retirement age. In addition, guaranteed income was provided for persons age 57 and older who lost their jobs.

The effect of this series of reforms is easily seen in Figures 5.13a–5.13d, which show the *distribution* of social security retirement ages for those workers attaining age 60 in 1972, before any of these changes; in 1978 and 1982, after the first reforms; and in 1986, after they were all in place. (These figures must be distinguished from those like Figure 5.12 for Germany, which shows hazard, or departure, rates; Figure 5.13 shows the distribution of retirement ages.) In the early 1970s, the modal retirement age was 65, as shown for the cohort that reached age 60 in 1972 (and age 65 in 1977). But as early as 1963, special allowances were provided for some workers who became unemployed at age 60 or older, perhaps reflected in the small spike at age 60. Beginning in 1972, a "resource maintenance" program provided grants equal to 60 to 70% of last earnings to persons who became unemployed between ages 60 and 64. The effect of these programs seems to be reflected in the increasing proportion of workers retiring at age 60, as shown in Figures 5.13b and 5.13c (1978 and 1982). In 1983, age 60 became the normal social security retirement age. Shortly after that, the modal retirement age did indeed become 60, as shown in Figure 5.13d for the cohort reaching age 60 in 1986.

As in Germany, the current labor force departure rates in France also correspond closely to social security provisions. The age-specific rates of departure from the labor force in France are shown in Figure 5.14. Approximately 60% of employees who remain in the labor force until the social security early retirement age – 60 – retire then. But even before that age, departure rates are substantial, apparently reflecting the guaranteed income provisions for employees who become "unemployed," even if they are not eligible for social security benefits. Thus, as in

177

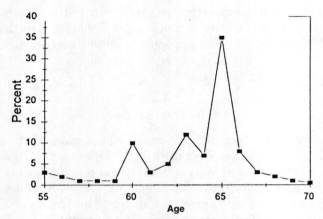

Figure 5.13a. Retirement Ages in France, Population Age 60 in 1972.

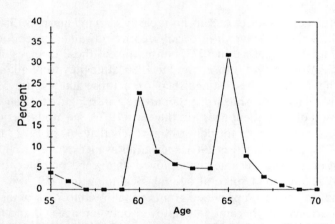

Figure 5.13b. Retirement Ages in France, Population Age 60 in 1978.

Germany, there is a strong incentive to take retirement benefits once they are available.

To summarize, these three country illustrations make clear the very close correspondence between retirement ages and the statutory social security eligibility for early and normal retirement benefits. In all three cases, there are large jumps in labor force departure rates at the early retirement age, in particular, and at the normal retirement age as well. The correspondence is demonstrated most convincingly by within-country changes in retirement behavior over time, which follow on changes in statutory provisions.

178

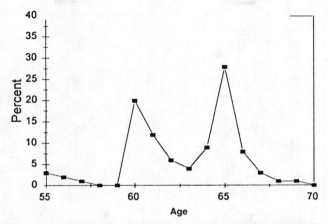

Figure 5.13c. Retirement Ages in France, Population Age 60 in 1982.

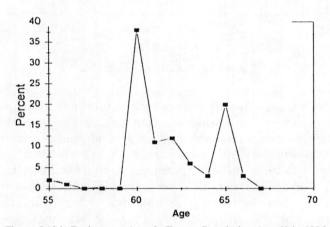

Figure 5.13d. Retirement Ages in France, Population Age 60 in 1986.

Tax Incentives to Retire:
Evidence across All Countries

In distilling the evidence from all of the countries studied in the NBER project, three features of the data stand out. First, as in the three country illustrations, there is a strong correspondence between early and normal retirement ages and departure from the labor force. Second, the social security provisions in most countries place a heavy tax burden on work past the age of early retirement eligibility and thus provide a strong incentive to withdraw from the labor force early. Third, the tax – and thus

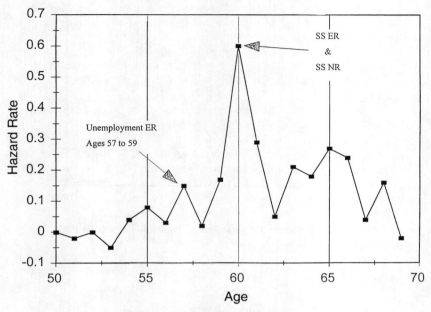

Figure 5.14. Hazard Rates for France.

the incentive to leave the labor force – varies substantially among countries. So does retirement behavior. Thus by considering comparisons across the countries we are able to draw general conclusions about the relationship between the tax penalty on work and retirement behavior.

In order to facilitate these comparisons, a central feature of the project was a detailed computation of the retirement incentives inherent in the provisions of that country's retirement-income system. This included, in some cases, not only social security programs but other quasi–early retirement options, such as disability insurance. By making the same analytic calculations, the individual studies provide a means of comparing the retirement incentives among the nations. In each case, the study considered the incentives facing a male worker born in 1930, and thus turning 65 in 1995, who earned the median earnings in each year for his cohort. He is assumed to have a wife who is three years younger and who does not work.

Results for the United States

To illustrate the nature of these calculations, it is useful to start with the U.S. case and then to move to a summary of the international findings; these U.S. results are presented in Diamond and Gruber (1998). Table

Table 5.1. *U.S. Base Case*

Last Year of Work (age)	Replacement Rate (fraction of earnings)	SSW ($)	SSW Accrual ($)	Accrual Rate	Tax/ Subsidy Rate
61	0.403	104,275	−1,019		
62	0.440	104,701	426	0.004	−0.028
63	0.476	10,476	65	0.001	−0.005
64	0.703	104,335	−432	−0.004	0.031
65	0.749	101,882	−2,452	−0.024	0.188
66	0.798	99,109	−2,773	−0.027	0.225
67	0.845	95,964	−3,145	−0.032	0.269
68	0.872	91,131	−4,833	−0.050	0.439
69	0.898	86,412	−4,718	−0.052	0.455

5.1 shows the basic results for the U.S. case. Each row represents the age of the worker in the last year of work; that is, the first row represents the effect of working during the 61st year and retiring on the 62nd birthday. The first column shows the net replacement rate. At the first point that benefits can be claimed, the replacement rate is 40%; that is, if the individual retires on his 62nd birthday, SS benefits will replace 40% of his forgone wages. This percentage rises over time as a result of actuarial adjustment, which rewards workers for delayed benefit claiming by increasing benefits. The major change occurs for retirement on the 65th birthday, when the wife turns 62, since at that point the spouse becomes entitled to dependent benefits. For the worker who works through his 69th year and collects on his 70th birthday, SS benefits replace almost 90% of his after-tax earnings.

The next three columns show the evolution of SSW over time. A worker who retires at the early retirement age will have accumulated $104,275 in SSW. If he works an additional year, his SSW will increase by about 0.4%, as shown by the accrual rate in the fourth column. That is, the U.S. system is roughly "actuarially fair" with respect to retirement at age 62; the fact that benefit receipt is delayed for a year and that the worker has to pay another year of SS taxes is compensated by the actuarial adjustment to benefits, and the fact that this next high-earnings year can replace a lower-earning year earlier in his career. As a result, as the final column shows, there is actually a subsidy for working at age 62 under the SS system: the median worker who chooses to work an additional year at age 62 sees a net wage bonus of 2.8%.

From age 62 through age 64, there are implicit taxes on work through the SS system, but these are small. However, at age 65, the implicit tax on work jumps up dramatically. For this worker, working during his 65th year means forgoing over \$2,450 in SSW, which amounts to almost 19% of what he would earn during that year. This is because the actuarial adjustment for working beyond age 65 is unfair, given the forgone year of SS benefits. This tax rate rises further with age, so that for the decision to work during the 70th year, the forgone SSW amounts to almost half of what he would earn during that year.[7]

The results in Table 5.1 illustrate the retirement incentives under SS for one type of worker, a married male with a nonworking spouse. Table 5.2 summarizes the incentives under SS for other types of workers, showing both the replacement rate for retiring at a given age and the tax/subsidy rate for another year of work. We first consider single male workers. For this group, the replacement rate is much lower than for their married counterparts, since they do not benefit from the dependent's benefit that accrues to the married male with a nonworking spouse. The tax rates on additional work are also higher at most ages for single workers, for the same reason: both the actuarial adjustment to benefits and the benefit recomputation from additional years of high earnings are worth more to married workers, since they get a 50% bonus on each extra benefit dollar.

We then consider low- versus high-earning workers. In particular, we show the results for workers at the 10th and 90th percentiles of the earnings distribution. Low-earning workers have a much higher replacement rate, and higher-earning workers have a correspondingly lower rate. Before age 65, there are small tax rates on work for higher-earning workers and larger subsidies for low earners; this is because the actuarial adjustment and benefit recomputation is worth much more to a low earner as a share of earnings. After age 65, however, when actuarial adjustments become "unfair," the tax rates rise much more for low-earning workers, since at their high replacement rates there is a greater penalty for unfair actuarial adjustments. This effect foreshadows somewhat what we see below for other nations.

International Comparison

Labor force participation and retirement incentives for all eleven countries in our study are summarized in Table 5.3. The countries are ordered

---

[7] The much higher tax rates after age 65 will be diminishing over time, as the Delayed Retirement Credit (DRC) provided to workers who work past that age is gradually increased from 5 to 8% over the next decade. The jump in the implicit tax on work in the 68th year is due to dependent benefits: if the worker delays claiming past age 68, that implies (given our assumed age difference) that dependent's benefits are delayed past age 65, so that the unfair DRC penalizes the dependent as well.

Table 5.2. *Additional U.S. Incentive Calculations*

Last Year of Work (age)	Single Worker		10th Percentile Earner		90th Percentile Earner	
	Replacement Rate	Tax/Subsidy Rate	Replacement Rate	Tax/Subsidy Rate	Replacement Rate	Tax/Subsidy Rate
61	0.430		0.530		0.247	
62	0.465	0.083	0.577	-0.064	0.267	0.024
63	0.503	0.143	0.627	-0.080	0.290	0.015
64	0.540	0.177	0.926	-0.035	0.432	0.028
65	0.568	0.327	0.990	0.187	0.465	0.117
66	0.598	0.352	1.056	0.238	0.501	0.140
67	0.627	0.385	1.119	0.445	0.536	0.165
68	0.657	0.412	1.156	0.673	0.559	0.272
69	0.687	0.442	1.193	0.660	0.583	0.281

Table 5.3. *International Summary*

Country	Non-Work at Ages 55 to 65 (% of age group)	Early Retirement Age	Replacement Rate at ER Age (% of earnings)	SSW Accrual in Next Year (%)	Implicit Tax on Earnings in Next Year (%)
Belgium	67	60	77	−5.6	82
France	60	60	91	−7.0	80
Italy	59	55	75	−5.8	81
Netherlands	58	60	91	−12.8	141
UK	55	60	48	−10.0	75
Germany	48	60	62	−4.1	35
Spain	47	60	63	4.2	−23
Canada	45	60	20	−1.0	8
U.S.	37	62	40	0.4	−3
Sweden	35	60	54	−4.1	28
Japan	22	60	54	−3.9	47

by the amount of "'non-work" of men between the ages of 55 and 65, which is explained above and shown in Figure 5.8.

The second column of the table shows the early retirement age under social security systems in each country. In several countries, there is no clearly defined early retirement age. For example, in Italy, one can retire upon the accumulation of thirty-five years of work, which we express as ER age 55 in the table, since our "sample" worker is assumed to begin working at age 20.

The third column shows the "replacement rate" of the social security system at that early retirement age. There is substantial variation in the replacement rates. In the United States, the replacement rate for this sample worker is about 40% of previous earnings. In France and the Netherlands, however, the replacement rate is 91%, and in the majority of countries it is over 60%.

The last two columns show the accrual rate of SSW and the associated implicit tax on earnings, respectively, for a worker who works for one year beyond the early retirement age. That is, these columns summarize the incentives facing a worker as he decides whether to retire when he reaches the age at which he is first entitled to benefits. As noted above, in the United States this accrual rate is positive, and the tax is negative, at the early retirement age, although the tax on work becomes substantial after age 65.

For the other countries, the story is generally quite different: delaying retirement past the age of early benefit entitlement leads to enormous reductions in SSW and associated very high tax rates on continued work. For example, in France, retiring at age 61 instead of age 60 implies a 7% reduction in the total value of one's SSW, which is 80% of earnings over that next year. That is, by working one more year, the worker forgoes in SSW four-fifths of what he will earn from work! Indeed, in the Netherlands, the tax rate is actually much greater than 100%; the median worker who continues in the labor force beyond the age of early benefits entitlement loses much more in SSW than he will earn from his job.

These enormous tax rates on continued work in many other countries are striking, particularly in contrast with the low tax rates in the United States. There are four reasons why the tax rate at the early retirement age is so much lower in the United States. First, the "replacement rate" is much lower in the United States, and thus wage earnings exceed Social Security benefits by much more than in other countries, such as France or the Netherlands. Aside from other features of the programs, higher replacement rates increase the retirement incentives in these other countries; the benefit forgone is much lower in the United States. Second, between age 62 and age 65, the U.S. system provides an actuarial adjustment to benefits if their receipt is delayed, which offsets to a large extent the fewer years of benefit receipt. There is no actuarial adjustment in countries such as France. Third, payroll tax rates to finance the program are much lower in the United States, which lowers the tax on additional work. Finally, the U.S. system allows higher earnings later in life to replace low earnings in earlier years; this is not true in many other countries.

Casual perusal of this table suggests a strong relationship between non-work and the tax rate on continued work. To see the relationship more clearly, it is useful to divide the countries into three groups: (1) those with high non-work: Belgium, France, Italy, the Netherlands, and the United Kingdom; (2) a medium non-work group: Germany, Spain, and Canada; and (3) those with low non-work: the United States, Sweden, and (in particular) Japan. The average replacement rate at early retirement in the first group is 76.6% of median earnings, and the average tax on continued labor earnings in that year is 91.8%. In the third group, with the least non-work, the average replacement rate at the early retirement age is 50%, and the tax rate on continued earnings is 24.7%. These comparisons point to a rather strong correlation between social security incentives and non-work.

There is no completely satisfactory way to summarize the country-specific incentives for early retirement. One crude measure is based on implied tax rates on continued labor earnings once a person is eligible for social security benefits. We sum the implied tax rates (expressed as fractions) on continued work from age 55 through age 69. We call this the "tax force" to retire. We begin with age 55 because even though age 60 is the official early retirement age for most of the social security systems in our study, in practice, these systems often offer important retirement incentives at earlier ages, as well as through related provisions that should be reflected in the comparisons.

The relationship is formalized in Figure 5.15, which presents scatter plots of the tax force to retire and the rate of non-work between ages 55 and 65. In panel A, non-work is plotted against the tax force values. The relationship is clear; there is a strong correspondence between the tax force to retire and non-work. The relationship is nonlinear, however. Thus, in panel B non-work is plotted against the logarithm of the tax force. The solid line in panel B shows the fit of the data by a regression of non-work on the logarithm of the tax force. This tax force measure can explain about 82% of the variation in non-work across our sample of countries. Thus these data suggest a strong relationship between social security incentives to quit work and older workers' departure from the labor force.

The correspondence between the two should be understood in a broader context, however. There are two distinct issues: First, while it seems apparent that social security provisions do affect labor force participation, it also seems apparent from the country studies in Gruber and Wise (1999) that in at least some instances the provisions were adopted to encourage older workers to leave the labor force. For example, anecdotal evidence suggests that in some countries it was thought that withdrawal of older employees from the workforce would provide more job opportunities for young workers. This possibility does not by itself bring into question a causal interpretation of the relationship between plan provisions and retirement. To the extent that it is true, it simply says that in some instances the provisions were adopted for a particular reason. And the data show that they worked.

The second issue, however, must temper a causal interpretation of the results. It could be argued that, to some extent at least, the social security provisions were adopted to accommodate existing labor force participation patterns, rather than the patterns being determined by the provisions. For example, early retirement benefits might have been provided to support persons who were unable to find work and thus already out of the labor force. While this is surely possible, the weight of the

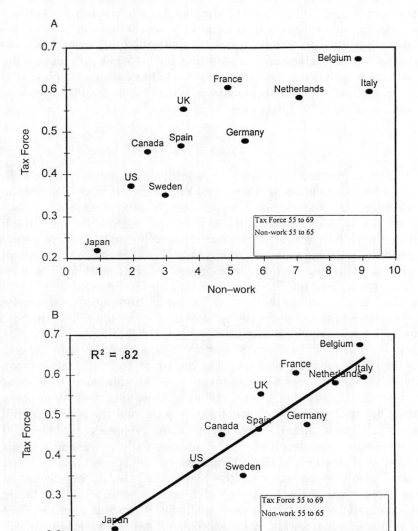

Figure 5.15. Effect of Tax Force on Non-Work.

187

evidence suggests otherwise. The German, French, and U.S. illustrations provide strong evidence that changes in plan provisions induced subsequent changes in retirement rates and not the other way around. In addition, as Axel Börsch-Supan has noted in Chapter 5-1, the decrease in the retirement age in Germany was not associated with high unemployment; more likely, it reflected sociopolitical forces that were otherwise independent of retirement decisions.

Conclusions

The populations in all industrialized countries are aging rapidly, and individual life expectancies are increasing. Yet older workers are leaving the labor force at younger and younger ages. In several countries in our study, participation rates for men 60 to 64 have fallen from over 70% in the early 1960s to less than 20% now. This decline in labor force participation magnifies population trends, further increasing the number of retirees relative to the number of persons who are working. Together, these trends have put enormous pressure on the financial solvency of social security systems throughout the world. Ironically, we argue, the provisions of the social security systems themselves typically contribute to the labor force withdrawal.

It is clear that there is a strong correspondence between the age at which benefits are available and departure from the labor force. Social security programs often provide generous retirement benefits at young ages. In addition, the provisions of these programs often imply large financial penalties on labor earnings beyond the social security early retirement age. Furthermore, in many countries, disability and unemployment programs effectively provide early retirement benefits before the official social security early retirement age. We conclude that social security program provisions have contributed to the decline in the labor force participation of older persons, substantially reducing the potential productive capacity of the labor force. It seems evident that if the trend toward early retirement is to be reversed, as will almost surely be dictated by demographic trends, changing the provisions of social security programs that induce early retirement will play a key role.

References

Baker, Michael, and Dwayne Benjamin. 1996. "Early Retirement Provisions and the Labour Force Behavior of Older Men: Evidence From Canada." Mimeo, Department of Economics, University of Toronto.

Blanchet, Didier, and Louis-Paul Péle. 1999. "Social Security and Retirement in France." In J. Gruber and D. Wise (eds.), *Social Security and Retirement around the World*. Chicago: University of Chicago Press.

Blundell, Richard, and Paul Johnson. 1999. "Social Security and Retirement in the United Kingdom." In J. Gruber and D. Wise (eds.), *Social Security and Retirement around the World*. Chicago: University of Chicago Press.

Boldrin, Michele, Sergi Jimenez, and Franco Peracchi. 1999. "Social Security and Retirement in Spain." In J. Gruber and D. Wise (eds.), *Social Security and Retirement around the World*. Chicago: University of Chicago Press.

Börsch-Supan, Axel, and Reinhold Schnabel. 1999. "Social Security and Retirement in Germany." In J. Gruber and D. Wise (eds.), *Social Security and Retirement around the World*. Chicago: University of Chicago Press.

Brugiavini, Agar. 1999. "Social Security and Retirement in Italy." In J. Gruber and D. Wise (eds.), *Social Security and Retirement around the World*. Chicago: University of Chicago Press.

Burtless, Gary, and Robert Moffitt. 1986. "Social Security, Earnings Tests, and Age at Retirement." *Public Finance Quarterly* 14:3–27.

Diamond, Peter, and Jonathan Gruber. 1999. "Social Security and Retirement in the United States." In J. Gruber and D. Wise (eds.), *Social Security and Retirement around the World*. Chicago: University of Chicago Press.

Gruber, Jonathan. 1999. "Social Security and Retirement in Canada." In J. Gruber and D. Wise (eds.), *Social Security and Retirement around the World*. Chicago: University of Chicago Press.

Gruber, Jonathan, and David Wise. 1999. "Social Security and Retirement around the World." In J. Gruber and D. Wise (eds.), *Social Security and Retirement around the World*. Chicago: University of Chicago Press.

Kapteyn, Arie, and Klaas de Vos. 1999. "Social Security and Retirement in the Netherlands." In J. Gruber and D. Wise (eds.), *Social Security and Retirement around the World*. Chicago: University of Chicago Press.

Lumsdaine, Robin L., James H. Stock, and David A. Wise. 1991. "Fenêtres et retraites." *Annales d'Économie et de Statistique* 20/21:219–42.

———. 1992. "Three Models of Retirement: Computational Complexity versus Predictive Validity." In D. Wise (ed.), *Topics in the Economics of Aging*. Chicago: University of Chicago Press.

———. 1994. "Pension Plan Provisions and Retirement: Men and Women, Medicare, and Models." In D. Wise (ed.), *Studies in the Economics of Aging*. Chicago: University of Chicago Press.

Oshio, Takashi, and Naohiro Yashiro. 1999. "Social Security and Retirement in Japan." In J. Gruber and D. Wise (eds.), *Social Security and Retirement around the World*. Chicago: University of Chicago Press.

Palme, Mårten, and Ingemar Svensson. 1999. "Social Security and Retirement in Sweden." In J. Gruber and D. Wise (eds.), *Social Security and Retirement around the World*. Chicago: University of Chicago Press.

Pestieau, Pierre, and Jean-Philippe Stijns. 1999. "Social Security and Retirement in Belgium." In J. Gruber and D. Wise (eds.), *Social Security and Retirement around the World*. Chicago: University of Chicago Press.

Stock, James H., and David A. Wise. 1990a. "Pensions, the Option Value of Work, and Retirement." *Econometrica* 58, 5:1151–80.

1990b. "The Pension Inducement to Retire: An Option Value Analysis." In D. Wise (ed.), *Issues in the Economics of Aging.* Chicago: University of Chicago Press.

Comment

AXEL BÖRSCH-SUPAN

As a participant in the project that led to this chapter, I am in a somewhat awkward position. If I deliver an acidic account of the shortcomings, I will shoot myself in the foot. If I praise the paper, nobody will believe my self-serving comments. As one says in German, our respected editor elected the goat to be the gardener. What should I do other than to shoot and to praise anyway?

Starting with the praise, this international comparison project is successful for at least three reasons. First, Gruber and Wise enforced a very strict framework. Every country did the same calculations, using similar sources. A tight template aimed to ensure strict comparability across countries. The project was not the first international comparison of retirement systems; however, many failed exactly because results were not as comparable as in this project.

Second, the project was able to exploit meaningful international variation. Retirement incentives are astoundingly different across countries that have otherwise fairly similar economic and social backgrounds. The chapter uses these differences to identify behavior, thereby largely avoiding the danger of relating behavioral differences only to differences in amorphous "culture."

Finally, all eleven papers on which the Gruber and Wise chapter is based have a single and stark message: Retirement incentives matter, and they matter systematically across the eleven countries in the project. This message serves as an organizing principle of the Gruber-Wise summary, making it an effective "issues brief" on the question of how workers respond to retirement incentives.

The core of the chapter is Figure 5.15, which plots the rate of nonwork against a summary measure of retirement incentives. Such countries as Belgium and Italy have large incentives to retire early, and, alas, non-work is frequent among persons aged 60 and older. In contrast, Sweden and the United States provide fewer incentives to retire earlier, with a corresponding higher old-age labor force participation. The correlation is strong, with and without Japan, which has by far the smallest early retirement incentives and the highest old-age labor force participation. My critical comments will be structured by the two variables in Figure 5.15. I will then comment on some institutional details that might blur the depicted relation. Finally, I pick up the most important issue: Can we infer causality?

The Dependent Variable: Non-Work

Gruber and Wise define "non-work" as the share of workers at ages between 55 and 65 who do not participate in the labor force. Looking only at men, this measure ranges from 22% in Japan to 67% in Belgium (Figure 5.8). One may quibble about weighing this measure by productivity (using, e.g., age and health) to obtain a more sophisticated measure of how much productive capacity is not being used in these countries. These are unimportant details, however, because all variants of this measure are strongly correlated. I am more disappointed that the chapter avoids a discussion of what we should associate with this measure. This blurs the conclusions for public policy. There are two extremes. One is the "puritan perspective" that associates non-work with the loss of productive capacity to the society, which might otherwise have a higher GDP. With this perspective, the policy conclusion from Figure 5.15 seems clear: Most European countries should abolish their costly early retirement incentives. The other extreme may be termed the "European view": Early retirement is a social achievement, a gift that could be afforded because of high productivity. Why turn back to a less favorable labor-leisure trade-off? This position is popular among many current European governments – and it helps, by the way, to keep the statistical unemployment rate low.

As economists, we try to shy away from value judgments. However, we know something about the divergence between private and social costs of early retirement, perverse redistributive effects between late and early retirees, and the labor supply distortions created, particularly in pay-as-you-go systems in which retirement income is raised by distorting taxes and contributions. Thus, there is more than the pure labor-leisure trade-off involved in an assessment of "non-work": There are clearly welfare costs of early retirement, which should be stressed in this analysis. Moreover, in addition to its relevance for policy conclusions, the content of "non-work" also has bearings on the causal interpretation of Figure 5.15, discussed below.

The Explanatory Variable: Tax Force

The crucial explanatory variable is the "tax force" of the early retirement provisions on earnings in old age. This is a very handy summary of the incentives, a measure comparable across countries, and a powerful concept in the political discussion.

While the concept is transparent, it requires nontrivial computations. Both numerator and denominator are sensitive to a host of assumptions. The denominator requires the projection of earnings if a worker would remain in the labor force. The project participants used age-earnings regressions for this task. There are at least three econometric issues that could not be handled comparably. First, actual earnings at old age suffer from selection bias because people do not randomly work longer or retire earlier. Getting rid of the selection bias would have required structural retirement models in each country, a new and large project in itself. Second and related, job choice may be endogenous to both the typical retirement age in an industry and the typical earnings trajectory in that industry. Third, only a few countries had panel data to identify age-earnings profiles. In most other countries, cross-sectional age and cohort effects are confounded, potentially biasing the tax force measures in directions and magnitudes that are hard to evaluate.

The numerator, the net present value of future social security benefits, is also more easily conceptualized than quantified. Most countries have more than one pathway to retirement, each with a different flow of pension benefits. Assuming rationality, one needs a "least-cost router" to compute the optimal choice for a worker at all possible retirement ages. Moreover, some of the pathways are probabilistic in nature. A notable example is disability: Some of the workers are granted this status, others not, and it is well known that this is not strictly correlated with health but affected by the leniency of the system, the business cycle, and pure chance. Finally, public pensions, on which most calculations concentrate, are often augmented by private incentives (such as severance payments), which were ignored because of lack of data.

The smoking gun for these kinds of problems is the astoundingly large tax rates in some countries, notably the Netherlands, where the tax on prolonging work at age 60 is a whopping 141% (Table 5.3). Why are there people working at all after age 60? By taking a sum over the entire early retirement window, Gruber and Wise smoothen the impact of such outliers such that the tax force measure used in Figure 5.15 does not feature such extreme tax rates.

Institutional Details

The point on private add-ons to public pensions leads to yet another institutional detail that is important for many European countries and underexposed in the Gruber-Wise analysis. In addition to the many formal pathways to retirement, many informal "preretirement" schemes have been invented, mainly in the 1980s. They have in common that employer and employee form a coalition at the taxpayers' expense. For example, severance pay is added to unemployment compensation so that workers well under early retirement age get the same replacement rate they would have gotten if they had retired much later. In Germany, about 20% of all male workers enter retirement through these schemes. We have no systematic data on the incentives created with these schemes because they are individually negotiated and vary even within a firm from occasion to occasion.

This is the point to remember that I am the goat in the garden. It is easy to find examples for institutional details that are left out in the Gruber-Wise project. We should turn the argument around and look at how full the glass really is. The individual studies mentioned at the outset of the chapter provide an amazing wealth of institutional detail that is in fact covered. The project focuses on a set of typical workers in each country, enrolled in the public pension system. Given the share of public pensions in total retirement income in the countries considered, and the care with which the project papers model public pensions, the glass is surely far more than half full.

Can We Infer Causality?

The chapter is very cautious in inferring causality. Figure 5.15 is certainly not the kind of econometric evidence that is robust to charges of reverse causality. As Gruber and Wise correctly stress, the point is not that retirement incentives could have been created in order to make workers retire earlier (e.g., to reduce the statistical unemployment rate). Even if it were so, this would not destroy a causal interpretation of Figure 5.15, because it would only show that the politicians achieved what they intended. This is an important result.

More destructive is the argument that low old-age labor force participation came first and the introduction of early retirement incentives later. This is a frequently heard argument in Germany, claiming that the lack of demand for labor created old-age unemployment, which then was converted into early retirement. This contradicts the story that Gruber and Wise are telling, which focuses on the supply of, rather than the demand for, labor. German evidence does not support this demand story. Figure 5-1.1 combines a variant of Figure 5.11 in the Gruber-Wise paper with two measures of the German unemployment rate.

The figure shows the sudden decrease in the average retirement age after the 1972 reform. It dropped steadily from about age 61.5 in 1971 to age 58.5 in 1981. In turn, unemployment first rose between 1970 and 1975 from 0.7% to 4.7% and then fell from 1975 to 1980. There is no systematic time-series correlation between mean retirement age and unemployment between the reform and 1980. Between 1980 and 1983, the unemployment rate rose from 3.8% to 9.1%, in a dramatic increase that eventually led to the collapse of the Social Democratic government. However, mean retirement age increased slightly from that point on. This positive time series correlation between mean retirement age and unemployment is the opposite of what a demand-induced change in old-age labor supply would suggest.

There is a second interpretation of the data with causality running counter to the direction proposed by Gruber and Wise. This story claims that the labor-leisure trade-off changed in response to a secular real-wage increase. The income effect dominated the substitution effect and lowered labor force participation. In response to this shift, the government introduced early retirement as a popular piece of legislation. It is not so easy to defuse this argument. Its weight can be assessed only when we better understand the public choice process that generated the current retirement system. The mean voter is fairly old in Germany (currently about age 47), possibly forcing the government to put more weight on generous retirement benefits and early retirement ages than on the tax and contribution burden of the younger voters. A superficial inspection of Figure 5.15 does not yield a straight correlation between the age of the median voter and the generosity of early retirement. However, we know that the median voter model is too simplistic an approach. Linking the Gruber-Wise results to a careful public choice analysis would be a worthwhile exercise.

Finally, let me draw some implications of the Gruber-Wise chapter for the current debate about social security privatization. If incentives matter so strongly, a retirement system that is sensitive to small policy changes creates problems. Getting the actuarial formula wrong (e.g., by projecting overly optimistic or pessimistic life expectancies) is likely to create large welfare losses in terms of a wrong average retirement age and a wrong resulting contribution rate in a pay-as-you-go system.

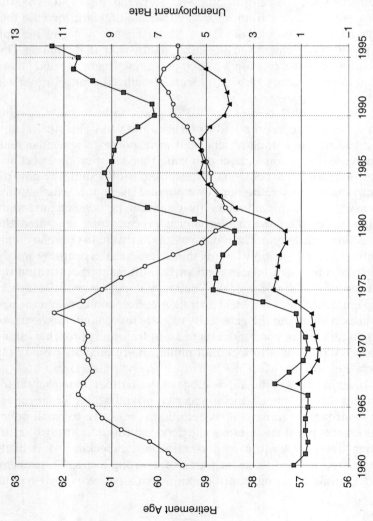

Figure 5-1.1. Average Retirement Age and Unemployment in Germany, 1960–95. *Notes:* "Retirement age" is the average age of all new entries into the public pension system. "Unemployment rate" is the general national unemployment rate. "Unempl. R. (50–55)" refers to unemployed men aged 50–55.

Comment

Privatization has the charm of creating actuarial fairness as a by-product through the rate of return equilibrium in the capital market, while pay-as-you-go systems need a constant adjustment of political parameters to remain (or become) actuarially fair, thereby creating additional incentives to tinker with the system for pork-barrel policy reasons.

Comment

MASSIMO LIVI-BACCI

A few years ago, I directed the dissertation of a student. She was working in the archives of the island of Elba, reconstructing the genealogies of the families in order to analyze their fertility and detect the onset of birth control and the pace of fertility decline in the particular environment of the island. The task was daunting: she had to transcribe several thousand handwritten records, translate the material into machine-readable format, input the data, write the appropriate program, and analyze the results. Once we discussed the plan and verified the completeness of the sources, she departed to start the data collection that, undoubtedly, would have taken a long time. After a surprisingly short period, she was back to me with a stack of computer printouts. "How could you transcribe the records in such a short period?" I asked, surprised. "My Dad, who has taken early retirement from" – and she mentioned a giant steel mill, then under public ownership – "has helped me; he has a passion for history and he has now enrolled in the University of Siena."

"But how could you so quickly do the data input, write the programs, and get the results so quickly?"

"My Mom, who was in the computer center of the same company and has also taken early retirement, helped me out." The plant was producing unneeded steel at a loss; redundant labor was encouraged to take early retirement with generous bonuses and inviting perks. My student's parents were, at the time, in their late forties, with decades of happy life before them.

Less intellectually minded young retirees have started their own independent businesses; others are working in the underground economy, and only a few have withdrawn from the labor market. The situation described by this anecdote is amusing but not uncommon in Europe since the 1970s. Employers needed to cut costs and increase

198

productivity to face competition; the powerful trade unions were fiercely fighting downsizing of employment. Governments stepped in, offering generous incentives that would please the workers, employers, and trade unions.

The concise, neat, and precise chapter of Jonathan Gruber and David Wise puts the wide problem of the relation among labor force partici-pation, retirement age, and incentives or disincentives provided by social security plans into an international perspective. The conclusion that "the social security program provisions have contributed to the decline of the labor force participation of older persons, substantially reducing the potential productive capacity of the labor force" finds support in the empirical analysis of the eleven countries retained in the study. Indeed, social security policies are responsible for the wide international varia-tion of participation rates: the ultragenerous regimes of most of Europe have encouraged early retirement much more than in Japan or the United States, where rules have been stricter and better designed. The chapter demonstrates that workers are good at calculating costs and benefits, and this is no surprise; what is surprising is that public policies so often forget this elementary fact.

The intricacy of the social security systems, built in layers as new pieces of legislation, or regulation, have been continuously superimposed on the old ones, makes it difficult to compare different systems; thus in-ternational comparisons require strong simplifications. The chapter, however, does not specify whether the calculation of the various rele-vant measures such as social security wealth, or the implicit tax on labor, refer to all workers, including the self-employed, or only to salaried workers. Moreover, in many countries central and local government employees have particular plans that differ from those of the private sector. The same applies to workers in agriculture. Perfect comparabil-ity probably cannot be achieved; however, the authors certainly know in which direction intercountry differentials would be changed were all workers included in the analysis.

A second question relates to another powerful incentive to leave the labor force: the possibility of augmenting one's retirement benefits with earnings from postretirement activity in the underground economy or self-employment. We can assume that the degree to which these options are open to the worker do influence departure rates after early retire-ment age; but most of the time they are not captured by the official sta-tistics. Labor statistics often fail to detect young retirees who work in the black economy; earning or income surveys may underestimate the earn-ings of the self-employed. These distortions affect certain countries more than others – Italy and Spain more than Germany or Sweden – thus affecting international comparisons. On the other hand, leaving the labor force is often the consequence of the need to take care of sick or disabled members of the family. In societies where the rate of institutionalization of the old is low – as in the Mediterranean countries – the burden of the care falls on their offspring, particularly women in middle age or early old age. This may determine early retirement, admittedly much more among women (not included in the analysis) than among men. The increasing aging of the population and the further trimming of old-age welfare may strengthen this effect on labor participation past middle age.

A third aspect – which the authors themselves have emphasized in their chapter – is the importance of refining the concept of "unused productive capacity" (1 – sum of labor participation rates). Activities not caught by surveys are a first possible bias, admittedly difficult to eliminate. The indicator could be refined by taking into account the different amount of work, with some sort of weighting, based, for example, on the hours worked. Another refinement could take into consideration productivity at different ages and in different economic sectors. Finally, the unemployed should be counted in the denominator, not in the numerators, of the activity rates. In the latter case, the level of unused productive capacity is reduced by a quantum proportional to unemployment and comparisons may be distorted.

A fourth question relates to the ongoing statutory changes in the retirement age. In the case of Italy, recent provisions for a gradual increase of normal retirement age and prospects for an acceleration of this increase have induced an abnormal outflow from the labor force in order to avoid being "trapped in" by the new legislation. As a consequence, current statistics may show, in the short term, a decline in the mean age at retirement, but this is a period effect and may not show up in real cohorts. Since many countries are under pressure to increase the statutory retirement age, this paradox may continue to show up here and there in the coming years.

The authors indicate that there is a strong negative association between social security incentives to leave work and participation rates among older workers. As to the interpretation of the relationship, they are rather cautious. Are generous provisions encouraging older workers to quit work, or are generous provisions adopted because older workers cannot keep their jobs or find new ones and therefore may become a political and social problem? A better understanding of the causal relationships is important if we want to draw policy indications. Social policy analysts might be able to tell us about the political debate leading to the formulation of particular social security provisions in different countries.

Comment

After the mid-1970s, many industrial sectors were in deep trouble, and generous provisions were seen as an easy way to keep social peace. Social security systems have been improperly used in order to cushion the dangerous effects of unemployment.

The authors very aptly conclude their chapter by saying that "it seems evident that if the trend toward early retirement is to be reversed, as will almost surely be dictated by demographic trends, changing the provisions of social security programs that induce early retirement will play a key role." The human life span can be divided into four parts of approximately the same length: one for growing up and learning; two parts for working; the fourth part for retirement and rest. Hence, by a rule of thumb, for every year of life gained, we have to work six additional months. In the second part of this century, life expectancy in rich countries has increased ten years or more, while mean age at retirement has declined by several years. Moreover, the life span is expected to increase further, and a life expectancy of thirty years at age 60 is within reach, at least among women. Trends in labor force participation have to be reversed, and very soon. This elementary truth is not yet clearly perceived by the public – indeed, a lower retirement age has been considered an irreversible conquest of the welfare state, hard won over decades of political pressures, trade union–employer confrontations, and long and hard negotiations. The notion that the improvement of the standard of living has brought many additional years of life to the average individual and that, for this very reason, retirement benefits and provisions have to be accommodated to this trend, is still extraneous to many older workers. Moreover, the bargaining power of the older population is increasing as societies age, and the political forces are reluctant to undertake the needed reforms. This explains – but does not justify – the reluctance of the political forces to undertake badly needed reforms.

CHAPTER 6

Aging, Fiscal Policy, and Social Insurance: A European Perspective

BERND RAFFELHÜSCHEN

Introduction

In most Member States of the European Union (EU), the achievement of sound and sustainable finances is high on the political agenda. Ever-growing debt burdens are inducing rising interest payments that force public decision makers to choose between economizing on other spending items and increasing already high tax loads, and with them their negative incentive effects. Throughout the EU, there is also a clear and present need to reform the welfare state, since population aging, rising unemployment rates, and lack of competitiveness in an integrated world economy are imposing more and more constraints on generous welfare programs.

This chapter investigates the demographic transition and its impact on the intergenerational effects of fiscal policy within the European Union. Traditional fiscal indicators based on cash-flow budgets fail to address the long-run effects of today's fiscal policy. Future liabilities of unfunded social security and health care systems are absent from current annual statistics, making the amount of outstanding public debt an unreliable indicator for assessing fiscal policy issues. Hence, we use the device of generational accounting developed by Alan Auerbach, Jagadeesh Gokhale, and Laurence Kotlikoff (hereafter AGK) in order to investigate the effects of current fiscal policy on living and future European generations.

The intergenerational analysis provided in this chapter is restricted to twelve of the fifteen Member States of the EU: Austria, Belgium, Denmark, Finland, France, Germany, Ireland, Italy, the Netherlands, Spain, Sweden, and the United Kingdom. A team of European and U.S. experts prepared these country studies at the request of the European

Commission's Directorate General XXI (Task Force on Statutory Contributions).[1] Because of severe problems with respect to the provision of
necessary data, we exclude Greece and Portugal from our analysis. For
Luxembourg, the necessary data are available, but because of the
country's small size, the standard tax incidence assumptions used for
other countries are not applicable.

The chapter is organized as follows. The section "Fiscal Policy and the
Welfare State in an Aging Society" starts by reporting the demographic
trends projected for Europe. The section then focuses on the impacts of
the future aging process on fiscal policy and social insurance in the twelve
countries covered by this study. The section "Measuring Intergenerational Redistribution" provides a brief description of generational
accounting and outlines an improved set of indicators for intergenerational redistribution to be utilized in this study. The section
"Cross-Country Studies: Challenges" presents the baseline results for the
selected EU Member States and investigates the sources of intergenerational imbalance. The section "Cross-Country Studies: Reforming
Social Security" reports results for the sustainability of the pay-as-you-
go social insurance of specific EU Member States. The final section summarizes the chapter's findings.

Fiscal Policy and the Welfare State in an Aging Society

Demographic Trends

During the period since World War II, virtually all industrialized countries have undergone a move from high levels of fertility just after the
war to historically very low birth rates since the 1970s. Moreover, all of
these countries have been characterized by a secular trend of increasing
life expectancy and by the increasing importance of international migration. Although the exact patterns and timing of these changes have
varied over time and across countries, most industrialized countries have

---

[1] Cf. Keuschnigg et al. (1999) for Austria, Dellis and Lüth (1999) for Belgium, Jensen and
Raffelhüschen (1999) for Denmark, Feist et al. (1999) for Finland, Crettez et al. (1999)
for France, Bonin et al. (1999) for Germany, McCarthy and Bonin (1999) for Ireland,
Franco and Sartor (1999) for Italy, Bovenberg and ter Rele (1999) for the Netherlands,
Berenguer et al. (1999) for Spain, Lundvik et al. (1999) for Sweden, and Cardarelli and
Sefton (1999) for the United Kingdom. The studies can be found in a special issue of
European Economy entitled *Generational Accounting in Europe* (European Commission
1999). See Raffelhüschen (1999a) for an executive summary and Raffelhüschen (1999b)
for a brief methodological description.

Table 6.1. *Trends in Fertility, Life Expectancy, and Population Size, 1995–2035*

	Gross Fertility Rate		Life Expectancy at Birth, Female			Population (millions)		
	1995	2015	1980	1995	2015	1995	2015	2035
Austria	1.4	1.5	76.1	79.0	81.6	8.0	8.3	8.0
Belgium	1.6	1.8	76.6	79.8	81.1	10.1	10.3	9.9
Denmark	1.8	1.9	77.4	77.9	78.0	5.2	5.5	5.7
Finland	1.8	1.8	77.6	80.5	82.0	5.1	5.2	5.0
France	1.7	1.7	78.4	81.6	83.2	58.0	61.2	60.2
Germany	1.4	1.4	76.8	78.7	81.1	81.7	82.8	76.0
Ireland	1.8	1.8	75.0	77.9	81.9	3.6	4.0	3.9
Italy	1.3	1.5	77.7	80.4	83.0	57.3	56.7	50.7
Netherlands	1.5	1.7	79.5	80.3	83.0	15.4	16.2	15.9
Spain	1.3	1.3	78.0	80.5	82.4	39.1	39.2	35.0
Sweden	1.7	1.8	79.1	81.5	83.3	8.8	9.3	9.4
UK	1.7	1.8	76.8	79.3	80.7	58.6	61.2	61.1
Average	1.5	1.6	77.5	79.9	82.0			

Source: Country studies in European Commission (1999).

one phenomenon in common: a significant "double-aging" of the population.[2] First, the elderly dependency ratio has increased, a process that is very likely to accelerate during the next four decades. Second, the share of the oldest old among the elderly population is also projected to rise significantly; that is, the general population aging will be accompanied by an aging of the elderly population itself.

In Europe, the double-aging is particularly pronounced, leading to historically unprecedented levels in both the elderly dependency ratio and in what might be labeled the oldest-old dependency ratio. As can be seen from Table 6.1, gross fertility in all of our twelve EU Member States is at present well below the level of 2.1 generally assumed necessary to maintain a stationary population. This holds for all countries except Ireland since about the mid-1970s. In general, fertility rates are lowest in the central countries (Austria, Belgium, France, Germany, the Netherlands) and the southern ones (Italy, Spain). In the northern countries (Denmark, Finland, Ireland, Sweden, United Kingdom), which began

---

[2] See Börsch-Supan (1991) or Franco and Munzi (1996) for a more detailed discussion of the double-aging phenomenon.

to experience the demographic transition as early as the late 1960s, the figures lie in a range only slightly below reproduction level. According to the most likely projections of future fertility, the rates will either stay constant or display minor increments in most countries; that is, the weighted average number will rise from 1.5 in 1995 to 1.6 in 2015.[3]

Table 6.1 also reports the female life expectancy at birth for the years 1980, 1995, and 2015. While countries within each subregion share common patterns of fertility, the same is not apparent when it comes to national mortality rates. For example, France and Sweden share the highest life expectancy in 1995, while Denmark and Ireland are last. Although the patterns of mortality vary significantly over the reported countries, an examination of the average trends reveals that life expectancy for females increases by one year every ten years. Similar patterns can be found for the lower life expectancy of males, which is about six years less than that of females.[4]

The overall population change in the selected Member States of the EU has been mainly determined by the recent changes in fertility and mortality. Of course, in particular countries, international migration has had and will continue to have significant impacts on the age structure. For example, in Germany, migrants rejuvenate the host population since immigrants are on average ten years younger (cf. Bonin et al., 2000a). In contrast, in Ireland immigration and emigration are of the same magnitude but emigrants are on average 4.4 years younger than immigrants. Thus, even the zero net influx leads to a more pronounced aging. For most of the selected countries, the net influx does not enlarge the population significantly in the long run, though for the first two decades most population projections include a very high level of asylum seekers. Thus, the overall population will increase between 1995 and 2015 by 2.6 percent because of both slightly increasing fertility rates and immigration. Between 2015 and 2035, however, the baby-boom generations will die, and the population will decrease by 5.3 percent, that is, by 0.25 percent on annual average. Deviations in individual countries from this hump-shaped trend occur for two reasons. First, in Denmark and in Sweden the combination of fairly high fertility and immigration leads to

[3] Gross fertility figures for 1995 are taken from the respective official statistics. The numbers for 2015 reflect the fertility assumptions that have been employed in the cross-country studies presented below. They rest either on official projections of the national census bureaus or on the assumptions of the national experts of the EU study.
[4] The most striking deviation from the average is the case of Denmark, where no significant rise in life expectancy was registered during the recent past. This is the reason why we also kept the figure constant for future periods in our calculations.

Table 6.2. *Projections of the Elderly and Oldest-Old Population, 1995–2055*

	Elderly Dependency Ratio[a]				Oldest-Old Dependency Ratio[b]			
	1995	2015	2035	2055	1995	2015	2035	2055
Austria	34.7	42.3	66.2	65.5	10.7	14.1	22.4	26.7
Belgium	39.0	45.3	60.5	58.5	11.2	15.6	21.8	22.7
Denmark	35.2	44.0	51.5	43.9	12.3	12.4	16.9	16.2
Finland	34.0	51.7	60.9	60.6	10.3	15.6	25.1	23.1
France	37.1	46.9	62.2	64.1	11.3	17.0	24.9	27.4
Germany	35.7	47.3	69.2	68.8	10.8	17.4	24.1	27.4
Ireland	30.2	37.5	59.2	75.1	9.6	10.9	20.3	31.6
Italy	39.5	53.0	79.7	78.4	11.5	20.6	29.0	38.4
Netherlands	30.5	43.6	65.3	61.0	9.6	12.9	23.6	24.8
Spain	38.1	45.1	74.5	90.4	11.1	17.0	26.2	44.6
Sweden	41.4	54.9	66.8	66.5	15.4	19.5	28.8	29.0
UK	37.7	43.8	57.8	56.2	12.9	14.4	20.2	21.5
Average	37.1	47.1	66.9	68.1	11.5	16.8	24.3	29.3

[a] Population aged 60+ as a percentage of those aged 20–59.
[b] Population aged 75+ as a percentage of those aged 20–59.
Source: Country studies in European Commission (1999).

an ever-growing population. Second, in Italy fertility is so low that the population is continuously decreasing.

Table 6.2 reports the present and projected dependency ratios for both the elderly (60+) and the oldest old (75+) for the selected EU Member States in 1995, 2015, 2035, and 2055. The evolution over time is determined partly by the relative sizes of existing age cohorts and partly by assumptions concerning future fertility, mortality, and immigration. The elderly dependency ratio – that is, those aged 60+ as a share of the working-aged (20–59) population – will increase from 37.1 percent in 1995 to 47.1 and 66.9 percent in 2015 and 2035, respectively.[5] There is a sort of "breathing space" between now and the beginning of the second decade of the next century. Between 2015 and 2055, however, the elderly dependency ratio is projected to rise rapidly. In 2035, three potential workers will supply two retirees with their old-age benefits. Since the potential workforce corresponds to approximately two-thirds of the working-age population, each European worker in the year 2035 will,

---

[5] As compared to Japan, this is slightly less, while the figures for the United States are much more moderate; see Kotlikoff and Leibfritz (1999).

on average, have to finance the transfers to one retiree. After that year, the ratio of elderly will stabilize at approximately 68 percent in the long run.

An examination of the relative weight of the oldest-old age group – that is, the ratio of those aged 75+ to the population of working-aged – reveals patterns similar to those of the elderly dependency ratio. During the period 1995–2015 we can identify the same breathing space, since the weighted average proportion of the oldest old is projected to increase from 11.5 percent to "only" 16.8 percent. In the following two decades, this rise will accelerate. By 2035 the number of very elderly will already be more than double the present level. The fact that trends in the proportion of the oldest old also differ from trends in the subgroup of elderly can be seen by focusing on the numbers for the year 2055. In contrast to the already stabilized elderly dependency ratio, the share of the oldest old continues to increase significantly until reaching its maximum shortly before 2055, when the last very old baby boomers have left the world.[6]

Both the elderly dependency ratio and the oldest-old dependency ratio vary considerably across the countries. In Austria, Belgium, Denmark, France, Ireland, Spain, and the United Kingdom, the increase in the elderly dependency ratio between now and 2015 is below average, while in Finland, Germany, Italy, and the Netherlands, the increases are in a range above average. For the period 2015–2035, the increase in the elderly dependency ratio will be very pronounced in Austria, Ireland, and Spain. In contrast, the increase will be far below average in the Scandinavian countries and about average in those remaining. A similar demographic transition can be found in the oldest-old dependency ratio. Such countries as Italy, Ireland, and Spain will face oldest-old dependency ratios in 2055 that are more than triple the corresponding 1995 figures, while in Denmark, the United Kingdom, and Sweden, for example, the increases amount to only 32, 67, and 88 percent, respectively. Hence, one can identify a sort of north-south succession in both the extent and the timing of the European aging pattern. In general, the demographic transition will be earlier the farther north a country is located, but the extent will be more pronounced in the southern areas of Europe.

---

[6] Not only the dependency ratios but also the sex composition of the population aged 60+ is of considerable importance when it comes to projecting social expenditure or calculating the intergenerational redistribution of today's fiscal policy in an aging society. Of course, females outnumber males significantly because of their higher life expectancy (see above). At present, there are on average slightly fewer men than women in the first decile of the subgroup of elderly while two out of three of the European oldest old are females. In the future, these proportions will stay approximately constant.

BERND RAFFELHÜSCHEN

Fiscal Policy Issues

With respect to economic performance, the European Union of the 1990s is still a highly diverse region. Although the divergence among the selected Member States declined significantly during the postwar period, the per capita GDP in 1995 varied from 11,000 ECU in Spain to 25,300 ECU in Denmark, that is, from 60 to 137 percent of the average (see Table 6.3). With respect to economic strength, one can still identify the traditional north-south gap. However, the GDP growth rates reveal three major trends. First, countries with a low per capita GDP do experience, on average, higher growth rates; that is, the EU Member States continue to converge. Second, there seems to be a growing coordination in the business cycle, though some countries remain subject to very special developments.[7] Third, the northern and southern countries had already recovered from the recession of the early 1990s in 1995, while the growth rates of the central ones remained low. Nevertheless, the similarity of the business cycle among the selected states is sufficient for the subsequent cross-country comparison.[8]

In all the countries studied, fiscal policy's top priority in the 1990s was fulfillment of the Maastricht criteria, which stipulated the conditions for joining the European Monetary Union (EMU). Besides the convergence of interest and inflation rates, the criterion highest on the political agenda included a ceiling on both the public deficit (3 percent of GDP) and public debt (60 percent of GDP) until 1997. Table 6.3 shows the major fiscal policy indicators, including the government deficit measured either as percent of GDP or as the primary deficit, that is, taxes minus non-interest expenditure. By 1995, the total government deficit had already fallen to a level of 4.7 percent of GDP, and it continued to fall below thereafter, reaching the 3 percent level. Not only did the sheer quantity decline significantly, but so did the variance. In 1995 the variability was still high, ranging from 7.7 percent of GDP in Sweden to only 1.9 percent in both Denmark and Ireland. By 1997, all of the reported countries are in a corridor of 4 percentage points.

Similar to the regular deficit is the development of the primary deficit. Such countries as Belgium and Italy face high regular deficits of 4.1 and

[7] For example, the Finnish recession was especially strong because of the total breakdown of former trade patterns with the East European countries. Another exceptional development is found in Germany with respect to the unification-induced delay in joining the worldwide recession of the early 1990s.
[8] As shown in Raffelhüschen (1997) for the Norwegian example, the results of generational accounting calculations are especially sensitive to the state of the business cycle. Hence, it is of particular importance for a cross-country comparison that the covered studies refer to a base year that displays a similar overall growth pattern.

Table 6.3. *Macroeconomic and Fiscal Indicators*

	Per Capita GDP, 1995		GDP Growth Rate			Deficit-to-GDP Ratio, 1995	
	in ECUs	% of average	1990	1992	1995	Regular	Primary
Austria	22,000	119.5	4.5	1.3	1.4	5.0	0.6
Belgium	20,300	110.3	3.7	1.7	1.9	4.1	−4.4
Denmark	25,300	137.3	1.4	0.2	2.8	1.9	−1.5
Finland	19,100	103.7	0.0	−3.6	4.2	3.8	2.7
France	20,200	109.8	2.4	1.1	2.2	5.0	1.7
Germany[a]	22,600	122.5	5.7	2.2	1.9	3.6	0.4
Ireland	13,100	71.1	8.4	4.6	10.7	1.9	−3.3
Italy	14,700	79.8	2.2	0.6	3.0	7.0	−3.1
Netherlands	19,800	107.4	4.1	2.0	2.1	4.1	−1.0
Spain	11,000	59.7	3.7	0.7	2.8	5.9	1.0
Sweden	20,300	110.1	1.4	−1.4	3.6	7.7	5.2
UK	12,700	68.8	0.4	−0.5	2.5	6.5	2.2
Average	18,400	100.0	3.2	0.7	3.3	4.7	0.0

	Taxes and Statutory Contributions (% of GDP)			Taxes, 1995 (% of GDP)	Social Expenditure as Share of GDP (%)		
	1985	1990	1995		1983	1995[b]	2040
Austria	43.6	41.6	42.3	27.0	26.5	32.2	38.4
Belgium	47.9	45.1	46.8	31.1	30.8	28.9	36.5
Denmark	49.1	48.7	51.4	49.7	30.1	33.5	48.0
Finland	40.8	45.4	46.3	31.6	—	33.1	39.5
France	44.5	43.7	44.6	25.3	28.3	30.4	40.2
Germany[a]	41.6	39.5	42.6	24.3	28.8	31.3	45.5
Ireland	38.6	35.9	36.3	30.8	24.1	20.4	24.3
Italy	34.7	38.8	40.7	27.8	22.9	24.7	34.7
Netherlands	45.5	45.1	45.4	26.2	33.4	31.9	44.3
Spain	30.0	35.1	34.8	22.5	19.5	23.6	28.2
Sweden	50.0	55.8	51.5	37.3	—	35.8	46.0
UK	38.2	35.7	34.9	28.2	23.9	28.1	33.4
Average	42.0	42.5	43.1	30.2	26.8	29.5	38.3

[a] Figures before 1992 refer to West Germany.
[b] 1994 for Ireland, Spain, and the United Kingdom.

Sources: Eurostat (1997); OECD (1988); Country studies in European Commission (1999). Projections for Austria, Finland, Ireland and Spain, own calculations.

7.0 percent of GDP, respectively, while at the same time realizing primary surpluses of 4.4 and 3.1 percent, respectively. This is due simply to a high debt-to-GDP ratio, reaching approximately 120 percent in both cases. In Austria, Germany, Denmark, Spain, and Ireland, the corresponding ratio was between 60 and 70 percent in 1997. The Netherlands and Sweden are slightly above this range, and France, Finland, and the UK are slightly below it. The similarity of the debt-to-GDP ratios and the corresponding interest load on public coffers explains the high correlation between the regular and primary deficits shown in Table 6.3.

In the selected EU Member States, the government deficits have been narrowed mainly through tax increases and structural spending reductions; broadening of the tax base and closure of existing tax loopholes have had only minor importance. In fact, the overall load of average taxes and statutory payments has increased from 42 percent of GDP in 1985 to 42.5 percent in 1990 and 43.1 percent in 1995. However, Table 6.3 reveals a significant variability in both the level and the growth of taxes. While taxation is highest in the Netherlands and the Scandinavian welfare states, the United Kingdom, Ireland, and the southern European countries fall below the average, and the central group of countries is close to the average.

On first inspection, the split between taxes and statutory social insurance contributions reported for fiscal year 1995 in Table 6.3 is surprising. On average, taxes make up 30 percent of GDP while contributions account for approximately 13 percent. There is, however, a tremendous divergence in the contributions component. Three countries range far below average: Ireland (5.5 percent) and the United Kingdom (6.7 percent), which both provide for only basic pension benefits and finance them through taxes, and Denmark (1.7 percent), where a generous basic pension scheme is financed nearly entirely through the general federal budget. On the other hand, the central group of countries, particularly France, Germany, and the Netherlands, rely much more upon separate off-budget authorities and contribution payments to finance their generous pay-as-you-go schemes. In fact, contributions account for almost 20 percent in these countries. We will come back to this issue subsequently.

Social Insurance Systems and Intergenerational Contracts

As mentioned above, most EU Member States have also narrowed their government deficits through structural spending reductions. However, the major spending reductions were in government consumption and investment expenditure. With respect to social expenditure, the opposite is true. Basically, all EU Member States have suffered from increasing structural unemployment, which necessitated tremendous benefit payments, and/or have enlarged their welfare programs. Hence, the average ratio of social expenditure to GDP has increased from 26.8 percent in 1980 to 29.5 percent in 1995. Exceptions do exist. Ireland, for example, has had both a very favorable age structure and economic development strengthened significantly by high direct investment from abroad.

As seen in Table 6.3, a high variability is hidden in the average numbers. In Italy, Ireland, and Spain, social expenditures ranged between 20 and 25 percent of GDP in 1995. Those of Belgium, France, and the United Kingdom lie between 26 and 30 percent, and Austria, Denmark, Finland, Germany, the Netherlands, and Sweden spend between 31 and 36 percent for that purpose. The north-south distinction clearly is present here, with all the Scandinavian welfare states spending more than one-third of their GDP on social programs, while southern European countries tend to spend only about one-fifth of GDP.

The last column of Table 6.3 reports the results of projecting total social expenditure for the period 1995 throughout 2040. Employing the growth rates estimated in OECD (1988), one finds that because of the aging of the population, social expenditures will increase, on average, from 29.5 percent to 38.3 percent of GDP. In fact, only Ireland and Spain will spend less than one-third of their GDP on social programs in 2040, while such countries as Denmark, France, Germany, the Netherlands, and Sweden will spend over 40 percent. Of course, these projections of age-related public expenditures have to be taken as first "guesstimates," since they focus exclusively on the initial per capita transfer levels for education, family benefits, health, unemployment, and pensions. Hence, they are not comparable with the results of the generational accounting method, which encompasses all types of financial transactions between the public and the private sector. Before turning to the methodological description, it might be in order to take a closer look at the items constituting the overall social expenditure, that is, those for pensions and public health care.

Table 6.4 shows the projections of pension and health-care expenditures as percentages of GDP for the period 1995 through 2050. On average, the demographic pressure induces an increase of pension expenditures from 8.9 percent of GDP in 1995 to only 9.0 percent in 2010, indicating the above-mentioned "breathing space." In 2020 and 2040, however, this item will increase to 13.0 and 13.6 percent of GDP,

211

Table 6.4. *Pension and Health Care Expenditures, 1995–2050*
(percent of GDP)

	Pension Expenditures				Health Expenditures		
	1995	2010	2030	2050	1995	2030-A[a]	2030-B[b]
Austria	8.8	10.2	14.4	14.9	7.4	10.3	10.7
Belgium	10.4	8.7	13.9	15.1	7.4	9.5	10.5
Denmark	6.8	7.6	10.9	11.5	5.6	7.0	7.8
Finland	10.1	10.7	17.8	17.7	6.9	9.4	9.9
France	10.6	9.7	13.5	14.4	7.0	8.9	11.1
Germany	11.1	11.8	16.5	17.5	6.2	7.8	10.0
Ireland	3.6	2.6	2.8	3.0	5.1	5.6	6.4
Italy	13.3	13.2	20.3	20.3	6.4	8.1	10.4
Netherlands	6.0	6.1	11.2	11.4	6.7	9.8	9.9
Spain	10.0	10.0	14.1	19.1	5.7	7.4	8.1
Sweden	11.8	12.4	15.0	14.5	6.2	7.9	9.0
UK	4.5	5.2	5.5	4.1	6.0	7.0	8.3
Average	8.9	9.0	13.0	13.6	6.4	8.2	9.3

[a] Health care costs grow in line with GDP.
[b] Health care costs grow one percentage point faster than GDP.
Source: OECD (1997).

respectively. In a cross-country comparison for the year 1995, the relative pension expenditure load is highest in Italy, Sweden, and Germany, while it is lowest in Ireland and the UK, that is, in countries providing only basic pension benefits. With respect to the lower end of the scale, the relative ranking of pension tax loads will still hold in 2030 and 2050. However, at the upper end, there will be a somewhat different situation. In 2030, the three most highly burdened countries will be Italy, Finland, and Germany, while in 2050 they will be Italy, Spain, and Finland.

The next highest item in overall social expenditure in Europe is health care. In 1995, on average, about 6.4 percent of GDP was spent on health care in the selected EU Member States listed in Table 6.4. Upon reaching the year 2030, the double-aging effects will have increased this spending to 8.2 percent of GDP if health care costs grow in line with GDP. Since this is very unlikely to happen, Table 6.4 also shows the projection for a scenario in which the growth rate of health care costs exceeds that of GDP by one percentage point. Under these conditions, health expenditures will make up 9.3 percent of GDP in 2030. Health expenditure patterns vary significantly across the listed countries, although the variance is surprisingly small. In fact, the highest relative expenditure item in 1995 is 7.4 percent in Austria, while the lowest is 5.1 percent of GDP in Ireland.

In the equal-growth scenario, the same countries will be highest and lowest, but the divergence between them will be much higher: the difference between the highest and the lowest expenditure-to-GDP figure increases from 2.3 percent in 1995 to 4.8 percent in 2030. In the case of faster-growing health treatment costs, the divergence will decline; but we will observe that more than 10 percent of GDP will be spent on health care in Austria, Belgium, France, Germany, and Italy. As also shown by the projections of the OECD (1988, 1997), the exploding pension and health care expenditures will to some extent be offset by reductions in educational expenditures and family benefits. As seen from Table 6.3, however, this effect is rather low. We will come back to the issues of financing the generous pension and health care schemes and investigate the tax loads implied by the double-aging process after having briefly described the method employed to do so.

Measuring Intergenerational Redistribution

The method of generational accounting was developed by AGK (1991, 1992, 1994) as an alternative to annual cash-flow accounting, which completely fails to reflect the intertemporal stance of fiscal policy.[9] While working on standardized accounts in a cross-country study, it is necessary to improve the generational accounting method with respect to the indicator of intergenerational redistribution. We will come back to the differences between the traditional and the improved method while outlining the modus operandi of this study.

Generational accounting begins by considering the government's intertemporal budget constraint,

$$B_t = \sum_{s=0}^{D} N_{t,\,t-s} + \sum_{s=1}^{\infty} N_{t,\,t+s}. \tag{1}$$

The left side of equation (1) reflects the current net debt (B) of the public sector in the base year t, which is typically positive for most countries. It

---

[9] For a brief description of the generational accounting method, see, for instance, Auerbach et al. (1994). A critical survey on the underlying theoretical conventions and empirical issues involved can be found in Haveman (1994), CBO (1995), and Diamond (1996). Buiter (1995), Fehr and Kotlikoff (1995), and Raffelhüschen and Risa (1997) emphasize in particular the importance of macroeconomic repercussions and static incidence assumptions. The method employed in this paper follows the standards developed in the European Commission's project (cf. Raffelhüschen, 1999b).

is either taken directly from the official statistics or – equivalently – calculated by discounting and adding together the projected government debt service for every future period. The net debt of the public sector induces spending, which must be paid for out of two possible sources: (1) the present value of net tax payments projected to be made by generations presently alive, or (2) the present value of net tax payments by future generations. Discounting is done at an assumed pre-tax real interest rate (r).

The terms on the right side of (1) incorporate all future taxes paid and benefits received. The latter include not only explicit transfer payments, in cash and in kind, but also projected future government purchases of goods and services, which are allocated to individual generations on a life-cycle adjusted per capita basis. Let D denote the maximum age of an individual, and let $N_{t,k}$ stand for the present value of the net tax payments, that is, taxes net of receipts, transfers, and imputed government expenditures, to be made in future years by all members of the generation born in year k. The first term on the right side of equation (1), $N_{t,t-s}$, then equals the sum of the present value of net taxes of all generations alive in the base year t. The last term in the budget constraint $(N_{t,t+s})$ stands for the sum of the present value of net tax payments made by future generations, that is, those born in year $t + 1$ and later. For further analysis, the net payments can be decomposed as follows:

$$N_{t,k} = N_{t,k}^m + N_{t,k}^f = \sum_{s=\max\{t,k\}}^{k+D} T_{s,k}^m P_{s,k}^m \left(1+r\right)^{t-s} + \sum_{s=\max\{t,k\}}^{k+D} T_{s,k}^f P_{s,k}^f \left(1+r\right)^{t-s}. \quad (2)$$

In equation (2), $T_{s,k}^m$ and $T_{s,k}^f$ refer to the average net payment made in year s by a representative male (m) or female (f) member of the cohort born in year k, while $P_{s,k}^m$ and $P_{s,k}^f$ stand for the number of members of the generation born in year k who survive until year s. Hence, the respective products represent the net taxes paid by all males or females of generation k in year s. The summation begins in year t for generations born prior to the base year, while for future generations – those born in year $k > t$ – the summation begins in year k. Irrespective of the year of birth of a generation, the discounting is always back to year t.

In order to calculate current generations' net payments, it is necessary to specify the demographic structure. This is done by using country-specific population projections, derived on the basis of official statistics that incorporate assumptions concerning future fertility, mortality, and net migration. As a second step, the net payments $T_{s,k}$ for all male and female agents of generation $k \leq t$ have to be calculated. Let i indicate the type of payment, that is, a particular tax or benefit. Then we can simply sum over all types of payments in order to derive

$$T_{s,k}^m = \sum_i h_{s-k,i,s}^m, \tag{3}$$

where $h_{s-k,i,s}^m$ stands for the average transfer received or taxes paid by male agents of age $s - k$ in year s. Of course, the same holds for female or average agents. Let $a = s - k$ represent the age of an individual and assume that both average payments and receipts grow in correspondence with overall productivity at a constant rate, g. Then the average tax or transfer for males in year $s > t$ can be obtained from

$$h_{a,i,s}^m = h_{a,i,t}^m (1+g)^{s-t}. \tag{4}$$

Equations (1)–(4) are already sufficient to calculate the net payments of living generations. For individuals of age 0 to D in the base year, we retrieve average payments for a broad range of tax and transfer payments from micro data. Thus, we derive age- and gender-specific profiles for each of them. Note that taxes include all forms of statutory payments to government, while transfers reflect both in-cash and in-kind benefits. In some instances, profiles may not vary according to age and gender. This is the case whenever the assumed incidence corresponds to this uniformly distributed profile or whenever sufficient information is not available. The cross-section profiles are extrapolated into the future according to equation (4). In other words, they are taken as being representative of the unobserved longitudinal data.[10] From that, one derives the net payments of the respective current generation as outlined in equation (2).

Dividing the present value of future net taxes of a living generation born in year $k \leq t$ by the population of that generation still alive in the base year yields the generational account of that particular cohort, either on average or distinguished by gender:

$$GA_{t,k} = \frac{N_{t,k}}{P_{t,k}}, \qquad GA_{t,k}^m = \frac{N_{t,k}^m}{P_{t,k}^m}, \qquad GA_{t,k}^f = \frac{N_{t,k}^f}{P_{t,k}^f}. \tag{5}$$

In fact, it should be emphasized that a generational account encompasses only taxes paid net of transfers received in a present value and rest-of-life projection. Because of the exclusively forward-looking concept, one

[10] While this approach is quite standard, its pitfalls are well noted in nearly every econometrics textbook. Given the fact that sufficient panel data are not yet available for most countries, the procedure might nevertheless be taken as a preliminary second-best approximation.

should never compare the accounts among living generations. Rather, the account should be viewed as reflecting the per capita burdens on particular generations of financing public spending as a whole. This holds for both current and future generations.

In order to illustrate the burden passed over from current to future generations via the continuation of today's fiscal policy, it is first necessary to compute the residual necessary to balance the intertemporal budget constraint. This residual can be interpreted as the gap with respect to those demands on future budgets that would ensure a sustainable fiscal policy.[11] In other words, it represents the true government debt (TD) or wealth of the base year t, written as

$$TD_t = Bt - \sum_{k=t-D}^{\infty} N_{t,k}.$$ (6)

The measure accurately reflects the additional burdens for future generations induced by currently living cohorts and thus makes explicit the government liabilities that are not included in the official debt figures. Such liabilities include, for example, entitlements to pension benefits that young people obtain in a pay-as-you-go system by paying their contributions.

The overall figure of true intertemporal debt has to be financed by the net tax payments of all future generations. How the burden of this required payment will actually be distributed among future generations is uncertain, because this distribution will be determined by policies adopted in the future. For illustrative purposes, however, we use the set of relative tax and transfer profiles shown in equation (4) for future generations. The burden future generations have to bear in order to service the true debt of the public sector is met by adjusting specific payments or by transfers through a scaling constant, γ_i, which may depend on the type of payment i. The net payments $T_{s,k}$ for future agents of a generation $k > t$ is thus given by

$$T_{s,k} = \sum_i \gamma_i h_{a,i,s},$$ (7)

where $h_{a,i,s}$ is the average transfer received or taxes paid by agents of age a in year $s > t$, while the scaling constant, γ_i, ensures that the public budget constraint in equation (1) is balanced.[12]

[11] A similar approach is found in Kotlikoff and Walliser (1995).
[12] The basic idea of this approach is to treat future and current generations absolutely identically, that is, to assume that future generations face the same fiscal policy as currently living agents. Auerbach (1997) provides first insights in this particular treatment; the basic idea was also first mentioned to me by Alan Auerbach in an e-mail.

Measuring the degree of intergenerational imbalance thus means specifying one particular hypothetical fiscal policy to serve as a valid fiscal indicator. For example, the vector γ_i might reflect a uniform proportional increase in all or specific taxes for all future generations. It could just as easily specify a decrease in all transfers necessary to ensure a sustainable and therefore intergenerationally balanced fiscal policy. In general, values of γ_i will differ from unity, indicating an unequal distribution among future and living generations. One may also state the intergenerational imbalance in terms of the absolute difference in the accounts of future and current newborns. Note that only base-year newborns can serve as representatives for current generations, since they are the only ones that are captured over their entire life cycle.

The resulting difference in lifetime net tax payments between current and future generations, given that the intertemporal budget constraint of the public sector holds, is used as an indicator of intergenerational redistribution. Of course, a priori, it is arbitrary which policy is deemed suitable as the basis of this indicator. Another illustration of intergenerational balance is to set the scaling constant, γ_i, for all current and future generations to a value that ensures a balanced intertemporal budget constraint. This corresponds, for example, to the tax increase or cut in transfer payments for *all* generations necessary to service the intertemporal liabilities of the public sector. Taking the intertemporal liabilities or hypothetical tax revenue increases as an indicator of intertemporal redistribution of the actual fiscal policy is the only appropriate way to compare the generational accounting results for different countries. Such international comparisons are, however, only meaningful if the underlying indicator – for example, the increase in income taxes – refers to equivalent bases, for example, tax increase as a percent of GDP.

In the traditional method of generational accounting, the residual of the intertemporal budget constraint is distributed equally among all future generations in a growth-adjusted manner. Moreover, government spending for the provision of public goods and services is not attributed (uniformly) to all present and future generations. Instead, only the residual distributed uniformly over future generations is increased. Since past tax payments and transfer receipts of living generations are not included in the calculations, the accounts represent present-value net payment burdens over the entire lifetime only for base-year newborns and, of course, all future generations, of which the generation born right after the base year is typically chosen as a representative. A comparison of these generations' accounts is used in the traditional method to reveal whether the current set of policies imposes a generational imbalance. This imbalance is typically quantified with the help of an index, π, defined as

$$\pi_t = \frac{GA_{t,t+1}(1+r)}{GA_{t,t}(1+g)}. \tag{8}$$

Conventionally, this ratio serves as an indicator of intertemporal redistribution; that is, a value of π exceeding unity indicates net payments of future generations that are $(\pi - 1)$ percent higher than those of current newborns. If π falls short of unity, the distribution is, of course, to the advantage of future generations in similar magnitude.

Measuring intergenerational redistribution with the help of one numerical indicator is a straightforward illustration, but it cannot be applied in certain cases. There are country-specific circumstances in which the indicator π is misleading. We will not go into a deep discussion of these issues here. Nevertheless, a short note might be in order. At just a first glance, the traditional indicator has a – seemingly technical – shortcoming, which can be easily seen by using some simple algebra: π is not defined at all if $GA_{t,t} = 0$, and it does not make sense if $GA_{t,t} <$ 0. Moreover, the indicator will quantitatively and qualitatively be very sensitive for $GA_{t,t} \approx 0$, since

$$\lim_{GA_{t,t}=0+\varepsilon, \varepsilon \to 0} \pi = \infty,$$

and

$$\lim_{GA_{t,t}=0-\varepsilon, \varepsilon \to 0} \pi = -\infty.$$

This asymptotic behavior (cf. Raffelhüschen, 1996) is empirically relevant for most countries if, as in this study, all non–age-specific expenditures (including government purchases of goods and services) are uniformly distributed over the generations. In fact, it leads in general to a generational account of base-year newborns that is negative. But the problem occurs in some cases, even when one employs the traditional method, in which general government expenditures are not allocated to individuals.[13] It is exactly these shortcomings that necessitate the methodological adjustments in measuring intergener-

---

[13] See, for example, the Danish country study found in Jensen and Raffelhüschen (1997). Another severe problem of measuring intergenerational redistribution with the help of the percentage difference π occurs whenever post–base-year migration is considered as simply augmenting the residential cohorts already alive in the base year. See Bonin et al. (2000a) for details.

ational balance developed in the course of working on the country studies of the European Commission (1999) project "Generational Accounting in Europe."

Cross-Country Studies: Challenges

The findings of all country studies referred to subsequently are fully compatible, since (1) all population projections rest on the same method; (2) all types of public receipts and expenditures (including education) are treated identically; (3) in all cases, the definition of government wealth is the same; (4) all policy reforms enacted in or prior to the base year are included in the projections; (5) all studies adjust for the traditional problems of measuring intergenerational redistribution in the way outlined above; and (6) all calculations are done with the identical software package. Former international comparisons found in the literature severely suffer from incompatibilities with respect to basically all these issues. Only the comparisons in Kotlikoff and Leibfritz (1999) and Kotlikoff and Raffelhüschen (1999) are nearly as standardized as those presented in this chapter.

Table 6.5 reports the net tax payments of current generations aged 0 to 100 in the base year 1995, as well as the net tax payments of future generations represented by the newborns of the year 1996. Of course, the accounts of future newborns reflect the γ-adjustments of equation (7) that are necessary to ensure that the public budget is balanced, that is, that the budget constraint in equation (1) is met. If not indicated otherwise, the accounts are calculated on the basis of an annual real GDP growth rate of 1.5 percent and an exogenous real interest rate of 5 percent.

What strikes one first while looking at the average accounts is the similarity in the shape of the current generation's net payments, expressing the typical life-cycle patterns in all country studies. With the exception of Italy, all countries display a generational account of base-year newborns that is negative. Although net payments to the public sector remain strictly negative during childhood and youth, the accounts turn positive at around age 10, and then steadily increase, reaching a maximum at around age 25 in most countries. This is simply due to both the discounting of future tax and contribution payments and the fact that more and more years of net transfer receipts are not taken into account in this exclusively forward-looking concept. Over the years of active labor market participation, the net payments are in general positive but falling, before turning negative at around age 45. After that age, there is a further decline, until a maximum of net present value transfers is reached

Table 6.5. *Generational Accounts for Selected Member States of the EU (thousands of 1995 ECUs)*

Generation's Age in 1995	Austria	Belgium	Denmark	Finland	France	Germany	Ireland	Italy	Netherlands	Spain	Sweden	UK	Average
-1	119.4	-16.9	-12.6	71.6	-7.7	82.6	-6.7	76.8	-12.5	62.0	36.1	29.8	37.6
0	-17.8	-29.1	-55.0	-83.2	-56.2	-35.1	-4.9	11.0	-52.8	-12.3	-99.0	-35.2	-39.4
5	-12.1	-5.3	-32.3	-42.4	-37.6	-11.7	5.2	25.9	-38.2	-6.0	-79.6	-25.2	-22.0
10	15.9	28.9	15.3	-16.8	-9.1	30.8	20.5	56.2	-2.6	6.0	-29.5	-5.9	8.7
15	57.5	78.3	66.4	25.5	34.4	79.3	37.4	98.8	39.9	20.2	22.1	17.5	47.6
20	81.3	134.0	121.0	63.7	82.5	118.8	49.4	122.2	83.8	37.0	78.5	36.5	83.5
25	78.7	161.0	142.7	87.4	106.6	130.7	49.8	119.4	106.7	50.1	104.9	48.4	98.2
30	62.6	146.0	141.3	80.5	103.3	116.6	31.8	97.3	100.5	52.7	111.4	48.4	90.2
35	39.0	118.0	126.9	63.2	93.8	86.3	17.5	65.0	84.2	47.3	105.2	40.3	72.9
40	11.5	82.9	94.6	29.2	69.8	44.1	8.7	11.8	59.7	33.7	84.5	25.4	45.1
45	-32.2	39.3	46.7	-11.5	37.4	-8.2	-2.6	-27.3	28.4	10.7	49.1	3.7	9.8
50	-83.7	-12.4	-14.7	-67.3	-13.7	-73.2	-16.6	-69.2	-9.3	-23.4	0.4	-22.2	-35.3
55	-148.3	-66.7	-67.7	-127.3	-69.5	-138.2	-33.0	-110.9	-48.2	-60.6	-61.2	-50.4	-83.5
60	-206.1	-102.0	-126.2	-159.4	-99.4	-194.4	-48.3	-143.8	-82.5	-91.8	-119.0	-69.8	-121.6
65	-211.2	-114.0	-146.0	-163.8	-127.3	-205.7	-58.5	-157.1	-110.2	-111.0	-152.0	-77.1	-136.8
70	-191.8	-110.0	-154.6	-148.6	-116.6	-182.2	-54.2	-151.4	-113.8	-109.4	-152.9	-73.8	-130.3
75	-167.5	-98.4	-158.0	-133.3	-94.9	-153.1	-46.2	-130.2	-115.0	-96.6	-139.6	-63.6	-116.7
80	-136.1	-84.9	-161.6	-114.7	-75.5	-121.0	-38.9	-101.9	-112.8	-80.0	-122.3	-51.7	-100.3
85	-106.0	-70.0	-161.0	-101.8	-57.8	-92.7	-32.7	-76.2	-105.8	-64.4	-100.1	-41.6	-84.3
90	-81.6	-55.5	-152.5	-83.3	-43.5	-68.8	-28.0	-55.5	-94.4	-48.9	-78.5	-29.0	-68.4
95	-59.7	-42.9	-113.4	-64.9	-31.0	-47.9	-21.0	-38.8	-80.3	-30.0	-58.4	-13.β	-50.1
100	-23.2	-16.1	-39.5	-24.5	-10.6	-16.9	-7.9	-14.6	-31.7	-12.2	-20.0	5.3	-17.7

Source: Country studies in European Commission (1999).

between 60 and 65, when an average agent in Europe retires. With further increasing age of the retirees, the absolute value of net transfers decreases, as fewer and fewer years of life expectancy remain.

In contrast to the very similar qualitative findings, the quantitative figures are fairly different. For example, an average European newborn in the base year 1995 will receive net transfers over the remaining life cycle amounting to 39,400 ECU. In contrast, an Italian newborn will have to pay 11,000 ECU, while an average Swedish newborn will receive approximately 99,000 ECU in present-value transfers. In fact this reflects the countries' tremendous divergence in the structure of youth assistance as they do not differ very much in educational expenditures. The difference is largely due to the attitude toward the young recipients: typically, the Scandinavian welfare states (and the Netherlands) pay welfare benefits or youth support directly, while the southern European approach is to donate these transfers indirectly via the head of the family.

With respect to the maximum amount of taxes paid over the remaining life span, the peak is reached at age 20 in Austria and Italy and at age 30 in Spain and Sweden, while all other countries peak at age 25. These maximum amounts vary from 48,400 ECU in the United Kingdom to 161,000 ECU in Belgium. This is more than triple the UK figure. In fact, between ages 20 and 40, Belgium and Denmark impose the highest tax burden, while the net tax load is lowest in the United Kingdom and Ireland between ages 20 and 35. The generational account turns negative between age 42 (Austria) and 51 (Sweden). Nevertheless, the time span covers a period of nearly 10 years, indicating once more the differences in tax-transfer patterns over the EU Member States.

With the exception of three countries, all average agents will reach their maximum amount of remaining transfer receipts upon reaching age 65. The exceptions are the archetypical European welfare states, that is, Denmark, the Netherlands, and Sweden. While in Sweden and the Netherlands, the peak is delayed by five and ten years, respectively, relative to the EU average. Denmark is a very special case, in which the maximum amount of transfers is received by the oldest old. The reason these Scandinavian countries deviate from the others in our sample is twofold. The first reason is of economic importance: all three have very generous long-term–care programs. The second reason is not of economic weight, involving only a data constraint: for all other countries, the benefits to the oldest old of health treatment and long-term care are assumed to be distributed fairly uniformly over the last years of living.

What is also striking when it comes to the transfer receipts of the elderly in Europe is, again, the tremendous divergence in the net payments. The variance reaches from fairly low amounts of 58,500 and 77,100 ECU in Ireland and the United Kingdom, respectively, to the maximum figures found in Austria and Germany, where a 65-year-old can expect to receive more than 200,000 ECU as a net transfer over his or her remaining life cycle. One might conclude that the elderly fare best in northern Europe and the central countries in our sample. This cannot, however, be concluded from focusing exclusively on the sheer absolute amounts, since the selected countries vary significantly with respect to income and living standard. Therefore, Table 6.6 reports the generational accounts of Table 6.5 scaled by the ratio of the average per capita GDP in the EU and the countries' per capita GDP as shown in Table 6.3.

When it comes to the maximum of GDP-scaled net transfer receipt, we find the highest values for Italy (196,800 ECU) and Spain (186,000 ECU), while formerly leading Austria (176,700 ECU) and Germany (167,900 ECU) are only third and fourth. From this it might be concluded that the elderly fare relatively best in the southern group of countries, not in the central or northern one. Nevertheless, this conclusion is still not valid, since today's elderly have, of course, paid their contributions to the respective pay-as-you-go schemes in the past. Avoiding the calculation of internal rates of return,[14] the ratio between the maximum net transfers received and the maximum net taxes paid gives some sort of "return-on-investment" intuition. From Table 6.7, it can be seen that in Austria and Spain, respectively, the maximum net transfer amounts to 2.6 and 2.1 times the maximum net tax payment of average agents. Among those countries with the lowest ratio, we find two typical European welfare states, Denmark and the Netherlands, in which both amounts are approximately of the same size. The lowest ratio is found for Belgium, a country in which the maximum net taxes paid exceed the maximum amount of net transfers received. Obviously, the intuitive north-south distinction in Europe with respect to the status of the welfare of the elderly cannot be confirmed by our figures.

Also with respect to the scaled maximum net tax payment over the remaining life span, we cannot confirm the ranking we found while focusing on absolute accounts. Surprisingly, the highest relative net tax payments in 1995 are faced by an average 20-year-old Italian, while the figure for Belgium, which was highest in absolute terms, comes only next. Another surprising result can be seen in the ranking of the lowest amount of maximum net tax payments. Ireland and the United

---

[14] For example, Schnabel (1998) provides a calculation of internal rates of return from social security contributions for current living generations in Germany.

Table 6.6. *Scaled Generational Accounts for Selected Member States of the EU (thousands of 1995 ECUs, scaled by per capita GDP as per cent of EU average)*

Generation's Age in 1995	Austria	Belgium	Denmark	Finland	France	Germany	Ireland	Italy	Netherlands	Spain	Sweden	UK	Average
-1	99.9	-15.3	-9.2	69.0	-7.0	67.4	-9.4	96.2	-11.6	103.9	32.8	43.3	40.5
0	-14.9	-26.4	-40.0	-80.2	-51.2	-28.6	-6.9	13.8	-49.2	-20.6	-90.0	-51.2	-37.4
5	-10.1	-4.8	-23.5	-40.9	-34.3	-9.5	7.3	32.4	-35.6	-10.1	-72.3	-36.6	-20.2
10	13.3	26.2	11.1	-16.2	-8.3	25.1	28.8	70.4	-2.4	10.1	-26.8	-8.6	9.9
15	48.1	71.0	48.3	24.6	31.3	64.7	52.6	123.8	37.1	33.8	20.1	25.4	48.0
20	68.0	121.5	88.1	61.4	75.2	96.9	69.5	153.1	78.0	62.0	71.3	53.1	82.6
25	65.8	146.0	103.9	84.3	97.1	106.7	70.1	149.6	99.3	83.9	95.3	70.4	97.1
30	52.4	132.4	102.9	77.6	94.1	95.1	44.7	121.9	93.6	88.3	101.2	70.4	88.8
35	32.6	107.0	92.4	60.9	85.5	70.4	24.6	81.4	78.4	79.2	95.6	58.6	71.3
40	9.6	75.2	68.9	28.2	63.6	36.0	12.2	14.8	55.6	56.5	76.8	36.9	43.4
45	-26.9	35.6	34.0	-11.1	34.1	-6.7	-3.7	-34.2	26.4	17.9	44.6	5.4	8.4
50	-70.0	-11.2	-10.7	-64.9	12.5	-59.7	-23.4	-86.7	-8.7	-39.2	0.4	-32.3	-36.3
55	-124.1	-60.5	-49.3	-122.8	-63.3	-112.8	-46.4	-138.9	-44.9	-101.5	-55.6	-73.3	-84.3
60	-172.4	-92.5	-91.9	-153.7	-90.6	-158.6	-68.0	-180.1	-76.8	-153.8	-108.1	-101.5	-121.9
65	-176.7	-103.4	-106.3	-158.0	-116.0	-167.9	-82.3	-196.8	-102.6	-186.0	-138.1	-112.1	-137.8
70	-160.5	-99.7	-112.6	-143.3	-106.2	-148.7	-76.3	-189.7	-105.9	-183.3	-138.9	-107.3	-131.3
75	-140.1	-89.2	-115.0	-128.5	-86.5	-124.9	-65.0	-163.1	-107.1	-161.8	-126.9	-92.5	-117.0
80	-113.9	-77.0	-117.7	-110.6	-68.8	-98.7	-54.7	-127.7	-105.0	-134.0	-111.1	-75.2	-99.7
85	-88.7	-63.5	-117.2	-98.2	-52.7	-75.6	-46.0	-95.5	-98.5	-107.9	-91.0	-60.5	-83.0
90	-68.3	-50.3	-111.0	-80.3	-39.6	-56.1	-39.4	-69.5	-87.9	-81.9	-71.3	-42.2	-66.5
95	-49.9	-38.9	-82.6	-62.6	-28.2	-39.1	-29.5	-48.6	-74.8	-50.3	-53.1	-18.9	-48.1
100	-19.4	-14.6	-28.8	-23.6	-9.7	-13.8	-11.1	-18.3	-29.5	-20.4	-18.2	7.7	-16.6

Source: Country studies in European Commission (1999).

223

Table 6.7. *Minima and Maxima in the Generational Accounts*
(thousands of 1995 ECUs)

	Unscaled Accounts			Scaled Accounts	
	Minimum	Maximum	Absolute ratio	Minimum	Maximum
Austria	−211.2	81.3	2.6	−176.7	68.0
Belgium	−114.0	161.0	0.7	−103.4	146.0
Denmark	−161.6	142.0	1.1	−117.7	103.9
Finland	−163.8	87.4	1.9	−158.0	84.3
France	−127.3	106.6	1.2	−116.0	97.1
Germany	−205.7	130.7	1.6	−167.9	106.7
Ireland	−58.5	49.8	1.2	−82.3	70.1
Italy	−157.1	122.2	1.3	−196.8	153.1
Netherlands	−115.0	106.7	1.1	−107.1	99.3
Spain	−111.0	52.7	2.1	−186.0	83.9
Sweden	−152.9	111.4	1.4	−138.9	101.2
UK	−77.1	48.4	1.6	−112.1	70.4
Average	−138.6	99.3	1.5	−139.2	98.0

Kingdom do still display comparatively low net tax loads for young individuals. Nevertheless, the lowest maximum is found for a 20-year-old Austrian.

The impact of today's fiscal policy on the distribution of net tax burdens between current and future generations is reported in Table 6.8. The first column shows the traditional indicator of intergenerational redistribution, the percentage difference between the accounts of future and current newborns, π. Because of changes in the sign, the indicator is not valid in the cases of Denmark, Finland, Sweden, and the United Kingdom. In Austria, Belgium, France, Germany, Ireland, the Netherlands, and Spain, both accounts are negative, while in Italy they are both positive. Obviously, π is not a helpful indicator for measuring intergenerational redistribution. Hence, we employ the set of indicators outlined in the section "Measuring Intergenerational Redistribution."

On average, the absolute difference in the net payment of current and future newborns amounts to 77,000 ECU, since base-year newborns receive approximately 39,400 ECU, while newborns in the following year would face a net tax burden of 37,600 ECU. Of course, the latter amount reflects the fact that it is the future generations who are made responsible for the service of the government's true liabilities, which make up 130 percent of GDP, on average, of the selected EU Member States.

Table 6.8. *Measuring Generational Balance*

	Percentage Diff. (pi)	Absolute Diff. (thousands of ECUs)	Incr. all Taxes for Future Gen. (%)	Incr. all Taxes (% of GDP)	True Liabilities (% of GDP)
Austria	350.1	137.2	82.7	6.5	192.5
Belgium	20.0	12.2	6.7	0.6	18.8
Denmark	−6.3	42.4	20.3	2.3	71.2
Finland	−520.1	154.8	91.5	8.8	253.2
France	548.6	48.5	33.8	2.6	81.3
Germany	158.6	117.7	58.9	4.7	136.0
Ireland	6.3	−1.8	−1.7	−0.1	−4.3
Italy	139.3	65.8	53.2	4.0	107.3
Netherlands	113.2	40.3	25.1	2.5	75.9
Spain	477.8	74.3	106.5	5.1	151.9
Sweden	−1,446.1	135.1	74.0	7.6	236.5
UK	−6,928.9	65.1	74.0	6.0	184.4
Average	−590.6	77.0	54.0	4.4	130.0
	Deviation from Average (%)				
Austria	−159.3	78.1	53.1	49.1	48.1
Belgium	−103.4	−84.2	−87.6	−86.2	−85.5
Denmark	−98.9	−45.0	−62.4	−47.2	−45.2
Finland	−11.9	101.0	69.4	101.9	94.8
France	−192.9	−34.7	−35.1	−38.3	−35.2
Germany	−126.9	52.8	9.1	7.8	4.6
Ireland	−101.1	−102.3	−103.1	−102.3	−103.3
Italy	−123.6	−14.6	−1.5	−8.2	−17.5
Netherlands	−119.2	−47.7	−53.5	−42.6	−41.6
Spain	−180.9	−3.5	97.2	17.0	16.9
Sweden	144.8	75.4	37.0	74.4	81.9
UK	1,073.1	−15.5	37.0	37.7	42.2

Source: Country studies in European Commission (1999).

Thus, future generations would face a net tax burden in excess of that for today's newborns by 54 percent. If, however, all generations share in the burden of today's fiscal policy through paying γ percent more in all taxes, the necessary tax increment would permanently increase the tax-to-GDP ratio by 4.4 percentage points.

Obviously, the present fiscal policy of the selected EU Member States is, on average, in severe imbalance to the advantage of currently living generations, or to put it in other words, today's fiscal policy is unsustainable. This is true for all countries except Ireland. Only in Ireland – which has recently been dubbed the Celtic Tiger – is fiscal policy intergenerationally balanced and sustainable, since vis-à-vis the explicit debt of 72 percent of GDP, there are implicit public assets inherited by future generations in approximately the same magnitude (see Figure 6.1). There is, indeed, a little surplus in the intertemporal budget constraint of Ireland, which makes it possible to decrease the tax-to-GDP ratio by 0.1 percentage points.

The intergenerational imbalances found in all other countries differ tremendously. In terms of true liabilities, the debt-to-GDP ratio is only 18.8 percent in Belgium, while the figure for Finland is as high as 253.2 percent. Besides Finland, only Sweden, with a true debt-to-GDP ratio of 236.5 percent, displays a similarly high redistribution to the disadvantage of future generations. The composition of these true liabilities reveals an interesting fact, which can be easily seen in Figure 6.1. In the case of Finland, the explicit net debt figure is negative, indicating that Finland has currently explicit public assets in the magnitude of 8 percent of its 1995 GDP. The implicit liabilities, however, correspond to over 260 percent of GDP. In contrast, Belgium has the highest explicit net debt figure, with over 120 percent of GDP. Since the major aim of the present fiscal policy is to generate high tax revenues and a primary surplus, the implicit liabilities are negative in nearly the same magnitude. In the Swedish case, the positive implicit liabilities amount to 200 percent of GDP, while the explicit debt figure adds another 37 percentage points.

In Austria, the United Kingdom, and Spain, the generational imbalance is also extreme. In these countries, the true debt figure corresponds to 192.5, 184.4, and 151.9 percent of GDP, respectively. A lower but still severe imbalance can be found in Germany and Italy, where the net debt-to-GDP ratios are 136.0 and 107.3 percent, respectively. Still substantial imbalances are run by the French, Dutch, and Danish governments. The latter two countries seem to be very similar with respect to generational policy, since in both cases we find an average explicit net debt combined with a very low implicit debt figure, resulting in a true debt figure of 76 percent for the Netherlands and 71 percent for Denmark. Moreover, both countries have very generous welfare systems. The reason for the rather low generational imbalance is simply the severe tax load on currently living (and future) generations.

Measuring the intergenerational redistribution in terms of the increase in all taxes for all generations necessary to pay off the entire public debt leads to an identical range in the imbalance of today's fiscal policy in the selected Member States of the EU. The change in the tax-to-GDP quota

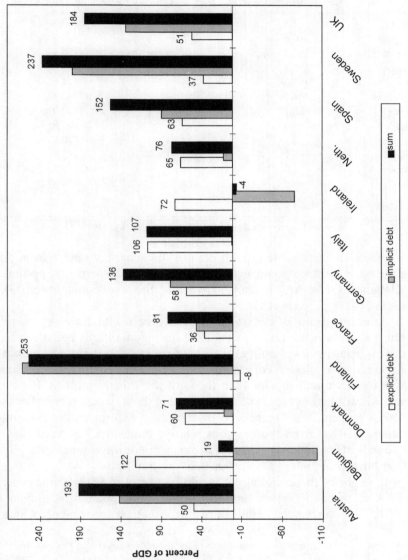

Figure 6.1. Composition of True Public Liabilities.

Table 6.9. *Sources of Generational Imbalance, Total Tax Increase Needed to Restore Generational Balance (percent of GDP)*

	Baseline Results	No Explicit Debt	No Demographic Change
Austria	6.5	4.8	2.3
Belgium	0.6	−3.5	−1.7
Denmark	2.3	0.4	0.1
Finland	8.8	9.1	3.8
France	2.6	1.4	1.6
Germany	4.7	2.2	−0.3
Ireland	−0.1	−2.5	−0.9
Italy	4.0	0.0	−2.8
Netherlands	2.5	0.4	−0.8
Spain	5.1	2.5	2.9
Sweden	7.6	6.4	5.1
UK	6.0	4.3	4.8
Average	4.4	2.4	1.0

Source: Country studies in European Commission (1999).

that ensures a sustainable growth path of the economy ranges from as high as 8.8 percentage points in Finland to as low as 0.6 percentage points in Belgium. Of course, in Ireland we find the above-mentioned tax decrease of 0.1 percent of GDP.

A different scaling of generational imbalance would, however, occur if one focused on the tax increase for future generations necessary to restore a balanced fiscal policy.[15] This is, of course, due to the divergence in the national tax bases. For example, we would find Spain on top, since its tax base is much smaller than those of the other countries. Future Spaniards would thus face tax loads exceeding those of current newborns by 106.5 percent. With respect to the absolute difference, the ranking differs somewhat from the previous relative indicators.[16] Nevertheless, for all indicators, the divergences are of only minor importance and only reflect differences in tax systems or in living standards.

In the light of these findings, it would be useful to know the specific sources of the generational imbalance and their quantitative impact. Table 6.9 summarizes the results of two hypothetical experiments, which

[15] The ranking with respect to the imbalance in fiscal policy would be in this case (from high to low): Spain, Finland, Austria, Sweden, the United Kingdom, Germany, France, Italy, the Netherlands, Denmark, Belgium, Ireland.

[16] The ranking with respect to the imbalance in fiscal policy would be in this case (from high to low): Finland, Austria, Sweden, Germany, France, Spain, Italy, United Kingdom, Denmark, the Netherlands, Belgium, Ireland.

address these important questions. The first experiment repeats the baseline for each country while setting the amount of the respective government's explicit net debt to zero. The second experiment calculates the generational imbalance resulting if the fairly advantageous age structure of the base year 1995 is kept constant. Of course, the first experiment illustrates the relative importance of the accumulated deficits of the recent past, while the latter addresses the pure demographic effects.

Table 6.9 reports for each country the increase in all taxes necessary to restore intergenerational balance as a percentage of GDP for the baseline, the explicit debt, and the demographic experiment. On average, the imbalance would be halved in the absence of any explicit debt, while approximately three-quarters of the imbalance would disappear if the age structure remained constant. Thus, the major part of the imbalance in the fiscal policy within the selected EU Member States stems from demographic trends. As a rule of thumb, roughly two-thirds of the imbalance can be attributed to the demographic transition, while one-third is due to the inherited explicit public debt.

As also shown in Table 6.9, the variance of the relative importance of explicit and implicit public indebtedness within the countries is rather broad. For example, in Finland the no-debt experiment indicates an increase of tax payments exceeding the baseline figure because this country has an explicit stock of public assets. But even if the demographic transition did not occur, Finnish fiscal policy would redistribute to the advantage of current generations. In contrast, Belgian fiscal policy would be sustainable in either of the two hypothetical experiments. In both cases, the baseline tax increase necessary to ensure sustainability would switch into a tax reduction. In the cases of Austria, Denmark, France, Spain, Sweden, and the United Kingdom, neither of the two experiments would fully eliminate the imbalance, while in the cases of Germany, Italy, and the Netherlands, a constant population structure would suffice.

In seven of the twelve selected countries – Belgium, Denmark, France, Ireland, the Netherlands, Spain, and the United Kingdom – the imbalance is mainly due to the explicit debt figures, although the demographic impact is mostly of only little less importance. In Austria, Finland, Germany, Italy, and Sweden, the imbalance stems predominantly from the demographic transition. Since the major source of generational imbalance is still the demographic trends and, in particular, the double-aging process, we will now consider the specific problems that arise in any attempt to maintain the financial sustainability of intergenerational contracts, mainly the pay-as-you-go pension, and to some extent the health schemes in the selected countries.

Cross-Country Studies: Reforming Social Security

Pension expenditures within the selected EU Member States range between only 3.6 percent of GDP in Ireland and 13.3 percent in Italy (refer back to Table 6.4). Moreover, long-term projections of expenditures for the next five decades make it clear that the pension system is not at all sustainable. Within the twelve selected EU Member States, there is, however, no such thing as *a* pension system – there are twelve. In fact, the pension schemes, which were set up at very different dates, vary considerably from country to country, with basically only one common feature: they are all financed via pay-as-you-go schemes.

This feature aside, European systems vary from the pure tax-transfer system in Denmark to the more or less pure insurance approach with a high linkage between benefits and contributions. These Bismarckian types of social security systems are found in, for example, Austria and Germany. Nevertheless, even in these countries, federal grants supplement the contributions, which already encompass over 20 percent of the payroll.

From the viewpoint of generosity, the divergence is also significant. On the one hand, there are fairly generous countries, such as Austria, Germany, and Italy, with replacement rates of close to 70 percent, while such countries as Ireland, the Netherlands, and the United Kingdom provide only for a basic pension ranging slightly above the poverty line. The normal retirement age is, on average, lower for females and varies overall between 60 and 67. However, in most countries the effective retirement age is much lower. When one takes into account the early retirement schemes and disability pensions, it is, on average, around age 60. A precise description of the current institutional settings of pension systems within the EU Member States is a mammoth task and far beyond the scope of this chapter.[17] Hence, this section will present some directions in which policy reforms for the unfunded social security schemes have aimed or will aim in the future.

In most of the selected EU Member States, reform of the unfunded pension schemes has been on the political agenda since the late 1980s. With the exception of Ireland – where the aging problem does not exist – all the governments have responded to the future challenges through specific policy amendments. In most cases, these were enacted before 1995. Hence, our baseline results include the economic effects of these reforms, but obviously the measures have been far from sufficient to

---

[17] An enumerative description of the actual institutional settings can be found in Franco and Munzi (1996, part 2).

restore generational balance and fiscal sustainability. Nevertheless, in some cases the fiscal imbalance would be very much higher had the social security reforms not been enacted.[18]

In principle, there are two basic strategies for social security reforms. First, there is the possibility of partially funding a hitherto unfunded system. A move toward funded pensions promises various benefits in an economy on an efficient growth path, but it also immediately triggers the well-known argument of the double burden on transitional generations.[19] The second reform strategy aims to redress the problems of an unfunded system without questioning the basic principle of pay-as-you-go financing. This can be done through various measures that either reduce entitlements or increase tax revenues. Of course, high and growing contribution rates will imply further distortions in labor markets that already are highly inefficient. Hence, it is mostly not increases in contribution rates but increases in federal grants that are the focus of the recent political debates. Subsequently, we will discuss these types of policy reforms in the context of specific country studies.

There are various ways in which entitlements can be reduced for either present or future elderly cohorts. First, the minimum years of contribution payments for eligibility can be increased. Second, existing entitlements can be reduced through a switch in the indexation of pension payments from gross wages to net wages or to consumer prices. Both measures were, for example, part of the French 1993 reform, the German pension reform of 1992, and the Italian reforms of 1993 and 1995. Third, new entitlements can be reduced by making the method of calculating the primary insurance amount (PIA) less favorable for the beneficiaries. This was done in a number of countries, including Austria, Belgium, France, Germany, Italy, Spain, and the United Kingdom.

As an example, Table 6.10 reports the effects of the recently introduced Spanish Toledo Agreement, which prolonged the period over which the PIA is calculated from the last eight to the last fifteen years of active labor market participation. The agreement stipulated that beginning in 1997 one year of past employment would be added each year until 2003, at which point the last fifteen years of employment would be taken into account. According to Berenguer et al. (1999), this will

---

[18] For example, in Italy the 1995 pension reform reduced the true liabilities from 181.4 percent to the baseline figure of 107.3 percent of GDP. If this reform will actually be carried through, this implies an elimination of implicit liabilities, as explicit public debt amounts to 105.9 percent of GDP.

[19] As shown by Breyer and Straub (1993) and Raffelhüschen (1993), the argument does not hold since pay-as-you-go systems tend to distort the labor-leisure choice. Kotlikoff et al. (1998) provide the results of similar experiments for the United States.

Table 6.10. *Reforming Public Pension Schemes in Spain, Denmark, and Finland (thousands of 1995 ECUs)*

Generation's Age in 1995	Spain		Denmark		Finland	
	Baseline	Toledo Agreement	Baseline	Increasing Retirement Age	Baseline	Increasing Contribution
0	-12.3	-11.4	-55.0	-53.3	-83.2	-71.8
5	-6.0	-5.0	-32.3	-30.3	-42.4	-30.2
10	6.0	7.2	15.3	17.8	-16.8	-4.1
15	20.2	21.7	66.4	69.3	25.5	38.0
20	37.0	38.7	121.0	124.4	63.7	75.4
25	50.1	52.2	142.7	146.8	87.4	97.6
30	52.7	55.1	141.3	146.2	80.5	88.9
35	47.3	50.1	126.9	132.6	63.2	69.7
40	33.7	37.0	94.6	101.5	29.2	33.7
45	10.7	14.4	46.7	55.0	-11.5	-8.7
50	-23.4	-19.2	-14.7	-4.7	-67.3	-66.0
55	-60.6	-57.5	-67.7	-55.4	-127.3	-126.8
60	-91.8	-91.8	-126.2	-126.2	-159.4	-159.4
65	-111.0	-111.0	-146.0	-146.0	-163.8	-163.8
70	-109.4	-109.4	-154.6	-154.6	-148.6	-148.6
75	-96.6	-96.6	-158.0	-158.0	-133.3	-133.3
80	-80.0	-80.0	-161.6	-161.6	-114.7	-114.7
85	-64.4	-64.4	-161.0	-161.0	-101.8	-101.8
90	-48.9	-48.9	-152.5	-152.5	-83.3	-83.3
95	-30.0	-30.0	-113.4	-113.4	-64.9	-64.9
100	-12.2	-12.2	-39.5	-39.5	-24.5	-24.5
Future generations	62.0	54.0	-12.6	-22.2	71.6	49.6
Absolute difference	72.3	65.4	42.4	31.0	154.8	121.4
True gov. debt (% of GDP)	151.9%	133.7%	71.2%	52.0%	253.2%	199.8%

Sources: Borgmann et al (2000); Jensen and Raffelhüschen (2000); Feist et al (1999)

eventually translate into a 7.2 percent overall reduction of the PIA for all newly retired persons. The comparison of the respective generational accounts before and after the reform illustrates the intergenerational impact of the Toledo Agreement. Because of the smooth phasing in of pension reductions, the accounts of the current elderly will remain unaffected. In contrast, those retiring in the period 1998 through 2006 will face the highest burdens, which amount at the maximum to additional net payments of 3,700 ECU for those age 45 in the base year. For future generations of Spaniards, the Toledo Agreement implies a reduced net payment of 54,000 ECU, which is 8,000 ECU less than the baseline figure. It services a stock of true public debt amounting to 133.7 percent of GDP. This is still a considerable intergenerational redistribution, but it is significantly lower than the imbalance indicated by a 151.9 debt-to-GDP ratio in the case of not enacting the Toledo Agreement.

As a fourth way of reducing pension entitlements, most European countries have changed the retirement age. In Austria, Belgium, Denmark, Finland, Germany, Italy, Sweden, and the United Kingdom, this was or will be done either by directly changing the legal retirement age or by decreasing the incentives for early retirement. As an example, we examine the generational impacts of a recently proposed reform that will reverse the strong tendency toward early retirement in Denmark. As in other European countries, the window of retirement opens with a specific early retirement scheme with relatively advantageous conditions, while the standard retirement age is 67 for both males and females. The proposed policy option will narrow this window by increasing the earliest retirement age stepwise from 60 to 63 through the years 2000–2002. Clearly, this announced reform would yield a twofold gain: not only would the workforce be expanded, leading to higher labor income taxes; there would also be a fall in the large number of recipients of public transfer payments.

The fourth and fifth columns of Table 6.10 report the generational impacts of this likely Danish pension reform, which solely adjusts the early retirement benefits and income tax revenues. As compared to the baseline figures, the burdens of current generations will rise with age until they top at the age of 55 due to the five-year announcement period. The current elderly, that is those aged 56 and above, will remain fully unaffected. With respect to intergenerational redistribution, we find a significantly reduced burden on future generations. This holds for both the absolute difference in current and future newborns' accounts, amounting to 31,100 ECU, as compared to 42,400 ECU in the baseline, and for the true debt, which will be reduced from 71.2 to 52.0 percent.

Obviously, raising the retirement age is a very effective way of approaching generational balance under the given demographic pressure. It cannot, however, be utilized to ensure full balance, since this would necessitate extremely high retirement ages. Moreover, one should keep in mind that this type of reform measure will predominantly burden older and therefore – in terms of life-cycle planning – not very flexible cohorts. Hence, an announcement made far in advance is an obligatory part of this type of reform proposals.

Another strategy of restructuring an unfunded system without calling the basic principle of pay-as-you-go financing into question aims to increase the revenues allocated to the elderly through the social security budgets. This can be done either through increasing the contribution rates or by increasing the federal subsidies. Interestingly, most European pension schemes are defined-benefit plans, though there is a political consensus that a target replacement ratio should not be ensured under all circumstances. As a case study, we consider the Finnish social security system, which is characterized by a particularly low effective retirement age.[20] The basic features of that system are fairly similar to those of the other Scandinavian countries.

The last two columns of Table 6.10 show the Finnish generational accounts for the baseline and for a policy option that gradually increases the contribution rates to public pension schemes by 0.235 percentage points annually over forty years. Starting at the 1995 total contribution rate of 20.6 percent, this ensures approximately constant per capita spending and increases the contribution rate to 30 percent by 2035. While this scenario does not affect 1995 pensioners at all, cohorts aged under 60 in 1995 pay a considerably larger amount of social security contributions over their remaining lifetime. For a 1995 newborn, the net transfer is reduced from 83,200 ECU in the baseline to 71,800 ECU in the reform scenario. This leaves future generations with generational accounts amounting to 49,600 ECU, and thus results in an absolute difference between generational accounts of 121,400 ECU, which is almost 22 percent lower than the baseline value. The fact that future generations' burden will be reduced can also be illustrated by focusing on the true debt figure, which decreases from 253 to 200 percent. Similar quantitative and qualitative findings can be derived from experiments that set the contribution rates endogenously, in a way that ensures a balanced social security budget through the years of the demographic transition.

[20] The effective retirement age is, on average, 58. The standard retirement age for unemployment pensions and disability retirement was increased stepwise from 55 to 58 until 1998.

234

In all three of these case studies, we focused exclusively on the impact of changes on the expenditure or receipt side of social security budgets that do not question the basic pay-as-you-go principle. What remains to be discussed is the move toward a (partially) funded system. However, in order to get a clear and unbiased picture of the demographic pressure as well as the impact of alternative reform scenarios, it is instructive to isolate generational accounts of those intergenerational contracts, which are the main source of the financial burden arising from the aging process. From a European perspective, these contracts include not only social security and health-care insurance, but also the long-term–care insurance recently introduced in Germany and the Netherlands.

As an example, Table 6.11 reports the isolated generational accounts of the three generational contracts in Germany for the baseline results and three hypothetical experiments.[21] In the baseline, the maximum net payment in the case of a 20-year-old average person amounts to 66,900 ECU. Already at age 38, the present value of remaining gross payments breaks even with the value of transfers received over the remaining life cycle. For a person age 65, the expected net transfers received during old age peak at 191,300 ECU and decrease thereafter.

Summing up all net-of-contribution demands of all currently living cohorts would imply a stock of implicit liabilities of all German social insurance amounting to 114.3 percent of GDP. This is high for Europe, but by far not the top of the range. In order to service this implicit debt, future Germans would have to face a change of 125.7 percent in total contributions. That would lead to a generational account of those born after the base year of 120,700 ECU, that is, 95,500 ECU more than the account of base-year newborns. Hence, overall contribution rates would have to be raised from approximately 32 percent of gross payroll in the base year to more than 50 percent in 2035, which, even in Europe, is an absolutely unrealistic policy.

The third and fourth columns of Table 6.11 offer two hypothetical reforms of the pay-as-you-go system that either increase contribution rates or cut benefits in order to balance fully the intertemporal social insurance budget constraint. The first case implies a social security payroll tax rate of 23.2 instead of 18.6 percent in the base year and all future

---

[21] The study on generational contracts in Germany draws from Raffelhüschen and Walliser (1999). In order to calculate separate generational accounts, only the respective profiles for contributions and transfers of social security, health care, and long-term care are taken into account. Federal grants to social security are neglected because in 1995 they corresponded to non–insurance-related expenditures. Overall, federal grants display the same incidence as the taxes necessary to finance them.

Table 6.11. *Reforming Social Insurance in Germany (thousands of 1995 ECUs)*

Generations's Age in 1995	Baseline Account	Increasing Contributions	Decreasing Transfers	Partial Funding
0	25.2	43.4	34.8	39.1
5	35.8	57.4	46.1	51.8
10	45.8	71.5	57.5	64.5
15	57.6	88.0	70.7	79.4
20	66.9	101.3	81.4	91.4
25	61.1	96.3	77.4	86.9
30	44.4	77.9	62.6	70.3
35	20.1	50.6	40.7	45.7
40	−10.6	15.5	12.5	14.0
45	−47.6	−27.0	−21.7	−24.4
50	−91.0	−76.7	−61.6	−69.2
55	−137.7	−129.8	−104.3	−117.1
60	−182.9	−180.5	−145.1	−162.8
65	−191.3	−191.0	−153.5	−172.3
70	−167.0	−167.0	−134.2	−150.6
75	−139.1	−139.1	−111.8	−125.5
80	−109.3	−109.3	−87.8	−98.6
85	−83.2	−83.2	−66.9	−75.1
90	−61.6	−61.6	−49.5	−55.6
95	−42.9	−42.9	−34.5	−38.7
100	−15.0	−15.0	−12.1	−13.6
Future gen.	120.7	43.4	34.8	39.1
Absolute diff.	95.5	0.0	0.0	0.0
Increase in all taxes (%)	125.7%	0.0%	0.0%	0.0%
Soc. ins. liab. (% of GDP)	114.3%	0.0%	0.0%	0.0%

Source: Raffelhüschen and Walliser (1999).

years, a health insurance payroll tax rate of 16.3 instead of 13.1 percent and a payroll tax rate of 2.1 instead of 1.7 percent for the recently introduced long-term–care insurance.[22] In contrast, generational balance in social insurance could also be restored through an immediate and per-

[22] Note that all these results are very optimistic, since they assume that per capita medical expenditures grow in line with the GDP. See also Table 6.4 for health care expenditure projections under alternative growth rates for the costs of treatment.

manent transfer reduction amounting to 19.6 percent of the 1995 level. In the case of Germany, this translates into a replacement rate of 57.5 percent instead of the present level of 70 percent of net labor income.

It is obvious by comparing the third and fourth columns of Table 6.11 that the share of the burden necessary to restore generational balance is more equally spread between currently living generations in the case of the benefit reduction. However, neither of these two extreme scenarios seems to be a realistic policy option. Most likely, there will be some kind of combination of the two extreme scenarios.

Reflecting a guess of what might result from future decision making, the last column of Table 6.11 reports the generational accounts of a partial funding system, assuming that half of what is necessary to restore intergenerational balance is financed via increased contribution rates while the other half is financed via benefit reductions. In order to keep the calculations simple, the exercise assumes that both reform measures are introduced without any pre-announcement period. As compared to the baseline, the resulting differences in the accounts are simply linear combinations of the extreme cases discussed above.

In the first decades, annual surpluses will occur, and social insurance schemes will operate as partially funded systems. When the demographic burden intensifies, these funds will be sufficient to partially finance the resulting deficits up to the year 2200. The impact on the net payments of currently living agents is fairly but not fully uniform. In absolute terms, working-age individuals would face net payments between 19,000 and 26,000 ECU above those of the baseline scenario, in which the future generations are heavily burdened. For a current newborn German, the mixed strategy implies an additional payment of 13,900 ECU, which corresponds approximately to the average load levied on the elderly.

The strategy of partially funding pay-as-you-go social insurance schemes while at the same time requiring the current elderly to participate in restoring intergenerational balance has several advantages in both the German and the European context. First, it is superior with respect to intergenerational as well as intragenerational equity. Second, it endows the German or European economy with capital, which might trigger an accelerating growth process in the future. At the same time, the policy increases labor productivity and thereby creates new job opportunities for those unemployed because of the high wages in the central and northern countries in the sample. Third, reduced benefits might open up a demographic "breathing space," which in turn could be used to decrease effective labor costs, which are very high in most of the EU Member States.

Summary

Throughout the European Union, there is a clear and present need to reform the welfare state, since an aging population, rising unemployment rates, and lack of competitiveness in a globalized world economy are imposing more and more constraints on national welfare programs. At the same time, growing debt burdens induce high interest payments, which also call the sustainability of present fiscal policy substantially into question and force public decision makers to economize on other spending items and/or increase the already high tax loads.

This chapter investigates the demographic transition and its impact on the intergenerational stance of current fiscal policy within the European Union with the help of generational accounting. The sustainability in aging societies of both the so-called generational contracts via pay-as-you-go welfare programs and explicit debt burdens are the focus of this analysis.

Our findings suggest that the present fiscal policy of the selected EU Member States is in severe imbalance to the advantage of currently living generations. This is true for all countries except Ireland. Only in Ireland there is a minor stock of true public assets, while in all other countries there are true public liabilities that are being passed on to future generations. The intergenerational imbalance is highest in Finland and Sweden, where the current government policies shift a true debt-to-GDP ratio of over 200 percent to future Finns and Swedes. In Austria, the United Kingdom, and Spain, the generational imbalance is also extreme. A lower but still severe imbalance can be found in Germany and Italy. Still substantial imbalances are run by the French, Dutch, and Danish governments, resulting in true debt figures of 70 to 80 percent of GDP. Finally, a minor imbalance to the disadvantage of future generations is found in Belgium.

There are two major sources of the generational imbalance, the stock of explicit public debt and the demographic trend. On average, the imbalance would be halved in the absence of any explicit debt. Without the double-aging of the population, approximately three-quarters of the imbalance would disappear. Hence, the major part of the generational imbalance within the selected EU Member States stems from the demographic trends. As a rule of thumb, roughly two-thirds of the imbalance can be attributed to the demographic transition, while one-third is due to the inherited explicit public debt.

The demographic burden for future generations runs through social insurance, especially the pay-as-you-go pension schemes, as well as the health system and the recently introduced pay-as-you-go insurance for long-term care. Hence, the analysis has identified, in the context of specific country studies, some directions in which policy reforms for the unfunded schemes have gone or will go. Among reform strategies, we investigated the possibility of partially funding hitherto unfunded systems, as well as reforms that do not call the basic principle of pay-as-you-go financing into question. We found that partially funding the social insurance schemes has advantages with respect to both long-run inter-temporal distribution and short-run labor market problems.

Whether funding strategies or in a broader sense the restructuring of the welfare states in Europe is politically and economically feasible remains an open question. There is, however, no doubt about the general need to adjust social policies in Europe to both the present economic conditions and the demographic challenges to be expected in the not-so-distant future. Of course, the well-known diversity of the European countries necessitates different ways of adjustment in, for example, the pure welfare state of the Scandinavian countries and the Bismarckian social insurance of Germany or Austria. Nevertheless, traditional solidarity and social safety nets do have to be better reconciled with economic efficiency and fiscal sustainability.

References

Auerbach, A. 1997. Quantifying the Current U.S. Fiscal Imbalance. *National Tax Journal* 50:387–98.

Auerbach, A., J. Gokhale, and L. Kotlikoff. 1991. Generational Accounts: A Meaningful Alternative to Deficit Accounting. In David Bradford (ed.), *Tax Policy and the Economy*, vol. 5. Cambridge, MA: MIT Press.

——— 1992. Generational Accounting: A New Approach for Understanding the Effects of Fiscal Policy on Saving. *Scandinavian Journal of Economics* 94:303–18.

——— 1994. Generational Accounting: A Meaningful Way to Evaluate Fiscal Policy. *Journal of Economic Perspectives* 8:73–94.

Berenguer, E., H. Bonin, and B. Raffelhüschen. 1999. The Spanish Need for a Broader Tax Base. In European Commission (1999).

Bonin, H., B. Raffelhüschen, and J. Walliser. 2000. Can Immigration Alleviate the Demographic Burden? An Assessment With Generational Accounts. University of Freiburg, Discussion Paper of the Institute of Public Finance, no 54. (*Finanzarchiv*, forthcoming.)

——— 1999. The German Squeeze: Unification and Ageing. In European Commission (1999).

Börsch-Supan, A. 1991. Implications of an Aging Population: Problems and Policy Options in West Germany and the United States. *Economic Policy* 12:104–39.

Bovenberg A., and H. ter Rele. 1999. Government Finances and Ageing in the Netherlands. In European Commission (1999).

Breyer, F., and M. Straub. 1993. Welfare Effects of Unfunded Pension Systems When Labor Supply Is Endogenous. *Journal of Public Economics* 50:77–91.

Buiter, W. 1995. Generational Accounts, Aggregate Saving and Intergenerational Distribution. NBER Working Paper no. 5087, Cambridge, MA: National Bureau of Economic Research.

Cardarelli, R., and J. Sefton. 1999. Rolling Back the UK Welfare State? In European Commission (1999).

CBO (Congressional Budget Office). 1995. Who Pays and When? An Assessment of Generational Accounting. Washington, DC.

Crettez, B., K. Feist, and B. Raffelhüschen. 1999. Generational Imbalance and Social Insurance Reforms in France. In European Commission. (1999).

Dellis, A., and E. Lüth. 1999. Does Belgian Fiscal Policy Cope with Debt and Ageing? In European Commission (1999).

Diamond, P. 1996. Generational Accounts and Generational Balance: An Assessment. *National Tax Journal* 49:597–607.

European Commission. 1999. Generational Accounting in Europe. *European Economy: Reports and Studies* no. 6.

Eurostat. 1997. *Statistical Yearbook 97*. Brussels.

Fehr, H., and L. Kotlikoff. 1997. Generational Accounting in General Equilibrium. *Finanzarchiv* 53:1–27.

Feist, K., B. Raffelhüschen, R. Sullström, and R. Vanne. 1999. Macroeconomic Turnabout and Intergenerational Redistribution in Finland. In European Commission (1999).

Franco, D., and N. Sartor. 1999. Italy: High Public Debt and Population Ageing. In European Commission (1999).

Franco, D., and T. Munzi. 1996. Public Pension Expenditure Prospects in the European Union: A Survey of National Projections. In Aging and Pension Expenditure Prospects in the Western World. *European Economy: Reports and Studies*, no. 3:1–26.

———. 1997. Aging and Fiscal Policies in the European Union. In The Welfare State in Europe – Challenges and Reforms. *European Economy: Reports and Studies*, no. 4:239–388.

Haveman, R. 1994. Should Generational Accounts Replace Public Budgets and Deficits? *Journal of Economic Perspectives* 8(1):95–111.

Jensen, S., and B. Raffelhüschen. 1997. Generational and Gender-Specific Aspects of the Tax and Transfer System in Denmark. *Empirical Economics* 22:615–35.

———. 1999. The Danish Welfare State: Challenges Ahead and Needs for Social Security Reform. In European Commission (1999).

Keuschnigg, C., M. Keuschnigg, R. Koman, E. Lüth, and B. Raffelhüschen. 1999. Restoring Generational Balance in Austria. In European Commission (1999).

Kotlikoff, L., and W. Leibfritz. 1999. An International Comparison of Generational Accounts. In A. Auerbach, L. Kotlikoff, and W. Leibfritz (eds.),

Generational Accounting around the World. NBER series. Chicago: University of Chicago Press.

Kotlikoff, L., and B. Raffelhüschen. 1999. Generational Accounting around the Globe. *American Economic Review* 89:161–6.

Kotlikoff, L., K. Smetters, and J. Walliser. 1998. The Economic Impact of Privatizing Social Security. In H. Siebert (ed.), *Redesigning Social Security*. Tübingen.

Kotlikoff, L., and J. Walliser. 1995. Applying Generational Accounting to Developing Countries. IED Discussion Paper series, no. 67. Boston: Institute for Economic Development, Boston University.

Lundvik, P., E. Lüth, and B. Raffelhüschen. 1999. The Swedish Welfare State on Trial. In European Commission (1999).

McCarthy, T., and H. Bonin. 1999. EU Transfers and Demographic Dividends in Ireland. In European Commission (1999).

OECD. 1997. Ageing in OECD Countries – A Critical Policy Challenge. *Social Policy Studies*, no. 20. Paris.

1988. *Ageing Populations – The Social Policy Implications*. Paris.

Raffelhüschen, B. 1993. Funding Social Security through Pareto-optimal Conversion Policies. *Journal of Economics*, Suppl. 7:105–31.

1996. A Note on Measuring Intertemporal Redistribution in Generational Accounting. Discussion Paper of the Institute of Public Finance no. 53, University of Freiburg.

1997. Generational Accounting in Europe – Feasibility Study. Mimeo, Freiburg and Brussels.

1999a. Generational Accounting in Europe. *American Economic Review* 89:167–70.

1999b. Generational Accounting: Method, Data and Limitations. In European Commission (1999).

Raffelhüschen, B., and A. Risa. 1997. Generational Accounting and Intergenerational Welfare. *Public Choice* 93:149–63.

Raffelhüschen, B., and J. Walliser. 1999. Unification and Aging: Who Pays and When? In A. Auerbach, L. Kotlikoff, and W. Leibfritz (eds.), *Generational Accounting around the World*. NBER series. Chicago: University of Chicago Press.

Schnabel, R. 1998. Rates of Return of the German Pay-As-You-Go System, Working Paper, 2/98, Department of Economics, University of Mannheim.

CHAPTER 6-1

Comment

DAVID N. WEIL

This is an interesting chapter to read, in part because it is so full of data and in part because reading about the fiscal/demographic mess in Europe makes me feel happier to be an American.

As one reads the chapter, it becomes clear that it is built on a huge base of data and analysis. Thousands of person-hours went into analyzing micro data and producing the generational accounts for each country that are summarized here. As in Chapter 5, by Jonathan Gruber and David Wise, the author of this chapter expended great effort in enforcing uniformity in the construction of individual country accounts, and we readers are able to reap the benefits.

I will begin by quickly reviewing the idea of generational accounts, before turning to some issues in their interpretation. The starting point for the analysis is to think about an individual's fiscal dealings with the government over the course of her life. The taxes that she pays and the transfers that she receives are the relatively easy flows to measure. An immediate complication arises, however, over how to deal with government spending other than transfers – in other words, with purchases. The approach taken here is to divide these purchases evenly over the entire population (i.e., not to try to allocate purchases by different age groups). Thus in this chapter, "transfers" include all government spending.

Once an individual's life has ended, we could imagine looking back at all of the taxes that she paid less transfers received and discounting these back to the time of her birth. This discounted sum, for the average individual in a birth cohort, is the generational account for that cohort. If it is negative, it means that the individual has received more from the government than she has paid in; if it is positive, it means that she has paid more than she has received.[1]

Generational accounts in this sense can only be measured ex post. The goal of this literature, however, is to create a measure of fiscal policy that can be calculated now. The starting point here is the cross-sectional profile of taxes and transfers, calculated from a combination of government accounts and micro data. Under the assumption that these profiles will remain unchanged, we can calculate the generational accounts for those currently alive as well as for those yet unborn.

Assuming that the cross-sectional tax and transfer profiles will remain unchanged raises a problem, however: running policy forward, the government's deficits are unsustainable. Thus, either taxes or transfers will have to be adjusted in the future to restore balance. In principle, any aspect of taxes or transfers could be changed to restore sustainability. In this chapter, it is assumed that only taxes will be adjusted and that the adjustment will be uniform in two senses: first, all tax rates will be adjusted by the same percentage; and second, the adjustment will be the same in all future years and will begin right away (although it will apply only to unborn generations – see below). The parameter γ that is calculated in the chapter is the size of the adjustment that will be required. For example, for Europe, on average, taxes will have to be adjusted upward by 4.4% of GDP in order to restore sustainability.

Once future taxes have been adjusted by γ, we can calculate the generational account for each birth cohort. The most interesting comparison is between the accounts of newborns and the accounts of those who have yet to be born (under the assumptions of this chapter, the generational accounts of all future generations, relative to GDP, are the same). This change in the generational account, which averages 77,000 ECU, is a measure of the degree of fiscal imbalance – it shows us how much fiscal policy will have to change to restore balance.

Note that there is an odd quality to this sort of comparison. It is not a statement about predicted, likely, or even feasible future paths of

---

[1] Distributing expenditures by age is pretty dicey; and valuing the services the government provides at cost is not necessarily correct either, since the government wastes some of the money it spends, and in other cases purchases are worth far more to taxpayers than they cost the government. For this reason, the *level* of the generational account may not be that informative. We wouldn't want to say that a cohort with a positive generational account – that is, a cohort that pays in more to the government than it receives – would have been better off if the government had not existed! This problem of interpretation is mitigated when we look at the change in the generational account over time (i.e., was one birth cohort better served by its dealings with the government than another?), which is what this chapter focuses on.

policy. For example, the scenario that underlies the calculations assumes that those currently alive (including newborns) will live their whole lives under the current tax and transfer regime, while all those yet to be born (including those born in the next year) will live their whole lives under the new regime. It is hard to imagine that any tax system could impose this sort of cohort-based taxation, and it is a safe bet that none will. The calculation is also done under the assumption that fiscal authorities will immediately shift tax rates in such a way as to restore long-term balance. Sadly, this is also a low-odds proposition.

These considerations make the point that the change in the generational account calculated here is not meant to be a prediction about what actual generational accounts of future cohorts will look like – rather it is meant to be a summary measure of fiscal policy and how large a change would be required to put it onto a sustainable path.

Having set up this machinery, the chapter turns to the question of how population aging is affecting fiscal balance in Europe. I thought that this was a very interesting exercise. The strategy is simple: calculate the change in taxes required to restore sustainability under current demographic projections and then compare it to the change that would be required if the current age structure of the population remained unchanged. The result is that, on average, the adjustment in taxes under no demographic change would only be one-third as large as the adjustment under current projections – in other words, demographic change is producing two-thirds of the needed adjustment.

My one quibble with this exercise is the author's focus on using the size of the currently needed adjustment as a scaling measure. I would rather ask the simpler question, How large an effect is demographic change having on the fiscal situation?, without comparing it to some other problem.

Let me now turn to a few issues in interpreting the results.

1. Is generational balance a good thing? The author writes that "our results suggest that present fiscal policy is in a severe imbalance to the advantage of currently living generations." It sounds as if it would be better (or at least more just) if this weren't so. But to say things like that, we need to have a welfare criterion, which we don't have here.

A natural welfare criterion would look at utility from consumption – we might want to smooth consumption, utility, or marginal utility, depending on the setup used. But if we look at the forecasts underlying the calculations in this chapter, it is surely the case that consumption is still rising, even after future taxes have been raised. Thus, by this criterion, it might be the case that we are not shifting enough taxes to future generations. (If the model had an effect of tax distortions, this could conceivably not be the case: shifting too great a fiscal burden onto future generations could push them beyond the top of the Laffer curve. But in this chapter, future GDP growth is exogenous, so tax distortions are not present.)

2. Is it better to have a smaller γ (i.e., a smaller required increase in taxes to restore sustainability)? The answer is no, I think. This can be seen most easily by looking at the cases of Belgium and Finland. Belgium has one of the smallest required increases in taxes (0.6% of GDP), while Finland has the largest (8.8%). But look at the reason why: Belgium has an explicit debt of 120% of GDP, while Finland has positive net government asset holdings. As a result, Belgium is running large primary surpluses in order to pay interest on its debt, while Finland is running modest deficits. When we look at the cross-sectional profiles of taxes and transfers, Belgium looks like the more fiscally responsible country. But surely a country is in better fiscal shape that is not massively in debt to start with.

3. More generally, the cross-sections on which these accounts are based are full of things that we do not necessarily want to forecast far into the future. For example, if a country enacts a program of changes in its transfer schemes that phases in over time (as would be the case with most reforms of state pensions that one can imagine), this policy will not show up in the generational accounts calculated here. The day after the reform was enacted, the generational account would be just as far out of balance as the day before.

4. Finally, the results presented here take no account of any uncertainties, either in possible future outcomes or in the calculations themselves. As Lee and Tuljapurkar show in Chapter 2, there is a great deal of uncertainty in forecasts of straightforward measures of demographic structure. This, as well as uncertainties about income growth, spending, etc., should be reflected in generational accounts. One approach to starting to deal with uncertainty would be to calculate ex ante generational accounts for some earlier point in time – 1970, say – and then to see how they perform ex post.

In conclusion, I would like to go back to a bigger question: why is it that we want to do these assessments of fiscal policy? What is the usefulness of measuring generational accounts, or even the conventional debt, for that matter?

The answer is that we want to know how we are doing – whether we are living beyond our means, and whether it would be better to change policy now, rather than later, when it would be more painful to do so.

The problem is that the future is a big, uncertain mess. Results concerning fiscal stance are very sensitive to subtle assumptions. This makes it very hard to use future-looking measures to assess where we are now. Of course, more conventional measures, such as debt and deficit, are also possible to manipulate – witness the shenanigans that were pulled in order to satisfy the Maastricht criteria. But surely the scope for manipulating generational accounts is all the greater.

Let me end with a controversial thought (I'm not sure I believe this myself, but the discussant's job is to be controversial): would it really be so horrible if we based fiscal policy on more old-fashioned, possibly more robust measures, such as the debt/GDP ratio, rather than on forward-looking measures? Suppose that we went into the demographic shock of the aging of the baby boom (2010–30) with a fairly small debt/GDP ratio and didn't worry about the fact that generational accounts were unbalanced, implicit liabilities unfunded, etc.?

The view from the generational accounting literature is that if we did this, tragedy would ensue. But I don't buy this view. Yes, we would have to make larger adjustments in benefits and taxes than if we had started the adjustment earlier. But these adjustments would be easier to do in the face of actual circumstances than in the face of forecasts. That is, there would be far more political will to cut benefits in the face of an immediate rise in the payroll tax than there would be in the face of forecasted increases.

To put this point another way, implicit liabilities really are different from explicit liabilities. A proponent of generational accounting could point out that implicit liabilities are easier to renege on than explicit liabilities. In the United States, for example, the 1983 reforms of Social Security had huge effects on the generational accounts of birth cohorts, but hardly received the attention that would have been devoted to a writedown of the conventional debt. Thus, a proponent of generational accounts would argue, policy making will be much easier if we use this sort of measure to guide our decisions, rather than waiting until we are faced with unpayable explicit liabilities. On the other hand, generational accounts are much harder to observe and explain to voters, and much easier to manipulate, than are conventional measures of fiscal policy. These qualities diminish their usefulness as policy-making tools.

The aging of the baby boom is a big event. But it is not World War II and maybe not even the productivity slowdown. I would wager that in 2030, were we to reconvene this conference, there will have been some other economic event that overshadows population aging: global warming, a world financial meltdown, or a comet hitting the planet, for example. (Indeed, 25% of respondents to a recent Gallup/USA Today poll expect that aliens will have visited the planet by 2025.)

This wager suggests that we should be humble in our forecasts about the future and that we might want to extend this humility to constructing measures of fiscal policy that rely too much on knowledge about the future.

Comment

DAVID R. WEIR

This chapter summarizes the results of several individual country studies of the fiscal prospects for the countries of the European Community. A common methodology – generational accounting – was applied in each country study, resulting in a common set of measures about the burden current policy leaves for future generations and the importance of population aging in raising that burden. A synthesis such as this one does not provide the methodological details or breadth of sensitivity analyses that would allow a reader to evaluate the sensitivity of conclusions to assumptions used in the calculations. That is a substantial limitation when dealing with generational accounting, because the method is in general highly sensitive to assumptions. The benefit of synthesis is that it clearly distinguishes what is common to all the countries from what is unique to each.

The primary motivation for the use of generational accounting in this chapter is to measure the extent of long-run fiscal imbalance. Social insurance transfers resources from workers to retirees and therefore makes fiscal policy vulnerable to population aging. Generational accounting, as applied here, results in a measure of the increase in taxes needed to balance the government's long-run budget constraint. This measure of future tax burdens is adequate as an indicator of fiscal imbalance, but it should not be confused with two other types of intergenerational analyses.

One possible extension of generational accounting would be a study of the impact on different cohorts of well-specified changes in fiscal policy. Many different time paths for tax increases or benefit cuts could eliminate the long-term deficit equally well, but who bears most of the burden under each? A few examples of this type of analysis are given at the end of the chapter, with several policy options considered for

248

Germany. The analysis is limited, however, in being only forward-looking: it indicates how the future net taxes of cohorts will change, but does not consider past taxes and benefits to compare lifetime accounts of cohorts.

Moreover, even if lifetime net taxes are used, generational accounting is not a complete analysis of the relative well-being of different generations. Consider, for example, how World War II might have affected generational accounts. Allied governments borrowed heavily to finance the war, leaving future generations saddled with the burden of paying for it. Young men died, removing some of the largest positive generational accounts. Generational accounting makes no distinction between selfish indulgence and investments. Of course, the current fiscal plight of Western Europe owes little to wars fought for the future of democracy. Nevertheless, important investments in a better future, such as the costs of German unification, may justify a rising burden on future generations. Similarly, higher future tax rates on higher future levels of income may result in a more equitable distribution of after-tax income than would be the case if current generations paid the bill. Generational accounting examines only the distribution of taxes and benefits through fiscal policy.

In Chapter 5, Gruber and Wise compare many of the same European countries and show the close negative correlation across countries between effective tax rates on work after age 60 and labor force participation of older men. High effective tax rates come not from direct taxes on work, but rather from the disincentive effects of generous retirement systems, in which continuing employment means forgoing benefits and therefore reducing lifetime wealth. Countries with generous retirement systems are thus doubly vulnerable to population aging, because the labor force participation response to generous policies reinforces the size of transfers to the older population. Given this clear pattern, one might have expected to find that the countries identified by Gruber and Wise as having high effective tax rates and low labor force participation would also appear in a generational accounting as those with the most unbalanced long-term budgets. But that is not the case. Belgium and Italy have very generous retirement systems according to Gruber and Wise, but are in relatively good balance according to Raffelhüschen's generational accounting. Conversely, Sweden and the United Kingdom have very bad long-term public finance but have retirement systems with the fewest disincentives for work.

What does explain the rather substantial differences across European countries in generational accounting? Figure 6-2.1 shows the answer: when the long-term fiscal shortfall is measured by the percentage

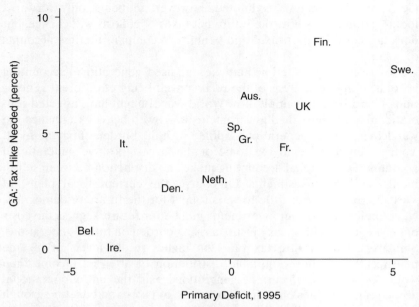

Figure 6-2.1. Long-Run Fiscal Imbalance and Current Deficits.

increase in taxes (on current and future generations) needed to balance the long-term budget, the best predictor of the size of the problem is the current primary deficit, that is, the extent to which current taxes cover current expenditures, excluding interest on the debt. Countries with the largest current deficits are also those with the largest long-run deficits. This is a useful reminder that not all problems of public finance are in the future; some are here and now.

Although it is somewhat surprising that cross-country differences in the generosity of retirement policy and in age at retirement are not stronger predictors of long-run fiscal problems, we should not overemphasize the importance of cross-sectional variation. Figure 6-2.1 also shows that all the countries face long-run deficits, whatever their current position. That is because all of them face the same set of demographic changes due to low fertility and increasing life expectancy. Because their demographic patterns are so similar, demographic change appears to explain little of the differences between them, even though it is the key factor behind long-run deficits in all the countries.

Demographic change accounts for two-thirds of the long-run deficit, according to the estimates in this chapter. That figure is based on a comparison of the baseline accounting using standard demographic

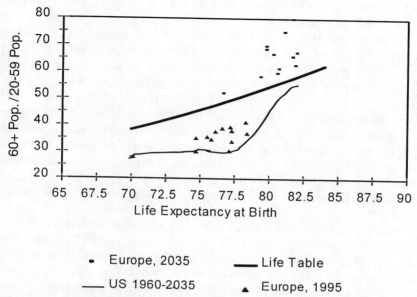

Figure 6-2.2. Elderly Dependency and Demographic Change in Europe and the United States.

projections with an alternative projection in which the age structure does not change. Another implication of the large difference between the two projections is that generational accounting estimates are highly sensitive to the demographic projections on which they are based. This suggests several directions for future development. Clearly a marriage of generational accounting with stochastic population projections (see Chapter 2, by Lee and Tuljapurkar) would provide a vehicle for assessing the range of possible fiscal futures.

Figure 6-2.2 provides a way to summarize the demographic changes in terms of their fiscal impact. The key variable for fiscal policy is the elderly dependency rate, shown on the vertical axis. It is determined partly by life expectancy, shown on the horizontal axis, and partly by past demographic forces, especially fertility. The solid black line shows the dependency rate that would prevail in a population that maintained exact replacement (zero population growth) at the given life expectancy. When fertility exceeds replacement, the dependency rate will be below the line. That is the case for all the European countries, as of about 1995, as it is for the United States. But most of Europe is substantially closer to the line than the United States, because the postwar baby boom was much less pronounced in Europe than in the United States. It is the large baby boom cohorts, now in their prime working years, that currently provide a favorable age structure.

Over the next forty years, both Europe and the United States will see elderly dependency rates rise. A part of that projected increase is due to rising life expectancies (horizontal movement), but the increase is much faster than gains in longevity alone would produce. In the case of the United States, the "birth dearth" of the 1960s and 1970s eliminates the baby boom "dividend" and will take the population close to replacement along the black line. In Europe, the situation is even worse. All the European countries are projected to land in the below-replacement range above the black line, where population dependency rates are even higher than would be expected given the life expectancy if fertility were at replacement levels. Low fertility is a big part of Europe's fiscal problems.

Because demographic change has such powerful influence on fiscal balance, a sound fiscal policy must encompass the policies that influence demographic behavior. In particular, fertility and migration have large consequences for the age structure of the population, and the policies that affect them cannot be isolated from their consequences. On the other hand, fertility should not be seen as a cure-all for the fiscal problems of an aging population. Raising children is also costly. The fact that a large share of those costs are borne privately, while the costs of aging are more visible on government accounts, could conceivably lead to distortionary policies, even if the public costs of education are included in the generational accounts. The use of generational accounting in this chapter clearly highlights the long-run fiscal problems of Western Europe and the role of demographic change in creating them. Finding solutions will be more difficult.

CHAPTER 7

Demographics and Medical Care Spending: Standard and Nonstandard Effects

DAVID M. CUTLER AND LOUISE SHEINER

It is a truism that demographic change will have major effects on the medical sector. Older people spend more on medical care than younger people, and the population will become increasingly aged over time. The share of the population over age 65, for example, is expected to nearly double by 2050, and the share of the population over age 85 is expected to more than triple. Even making the unrealistic assumption that medical costs increase at the rate of GDP, the increased age of the population alone will cause Medicare spending to nearly double as a share of the economy by 2050 and government nursing home spending to triple.

But a moment's thought demonstrates the difficulties with these conclusions. Clearly, medical spending rises with age. But why? Partly, the reason is that disability rises with age, and people who are disabled use more medical resources than people who are not disabled. If we are interested in understanding how demographic change will affect medical spending, therefore, we need to forecast the rate of disability in the economy. The simple projection described above assumed disability rates were constant by age, but substantial recent evidence (see Manton et al., 1997, and references cited therein) suggests that disability rates have been falling over time and are likely to continue falling in the future. Certainly, people are living longer than they used to, and thus fewer people at any one time will be in the position of requiring high-tech, high-cost end-of-life care.

Medical spending also depends on the age and sex distribution of the population. People living with others are less likely to enter a nursing home than people living alone. Thus medical spending in the future will depend on marriage rates among the elderly, the number of male and female elderly, and relationships between children and their parents. This too needs to be understood. And on top of these demographic changes are forecasts for increasing medical care costs holding constant health status. Growth of per person medical care costs at anywhere near its historical rate – nearly 2.5 percentage points above GDP growth – would send public medical costs through the roof. Of course, the increase in per person medical spending that we have witnessed is not an immutable law of nature. It is driven by technological change in medicine and depends on the rate of progress in medical technology and on how technologies are utilized.

The coming demographic change may well lead to increases in medical spending in the future, but the simple analysis commonly used to evaluate this question is not adequate to evaluate its magnitude or consider policy alternatives.

In this chapter, we examine the link between demographic change and medical spending and consider the implications of different policies to limit the fiscal consequences of aging. We show that demographic change will almost certainly lead to major increases in public spending on medical care, but the link is nowhere near as clear as conventional wisdom suggests. We begin with a simple decomposition. Average medical spending depends on the number of people of each age and average medical care utilization at each age. The age distribution of the population is largely determined by fertility and mortality rates,[1] and forecast changes in fertility and mortality clearly imply increased medical spending over time. The burden is further exacerbated because a smaller share of people will be working and paying taxes in the future, thus reducing the public revenues available to pay for increased medical costs.

Medical spending by age is more complicated, but also more important, since changes in age-specific medical spending have a substantively greater impact on future medical costs than do changes in the age distribution of the population. Forecasting age-specific medical spending is difficult. We consider first spending on acute medical care. We show that acute-care medical spending can be explained well by disability and proximity to death; once these factors are taken into account, age itself has a rather small effect. People use more services when they are disabled and in the period just before death. Since disability and death rates are falling, relative medical spending by age will likely flatten over time. Offsetting this, however, is the increase in spending for any level of disability and time until death. Over time, society spends more on a given health state than it did in the past. Forecasting the rate of this techno-

---

[1] Immigration also affects the age distribution, but to a smaller extent.

logical change is crucial, but not well understood. We present a range of arguments consistent with both a more rapid and a less rapid growth of health-specific spending in the future than in the recent past.

We then turn to long-term care. While long-term-care spending is small for the nation as a whole, it is large for the public sector; about 10 percent of public medical spending is devoted to nursing home care. Many of the issues relevant for acute care are also relevant for long-term care. As disability declines and people are farther away from death, the need for long-term care will fall. This will be offset by increased costs conditional on using services. But there is another important effect as well: the demand for formal long-term care depends on the availability of informal care (Lakdawalla and Philipson, 1998). Our analysis, however, shows that the availability of informal care is not likely to rise much – while mortality reductions mean that there will be fewer widowed spouses, the projections indicate that never having been married will also increase, leaving these elderly without spouses or children to care for them. If these projections are correct, then on net the availability of informal care will not change much.

On net, our results confirm the conventional wisdom – medical spending will almost certainly become more difficult to afford in the future. But many of the factors we identify will have important implications for the magnitude of the spending increase and for optimal policy design.

We use our results to briefly remark upon policy options for medical care reform. In contrast to the case of Social Security reform, we do not find a large effect of potential increases in the age of eligibility on the long-term ability to finance medical spending. This is partly because the oldest old spend much more on medical care than the youngest old, so that cutting off the youngest old from receiving benefits saves much less than the share of the young elderly in the elderly population, and partly because if the eligibility age is raised, many more people will likely qualify for Medicare under disability rules. Since medical spending is so skewed to high spenders, having even a fraction of the high spenders remain on the public rolls would eliminate much of the savings from increasing the eligibility age. We suggest instead that policy will need to focus on the *management* of medical care costs overall more than on the *distribution* of costs among different participants.

The chapter is structured as follows. In the first section, we review basic factors affecting medical spending over time: demographic change and per person medical costs. In the second section, we consider trends in the health of the elderly. We show that by essentially all measures, the elderly are healthier than they used to be. The third and fourth sections then examine the factors predicting changes in acute medical spending and

Table 7.1. *Forecast Changes in Demographics and Medical Spending by Age*

Age	Population Distribution, 1990 (%)	Population Distribution, Projection to 2050 (%)			Medical Spending, 1987 ($ per capita)	
		Low	Intermediate	High	Total	Public
<20	28.9	27.3	23.2	18.9	745	198
20–64	58.8	55.6	55.6	55.8	1,535	395
65+	12.3	17.0	20.8	25.3	5,360	3,356
65–69	4.0	4.8	5.4	6.0	3,728	2,298
70–74	3.1	3.9	4.4	5.1	4,424	2,860
75–79	2.4	3.2	3.8	4.5	5,455	3,612
80–84	1.5	2.5	3.1	3.9	6,717	4,384
85+	1.3	2.7	4.0	5.8	9,178	5,547

Sources: Population forecasts are from the Social Security Administration. Medical spending forecasts are authors' calculations.

long-term-care spending in the future. The fifth section considers potential policy responses to demographic change. The last section sums up our conclusions.

A Framework for Analysis

We start off with a basic framework for evaluating the role of demographic change in affecting medical spending. We denote the number of people in age group a in year t as $N_a(t)$. The average health status of people in age group a in year t is $h_a(t)$, and the average medical spending conditional on health status is $m_a(t)$. For the population, medical spending is therefore given by

$$\text{Medical Spending } (t) = \sum_a m_a(t) \cdot h_a(t) \cdot N_a(t). \qquad (1)$$

In equation (1), medical spending may be total medical costs, in which case this is spending for the population as a whole, or it may be spending by the public sector, in which case it is per person public medical spending. We focus particularly on public spending through Medicare and Medicaid.

Each of the three factors in medical spending – spending conditional on health, the average health of different age groups, and the age distribution of the population – will change over time. Table 7.1 shows information about population change through the middle of the next century. The elderly currently represent about 12 percent of the population. According to Social Security projections – used also by the actuaries of the Medicare Trust Funds – this share is expected to almost double by 2050, to 21 percent of the population. Even under the low, or optimistic, scenario, the share of the population that is elderly increases to 17 percent. The high, or pessimistic, scenario, which many researchers have identified as more likely than the intermediate scenario, has an elderly share of the population of 26 percent in 2050.

Furthermore, the average age of the elderly is increasing, as the ranks of the oldest old (those 85 and over, for example) are growing the fastest. Indeed, as Table 7.1 shows, under the intermediate assumptions, the population aged 85 and over more than triples – going from just 1.3 percent of the population in 1990 to about 4 percent in 2050.

Forecasting the first two terms – average medical spending conditional on health status and the average health of the population – is more difficult. The first term, expenditures given health status, depends on relative prices, relative intensity of treatment, and the state of medical technology. The second term is related to the needs of the population.

Official HCFA Projections

Actuaries at the Health Care Financing Administration (HCFA) forecast Medicare spending for the Board of Trustees of the Federal Hospital Insurance (Medicare Part A, or inpatient services) and the Federal Supplementary Medical Insurance (Medicare Part B, or outpatient services) Trust Funds. The trustees issue a report on the financial health of the trust funds each year. In their most recent reports, they make the following assumptions.

Expenditures Given Health Status

For the short run, HCFA uses recent trends in Medicare spending and legislative changes enacted in the Balanced Budget Act of 1997 to forecast the growth of spending given health status. For the longer run, it assumes that spending growth, given health status, stabilizes. In particular, it assumes that for Medicare Part A, spending per unit of service grows at the rate of average hourly earnings. For Part B, it assumes that spending per enrollee grows at the rate of per capita GDP.[2]

---

[2] This difference is attributable to the different funding mechanisms of the two programs. Part A is funded through a payroll tax, so in the absence of demographic changes, growth according to wages could be financed with a constant tax rate. By contrast, Part B is financed out of general revenues, so using the growth of GDP is more natural.

Figure 7.1 shows the difficulty of this projection. The figure shows the growth rate of real medical spending in different decades from 1929 to the present.[3] Growth rates were relatively low in the pre–World War II era, increased rapidly from 1950 through 1990 and then slowed in the 1990s. On average, medical spending growth has exceeded income growth by 2.5 percent per year, although at particular points the gap has been much smaller (1.0 percentage point in the 1990s), as well as much larger (4.0 percentage points in the 1960s).

Health Status of the Population
HCFA does not explicitly forecast the health of the population, but does so implicitly. For Part A services, the actuaries assume that health needs are constant across age and sex. This effectively means that medical needs change only as the population changes.

The last two columns of Table 7.1 show the consequences of this assumption. Medical spending is highly skewed to older ages. The average person over age 65 spends 3.5 times as much on medical care as the average working-age person. And the oldest elderly (age 85+) spend six times the amount spent by the working-age population. As the last column shows, the disparity is even greater for public medical spending. Thanks to generous Medicare and Medicaid benefits, the average elderly person spends more than 8.5 times more of public dollars on medical care than the average working-age person. The ratio is 14:1 for the oldest elderly.

For Part B, the actuaries assume that needs are constant over time (for example, without even any adjustment for age and sex composition changes). This is somewhat puzzling, since outpatient service use does increase with age. Within the current framework, adding an adjustment for differential service use by age seems natural.

Projected Growth
Figure 7.2 presents projections of Medicare spending using the Trustees' projections. The upper panel shows the growth of total real Medicare spending; the lower panel shows Medicare as a share of GDP. The Trustees forecast that Medicare spending will rise from its current 2.5 percent of GDP to nearly 6.5 percent of GDP by the middle of the next century.

The projections assume a reduction in Medicare spending growth over the next few years, stemming from the provisions of the Balanced Budget Act of 1997, which cut Medicare substantially in the short term. After

---

[3] This is not adjusted for changes in the health status of the population. There is no commonly accepted set of adjustments for this.

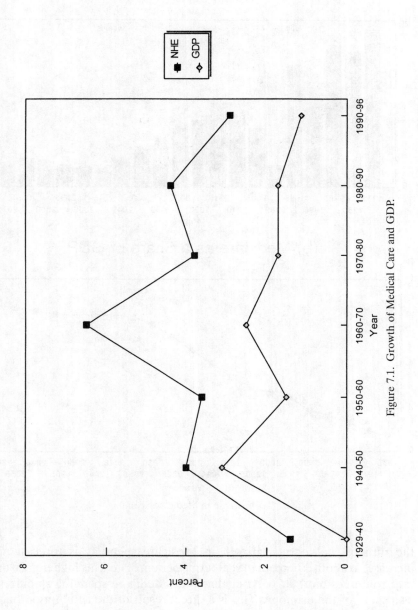

Figure 7.1. Growth of Medical Care and GDP.

259

(a) Growth of Real Medicare Spending

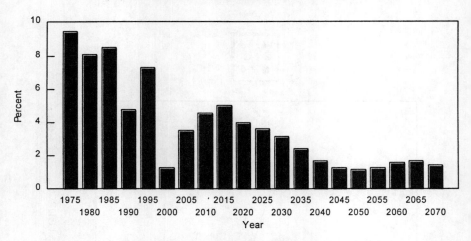

(b) Medicare as a Share of GDP

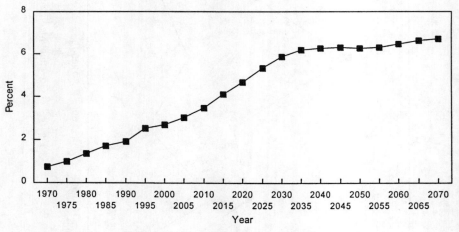

Figure 7.2. Increase in Medicare Spending.

the turn of the century, growth in Medicare spending is forecast to increase, to about 3 percent in real terms per enrollee. This higher growth rate continues until 2020. After that year, Medicare spending stabilizes as a share of the economy. This is a direct result of the assumption that spending per enrollee increases at the rate of wage growth (Part A) or GDP growth (Part B).

Table 7.2. *Share of Marginal Survivors by Age*

| Mortality Structure in: | % in Age Group Alive in 1990 Who Would Have Been Dead under Mortality Rates of Indicated Year | | | |
	65+	65–74	75–84	85+
1960	23	14	25	49
1970	18	12	20	35
1980	6	4	7	12

Source: Based on Social Security Life Tables.

The Health of the Elderly

As noted above, a crucial issue in forecasting medical spending is forecasting changes in the health of the population. The most important health issues affecting medical spending concern the elderly. Before considering alternative projections, we first discuss evidence on trends in the health of the elderly population.

The starting point in evaluating the health of the elderly is the decline in mortality over time. An individual born in 1960, according to the cross-sectional mortality profile for that year, had a 71 percent chance of reaching age 65;[4] the same person born in 1990, according to the 1990 mortality profile, had a 90 percent chance of reaching age 65. Changes in mortality within the elderly population have been even more dramatic. A person reaching age 65 in 1960 had a 26 percent chance of surviving to age 85. A person reaching the same age in 1990 had a 38 percent chance of surviving to age 85.

Table 7.2 shows the magnitude of survival improvements another way. We calculate the share of "marginal" survivors in 1990 in comparison to 1960, 1970, and 1980. The first column of the table, for example, shows the share of the 65+ population alive in 1990 who would not have been alive under the mortality rates prevailing in 1960, 1970, or 1980. The share of marginal survivors ranges from 6 percent in relation to 1980 to 23 percent in relation to 1960. As the second through fourth columns show, the share of marginal survivors is substantially greater at older ages. Half of the population age 85 and older that was alive in 1990 would not have been alive under the mortality structure prevailing in 1960.

---

[4] That is, having the period life table from 1960. This is not the same as the cohort life table for people born in 1960 or earlier.

Table 7.3. *Percentage of Elderly in Last Year of Life*

Age	1990	2010	2030	2050	2070
65+	5.0	5.0	4.2	4.7	4.4
65–69	2.3	2.0	1.8	1.7	1.5
70–74	3.3	3.0	2.7	2.5	2.3
75–79	5.0	4.6	4.1	3.8	3.5
80–84	7.6	6.9	6.2	5.7	5.2
85–89	11.5	10.6	9.5	8.7	7.9
90–94	17.5	16.2	14.5	13.2	12.0
95 +	27.0	25.3	23.1	20.2	19.3
Average Age at Death	79.5	81.1	80.1	83.1	83.5

Source: Data based on Social Security life tables.

The period just before death is generally one of high disability. Medicare spending, for example, is seven times greater for those in the last year of life than for those who are not in the last year of life (Lubitz and Riley, 1993).[5] As the population lives longer, changes in the share of people in the last year of life will change disability rates. Table 7.3 reports the probabilities that a person is in the last year of life between 1990 and 2070 based on Social Security mortality assumptions. For each age group, the probability of being in the last year of life declines substantially over the projection horizon. Among people age 85–89, for example, the probability of dying within a year falls from 11.5 per cent to 7.9 per cent, a one-third reduction.

For Medicare as a whole, however, the changes are more muted. When younger people do not die, they become older people, for whom the probability of death is greater. Between 1990 and 2030, the percentage of all Medicare beneficiaries in their last year of life declines from about 5 per cent to 4.2 per cent. After 2030, the fraction of Medicare beneficiaries in their last year of life begins to climb again, as the baby boom population moves into its 80s and 90s.

Increasing longevity may have other effects on the health of the elderly population, however, beyond its implications for the share of people near death.[6] The increasing importance of marginal survivors at older ages has led some to predict that the health of the surviving pop-

---

[5] Put another way, the 5 percent of Medicare beneficiaries who die in any year use 30 percent of all Medicare resources.

[6] Poterba and Summers (1982) present a detailed discussion of changes in the frailty of the surviving population.

ulation is worse. Suppose, for example, that treatment for people who have had a stroke improves, so that more people survive a stroke than did in the past. This would increase the share of marginal survivors in the population but create additional medical needs for those alive. Stroke survivors need acute services, rehabilitation care, and frequently long-term care as well. If there are more marginal stroke survivors with high medical needs, the health of the living population would, on average, decline, even as longevity improved.

But there are other scenarios about the relation between longevity and medical care needs. To use the stroke example, one alternative scenario is that the incidence of strokes is falling over time, so more people are surviving to older ages without any debilitating condition. In the case of cardiovascular disease, better prescription drugs (such as antihypertensives) and improved behavioral factors (better exercise, reduced smoking, reduced salt intake) have all reduced the risk of a major cardiovascular disease incident. Estrogen replacement therapy and increased attentiveness to physical surroundings may reduce the risk of hip fractures.

Health may also improve because we are better at caring for people after disease, so that those who survive are in better health. The improvement in health among those who would have survived the disease in all time periods may then outweigh any reductions in health from more marginal survivors. Changes in medical practice have almost certainly had this effect. In the case of cardiovascular disease, thrombolytic therapy delivered soon after an acute incident dramatically reduces the adverse consequences. Thrombolytic therapy was unknown in 1960 but was used commonly in 1990. Improvements in physical or occupational therapy have the same effect: they improve the health of survivors. And behavioral factors, such as reduced salt and antihypertensive therapy, even as they prevent cardiovascular illness, also reduce its adverse consequences when it occurs.

Whether, on net, increases in longevity are associated with improvements or reductions in average health is therefore an empirical question. We present evidence on this question here, although readers interested in more detail might examine a wealth of recent papers (for example, Fries, 1989; Manton et al., 1997; Hoffman et al., 1996; Vita et al., 1998; Fries et al., 1993). Some first evidence on this question is provided by the recent history of mortality reduction. As Figure 7.3 shows, the dominant source of improved longevity in the past thirty years has been reductions in cardiovascular disease mortality – deaths from coronary heart disease and cerebrovascular disease (stroke). Mortality from these sources has fallen nearly 3 percent annually since the late 1960s.

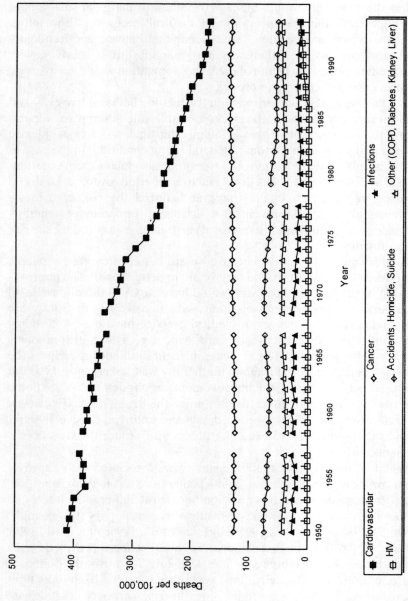

Figure 7.3. Mortality by Cause of Death, 1950–94. *Source:* National Center for Health Statistics, unpublished data.

Several papers have analyzed the sources of the reduction in coronary heart disease (CHD) mortality, a major source of cardiovascular disease death. Roughly one-third of the reduction in CHD mortality is attributable to reduced incidence of CHD (primary prevention). CHD incidence has fallen about 1 percent per year in the past three decades (Sytkowski et al., 1990; Sempos et al., 1988; Hunink et al., 1997). Declines in disease incidence are almost certainly associated with increases in the average health of the surviving elderly population.

Survival after a CHD incident accounts for the remaining two-thirds of the improvement in CHD mortality. Increased survival after CHD is partly a result of improved acute treatment (for example, bypass surgery) and partly a result of better postacute treatment (secondary prevention). Secondary prevention generally included behavioral changes (reduced smoking, better exercise, reduced salt intake) and prescription drugs (antihypertensives, antilipidemics) that prevent long-term coronary damage and another serious incident. The role of acute treatment and secondary prevention in improved health likely varies over time. Older literature examining changes in CHD mortality in the late 1960s and 1970s found that secondary prevention was more important than acute treatment (Goldman and Cook, 1984), but more recent studies from the 1980s place more weight on intensive treatments (Hunink et al., 1997).

In all time periods, though, at least one-half, and perhaps as much as three-quarters, of the health improvement is a result of primary and secondary prevention, rather than advances in high-tech medicine. Increased prevention, both primary and secondary, almost certainly results in better health among the surviving population. Given the dominance of these factors in explaining improved health, we suspect that reduced mortality has not been accompanied by a less healthy surviving population.

There are some empirical data to back this up. Measuring "health," of course, is quite difficult, since health is a multi-attribute concept, with both physical and mental dimensions. As a result, there is no one summary measure that one can look at to examine changes in health. We therefore examine several measures of health among the elderly.[7]

Table 7.4 shows a first measure of health: how many restricted-activity days and bed days an average person had in the previous year. Data on restricted-activity days are available in the National Health Interview Surveys (NHIS) since 1969. We examine restricted-activity days at five-year intervals (1970, 1975, 1980, 1985, 1990, and 1995).

---

[7] Poterba and Summers (1982) discuss a number of different measures of disability.

Table 7.4. *Restricted-Activity Days among the Elderly*
(number of days)

Age	1970	1975	1980	1985	1990	1995
Restricted-activity days (past year)						
65+	33.1	39.2	40.7	32.4	32.3	33.2
65–74	29.2	35.9	37.0	29.2	27.5	29.4
75–84	37.7	43.1	45.1	36.0	37.2	37.3
85+	45.0	48.6	51.4	43.6	50.1	46.8
Bed days (past year)						
65+	13.7	14.4	14.1	14.7	14.2	13.5
65–74	11.1	12.3	11.8	12.2	11.4	11.3
75–84	15.4	16.1	15.8	16.5	16.3	15.5
85+	26.2	23.3	24.5	26.7	27.3	22.8

Sources: Data are based on the National Health Interview Survey. Survey years are a three-year window around the indicated year (for example, 1969–71 for 1970) except for 1995, which uses data from 1993–95.

Because the sample sizes are small for some of the demographic groups (particularly the oldest old), we pool three years of data for each estimate. For example, data for 1970 are formed by pooling data from the 1969, 1970, and 1971 surveys.[8]

We report restricted-activity days and bed days for the elderly population as a whole and for the population in different age groups. In each case, the data are standardized by age and sex. For example, the estimate of restricted-activity days for 65- to 74-year-olds is a weighted average of the rates for 65- to 69-year-old men and women and 70- to 74-year-old men and women.[9]

The average number of restricted-activity days for the elderly is relatively high: about 30 to 40 per year. The oldest elderly have more restricted-activity days than the younger elderly, but the difference is not very large. Examining the data over time shows a clear pattern. Over the 1970s, restricted-activity days increased. For the elderly as a whole, the number of restricted-activity days rose from an average of 33.1 in 1970 to 40.7 in 1980, or 2.0 percent annually. This is true for each subgroup of the population.

[8] Because the 1996 NHIS data are not available, the 1995 estimates are based on surveys in 1993, 1994, and 1995.
[9] The weights are the 1990 population in each age-sex group.

This increase in restricted-activity days was taken by many to be a sign that marginal survivors were reducing the health of the elderly population (for example, Crimmins et al., 1997). Some discussion in the early 1980s highlighted the difficult burdens this increase in the share of marginal survivors was likely to have for Medicare and for society. But others saw the change as a reporting phenomenon: people may have reported themselves in worse health, but underlying health might not have changed or might even have improved (Waidmann et al., 1995). One reason for this is that disability is a qualification element for several public programs, such as disability insurance or Supplemental Security Income. In addition, people might report more disability because they have been diagnosed with more diseases. People with scattered aches and pains may not report themselves as restricted in activity if they know that all elderly people feel similarly. But when doctors label the condition (for example, rheumatoid arthritis), people may come to believe they are restricted in activity because of a medical condition.[10]

This debate has been muted by the experience of the 1980s and 1990s, however. Since 1980, restricted activity days have fallen, by 1.3 percent per year, on average. The decline was for all age groups. Whatever one believes about the 1970s, therefore, the data since 1980 clearly suggest health improvements among the elderly.

The bottom rows of Table 7.4 show trends in days in bed. Bed days rose from 1970 through 1985, at an annual rate of 0.5 percent. Since 1985, bed days have fallen by 0.8 percent per year. Again, the decline is common for all age groups. Unlike restricted-activity days, bed days declined rapidly in each of the two five-year intervals.

Table 7.5 examines whether the elderly can engage in "major activities," defined as working, keeping house, school, something else, or unknown. In the NHIS interviews, people are asked to categorize themselves as unable to perform their major activity, limited in the kind or amount of the major activity, limited in other activities but not their major activity or not limited. Consistent data on this question have been available since 1982. About 40 percent of the elderly have some limitations in activities, although for only 10 percent of the elderly does the limitation prevent them from performing their major activity. The share of the elderly limited in their major activity fell between 1985 and 1995, but the decline has been relatively modest −0.4 percent overall and

---

[10] In similar surveys, one finds that children in richer families have more chronic conditions than children in poorer families. This is almost certainly due to more frequent diagnosis and labeling of conditions among the children of rich families, rather than true increases in disability.

Table 7.5. *Ability to Perform Major Activity among the Elderly (percent)*

	1985	1990	1995
Ages 65+			
Unable to perform major activity	10.6	10.3	10.4
Limited in kind/amount of major activity	13.2	12.1	12.0
Limited in other activities	15.4	15.5	15.6
Not limited	60.7	62.1	62.1
Ages 65–74			
Unable to perform major activity	10.9	10.4	10.8
Limited in kind/amount of major activity	11.4	10.2	9.9
Limited in other activities	14.0	13.5	13.3
Not limited	63.7	65.9	66.0
Ages 75–84			
Unable to perform major activity	7.8	7.8	7.6
Limited in kind/amount of major activity	14.0	13.1	12.8
Limited in other activities	18.6	19.6	19.9
Not limited	59.6	59.5	59.7
Ages 85+			
Unable to perform major activity	19.6	19.6	18.7
Limited in kind/amount of major activity	24.6	22.9	24.4
Limited in other activities	13.6	14.0	15.6
Not limited	42.2	43.5	41.3

Note: Major activity is defined as one of the following: working; keeping house; school; something else; unknown.

Source: Data are from the National Health Interview Survey.

0.2 percent per year for those unable to perform their major activity. The declines are present for each of the age groups.

In addition to physical health, we also want to know about mental health. Unfortunately, the NHIS does not ask about mental functioning. But the survey does ask people to self-rate their health. Presumably, people consider their mental as well as physical health in answering such questions. Table 7.6 shows the self-reported health of the elderly. Prior to 1982, the choices were excellent, good, fair, or poor. After 1982, very good was added as an additional category. Because of this change, the share of people in excellent, very good, or good health cannot be reliably compared over time. But the share of people in fair or poor health can be determined. As the table shows, the share of people in fair or poor health has declined uniformly since 1975. In 1975, 32 percent of the

Table 7.6. *Self-Reported Health Status of the Elderly*
(percent)

	1975	1980	1985	1990	1995
Ages 65+					
Excellent	28.6	28.8	16.0	16.4	15.8
Very good	—	—	20.5	22.9	22.9
Good	39.4	40.1	32.3	32.2	33.3
Fair	22.8	22.4	20.9	19.1	19.0
Poor	9.3	8.6	10.4	9.3	8.9
Ages 65–74					
Excellent	29.0	29.0	17.0	18.0	17.0
Very good	—	—	20.9	24.0	23.8
Good	41.0	40.3	32.8	32.3	33.2
Fair	21.7	22.8	20.2	17.7	18.0
Poor	8.2	8.1	9.2	8.1	7.9
Ages 75–84					
Excellent	28.0	29.0	15.0	14.0	14.0
Very good	—	—	19.6	21.5	21.7
Good	40.0	39.8	31.9	32.6	33.6
Fair	22.5	22.6	22.0	21.2	20.6
Poor	9.6	9.0	12.0	10.5	10.3
Ages 85+					
Excellent	32.0	30.0	16.0	14.0	13.0
Very good	—	—	20.4	20.1	19.7
Good	39.9	39.9	29.6	30.6	32.1
Fair	18.7	19.2	21.4	21.1	22.5
Poor	9.7	11.3	12.9	14.0	12.7

Source: Data are from the National Health Interview Survey.

elderly were in fair or poor health; by 1995, the share was 28 percent, an 0.7 percent annual decline. The decline in the share of people in fair or good health has occurred only among the younger elderly population. The share in both fair and poor health has increased for the population age 85 and older.

A separate way to measure disability is to measure specific physical functions. Researchers have identified two types of impairments that indicate directly people's physical and mental activity: impairments in activities of daily living (ADLs), such as the ability to walk, dress, and bathe oneself; and impairments in instrumental activities of daily living (IADLs), such as the ability to cook, clean, or manage money. The

Table 7.7. *Disability Rates among the Elderly (percent)*

Age and Extent	1982	1984	1989	1994
All ages	24.9	24.9	23.3	21.3
IADLs	5.6	6.0	4.7	4.3
1–2 ADLs	6.6	6.7	6.5	5.9
3–4 ADLs	2.9	3.0	3.6	3.2
5–6 ADLs	3.6	3.3	2.8	2.8
Institutionalized	6.3	6.1	5.7	5.2
By age				
65–74	13.8	13.0	11.8	10.9
75–84	29.1	29.4	27.9	24.1
85+	61.9	63.9	59.8	56.6

Source: Data are from the National Long-Term Care Survey.

National Long Term Care Survey (NLTCS) has measured the rate of impairments in ADLs and IADLs since the early 1980s.

Table 7.7 shows changes in disability rates from this survey (taken from Manton et al., 1997). Disability fell substantially from 1982 through 1994, at a 1.3 percent annual rate. The decline in disability is more significant for the greatest levels of disability. Institutionalization rates, for example, fell by 1.6 percent annually, and the rate of very severe disability in the community (five to six ADLs) fell by 2.1 percent annually. The decline in disability also appears to have increased over time. The rate of disability decline was 1.3 percent between 1984 and 1989 and 1.8 percent between 1989 and 1994.

The evidence that disability rates were declining in the United States spurred efforts to examine this issue in other countries. Table 7.8 shows evidence on disability rates in other industrialized countries. The first four columns show rates of severe disability (usually three or more impairments in activities of daily living). The last three columns show institutionalization rates. In most countries, disability rates have been declining over time. The decline is only modest in some countries (for example, the United Kingdom) but is rapid in others (for example, Japan). The average rate of decline among countries where disability rates are falling is 2.3 percent per year. In only two countries have rates of severe disability increased (Australia and Canada), but in each of these countries the institutionalization rate is falling.

Institutionalization rates have been falling as well in four of the five countries for which there is time series data. The decline has generally

270

Table 7.8. *Disability Changes among the Elderly in OECD Countries (percent)*

Country	Years	Serious Disability Rate			Institutionalization Rate		
		Year 1	Year 2	Annual Change	Year 1	Year 2	Annual Change
U.S.	1982, 94	13.3	12.4	−0.6	5.7	5.1	−0.9
Australia	1985, 96	17.0	17.3	0.2	6.7	6.5	−0.3
Canada	1985, 91	9.3	10.4	1.9	7.8	7.6	−0.4
France	1990, 94	3.2	2.4	−7.2	6.3	6.5	0.8
Germany	1986, 95	25.0	19.5	−2.8	—	—	—
Japan	1989, 96	10.3	8.8	−2.2	7.5	5.1	−5.5
Sweden	1975, 95	22.0	18.0	−1.0	—	—	—
UK	1980, 94	8.8	8.7	−0.1	—	—	—

Source: OECD.

been less rapid than the decline in the rate of severe disability. The one exception is France, where institutionalization rates have been increasing. But this may just be a change in the location of care; rates of severe disability in France have been declining rapidly.

In total, the evidence clearly suggests that for the past fifteen to twenty years the health of the surviving elderly has improved. There is more debate about what was happening to health prior to that time.

In forecasting health status, we care not just about changes in the health of the elderly, but also about why health is improving. If disability declines are a result of increased medical spending, one would not want to forecast a reduction in medical spending resulting from declining disability without also factoring in the increase in medical care costs needed to produce the disability decline.

Over the span of the past few centuries, it is clear that high-tech medicine has *not* been the most important factor contributing to reduced disability. Factors such as income and nutrition (Fogel, 1994; McKeown, 1976), lifestyle changes, technology such as refrigeration (Manton et al., 1997), and public health (Preston, 1996) have been far more important than medical care in increasing longevity. These factors do not involve expensive medical interventions. More recent evidence, however, assigns a much greater role to high-tech medical interventions in improved health, at least as regards coronary heart disease. This argues that future improvements in health might require additional medical spending.

How much disability reduction in the past depended on medical spending and to what extent it will in the future are open questions. Researchers have not yet focused on the reasons for the reduction in disability, although Manton et al. (1997) speculate that reduced disability is more attributable to factors such as the spread of aspirin after a cardiovascular disease illness or estrogen replacement therapy for elderly women than to expensive medical interventions.

The potential for future reductions in risk factors, and thus reduced disability, is certainly large. Smoking rates are still high, particularly among the less educated; rates of obesity have been increasing; and high cholesterol is prevalent. In addition, many low-cost medical interventions – such as beta blockers after a heart attack – have not diffused widely. Thus, one scenario is that we will learn even more about medical risks, and the spread of knowledge about risk factors will lead to substantial disability reductions. An alternative scenario, however, is that the marginal product of risk factor reduction will decline, leading to a reduction in the "exogenous" component of disability decline. We consider both scenarios in our spending forecasts.

Demographics and Medical Care Spending

Forecasting Acute Care Medicare Spending

In this section, we examine how changes in disability and per person medical spending will affect Medicare spending on acute care services in the future.

Changes in the Age of Death

The first factor affecting medical spending is the increasing age of death. Increases in the age of death will have two effects on Medicare spending. First, fewer people will be in the last year of life, and people in the last year of life spend more on medical care than those further away from death. Thus, increases in the average age of death will increase the average healthiness of the population and thus reduce Medicare spending.

In addition, analysts have also noted another feature of Medicare spending: the older the beneficiary, the less Medicare spends in the last year of life (Lubitz et al., 1995). Table 7.9 shows data on spending in the last year of life, taken from Lubitz and Riley (1993). Spending in the last year of life averages about $15,500 for the young elderly (those age 65–74). Average spending then falls to about $13,000 for those age 80–84 and declines to below $9,000 for those age 90 and older. Spending among survivors, in contrast, is much more constant by age.

The reason for the change in end-of-life spending as people age is not entirely clear. It may be that providers are less likely to use aggressive medical technology on the very old. Alternatively, the very old might be more likely to die from "natural causes" than from debilitating disease.

Table 7.9. *Medicare Expenditures in Last Year of Life, 1988 (per capita dollars)*

Age at Death	Medicare Spending	
	Survivors	Decedents
65–69	1,455	15,436
70–74	1,845	15,778
75–79	2,176	14,902
80–84	2,403	12,838
85–89	2,578	11,422
90+	2,258	8,888

Source: Based on Lubitz and Riley (1993).

Table 7.10. *Annual Growth Rate of Real Medicare Spending by Age (percent)*

Age	1967–77	1977–82	1982–87	1987–92	1992–95
65–66	7.8	5.3	3.5	2.9	3.0
67–68	6.9	6.3	3.3	3.7	3.6
69–70	7.0	6.5	4.1	3.4	3.6
71–72	6.7	7.1	4.9	2.9	3.5
73–74	7.1	6.6	4.7	3.6	3.6
75–79	6.6	6.8	4.5	4.3	3.3
80–84	6.0	7.1	3.8	4.3	6.4
85+	5.5	6.4	3.9	4.8	7.4
Average	6.8	6.7	4.2	4.1	4.9

Source: Data are based on Medicare program statistics.

But if this trend continues, the gradual increase in the average age at death implicit in the Social Security assumptions means that costs associated with dying will decrease.

As the average age of death increases and as the health of the elderly increases, it is possible that the oldest old will be treated more aggressively in the future than in the past – muting if not eliminating this source of savings. For example, if 90-year-olds are not considered particularly infirm in the future, doctors may be more likely to use invasive technologies on this group than they might have been in the past.

Substantial changes in the distribution of medical spending by age have occurred in the past few decades. Cutler and Meara (1998) show that between 1963 and 1987 medical spending among the over-65 population rose by 8 percent per year in real, per person terms, compared to 5 percent for the population age 1–64.[11]

Changes in the age distribution of medical spending within the elderly population are more subtle. Table 7.10 shows the growth of real Medicare spending per person for different ages. Between 1967 and 1977, medical spending growth was more rapid for the younger elderly population than for the older elderly population. In the subsequent decade (1977–87), spending growth was relatively constant by age group, and in the following eight years (1987–95) growth rates were much greater for the older elderly population than for the younger elderly population.[12] This pattern is somewhat different than for medical spending as a whole, mea-

---

[11] Medical spending increased by 10 percent annually for infants.
[12] Fuchs (1998) has also shown that in this latter period increases in the use of technology were much greater for the oldest old than for the elderly as a whole.

Table 7.11. *Forecasts of Medicare Acute Care Expenditures,*
Accounting for Changes in Age at Death and Disability among
Survivors (dollars per beneficiary)

Simulation	1992	2010	2030	2050	2070
Forecast holding constant age-specific spending					
All	3,232	3,342	3,272	3,510	3,518
		[1.03]	[1.01]	[1.09]	[1.09]
Forecast accounting for change in age of death					
All	3,232	3,261	3,121	3,287	3,240
		[1.01]	[0.97]	[1.02]	[1.00]
Forecast accounting for change in age of death and allowing for reduction in disability among survivors					
1% annual reduction	3,234	3,138	2,903	2,947	2,825
		[0.97]	[0.90]	[0.91]	[0.87]
1.5% annual reduction	3,234	3,083	2,822	2,838	2,713
		[0.95]	[0.87]	[0.88]	[0.84]

Note: Numbers in brackets are the ratio to spending in 1992.

sured in repeated national medical expenditure surveys. Cutler and Meara (1998) show that medical spending growth during 1963–70 and again during 1970–77 was greater for the older elderly population than for the younger elderly population. It may be that out-of-pocket costs rose more rapidly for the older elderly than did Medicare costs.

Data on the share of Medicare spending in the last year of life suggest little change in this relationship over time. Lubitz and Riley (1993) show that payments for elderly Medicare beneficiaries in the last year of life represented 28.2 percent of Medicare payments in 1976, 30.8 percent in 1980, 27.4 percent in 1985, and 28.6 percent in 1988. In the absence of firm data on how Medicare cost growth will differ by age or time until death in the future, we assume that growth will be the same over time.

Table 7.11 shows how average Medicare spending per beneficiary will change with changes in the age of death. The first row of the table shows spending, assuming a constant profile of spending by age. This is the assumption that the Medicare Trustees make in their current projections (at least for inpatient spending). To focus on the health status issues exclusively, we assume no growth of real spending per person. As the population ages, projected spending rises, by 3 percent in 2010 and 9 percent in 2050.

The next row of the table shows alternative projections accounting for increases in the age of death. In this scenario, spending per person falls over time. Even though the average age of the elderly population is higher, fewer people are in the last year of life, and people who are in the last year of life are older and thus spend less. By 2010, costs are about 2 percent lower than they would be if mortality remained constant, and by 2050 they are 6 percent lower. The reductions in cost are roughly constant across age groups.

Changes in Disability Rates among Survivors

In addition to reduced disability because fewer people are near death, there may also be reduced disability among survivors. As noted above, disability rates have declined over time, at anywhere from 0.5 percent to 1.5 percent per year, depending on the measure and time period. An appropriate projection would account for continued changes in disability rates as well.

To examine the impact of potential changes in disability, we need to determine how much more care people with disabilities use than those without disabilities. Table 7.12 presents the results from a regression of Medicare expenditures on age and disability. We use data from the 1992 Medicare Current Beneficiary Survey. Since we have accounted for decedents separately, we include only those who did not die in either 1992 or 1993.[13]

The first column of the table shows average Medicare spending for survivors by age. Costs for the young elderly are about $1,850 per person. For the oldest elderly (age 85 and older), costs are $1,700 higher per year. The second column includes the number of ADL and IADL impairments for the individual. The number of impairments is measured in the last quarter of 1991, before any of the Medicare spending. Thus, problems of reverse causality between sickness, spending, and impairments are avoided.[14] The regressions show that a large part of the relationship between health costs and age is better attributable to the relationship between disability and age. Once disability is accounted for, the relationship between health expenditures and age is much weaker. For example, two-thirds of the effect of being over age 85 is accounted for

---

[13] People with a missing death code are eliminated from the sample.

[14] Imagine that older people get sick and spend more on medical care, but still develop a disability. A survey taken at the end of the year would find that disabled people spent more, and this would explain the age effect. By using disability measures at the beginning of the year, we avoid this situation.

Table 7.12. *Effect of Disability on Medicare Expenditures*

Independent Variable	(1)	(2)
Constant	1,848	1,357
	(159)	(163)
70–74	351	360
	(217)	(215)
75–79	698	560
	(236)	(234)
80–84	1,200	711
	(270)	(271)
85+	1,736	612
	(312)	(434)
Number of IADLS	—	252
		(69)
Number of ADLs	—	490
		(86)
N	6,913	6,913
R^2	0.006	0.03

Note: Numbers in parentheses are standard errors.

Source: Regressions use data from the Medicare Current Beneficiary Survey.

by disability instead of age. Indeed, medical spending for survivors, holding constant the level of disability, actually declines from ages 80–84 to ages 85+. The ADL and IADL coefficients, in contrast, are large. Every additional ADL increases average spending by $250 per year, and each additional IADL increases average spending by nearly $500 per year.

We use these results to simulate what would happen to survivor costs were disability to continue declining in the future. As a benchmark forecast, we assume that the average level of ADLs and IADLs will decline by 1 percent per year (forever). The regressions in Table 7.12 translate these changes into average spending per beneficiary. We then add our projections of Medicare expenditures in the last year of life to get an estimate of average Medicare expenses, per beneficiary, arising from changes in mortality and disability.

The third and fourth rows of Table 7.11 show these projections. Reductions in disability rates of 1 percent annually along with the increase in age at death would have a very large effect on Medicare spending. Average spending per person would decline by 3 percent by 2010 and by 13 percent by 2050. Recall that the naive forecast, holding constant age-specific disability rates, is for a 9 percent increase in spending by 2050, so that changes in health would have a cumulative effect of 22 percent on per beneficiary spending on medical care. If disability declines for survivors were 1.5 percent per year, average spending would be 16 percent lower by 2050.

Changes in Disability-Specific Spending

A third factor influencing costs is changes in spending per level of health – the first term in equation (1). Forecasting the rate of increase in disability-specific Medicare spending is hazardous. Five decades ago, when medical spending was 5 percent of GDP but beginning to rise, it was commonly assumed that it would not reach 10 percent. But it did. Two decades ago, when medical spending was 10 percent of GDP, it was commonly thought that spending could not reach 15 percent of GDP. It has. Today, it is common to assume that medical spending cannot continue to increase indefinitely at its current rate, as the Medicare Trustees do. But, of course, there is no reason it cannot.

More fundamentally, the question is not whether medical spending per person will increase, but what drives medical spending. A voluminous recent literature has examined the sources of increase in medical costs over time (see Cutler and Sheiner, 1998, for a review). The uniform conclusion is that medical spending increases are driven by changes in

Table 7.13. *Projected Growth in Medicare Spending under Two Assumptions (percent of GDP)*

	1992	2010	2030	2050	2070
Medicare costs grow with GDP per capita					
Holding constant age-specific spending	1.7	1.8	2.7	3.1	3.3
Accounting for change in age of death and					
1% reduction in disability	1.7	1.7	2.4	2.5	2.6
Medicare costs grow at historical rate of increase relative to GDP					
Holding constant age-specific spending	1.7	2.9	7.1	12.8	22.3
Accounting for change in age of death and					
1% reduction in disability	1.7	2.7	6.1	10.4	17.2

medical technology. As technology advances, people can be treated in increasingly sophisticated ways, increasing length or quality of life, but incurring substantial expense.

Thus, to address this question we need to forecast the rate of technological change in medicine. Difficult questions produce a multiplicity of answers, and this question is no exception. It is useful to think about this question by considering the process of treating disease.[15] A half-century ago, most diseases were untreatable. We did not know what caused them or what to do about them. Spending was low (although the morbidity costs of disease were high). As knowledge expands, the ability to treat disease improves. Initially, most treatments are curative – they treat people who have the disease, rather than prevent the disease from developing. An example is bypass surgery for heart attacks. Bypass surgery is designed to restore blood flow after a heart attack, not to prevent a heart attack from developing. Treating disease after it occurs is more expensive than not treating disease (although it may be a good use of money). The final stage is prevention. Prevention is typically cheaper than treatment on an average cost basis. For example, it is cheaper to give someone antihypertensive medication than to give the same person bypass surgery. But for the population as a whole, the cost issue is more difficult. Because prevention is generally given to many more people than treatment, the total costs of prevention may be greater. The additional spending on prevention, of course, may be worth the money.

Over the past half-century, many diseases have moved from untreatable to curable after the fact. Not surprisingly, this has come at substantial expense. One argument about future spending is that even more diseases will move from untreatable to treatable. For example, Alzheimer's disease is largely untreatable now, but may be treatable (at very high cost) in the near future. Mapping the genetic sequence promises to expand our range of knowledge about disease tremendously, with potentially large implications for costs.

A separate argument, however, is that as we make more fundamental advances in medical knowledge, we will be able to prevent more diseases from occurring, and this may reduce costs. For example, better antihypertensive medication over time has almost certainly contributed to the substantial reduction in coronary heart disease incidents in recent decades. Cost-effectiveness analyses generally suggest that preventive

---

[15] See Thomas (1976). Thomas refers to these situations as nontechnology, halfway technology, and high technology.

care for CHD is far more cost-effective than ex post treatment (Garber and Phelps, 1997; Meltzer, 1997).

The structure of the medical system will also play some role in the rate and composition of technological change in medicine. In the era of traditional indemnity insurance, the incentives favored technology that improved health, even if only marginally and at great additional expense. In the new, managed care era, there may be more emphasis on technologies that either save money or do not involve such large expenses. The rate of application of new technologies may also be curtailed by managed care. Cutler and Sheiner (1998) find some evidence that technology diffusion has been slowed by managed care.

It is clear that any forecast of growth in disability-specific medical care costs is perilous. Rather than make one assumption, we consider a number of alternatives. The first alternative, presented for convenience more than for projection accuracy, is that real per person medical care costs will not increase over time. This is the assumption embedded in Table 7.11. Our second assumption is that medical spending will increase in the future at the rate of GDP growth. This is consistent with the long-range assumptions made by the actuaries of the Medicare Trust Funds. The final assumption is that medical care costs will increase by 2.5 percent more than GDP growth, the average additional rate of increase in the post–World War II period.

Table 7.13 shows average medical spending as a share of GDP under the latter two assumptions. It is clear that increases in medical spending conditional on health status will have a substantial effect on overall Medicare costs. Even with a reduction in mortality and a 1 percent annual decline in disability, Medicare spending as a share of GDP would increase more than sixfold by 2050.

Just as we are uncertain about the future course of disability, we are also uncertain about the average rate of increase in medical spending over the next seventy-five years. The level of spending implied by the projections in Table 7.13 is extremely high, particularly in relation to historical government budgets. Some fundamental change in the medical system or in people's attitudes toward medical spending may occur before then.

Summary

Our results suggest that demographic and cost factors are both important in forecasts of acute care spending. A dominant role is clearly played by increasing costs per health state. But demographic change – most notably the potential for significant reductions in disability among the elderly and increasing life expectancy – are also important.

Nursing Home Use and Expenditures

A similar framework can be used to analyze the impact of changing demographics on nursing home use. Because nursing home use is much more common among the very old than among the younger aged, the aging of the population is expected to have a dramatic effect on nursing home use. But public attention to the nursing home problem has been much smaller. Only about 50 percent of nursing home costs are paid for by the public sector (mostly by Medicaid), and these funds are financed out of general revenue. Hence, there is no Trust Fund insolvency issue to concentrate attention.

The Determinants of Nursing Home Care

In order to project future nursing home use, it is important to determine which factors are associated with nursing home use. Once again, nursing home use increases with age, but why? The health status of the individual is clearly important, but so are other socioeconomic factors, such as sex, race, marital status, number and location of children, income, wealth, etc. We particularly focus on variables that are likely to change in the future – age, disability, marital status, and proximity to death.

Table 7.14 reports regression results from the 1992 Medicare Beneficiary Survey on the use of nursing home care. The first set of columns are for men, and the second set are for women. The first column of each set reports the results of a regression using only age group dummies as the independent variables. Nursing home use increases substantially with age, particularly for the 80–84 and 85+ age groups. The increase in nursing home utilization as one ages is 10 percentage points for men and 25 percentage points for women. That difference, combined with the larger number of elderly women than elderly men, implies that nursing home use is substantially concentrated among older women.

The second column of each set includes marital status variables. Because nursing home use is so much higher for those 85 and over, we allow the coefficient on marital status to differ for that age group. As the coefficients indicate, being unmarried (widowed, divorced, or never married), increases nursing home use substantially, particularly for those age 85 and over. The data set we use does not contain good information on whether people have children; we suspect that the much larger effect on nursing home use of never having been married than of being widowed or divorced is a proxy for the lack of children. Controlling for marital status substantially reduces, but does not eliminate, the effect of

Table 7.14. *Probability of Nursing Home Use*

Independent Variable	Men				Women			
	(1)	(2)	(3)	(4)	(5)	(6)	(7)	(8)
Constant	1.02	-0.12	-2.96	-3.07	0.83	-0.62	-4.42	-4.39
	(0.69)	(0.60)	(0.55)	(0.54)	(0.72)	(0.78)	(0.70)	(0.70)
70–74	0.49	0.71	0.55	0.49	0.89	0.77	0.84	0.70
	(0.82)	(0.80)	(0.71)	(0.71)	(0.97)	(0.97)	(0.84)	(0.84)
75–79	2.13	2.08	1.01	0.79	2.72	2.20	0.78	0.41
	(0.91)	(0.89)	(0.79)	(0.79)	(1.02)	(1.03)	(0.90)	(0.90)
80–84	6.43	6.46	2.91	2.53	9.62	8.61	4.45	4.01
	(1.07)	(1.04)	(0.94)	(0.95)	(1.12)	(1.16)	(1.02)	(1.02)
85+	10.39	5.02	-2.61	-3.18	26.35	17.45	-5.49	-6.05
	(1.29)	(1.61)	(1.66)	(1.66)	(1.17)	(3.19)	(2.91)	(2.89)
Divorced	—	1.49	0.62	0.63	—	2.83	0.38	0.48
		(1.58)	(1.1)	(1.13)		(1.45)	(1.27)	(1.26)
Divorced* Age 85+	—	8.84	15.28	1.59	—	0.73	-0.23	-0.62
		(2.53)	(5.46)	(5.45)		(6.01)	(5.24)	(5.21)
Widowed	—	2.74	0.15	0.03	—	2.70	1.30	1.15
		(1.26)	(0.88)	(0.87)		(0.80)	(0.70)	(0.70)

Widowed* Age 85+	—	17.35	3.89	3.67	—	8.15	0.77	0.47
		(6.08)	(2.31)	(2.31)		(3.35)	(2.93)	(2.91)
Never married	—	14.98	12.55	12.56	—	7.19	6.12	5.97
		(1.58)	(1.42)	(1.42)		(1.78)	(1.55)	(1.54)
Never married* Age 85+	—	26.0	19.07	19.23	—	13.45	3.15	2.82
		(5.93)	(5.35)	(5.33)		(5.12)	(4.48)	(4.45)
ADLS	—	—	1.62	1.60	—	—	1.69	1.54
			(0.33)	(0.33)			(0.33)	(0.33)
ADIS* Age 85+	—	—	1.79	1.68	—	—	2.35	2.28
			(0.90)	(0.90)			(0.67)	(0.67)
IADLs	—	—	3.53	3.37	—	—	3.19	3.05
			(0.27)	(0.27)			(0.27)	(0.27)
IADLs* Age 85+	—	—	-0.19	-0.11	—	—	4.17	4.09
			(0.72)	(0.72)			(0.57)	(0.56)
Within 1 year of death	—	—	—	4.14	—	—	—	8.18
				(0.92)				(1.05)
N	3,040	3,037	3,037	3,037	4,839	4,828	4,828	4,828
R^2	0.03	0.08	0.26	0.26	0.12	0.13	0.4	0.4

Note: Numbers in parentheses are standard errors.

Source: Data are from the Medicare Current Beneficiary Survey.

283

age on nursing home utilization. Additional utilization for the very elderly in these regressions is 5 and 17 percent.

The third column adds the number of ADLs and IADLs to the regressions. Both measures of disability are important predictors of nursing home use. For women, the impact of ADLs and IADLs is substantially larger for those 85 and over than for those below age 85. In general, including measures of disability reduces the impact of marital status on nursing home use. Indeed, for women, the effect of marital status in these regressions is generally not statistically significant.

The final columns include a variable for whether death is imminent, defined as within the next two years.[16] Impending death has a large effect on nursing home utilization. For men, being within two years of death raises nursing home use by about 4 percent; for women, the effect is larger, about 8 percent. Including proximity to death does not reduce the impact of ADLs and IADLs. Disability still has an important effect on nursing home utilization.

We use the regression coefficients to simulate nursing home use among the elderly in the future. The results are shown in Table 7.15. The first pair of rows in the table shows future nursing home utilization, assuming that rates of use remain constant by age and sex. This is the type of forecast that is most similar to current estimates of acute care spending in the Medicare Trust Funds. The effect of population aging is quite apparent. Average nursing home use increases between 1992 and 2010, reflecting the increasing share of those age 85 and over in the elderly population. Between 2010 and 2030, the share of those age 85 and over actually declines, leading to a decline in nursing home use back to the 1992 level. The rate of use climbs again to roughly 7 percent by 2050 and remains there.

The marital status of the elderly will change quite significantly over the next fifty years. Table 7.16 presents the Social Security Administration's marital status projections. Overall, marriage rates for men decline, by nearly 10 percentage points, while marriage rates for women rise, by about 6 percentage points. However, rates of marriage for those 85 and over increase for both men and women, as substantial declines in the rate of widowhood offset increases in the divorce rate. The fraction of the elderly who have never been married tends to increase over time.

We evaluate the importance of these changes in marital status by using the regression coefficients presented above. The second pair of

---

[16] Unfortunately, we cannot date the death exactly. For calendar year 1992, we know if the person died between September 1992 and March 1994.

Table 7.15. *Forecasts of Nursing Home Utilization, Accounting for Age at Death, Disability, and Changes in Demographics (percent)*

Simulation	1990	2010	2030	2050	2070
Forecast holding constant age- and sex-specific utilization					
Nursing home utilization rate	5.2	6.1	5.3	7.2	7.1
		[1.17]	[1.02]	[1.39]	[1.36]
Share of GDP accounted for	1.0	1.4	2.1	3.2	3.5
Forecast holding constant age-, sex-, and marital status–specific utilization					
Nursing home utilization rate	5.2	5.9	5.5	7.6	7.7
		[1.13]	[1.05]	[1.46]	[1.47]
Share of GDP accounted for	1.0	1.4	2.2	3.3	3.8
Forecast holding constant age-, sex-, and marital status–specific utilization, and allowing for 1% annual reduction in disability rate over time					
Nursing home utilization rate	5.2	4.5	3.6	4.1	3.4
		[0.87]	[0.68]	[0.78]	[0.65]
Share of GDP accounted for	1.0	1.0	1.4	1.8	1.7
Forecast holding constant age-, sex-, and marital status–specific utilization, and allowing for changes in disability over time and changes in time until death					
Nursing home utilization rate	5.2	4.3	2.8	3.3	2.5
		[0.83]	[0.55]	[0.63]	[0.48]
Share of GDP accounted for	1.0	1.0	1.1	1.4	1.2
Forecast holding constant age-, sex-, and marital status–specific utilization, and allowing for changes in disability and time until death and growth of nursing home costs at 4% per year					
Share of GDP accounted for	1.0	1.7	3.3	7.3	10.9

Note: Numbers in brackets are the ratio to spending in 1990.

rows in Table 7.15 shows the results. All told, these patterns do not have a substantial effect on nursing home use, as increases in marriage (which would reduce nursing home use) are offset by increases in the fraction of people never married (and hence the fraction with no children to take care of them). While the pattern varies over time, in general, changes in marital status slightly increase the likely rate of nursing home use.

The next pair of rows shows the effect of a 1 percent annual reduction in disability rates on nursing home utilization. If the trend toward reduced disability continues, it will substantially reduce the demand for nursing home care. Rather than nursing home use increasing to 7.1 percent by 2070, including the effects of marriage and disability leads to

Table 7.16. *Marital Status of Elderly Population*
(percent)

Marital Status	1990	2010	2030	2050	2070
Males 65+					
Married	74.1	73.0	68.9	65.9	65.5
Widowed	15.4	14.9	13.0	13.6	12.7
Divorced	5.0	7.3	9.5	8.5	8.5
Never married	5.5	4.8	8.6	11.9	13.3
Males 85+					
Married	45.5	54.2	55.3	51.4	52.7
Widowed	46.5	38.5	35.6	34.0	31.9
Divorced	2.8	4.7	6.7	8.5	7.9
Never married	5.2	2.6	2.4	6.0	7.6
Females 65+					
Married	39.7	41.4	44.8	41.9	43.5
Widowed	50.6	45.1	34.2	35.8	33.7
Divorced	4.2	9.1	14.9	13.8	13.4
Never married	5.5	4.4	6.1	8.5	9.4
Females 85+					
Married	13.4	13.3	15.4	17.1	17.9
Widowed	77.1	77.4	70.0	62.1	60.5
Divorced	3.0	4.6	10.8	14.8	13.5
Never married	6.5	4.7	3.8	6.0	8.1

Source: Based on Social Security Administration forecasts.

the conclusion that disability declines would reduce nursing home use to roughly half that level, or 3.4 percent in 2070. The reduction in nursing home utilization, relative to the first row in the table, is 71 percent. Even by 2010, the difference is substantial. Of course, it is not clear whether the recent trend of decreasing disability among the elderly will continue – particularly over 75 years. But if it does, these numbers suggest that the impact on nursing home use would be quite substantial.

The next pair of rows adds the effect of fewer elderly being near death and thus facing the infirmities of end-of-life care. Including changes in the share of elderly near the end of life also lowers our projections of nursing home use, particularly after several decades. By 2050, nursing home utilization would decline by over 50 percent, in comparison to the 35 percent increase in utilization in the baseline forecast. It is clear that accurately forecasting nursing home use in the future requires assumptions about utilization before death, and disability rates by age are very hard to forecast accurately.

Table 7.15 also shows the impact of these changes on the share of GDP accounted for by nursing home care. In the first four blocks of the table, we assume that the average price of nursing home care increases at the rate of GDP per capita. Assuming constant nursing home utilization by age and sex, the share of GDP accounted for by nursing home care will more than triple by 2050. Under the most optimistic scenario, of decreasing death and disability, the share barely climbs at all – ending up in 2070 only 20 percent above the level in 1992.

The last row of the table shows the important role that changes in the cost of a nursing home have on the estimates. Between 1965 and 1995, the cost of a day in a nursing home increased by about 4 percent annually, in real terms. In the last row of the table, we forecast nursing home spending, assuming this growth rate continues into the future. Under this scenario, nursing home costs increase from 1 percent of GDP in 1990 to 7.3 percent of GDP in 2050, even given the optimistic assumptions about mortality and disability.

In contrast to the case of acute care medicine, there is relatively little research on the factors explaining the growth in nursing home costs per day. Nursing homes are less technologically sophisticated than acute care hospitals, so one would imagine that technological change would have less of an effect on nursing home costs. But other factors, such as changes in the average sickness of the elderly in nursing homes, may be important. Understanding the reasons for the underlying growth in nursing home costs, as well as the likely future course of disability reductions and death, are important issues in medical forecasting.

Policy Options for Medicare Reform

Even under optimistic assumptions about reductions in disability and increases life expectancy, Medicare and Medicaid financing remains a significant burden for the public sector. Some reform of these programs will clearly be needed.

Current cost containment policies in these programs are not well designed for the long-term problems of the system. Over the past decade, cost reductions in Medicare and Medicaid have been achieved by reducing *prices paid* for services. For example, payments to hospitals for each admission have increased less rapidly than the growth of input prices would warrant. The same is true of payments to physicians. But as we noted above, the fundamental driver of medical care cost increases is increases in the *quantity* of services provided. Reductions in prices will never be sufficient to offset increases in the quantity of services over time.

Thus some alternate form of cost reduction is necessary. We do not discuss reform options in great detail here, but we do note a couple of issues on which our results have bearing. One common reform option is to increase the age of eligibility for Medicare benefits, along the lines of the scheduled increase in the Social Security normal retirement age. Our results suggest that the cost savings from such a policy would be smaller than for Social Security. There are two reasons for this. First, because medical costs increase with age, the young elderly use a smaller share of medical care services than the older elderly. As Table 7.17 shows, 30 percent of the elderly population are between ages 65 and 69, but that group accounts for only 22 percent of Medicare resources. The disparity in Medicaid resources is even greater, since the young elderly are much less likely to be in a nursing home than the old elderly.

Second, increasing the age of eligibility will almost certainly be offset at least partly by increased Medicare eligibility through disability.[17] Because medical care spending is so skewed – the top 10 percent of users age 65–69 account for three-quarters of Medicare spending in that age group (see Table 7.17) – even a moderate offset of increased disability for the very sick would substantially reduce the potential savings from increasing the age of Medicare eligibility.

Perhaps more important will be efforts to reduce overall medical care spending for the elderly population. As noted above, technological change in medical care is a key determinant of the long-term growth of medical care costs. One might thus evaluate policies in terms of their long-term impact on the diffusion of medical technology. For example, Cutler and Sheiner (1998) show that increases in managed care enrollment over time have reduced the rate of growth of medical spending, in part by reducing the diffusion of high-cost medical technology. In light of these results, it may be that policy should focus on the *management* of medical care more than on just the *division of costs* among different participants.

Conclusion

Medicare and Medicaid costs are extremely difficult to project. Expenditures in the future will depend on what happens to the underlying health of the elderly, what technologies will be available, and how the

---

[17] Currently, about 10 percent of Medicare enrollees receive coverage because they are disabled but not yet age 65.

Table 7.17. Distribution of Medicare Spending by Age, 1992

	Ages 65–69		Ages 70–74		Ages 75–79		Ages 80–84		Ages 85+	
	Mean	Cum. %	Mean	Cum. %	Mean	Cum. %	Mean	Cum. %	Mean	Cum. %
Share of population	29%		29%		19%		13%		12%	
Mean per capita spending	$2,250		$2,656		$3,253		$3,582		$4,325	
Share of total spending	22%		24%		21%		16%		17%	
Percentile										
Top 1 %	$58,740	27%	$52,646	21%	$60,996	20%	$53,317	15%	$61,866	15%
95–99th	19,840	62	22,054	54	24,301	49	24,539	42	27,155	40
90–94th	7,441	78	9,913	72	12,944	69	14,116	62	15,379	57
70–89th	1,917	95	2,882	94	3,894	93	5,227	91	7,091	90
50–70th	399	99	601	99	810	98	1,146	98	1,608	98
1st–50th	44	100	74	100	114	100	161	100	204	100

Source: Data are based on the Medicare Current Beneficiary Survey.

health care market is organized. In this chapter, we have taken a first step in evaluating how improvements in the health of the elderly could affect medical spending. Our analysis suggests that changes in the underlying health of the population can help restrain the growth of health care spending in the future, although they do not undo the effects of continued rapid growth in health costs. Our initial examination of Medicare spending over time suggests that there is no clear and consistent relationship between increases in overall health costs and changes in age-specific spending. Nonetheless, future technological advances could have differential effects on health spending by age group. We believe that this is an important topic for future research.

References

Crimmins, Eileen M., Yasuhiko Saito, and Sandra L. Reynolds. 1997. "Further Evidence on Recent Trends in the Prevalence and Incidence of Disability among Older Americans from Two Sources: The LSOA and the NHIS." *Journal of Gerontology: Social Sciences* 52B(2):S59–71.

Cutler, David, and Ellen Meara. 1998. "The Medical Costs of the Young and Old: A Forty Year Perspective." In David Wise, ed., *Frontiers in the Economics of Aging*. Chicago: University of Chicago Press.

Cutler, David, and Louise Sheiner. 1998. "Managed Care and the Growth of Medical Expenditures." In Alan Garber, ed., *Frontiers in Health Policy Research*, vol. 1. Cambridge, MA: MIT Press.

Fogel, Robert W. 1994. "Economic Growth, Population Theory, and Physiology: The Bearing of Long-Term Processes on the Making of Economic Policy." *American Economic Review* 84(3):369–95.

Fries, James F. 1989. "The Compression of Morbidity: Near of Far?" *Milbank Quarterly* 67:208–32.

Fries, James F., et al. 1993. "Reducing Health Care Costs by Reducing the Need and Demand for Medical Services." *New England Journal of Medicine.* 329(5): 321–25.

Fuchs, Victor. 1998. "Health Care for the Elderly: How Much? Who Will Pay for It?" NBER Working Paper 6755.

Garber, Alan M., and Charles E. Phelps. 1997. "Economic Foundations of Cost-Effectiveness Analysis." *Journal of Health Economics*, no. 1, 1–31.

Goldman, Lee, and E. Fran Cook. 1984. "The Decline in Ischemic Heart Disease Mortality Rates: An Analysis of the Comparative Effects of Medical Interventions and Changes in Lifestyle." *Annals of Internal Medicine* 101(6): 825–36.

Hoffman, Catherine, Dorothy Rice, and Hai-Yen Sung. 1996. "Persons with Chronic Conditions: Their Prevalence and Costs." *Journal of the American Medical Association* 276(18):1473–79.

Hunink, Maria G. M., et al. 1997. "The Recent Decline in Mortality from Coronary Heart Disease, 1980–1990: The Effect of Secular Trends in Risk Factors and Treatment." *Journal of the American Medical Association* 227(7):535–42.

Lakdawalla, Darius, and Tomas Philipson. 1998. "The Rise in Old Age Longevity and the Market for Long-Term Care." NBER Working Paper 6547.

Lubitz, James D., and Gerald F. Riley. 1993. "Trends in Medicare Payments in the Last Year of Life." *New England Journal of Medicine* 328:1092–96.

Lubitz, James, James Beebe, and Colin Baker. 1995. "Longevity and Medicare Expenditures." *New England Journal of Medicine* 332(15):999–1003.

Manton, Kenneth, Larry S. Corder, and Eric Stallard. 1997. "Chronic Disability Trends in Elderly United States Population: 1982–1994." *Proceedings of the National Academy of Sciences* 94:2593–98.

McKeown, Thomas. 1976. *The Modern Rise of Population*. New York: Academic Press.

Meltzer, David. 1997. "Accounting for Future Costs in Medical Cost-Effectiveness." *Journal of Health Economics* no. 1, 33–64.

Poterba, James, and Lawrence Summers. 1982. "Public Policy Implications of Declining Old Age Mortality." In Gary Burtless, ed., *Work, Health, and Income Among the Elderly*. Washington, DC: Brookings Institution.

Preston, Sam. 1996. "American Longevity: Past, Present, and Future." Syracuse University Center for Economic Policy Research Policy Brief.

Sempos, C., R. Cooper, M. G. Kovar, and M. McMillen. 1988. "Divergence of the Recent Trends in Coronary Mortality for the Four Major Race-Sex Groups in the United States." *American Journal of Public Health* 78(11):1422–27.

Sytkowski, P. A., W. B. Kannel, and R. B. D'Agostino. 1990. "Changes in Risk Factors and the Decline in Mortality from Cardiovascular Disease: The Framingham Heart Study." *New England Journal of Medicine* 322(23):1635–41.

Thomas, Lewis. 1975. "The Lives of a Cell: Notes of a Biology Watcher." New York: Bantam Books.

Vita, A. J., R. B. Terry, H. B. Hubert, and J. F. Fires. 1998. "Aging, Health Risks, and Cumulative Disability." *New England Journal of Medicine* 228:1035–41.

Waidmann, Timothy, John Bound, and Michael Schoenbaum. 1995. "The Illusion of Failure: Trends in the Self-Reported Health of the U.S. Elderly." *Milbank Quarterly* 73:253–87.

Comment

VICTOR R. FUCHS

This chapter is concerned with projecting medical care expenditures, especially expenditures on the elderly. I heartily approve of such concern. Within the next two decades, financing health care for the elderly is likely to pose a much greater national problem than "saving social security" (Fuchs 1999a, 1999b). Change in the age distribution of the elderly, the subject of the chapter, is one element in projecting future expenditures. The authors argue that the standard method of projection – based on cross-sectional age-specific expenditures – overstates future expenditure increases for two reasons: (1) improvement in age-specific health status (e.g., lower mortality) leads to lower age-specific expenditures; and (2) end-of-life costs tend to be lower at older ages.

The first point was made by Kenneth Manton (1982); he suggested: "As mortality rates decline at a given age, there would be some compensating decline in the rate of utilization of certain health services (e.g., nursing home care) before that age" (p. 205). I explored this question empirically (Fuchs, 1984) by noting that health care expenditures at any given age are very strongly related to survival status. (The authors' Table 7.9 shows that survival status is a much stronger predictor of expenditures than age per se.)

If age-specific expenditures are adjusted for age-specific survival status, the tendency for expenditures to rise monotonically with age disappears, as can be seen in Table 7-1.1.[1] The quantitative importance of

---

[1] The adjustment was made by a method analogous to the indirect method of calculating age-adjusted death rates. I assume that each person's expenditures depended only on that person's survival status, using three categories: last year of life, next-to-last year of life, and "survivor." I estimate a "predicted" expenditure for each age group by multiplying the proportion in each survival status by the all-group average expenditure for each survival status and summing across the three statuses. The higher the death rate of

Comment

Table 7-1.1. *Reimbursement per Medicare Enrollee by Age, 1976 (dollars)*

	Actual	Adjusted for Survival Status
Age		
67–78	518	624
69–70	555	649
71–72	603	679
73–74	657	712
75–79	736	732
85+	866	595

Source: Health Care Financing Administration (1982). Adjusted expenditures calculated by Fuchs.

Table 7-1.2. *Effect of Change in Age Distribution of Medicare Enrollees on Reimbursement per Enrollee, 1975–95 (percent per annum)*

	"Standard" Method	"Nonstandard" Method
Reimbursement per aged enrollee (in constant dollars)	5.21	5.21
Change in age distribution	0.13	
Change in age distribution adjusted for survival status		0.01

Sources: Reimbursement values from Health Care Financing Review, Medicare and Medicaid Statistical Supplement, 1997, deflated by the GDP deflator. Age distribution change based on column 1, Table 7-1.1. Adjusted age distribution change based on column 2, Table 7-1.1.

this adjustment, however, is very small, at least for the period 1975–95. Table 7-1.2 shows that the effect of changes in age distribution estimated from the actual cross-sectional age pattern (column 1 of Table 7-1.1) was 0.13 percent per annum. When the cross-sectional pattern is adjusted for survival status (column 2 of Table 7-1.1), the effect falls to 0.01 percent per annum. The difference is of little consequence, however, when compared with the rate of change of age-specific expenditures of over 5.0 percent per annum. Additional adjustment for any age-specific

the group, the higher would be its predicted expenditures. The ratio of actual to predicted expenditures for an age group tells us whether expenditures are relatively high or low after adjusting for its death rate. This ratio multiplied by the average expenditure for all groups yields the adjusted expenditure for the group.

differences in disability that are independent of changes in survival status might modestly increase the difference between the "standard" and "nonstandard" methods, but the accuracy of future projections will depend much more on better estimates of trends in age-specific expenditures than on fine-tuning the age distribution adjustment. Moreover, the "nonstandard" approaches have problems of their own.

Neither the authors' criticism of the "standard" method nor the calculations presented in Tables 7.1 and 7.2 are truly dynamic – they fail to take into account how changes in age-specific survival status can affect physician and patient decisions regarding medical interventions. Although medical care utilization is usually positively associated with poor health, among the elderly the reverse relationship sometimes obtains. There are many interventions, particularly major surgical procedures, that would not be undertaken on elderly patients in poor health but would be undertaken if the patient were in good health.[2]

Furthermore, as reduction in age-specific mortality changes the age distribution of the population, there are likely to be feedback effects on the focus of medical R&D. An increase in the number of elderly will induce more R&D directed toward the health problems of aging; the result is likely to be higher expenditures per person than would be predicted from either standard or nonstandard models. It is clear from Figure 7-1.1 that expenditures between 1987 and 1995 rose more rapidly at older ages.

A dynamic view of the determinants of age-specific expenditures also raises questions about the authors' second point, namely, that end-of-life costs are lower at older ages. Cutler and Sheiner interpret their Table 7.9 as saying that expenditures in the last year of life are negatively correlated with age (i.e., years since birth). The same data could be read as saying that expenditures in the last year of life are positively correlated with life expectancy (i.e., years until death). In 1988 life expectancy at ages 65–69 was approximately 15.2 years; at ages 90–94, it was approximately 3.6 years. Indeed, if we divide per person expenditures on decedents by life expectancy, we find that those expenditures per year of life remaining rise with age, from $1,016 at ages 65–69 to $2,469 at ages 90–94.[3]

These calculations suggest that as age-specific mortality declines, the age pattern of expenditures per decedent that is observed in cross-

---

[2] Patients with chronic problems of the lungs, kidneys, liver, or other major organs are usually considered poor candidates for hip and knee replacements, abdominal surgery, and many cardiovascular procedures.

[3] The figure for 90–94 is an underestimate because I used the authors' data for 90+.

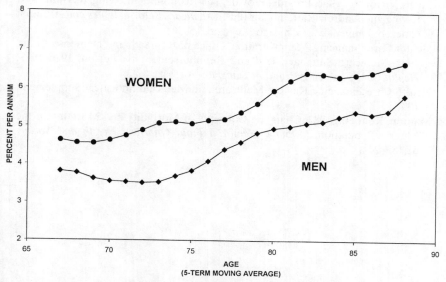

Figure 7-1.1. Annual Rate of Change in Medicare Payments per Person by Age and Sex, 1987–95. *Source*: Fuchs, 1999b.

section will probably also change. In one brief paragraph, the authors make note of this possibility but nevertheless conclude that costs associated with dying will decrease. This is far from certain. When life expectancy at age 90 is only a few years, it is not surprising to observe that medical care expenditures on 90-year-olds in the last year of life are rather modest. If, however, life expectancy at 90 were to increase to ten years, we could confidently expect that expenditures for 90-year-olds in the last year of life would be considerably greater.

I hope this chapter will stimulate badly needed research on *all* the determinants of changes in health care expenditures on the elderly, including health status, technological innovations, and insurance coverage.

References

Fuchs, Victor R. 1984. "Though Much Is Taken": Reflections on Aging, Health, and Medical Care. *Milbank Memorial Fund Quarterly/Health and Society* 62:143–66.

Fuchs, Victor R. 1999a. Health Care for the Elderly: How Much? Who Will Pay for It? *Health Affairs* 18 (January–February): 11–21.

Fuchs, Victor R. 1999b. Provide, Provide: The Economics of Aging. In Thomas R. Saving and Andrew Rattenmaier (eds.), *Medicare Reform: Issues and Answers.* Chicago: University of Chicago Press, pp. 15–36.

Health Care Financing Administration, Office of Research and Demonstrations. 1982. Medicare Summary, Use and Reimbursement by Person, 1976–1978. *Health Care Financing Program Statistics* (August).

Health Care Financing Review, Medicare and Medicaid Statistical Supplement. 1997.

Manton, Kenneth. 1982. Changing Concepts of Morbidity and Mortality in the Elderly Population. *Milbank Memorial Fund Quarterly/Health and Society* 60:183–244.

CHAPTER 8

Projecting Social Security's Finances and Its Treatment of Postwar Americans

STEVEN CALDWELL, ALLA GANTMAN,
JAGADEESH GOKHALE, THOMAS JOHNSON,
AND LAURENCE J. KOTLIKOFF

Introduction

The Social Security system's long-term finances are in crisis. Under intermediate assumptions, the system's payroll tax must be raised by 38 percent if we want to pay promised benefits on an ongoing basis. This represents five cents per dollar earned by the typical American worker. Moreover, this tax hike must be implemented immediately and be permanent. Under high-cost assumptions, the situation is worse: Payroll taxes need to be raised by 58 percent, meaning that typical workers will have to surrender seven more cents per dollar earned to the Old Age Survivors and Disability Insurance System (OASDI).

The true size of Social Security's fiscal problem is more than twice as large as the system's Trustees are publicly acknowledging in their

Though not listed as a coauthor, Melissa Favreault made indispensable contributions to the development of CORSIM, especially OASDI-related parts of CORSIM, as part of her doctoral dissertation work at Cornell. We also benefited from her advice during the preparation of the CORSIM runs reported in this chapter and from her feedback on an earlier draft. We thank Bill Richie and Felicitie Bell of the Social Security Administration Office of the Actuary for providing essential data and critical advice. Deborah Bailey, Lee Cohen, and Howard Iams of Social Security's Office of Research, Evaluation and Statistics permitted us to report initial results from their ongoing evaluation of CORSIM. We also thank Steven McKay and Tim Zayatz of Social Security's Office of the Actuary for critically important and extensive assistance in clarifying OASI benefit determination rules. Alan Auerbach, Nada Eissa, Ken Wachter, and Ronald Lee provided valuable feedback on an earlier draft. Laurence Kotlikoff and Steven Caldwell are grateful to Merrill Lynch & Co. for research support on a previous project that was the groundwork for this study. Finally, we thank Economic Security Planning, Inc., for permitting our use for this study of SSBC – a detailed OASI benefit calculator. All opinions expressed here are strictly those of the authors and are not necessarily those of the Federal Reserve Bank of Cleveland, Boston University, Cornell University, Merrill Lynch & Co., or Economic Security Planning, Inc.

297

Trustees' Report.[1] The reason is that the Trustees have instructed the actuaries to consider benefits and taxes over only the next seventy-five years. Although seventy-five years seems like a long time, there are huge deficits looming in years 76 and beyond. In systematically ignoring those longer-term shortfalls, the Trustees are dramatically understating the true dimensions of the long-run revenue shortfall.[2]

In addition to appreciating the Social Security actuaries' assessment of the system's true long-run solvency, it's important to know how they are arriving at their projections. This chapter describes, in general terms, the actuaries' methodology and contrasts it with an alternative one based on a microsimulation approach to forecasting benefit and tax payments. Our understanding of the actuaries' approach is based on extensive discussions with Bill Richie, one of Social Security's top actuaries. Nonetheless, our understanding is constrained by the fact that the actuaries do not have a detailed written description of their procedures.

Beyond describing, to the extent we can, the actuaries' forecasting method and contrasting it with our own, the chapter attempts to assess the accuracy of the actuaries' forecasts by comparing their low-cost, intermediate-cost, and high-cost projections with those derived from our own microsimulation model. Our model, described in Caldwell et al. (1999), combines CORSIM (a socioeconomic microsimulator) with SSBC (a detailed OASI Social Security benefit calculator).[3]

The term "attempts" needs to be clarified. The actuaries project only aggregate benefits; for example, they do not project benefits for different demographic and socioeconomic subgroups, including large ones, such as male and female birth cohorts.[4] In contrast, our model projects

[1] Steve Goss, Social Security's Deputy Chief Actuary, provided estimates of Social Security's untruncated long-term liabilities under intermediate assumptions; we are most grateful for his help.
[2] The problem with myopic forecasting is not new. Roughly a third of the blame that can be levied on the 1983 Greenspan Commission for not fixing Social Security's long-term finances once and for all can apparently be traced to the commission's use of a truncated projection horizon.
[3] CORSIM contains its own calculator of Social Security taxes and benefits, but for this chapter we chose to use the SSBC calculator because it was more detailed and had been more thoroughly tested. We should add, however, that using CORSIM with its own calculator has certain advantages. First, the CORSIM calculator includes DI, so that the full OASDI program is simulated, not only OASI. Second, CORSIM calculates taxes and benefits for the full population, rather than for selected cohorts. For extensive OASDI simulations using CORSIM's own tax and benefit calculators, see Favreault (1998) and Favreault and Caldwell (1997, 1998).
[4] The actuaries do appear to have the capacity to form separate benefit projections for cohorts differentiated by sex.

benefits and taxes by extremely detailed demographic and socioeconomic subgroups, but only for birth cohorts we define as "postwar Americans." These cohorts include native-born Americans as well as immigrants to the United States who were born or are projected to be born between 1945 and 2000.

Since we do not consider all Social Security benefit recipients or taxpayers, just those born between 1945 and 2000, we are unable to project total benefits and total taxes in any future year. However, we are able to estimate, for any given year, total benefits received by and taxes paid by postwar Americans.

For the year 2050, our postwar population ranges in age from 50 to 105. Since most OASI benefits are paid to those age 60 and above, it seems worthwhile to compare the Trustee's aggregate benefit projections for 2050 and neighboring years with our own. For the year 2010, our postwar population ranges in age from 10 to 65. For the year 2020, it ranges in age from 20 to 75. Since virtually all OASI taxes are paid by workers between the ages of 15 to 75, it seems worthwhile to compare the Trustee's aggregate tax projections for the period 2010–2020.

The chapter's final objectives are fourfold: first, to calculate the internal rate of return that different types of postwar Americans can expect, on average, to earn on their OASI contributions in the form of OASI benefits; second, to calculate OASI lifetime net tax rates for different types of postwar Americans; third, to determine the sensitivity of these calculations to the three sets of demographic and economic assumptions considered by the actuaries; and fourth, to indicate how the internal rates of return will change in response to tax hikes or benefit cuts.

Our findings suggest three things. First, there may be a somewhat smaller imbalance between long-run benefits and payroll tax revenues than is being forecast by the actuaries. Although our projections of aggregate taxes are quite close to those of the Social Security actuaries for years when comparisons are meaningful, our projected benefit payments are roughly 15 percent smaller, again, for years when we can form comparisons given the nature of our data. Second, assuming no change in current law, postwar Americans will earn less than a 2 percent real rate of return on their contributions to Social Security. If one assumes that postwar Americans could otherwise invest their contributions at a 5 percent real rate, this below-market rate of return translates into lifetime net Social Security tax rates of more than five cents per dollar earned. Third, implementing the tax hikes or benefit cuts that the actuaries suggest would fully resolve Social Security's long-term fiscal imbalance will leave today's newborns receiving a real return on their contributions of only 1 percent or thereabouts.

The next section describes the Social Security actuaries' long-term forecasting methodology. The third section describes in general terms our microsimulation model, relegating details to the Appendix. The fourth section compares projections based on the two methodologies. The fifth section presents internal rate-of-return and lifetime net-tax-rate calculations based on current policy under intermediate, high-cost, and low-cost assumptions. It also shows how these internal rates of return will change if the payroll tax is immediately and permanently increased by close to 40 percent or benefits are immediately and permanently cut by 25 percent. These are the alternative immediate and permanent tax hikes and benefit cuts needed to achieve present value budget balance for the Social Security system under intermediate assumptions. The final section summarizes and concludes the paper.

Social Security's Long-Term Forecasting Methodology

Figures 8.1 through 8.9, provided by Bill Richie of the Social Security Administration's Office of the Actuary, describes, via a flow diagram, how Social Security arrives at its short- and long-term forecasts. As mentioned, the actuaries do not have a written description of what they are doing within each of the boxes in their diagram, so our understanding of their methodology is limited to what we can infer from the diagram and from discussions with the actuaries.

Figure 8.1 provides an overview. It indicates that demographic projections are used to form economic projections. The economic projections (including the projection of payroll-taxable labor income) are, in turn, used to project taxable income to the system. The economic projections are also used in conjunction with the demographic projections to project benefit outgo. By comparing projected tax income and benefit outgo, the actuaries arrive at the system's actuarial status.

Figure 8.2 shows how the demographic projections are formed. The actuaries start with the mortality, immigration, and fertility assumptions chosen by the Trustees. They use these in concert with National Center for Health Statistics (NCHS), Immigration and Nationalization Service (INS), and Census data to produce annual birth rates, death rates, marriage rates, divorce rates, and immigration rates. All these rates are generated on an age- and sex-specific basis. These rates are then used to forecast total population by age, sex, and marital status. As Figure 8.1 shows, these totals are ultimately used to form economic projections

300

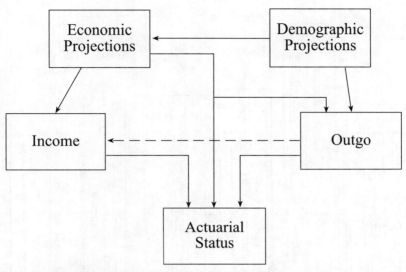

Figure 8.1. Overview of OASDI Projection Methodology. *Source*: Prepared by Social Security Administration, Office of the Chief Actuary, January 1999.

concerning labor supply and other variables as well as benefit (outgo) projections.

Figure 8.3 considers short-range economic projections. The first steps in forming these projections involve using (a) Bureau of Labor Statistics (BLS) survey data in conjunction with the demographic outputs shown in Figure 8.2 to generate totals of workers, wage workers, and self-employed workers and (b) Social Security Administration (SSA) employment and earnings data and BLS employment data to get total covered wages and self-employment income. Knowing total labor income, covered labor income, and the totals of those paying Social Security taxes suffices to generate average covered earnings and ratios of taxable to total earnings. At this point, the actuaries use (a) SSA data on the historical distribution of covered wages, as between sectors and between the non–self-employed and the self-employed, and (b) quarterly wage data from SSA administrative records to produce short-run forecasts of payroll tax revenues.

The process of producing long-range revenue projections is detailed in Figure 8.4. The basic idea appears to be to use labor force data on participation and unemployment rates by age and sex as well as demographic projections to forecast future levels of employment. This

301

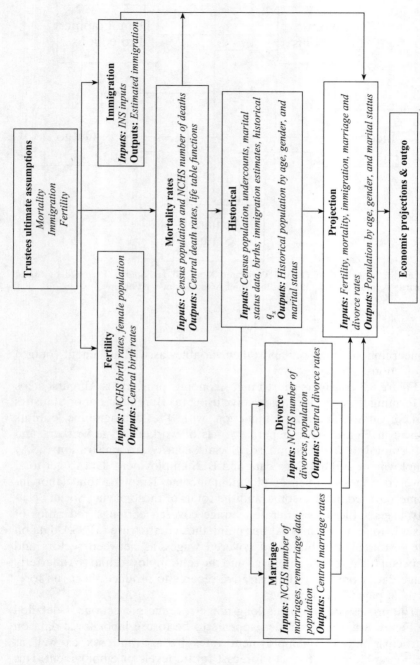

Figure 8.2. Demographic Projections. *Source:* Prepared by Social Security Administration, Office of the Chief Actuary, January 1999.

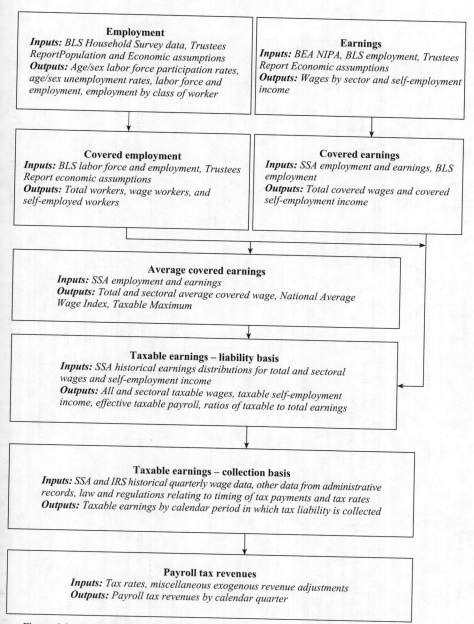

Figure 8.3. Short-Range Economic and Revenue Projections. *Source*: Prepared by Social Security Administration, Office of the Chief Actuary, January 1999.

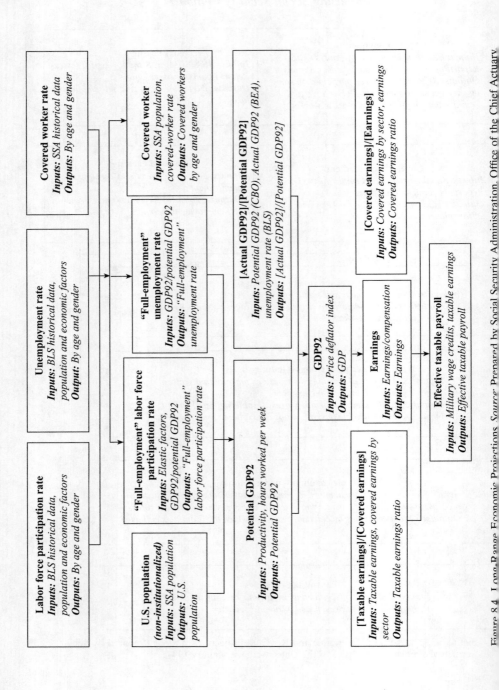

Figure 8.4. Long-Range Economic Projections. *Source:* Prepared by Social Security Administration, Office of the Chief Actuary.

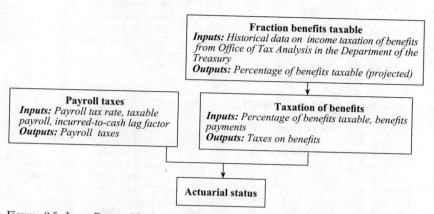

Figure 8.5. Long-Range Noninterest Income. *Source*: Prepared by Social Security Administration, Office of the Chief Actuary, January 1999.

forecast is then combined with a labor-productivity growth rate assumption to forecast total GDP. Armed with their estimate of the time path of future GDP, the actuaries appear to use GDP income shares to estimate total future labor income. These figures are adjusted by extrapolations of historical ratios of covered earnings to total earnings and of taxable earnings to covered earnings and then used to estimate the OASDI tax base and, given projected future tax rates, future total Social Security payroll taxes (see Figure 8.5).

Figures 8.6 through 8.9 consider the formation of aggregate benefit projections and their taxation under the federal income tax. The actuaries start with estimates of the fully insured population based on historical data. As each year passes, they update the fully insured population. Next, they use ratios of certain beneficiary types (e.g., retirees and widows) to the fully insured population to figure out how many beneficiaries of each type there will be in each year in the future. In the process, they also determine how many new beneficiaries of each type ("newly entitled beneficiaries") will appear each year. For those receiving benefits as of the starting year of the projection, the procedure is to simply grow their benefits through time at the inflation rate. For newly entitled beneficiaries, their procedure entails assigning an average benefit based on a sample of 20,000 newly entitled workers, whose earnings histories are updated and adjusted for projected productivity and other changes through time. The adding together of the benefits paid to existing beneficiaries and those paid to new ones leads to a projection of total benefit payments.

Disability-insured (DII) population
Inputs: FI population, historical DII population
Methods: Regression equations relating DII population to FI population by 5-year age group
Outputs: DII population (projected)

Fully-insured (FI) population
Inputs: Covered worker rates, SS area population, historical FI population, historical non-FI population by number of QCs, mortality rates
Methods: Project FI by single year of age
Outputs: FI population (projected)

Disabled-worker beneficiary (DIB) population
Inputs: DII population, historical data on DIBs in force and in current-pay by single year of age, historical DIB awards and terminations by single year of age, assumed annual changes in incidence, assumed annual changes in termination rates by cause (death, recovery, other)
Methods: Project DIBs by single year of age
Outputs: DIB population by single year of age at end of each projected year, DIBs converting to OABs during year

Average benefits for newly entitled beneficiaries
Inputs: Sample of newly entitled beneficiaries, grouped by male OAIB, female OAIB, male DIB, female DIB, young survivor (child or mother/father), disabled widow(er), or aged widow(er); Newly entitled beneficiaries by single year of age (male and female OAIBs) or age group (other categories); AWI; COLA
Methods: Project the sample forward for each year of projection and calculate an average benefit by age (group)
Outputs: Average benefits for newly entitled by category

Auxiliaries of DIB population
Inputs: DIB population by single year of age at end of each year; Auxiliaries of DIB population by category (young wife, young husband, aged wife, aged husband, minor child, disabled child, student child), by quarter (historical), in force, in current pay, awards, and terminations
Methods: Interpolate DIB population by quarter; Relate auxiliary awards to historical auxiliary awards and projected DIB awards; Project auxiliary termination rates based on historical trends
Outputs: DIB and auxiliary populations (in force and in current pay) by category, by quarter

Average benefits for beneficiaries in current pay
Inputs: Average benefits for newly entitled by category; Average benefits for beneficiaries in current pay (historical); Number of awards and terminations; Factors for increasing average benefit due to selective mortality, post-entitlement earnings, and other reasons
Methods: Project average benefit in current pay by adding benefits to newly entitled and subtracting benefits to newly terminated
Outputs: Average benefits for beneficiaries in current pay by category and by quarter (DI) or semiannual period (OASI)

Benefit payments
Inputs: Average benefits for beneficiaries in current pay by category and by quarter (DI) or semiannual period (OASI); Beneficiary populations by category; Factors for retroactive benefits; AERO payments (historical); Lump sum death payments
Methods: Benefits in current pay equal number of beneficiaries times average benefit; Retroactive benefits equal factor times awards; Factor applied for AERO payments
Outputs: Benefit payments by quarter

Short-range progress of funds

Figure 8.6. Short-Range Benefit Payments. *Source*: Prepared by Social Security Administration, Office of the Chief Actuary, January 1999.

Retired worker and insured widow(er) beneficiary population
Inputs: Fully insured population; OAIB and insured widow(er) population in force and in current pay by single year of age (historical); OAIB and insured widow(er) awards and terminations by single year of age (historical); Assumed annual changes in incidence rates
Methods: Project OAIBs and insured widow(er)s by single year of age, with all fully insureds being OAIBs or insured widow(er)s by age 70
Outputs: OAIB and insured widow(er) population by single year of age at end of each projected year

Young Auxiliary of Retired or Deceased Worker Beneficiary Population
Inputs: SS area population by single year of age; Historical data on young auxiliaries of retired or deceased worker beneficiary population by category (young wife, young husband, mother, father, minor child of retired worker, disabled child of retired worker, student child of retired worker, minor child of deceased worker, disabled child of deceased worker, student child of deceased worker), by single year of age, in force, in current pay, awards, and terminations
Methods: Project auxiliaries by single year of age
Outputs: Young auxiliary beneficiary population by single year of age at end of each projected year

Aged Auxiliary of Retired or Deceased Worker Beneficiary Population
Inputs: OAIB population, in broad age groups, interpolated to semiannual figures; SS area population, in broad age groups, semiannual; Aged auxiliaries of retired or deceased worker beneficiary population by category (disabled widow(er), aged wife, aged husband, widow, widower, parent), by semiannual period (historical), by broad age group, in force and in current pay
Methods: Regression equations relating auxiliaries by broad age group to dependent variable(s) (SS area population, OAIB population, or whatever is appropriate)
Outputs: Aged auxiliary beneficiary population by broad age group at end of each semiannual period

Lump-sum death payments
Inputs: Fully insured population; Mortality rates; Number of lump sum death payments (historical)
Methods: Calculate number of insured deaths; Apply factor for number of lump sum death payments
Outputs: Amount of lump sum death payments by quarter

307

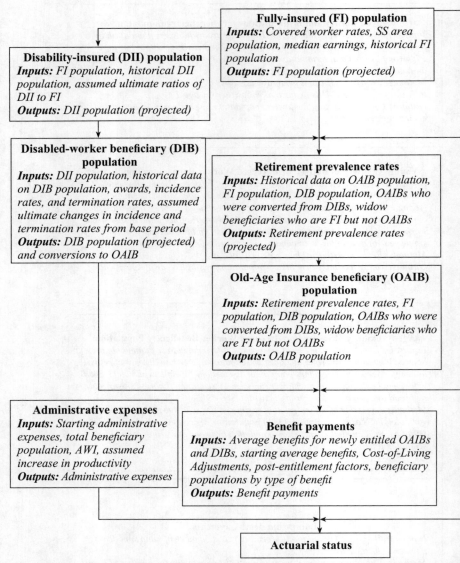

Figure 8.7. Long-Rage Outgo. *Source*: Prepared by Social Security Administration, Office of the Chief Actuary, January 1999.

Widow prevalence rates
Inputs: Historical data on widow beneficiary population, SS area
widowed population, married men in SS area population, married
men in SS area population who are FI, mother beneficiary population,
and widow beneficiaries with benefits totally offset for government
pensions
Outputs: Widow prevalence rates (projected)

Widow beneficiary population
Inputs: Widow prevalence rates, SS area widowed population,
married men in SS area population, married men in SS area population
who are FI, mother beneficiary population, and widow beneficiaries
with benefits totally offset by government pensions
Outputs: Widow beneficiary population (projected)

Average benefits for newly entitled OAIBs and DIBs
Inputs: Sample of newly entitled OAIBs and DIBs, SS
area population, covered workers, average taxable
earnings, National Average Wage Index (AWI), percentage
of covered workers with maximum taxable earnings
Outputs: Average benefits for new entitlements

Railroad interchange
Inputs: Data from Railroad Retirement Board,
AWI, covered workers, average benefits for OAIBs
Outputs: Net payments to RRB

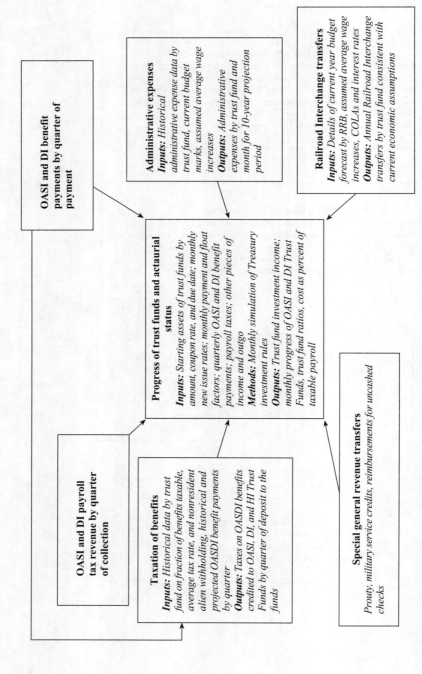

OASI and DI benefit payments by quarter of payment

Administrative expenses
Inputs: Historical administrative expense data by trust fund, current budget marks, assumed average wage increases
Outputs: Administrative expenses by trust fund and month for 10-year projection period

Railroad Interchange transfers
Inputs: Details of current year budget forecast by RRB, assumed average wage increases, COLAs and interest rates
Outputs: Annual Railroad Interchange transfers by trust fund consistent with current economic assumptions

Progress of trust funds and actuarial status
Inputs: Starting assets of trust funds by amount, coupon rate, and due date; monthly new issue rates; monthly payment and float factors; quarterly OASI and DI benefit payments; payroll taxes; other pieces of income and outgo
Methods: Monthly simulation of Treasury investment rules
Outputs: Trust fund investment income; monthly progress of OASI and DI Trust Funds, trust fund ratios, cost as percent of taxable payroll

OASI and DI payroll tax revenue by quarter of collection

Taxation of benefits
Inputs: Historical data by trust fund on fraction of benefits taxable, average tax rate, and nonresident alien withholding, historical and projected OASDI benefit payments by quarter
Outputs: Taxes on OASDI benefits credited to OASI, DI, and HI Trust Funds by quarter of deposit to the funds

Special general revenue transfers
Prouty, military service credits, reimbursements for uncashed checks

Figure 8.8. Short-Range Progress of Funds. *Source:* Prepared by Social Security Administration, Office of the Chief Actuary, January 1999.

310

Actuarial Status

Inputs: Trust fund at start of projection period, income (noninterest) variables, outgo variables, real interest rate, CPI assumption

Outputs: Progress of trust fund, trust fund ratios, actuarial balances

---

Figure 8.9. Long-Range Actuarial Status. *Source*: Prepared by Social Security Administration, Office of the Chief Actuary, January 1999.

The CORSIM-SSBC Model

Our microsimulation model combines two submodels: CORSIM and SSBC.[5] CORSIM is a dynamic microsimulation model of the U.S. population developed by Steven Caldwell of Cornell University and his associates.[6] The model is similar in form and purpose to other policy-oriented dynamic microsimulation models developed around the world.[7] CORSIM starts with a representative sample of Americans alive in 1960. It then "grows," or "ages," this sample of persons and households through time, demographically and economically. For example, persons are born, age, attend school, leave the family of origin, marry and start new families, work and earn money, become disabled, retire, and die. Households form, gain and lose members, migrate among states, pay taxes, make expenditures, and accumulate assets. In effect, the model simulates a longitudinal annual survey of American persons and households;

---

[5] This section draws on Favreault (1998) and Caldwell et al. (1999).

[6] Large-scale dynamic microsimulation modeling traces back to the seminal contributions of Guy Orcutt (1957). The first operational model is described in Orcutt et al. (1961). In the 1970s, Orcutt directed the team at the Urban Institute that constructed the DYNASIM model (Orcutt, Caldwell, and Wertheimer, 1976). CORSIM, under development since 1987, is descended from DYNASIM.

[7] Other prominent large-scale, policy-oriented dynamic microsimulation models developed for the United States include DYNASIM2 (see Zedlewski, 1989) and PRISM (see Kennell and Sheils, 1990). Anderson (1998), Ross (1991), and Citro and Hanushek (1991) review microsimulation models and alternative modeling strategies. Outside the United States, dynamic microsimulation models have been developed and used extensively for public pension analysis. Examples include the following: DYNACAN in Canada (Morrison, 1998); MOSART in Norway; NEDYMAS in the Netherlands; LIFEMOD in Great Britain; HARDING in Australia; the RFV/ATP model in Sweden; and the Frankfurt model in Germany. All but DYNACAN are discussed in Harding (1996). Smaller, demographically oriented microsimulation models in the United States include SOCSIM (see Hammel et al., 1976) and CAMSIM (see Smith, 1987) and are reviewed in Bongaarts, Burch, and Wachter (1987) and DeVos and Palloni (1989).

311

population representation is maintained by subtracting decedents and adding births and immigrants each year. For this chapter, the population is "aged" from 1960 to the year 2090.

SSBC uses a subset of CORSIM's completed lifetime demographic and economic experiences to determine OASI retirement, spousal (including divorced spouses), widow(er), mother, father, and children benefits, as well as OASI taxes. It does so by taking into account Social Security's earnings test, family benefit maxima, actuarial reductions and increases, benefit recomputation, eligibility rules, the ceiling on taxable earnings, and legislated changes in the normal retirement age.[8]

Microsimulation

Microsimulation begins with a population sample, and then "grows"/"ages" this population in discrete intervals, such as a month or year. Through the "aging" process, the model simulates life histories for each sample member. Life histories refer to sample members' demographic, economic, health, and social experiences through time. The simulation is generated by a set of mathematical algorithms that combine deterministic and stochastic elements.

The processes for continuous variables, such as earnings, are typically represented by regression equations with a deterministic component, which is based on the sample member's socioeconomic characteristics, and an error component, which is drawn from a prespecified distribution with strongly autoregressive properties. Discrete-state changes (e.g., the transition from unmarried to married, from living to dead, from not working to working) are typically represented as logistic functions. These logistic functions determine the probabilities of various state changes for each sample member as functions of the member's socioeconomic characteristics.[9] Because stochastic components are pervasive in dynamic microsimulation models, solutions for these models depend on the particular stochastic outcomes for each model run. A particular individual's outcome in a single run might differ from that of another person who is

---

[8] Although SSBC considers the OASI system in great detail, it leaves out the DI portion of Social Security. It also ignores the taxation of Social Security benefits under federal and state income taxes. Both of these omissions lead to an understatement of Social Security's redistribution from the lifetime rich to the lifetime poor.

[9] They are typically evaluated by taking a random draw from a uniform distribution whose values range from 0 to 1. If the value of the draw, say, 0.7, is higher than the probability predicted by the logistic function, say, 0.6, the sample member experiences the change in question. If not, the sample member remains in the initial state. In either case, it is necessary to update the member's record, since this information may be relevant for future transitions.

observationally identical. Furthermore, the very same individual might display different outcomes across model runs. One can reduce this Monte Carlo variability by averaging outcomes across multiple model runs, though this exacts a high price in computational resources. Fortunately there exist more practical variance reduction techniques.[10]

Alignment

CORSIM incorporates an array of alignment, or benchmarking, processes. Alignment is treated as an integral part of module development, with the particular aim of enabling modules to employ and reconcile data drawn from diverse sources and analytic levels. Initial micro-level outcomes in CORSIM are aligned, or benchmarked, to credible historical estimates (or future projections) at subgroup, group, and aggregate levels. For example, initial values of CORSIM-simulated earnings for persons with particular characteristics are averaged to calculate a CORSIM-simulated group mean. A credible historical estimate of mean earnings for that group – based on *Current Population Survey* (CPS) data – is compared to the CORSIM mean for the same group. Any difference between the CORSIM mean and the CPS mean is used as the starting point of an alignment process. The alignment process depends upon the underlying function. If the underlying function is linear, the alignment is a simple linear scaling. If the underlying function is nonlinear, as is the case for discrete outcomes, the alignment is nonlinear; see Johnson (1996) and Neufeld (1996a).

Once the alignment processes and parameters are determined, the population is passed again through CORSIM, at which time a modified, aligned earnings is simulated for each woman in the group. These

[10] Neufeld (1996b) provides an overview of these techniques. One approach, called the "sidewalk" method, entails keeping a running sum of probabilities, called the sidewalk variable and initialized at 0.5, to decide when events occur. When a unit's contribution to this sum causes the sum to reach or exceed an integer value, then the unit experiences the event (as opposed to the unit's experiencing the event when its probability exceeds a random draw). The sidewalk method preserves the principle that probabilities of greater magnitudes result in greater likelihood of experiencing the event. One of the key advantages of the sidewalk method is that the actual number of events experienced by a group never exceeds the expected number of events by more than one. Further, the method prevents the elimination of entire high-event-probability subgroups. It has the potential disadvantages of imposing negative dependence of events for related individuals when the initial database is structured so that individuals within families are processed sequentially and also of nonrepeatability across passes in the same run. To combat this limitation, Neufeld developed a "hybrid random number method," in which the advantages of the sidewalk method are combined with a more traditional tabular method. In this strategy, probabilities are subject to minor adjustment in order to ensure that the expected number of events will be nearly realized.

313

modified earnings cause the mean group earnings to closely track the historical benchmark. For some modules, multiple alignments are carried out to make simulated outcomes track multiple historical benchmarks. For example, aggregate earned income in CORSIM is aligned to historical National Income and Product Account estimates (or projections). Given alignment, CORSIM outcomes at the micro level track multiple historical (or projected) benchmarks, while retaining distributive richness at the micro level. This enables CORSIM to draw upon, reconcile, and integrate diverse sources and levels of historical data.[11]

Of particular importance for this study is our benchmarking of CORSIM's aggregate labor income in the future to projections of aggregate labor income (including proprietorship income) provided by the Social Security actuaries. Specifically, the actuaries provided three separate projections, corresponding to their high-cost, intermediate, and low-cost forecasts. We used each of these projections in producing three CORSIM data sets – one based on high-cost demographic and economic assumptions, one based on intermediate demographic and economic assumptions, and one based on low-cost demographic and economic assumptions.

Simulating with CORSIM

CORSIM begins in 1960, with an initial population consisting of the 1960 U.S. Census Public Use Microdata Sample (PUMS). The PUMS is a one-in-one-thousand sample, so when CORSIM runs with the full PUMS, all simulated counts are scaled by a multiple of 1,000 to represent national totals. To make the size of the file more manageable, a subsample of approximately 50,000 persons was drawn from the full 1960 PUMS and used for the runs reported in this chapter. The Census survey does not provide all the information needed as baseline data; the remaining information is imputed to the 1960 sample from a variety of sources. CORSIM "grows" the 1960 sample demographically and economically in one-year intervals through the year 2100. As detailed in Caldwell et al. (1996) and in the Appendix to this paper, CORSIM updating processes are implemented by modules that consist of stochastic equations, alignment procedures, and/or deterministic algorithms. As Table 8.1 makes clear, the stochastic equations are tested and estimated using – whenever possible

---

[11] Alignment also plays the critical function of ensuring that inputs to successive processes are accurate. For example, if one misspecifies the fertility function and does not subsequently align its predictions, even perfectly specified functions for work and earnings will generate inaccurate outputs, since both are dependent upon fertility outcomes.

Table 8.1. *CORSIM Modules Used in This Study*

Annual Process	Groups Subject to Process and Functional Form	Process Determinants	Data Used in Process Estimation	Alignment Data
Individual demographics				
Fertility	30 groups (among women); age <30, have child, marital status, race, work status Logistic	Age, birth$_{t-1}$, birth$_{t-2}$, duration of current marriage, earnings, family income, homeowner status, marital status, parity, schooling status, work status (F/T, P/T)	NLS:1969–87	Vital Statistics, 28 groups SSA total fertility rate
Mortality	51 groups; age, sex, race, marital status Logistic	Age, birthplace (U.S. or other), education, employment status, family income, marital status, year	NLMS:1980–89	Vital Statistics, 88 groups SSA age-sex adjusted death rate
Family demographics				
Enter marriage market for first time	20 groups; race, schooling status, sex, weeks worked Logistic	Age, age^2, education, ln(earnings), number of children, weeks worked	NLS:1973–87	Census, 16 groups
Assortative mating	*All* nonrelated opposite-sex *pairs* in marriage market at *t* Logistic to estimate probability of match; highest joint ratings married, others return to market for possible marriage at *t* + 1	Age difference, age difference*(1 if female older, 0 otherwise), abs((male's total income –female's total income)/ 1,000), difference in education, labor force	Census:1980 PUMS	None

continued

315

Table 8.1. *(continued)*

Annual Process	Groups Subject to Process and Functional Form	Process Determinants	Data Used in Process Estimation	Alignment Data
		participation interactions, male's education*(1 if older, 0 otherwise), racial interactions, state of residence, woman's number of children		
Marital dissolution (divorce only; widowhood determined by mortality)	4 groups; earning status of wife, presence of children under 18 Logistic	Age difference, duration of union, husband's wages, race, wage advantage	PSID:1968–87	NCHS, 14 groups
Reenter marriage market upon widowhood, divorce	7 groups; age (under 60/61+), race, sex, widowed or divorced Logistic	Age, age^2, education, ln(income), divorced (vs. widowed), has child, (1 – nowork)*loginc, weeks worked	PSID:1968–87	NCHS, 26 groups
Individual social and economic attainments				
Education: Grade attendance, completion	33 groups; grade level (17 definitions, from preschool to beyond third year of graduate school), race, sex, schooling status Logistic	Age, have child, living own, marital, status, on parents' education, parents own home	HSB:1980–86; NLS:1979–87	CPS, 2 groups

316

Work status (0/FT/PT)	174 groups; age, have child, living with parents, material status, race, sex, weeks$_{-1}$ > 47 = 0, weeks$_{-1}$ > 47 Probit	Age, education, have child, married$_{-1}$, marital status, number of kids, percent unemployment, youngest child's age	PSID:1972–87	Census and CPS, 35 groups SSA coverage rate, 2 groups
Number of weeks worked	58 groups; age, have child, marital status, race, sex, weeks$_t$ < 47, weeks$_t$ > 47 Regression	Age, education, have child, married$_{-1}$, number of children, percent unemployment, youngest child's age	PSID:1972–87	None
Weekly earnings rate	116 groups, age, have child, marital status, race, sex, weeks worked, weeks$_{t-1}$ Regression	Age, earnings$_{-1}$, education, education*earnings$_{-1}$, married$_{-1}$, number of children, percent unemployment, youngest child's age	PSID:1972–87	Census and CPS, 70 groups NIPA
Age of receipt of Social Security retirement benefits	Screen for eligibility Logistic for workers	Age, change in work hours$_{-1,t}$, coverage, earnings, education, homeowner, live alone, ln(asset income), ln(change in absolute value of income$_{-1,t}$), marital disruption$_{-1,t}$, marital status, race, sex, work hours	PSID:1986–91	SSA data, 1961–95, 12 groups

Sources: PSID – Panel Study of Income Dynamics; SSA – Social Security Administration; PUMS – U.S. Census Public Use Microdata Sample; HSB – High School and Beyond; NCHS – National Center for Health Statistics; NLS – National Longitudinal Survey; NLS-Y – National Longitudinal Survey of Youth; NLMS – National Longitudinal Mortality Study; CPS – Current Population Survey; NIPA – National Income and Product Accounts.

– large, nationally representative, longitudinal micro data files. Data used for the rule-based algorithms and for alignment are drawn from a variety of other program descriptions and data files.

In an effort to capture behavioral heterogeneity across socioeconomic subgroups, CORSIM often represents a single process by means of separate equations for multiple subgroups (Caldwell, 1985). A variable highly predictive of the outcomes of one group may be irrelevant for determining the outcomes of a second group and may act in the opposite direction for a third group.[12] In addition, when benchmarking group-level or aggregate-level outcomes generated by the micro-level equations, one might wish to ensure that a particular distribution of outcomes across social groups – as indicated by group-level estimates from a credible source – is maintained. For example, the benchmarking (alignment) factors attempt to account for both period and cohort effects. Yet period and cohort factors (changes in laws, political events, natural disasters) might have dissimilar effects on members of different social groups. As a result one might prefer to define these effects differently for as many socially relevant groups as possible.[13]

Of course, extensive cross-sectional alignments do not guarantee longitudinal realism. Simulating accurate proportions of the total population working, and even accurate distributions of work status across demographic groups for each year, does not ensure realistic work histories. We try to achieve life history realism in CORSIM by (1) extensive use of lagged endogenous variables, and (2) realistic life paths for related behaviors. However, we often find that these two strategies alone are insufficient to create full life path realism (Caldwell, Favreault, and Swan, 1996). A third strategy is typically required: including substantial autoregressive properties in disturbance terms. In the CORSIM simulation of weekly earnings, for example, error terms varying in size by subgroup are added to the deterministic components for subgroups based on education, prior work status, and other factors. However, if these error terms

---

[12] For example, the presence of children in the household may differentially influence the labor market behavior of men and women. Children under age 5 are likely to increase the probability that a man works, but decrease the probability that a woman works. In such a case, one needs to estimate equations predicting labor market outcomes for men and for women separately and may even wish to consider estimating separate equations for those individuals who have or don't have young children.

[13] The marriage rate for a particular age group, for example, is an outcome that one would expect to vary substantially across years given changes in the number of eligible males and females in the population, shifts in the economy, and changing social norms about the acceptability of remarriage and cohabitation. The micro equations capture several of these dimensions, but alignment ensures that appropriate totals are achieved for different age-sex groups in each year.

are not correlated over time, earnings can shift unrealistically from year to year. One strategy we have used is to correlate one's probability of working in a given period with the probability from all previous periods by assigning what we refer to as "permanent luck" factors to all members of the sample.[14]

Validating CORSIM

How credible is CORSIM at simulating Social Security outcomes? Given the size and complexity of the model, a full-scale treatment of its performance lies beyond the scope of this chapter.[15] However, some discussion of model validation is desirable.

Three levels of CORSIM validation can be loosely distinguished, in ascending order of challenge. The first level of validation, paralleling the traditional procedures of standard analytic research, takes place during the specification, testing, and estimation of individual microdynamic modules. Validation at this level focuses on the fit of a particular specification to (1) theory and previous research, and (2) suitable empirical data. For example, in the CORSIM microdynamic mortality module, the probability of death for a specific individual is specified as a direct (nonlinear) function of the individual's age, race, gender, income, educational attainment, employment status, place of birth (United States or not), and marital status. To arrive at a final specification, multiple credible alternatives were tested and compared; subsamples drawn from the National Longitudinal Mortality Study (NLMS) were used. Once the final specification was chosen, final parameter estimates were obtained

---

[14] One can consider these as terms that capture unobserved heterogeneity – like differences in motivation and even social grace. These factors, which are drawn from a normal distribution centered on zero, are then added to the individual's probability of working and the level of work effort (full-time versus part-time). Comparisons of year-to-year transitions observed in the PSID sample more closely resembled CORSIM patterns after this modification was made. Similarly, we impose structure on error terms in the earnings equations, dividing this error into two components: a transitory component drawn each year and then a lagged component. Weights for these respective components vary across social groups. Swan (1997) details related issues.

[15] For a discussion of general strategies for validating dynamic microsimulation models, see Caldwell (1996) and Caldwell and Morrison (1999). For results from validation tests aimed specifically at assessing CORSIM's capacity to simulate Social Security outcomes, see Favreault (1998) and Favreault and Caldwell (1997, 1998); note, however, that these validation results, as well as the validation results reported in this section of the chapter, are based on simulations using the CORSIM OASDI benefit calculator, not the SSBC OASI benefit calculator used in other sections of the chapter. Since we believe the SSBC calculator to be more accurate than the CORSIM calculator, we expect that validation tests in which the SSBC calculator was used would track historical benchmarks at least as well as those using the CORSIM calculator.

by fitting to the full NLMS sample. The estimated parameters were highly significant according to traditional criteria, and the parameter patterns were generally consistent with patterns suggested by theory and/or found in previous research. Specification, testing, and estimation exercises such as these constitute the first level of validation for stochastic modules in CORSIM.

Once the equations that survived the first level of validation testing are coded into CORSIM, the full set of equations (together with other components of CORSIM) is used to generate a "base" simulation covering the 1960–1997 historical period. This historical simulation invites a second level of performance testing. The validation yardsticks for this second level consist of particular historical benchmarks drawn from the 1960–1997 period. Validation tests at this second level still focus on the performance of each individual module, taken one at a time. But unavoidably, they also test the performance of modules supplying input variables to each individual module. An eventual outcome of the second level of validation is alignment to historical benchmarks, as discussed in the section on alignment above. But efforts to improve the underlying structure of a module take priority.

An example, again using the mortality module, would be useful. During each simulation, CORSIM-simulated *individual-level mortality probabilities* are summed and averaged to yield CORSIM-simulated *group-level mortality rates*. The CORSIM-simulated group-level mortality rates for each year over the 1960–1997 period are then compared to government estimates of group-level mortality rates over the same period. Government mortality estimates are provided for each of seventy-six groups defined by age, sex, and race. CORSIM-simulated individual-level probabilities are summed and averaged to generate rates for exactly the same groups. Differences between CORSIM-simulated and government-estimated mortality rates for each of seventy-six groups over the 1960–1997 period can arise from various sources, notably including specification and estimation flaws in the CORSIM mortality module (Caldwell, 1996). The pattern of these differences across time and across groups can suggest directions for further improvement in the CORSIM mortality module.

Second-level validation tests probe well beyond the more conventional first-level validation tests. To examine how well a mortality module based upon longitudinal micro-data fits group-level time series data, we impose a performance test that goes beyond conventional in-sample and out-of-sample tests of statistical fit. *In-sample* tests, of course, are relatively weak because the yardstick for measuring performance is typically the same data used for model selection and estimation. Conventional *out-of-sample* tests provide a stronger performance test because the yardstick is "fresh" data not used in model selection and estimation. However, the extra testing strength brought about by using new data are limited by the fact that typically the new data are *the same type* as the data used for the original model selection and estimation. Second-level CORSIM validation is *out-of-type* performance testing, because the performance yardstick is data that are not only new, but also different in kind from the data used in the first place for model selection and estimation (Caldwell, 1996). To continue the mortality example, in-sample and out-of-sample tests conducted as part of the first level of validation used micro-level longitudinal data as performance yardsticks. But out-of-type tests conducted as part of the second level of validation used group-level time series data (U.S. Census Vital Statistics) as performance yardsticks. In developing CORSIM modules, we believe that out-of-type performance yardsticks provide important diagnostic information beyond that yielded by conventional in-sample and out-of-sample measures.

Nevertheless, however stringent the performance tests posed by the first and second levels of CORSIM validation, the most important validation occurs at the third level, in which the full *system* of interacting modules is tested as a unit. Even if individual modules perform well according to the first two standards, the system of interacting modules can easily wander off track. Given CORSIM's starting point in 1960, many system-level historical yardsticks for assessing CORSIM's performance are available. Potential measures include historical (or projected) data (a) on univariate stocks and flows; (b) on multivariate stocks and flows; (c) from cross-sectional and over-time designs; and (d) at micro, group, and aggregate levels. For example, how well do CORSIM-simulated multivariate population distributions match historical distributions measured by censuses (e.g., the 1990 Census)? How well do CORSIM-simulated earnings histories match those measured in national longitudinal surveys (e.g., the Panel Study of Income Dynamics)? How well do CORSIM-simulated bivariate relationships between home ownership and earnings within subgroups match those measured in cross-sectional surveys (e.g., the Survey of Consumer Finances)? The list of potential yardsticks to test the system-level realism of CORSIM is very large. The number and variety of performance-testing yardsticks should be treated as an asset for dynamic microsimulation models generally and for CORSIM specifically.

Since the third level is the most demanding and important kind of validation and since OASDI projections are system-level CORSIM outcomes, we illustrate this kind of validation with specific examples. One example concerns simulating the growth of female-headed families over the 1960–1997 period. Though this outcome is less immediately relevant to Social Security than the examples to follow, it readily illustrates system-level validation. Recall that CORSIM modules generate flows or events, with associated stocks as consequences. For example, the stock of population in CORSIM is an outcome of birth, death, and net immigration flows. Each of the three flows is aligned, but the population stocks are not aligned and hence present opportunities for independent validation. Especially useful validation opportunities are created when specific population groups are the outcomes of multiple flows. The group defined as female-headed families (with at least one child under 18 living in the household) is an example. Six distinct CORSIM events generate new additions to the stock of female-headed families, and seven distinct events generate exits.[16] A validation test using the stock of female-headed families as yardstick therefore tests the cumulative effects of thirteen distinct CORSIM processes (and indirectly tests all processes that in turn influence those thirteen flows, i.e., virtually the entire CORSIM model). Figure 8.10, drawn from Morris and Caldwell (1999), displays the CORSIM-simulated number of female-headed families in the United States over the 1960–1997 period, compared to historical estimates. The intertemporal patterns of the two series are roughly similar, although differences are apparent in the levels. Because thirteen processes directly and cumulatively generate the number of female-headed families in CORSIM, accounting for differences between the two series might benefit from examining the matches among component flows. Unfortunately, in the case of female-headed families, not all component flows are documented with reliable historical data. In such cases examining the matches between simulated and historical flows becomes troublesome. In fact, when conventional historical data are weak or absent, one might argue that CORSIM-based estimates provide the best available historical estimates. One argument for such a claim is that CORSIM forces consistency on diverse data sources, including data on flows and stocks (Morris and Caldwell, 1999).

Given the topic of this chapter, we now turn to validation tests that connect directly with Social Security issues. Numerous such tests are described in Favreault (1998), from whose dissertation we select two

---

[16] New entries to female-headed–family status in CORSIM can arise when a child is born (to a single woman), a divorce occurs, a husband dies, an unmarried mother moves out of her family of origin, a single woman adopts a child, or a female-headed family emigrates. Exits can arise when a single mother marries, a divorced or widowed mother remarries, a mother dies, an only child dies, or an only child leaves home, or marries, or turns 18.

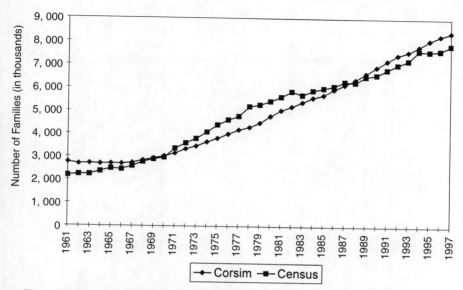

Figure 8.10. Number of Female-Headed Families in the United States, 1961–97. *Source*: CORSIM and Census data.

examples. Both examine CORSIM's capacity to simulate monthly Social Security benefits for retired female workers. Social Security benefits depend on each individual's earnings history, age, marital status, and spouse's earnings. Simulating benefits for retired female workers is particularly challenging, since female worker benefits are more likely than male worker benefits to depend on the joint distribution of the husband's and wife's earnings histories. Moreover, female earnings histories tend to be more variable, and more difficult to predict, than male earnings histories. Therefore, simulating realistic retired female worker benefits poses a challenge. Figure 8.11 displays average benefits for retired female workers over the 1961–1997 period. One series was simulated by CORSIM; the other series was drawn from Social Security administrative data.[17] The two series are similar. Even in 1997, at the end of the comparison period – by which point CORSIM has simulated thirty-seven years in the life of each retired worker – the difference between the two series is only 1.1 percent.

Averages, however, are notorious for concealing more than they reveal. Microsimulation is unique among modeling paradigms in its

[17] The historical estimate is taken from table 8.5.C2 in the 1997 Statistical Supplement published by the Social Security Administration.

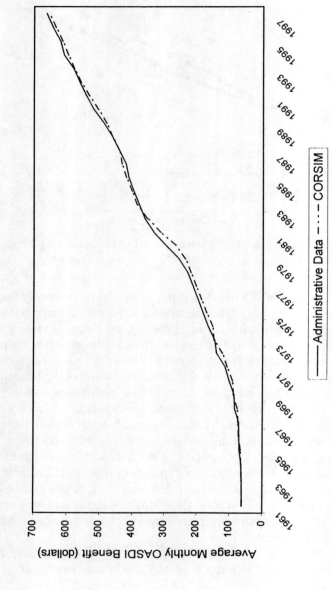

Figure 8.11. Average Monthly OASDI Benefit for Female Retired Workers, 1961–97. *Source:* CORSIM and administrative data.

claimed capacity to generate the full distributions underlying averages. But this claim amounts to little if the distributions are not validated. For example, Figure 8.11 suggests that CORSIM might be able to simulate realistic *average* monthly benefit levels for retired female workers, but the more difficult question concerns CORSIM's capacity to simulate realistic *distributions* of monthly benefit levels for retired female workers. Any claim that CORSIM can provide credible forecasts of the distributive impacts of Social Security reform proposals carries little weight in the absence of a demonstrated capacity to simulate historical benefit distributions. Figure 8.12 displays the results of one test of CORSIM's distributive realism. For the same group of retired female workers whose average benefit levels were examined previously, the figure compares the CORSIM-simulated distribution of monthly OASDI benefit levels in 1997 to the distribution as measured by Social Security administrative records.[18] Though differences are evident – CORSIM seems to overestimate the proportion of retired female workers receiving very high and very low benefits – the overall match of the two distributions is reasonably good. This is a relatively exacting validation test because – as was previously noted – by 1997 CORSIM has simulated thirty-seven years in the life of each retired worker.

One might reasonably argue that validation tests by model developers are less persuasive than validation tests by outsiders. Equally reasonably, one could argue that outsiders with Social Security policy expertise would be especially good at testing CORSIM's capacity for credible Social Security policy analyses. Fortuitously, researchers in the SSA's Office of Research, Evaluation and Statistics (ORES) are conducting a series of validation tests aimed at assessing CORSIM's suitability for Social Security policy analysis (Bailey, Cohen, and Iams, 1998). These researchers have the additional advantage of access to official Social Security earnings records and to a recently constructed exact match of these earnings records to respondents drawn from the Survey of Income and Program Participation (SIPP). The researchers are seeking to determine CORSIM's capacity for simulating realistic distributive impacts and realistic cost analyses at the same time. Initial evaluations have focused on individual and family earnings in CORSIM. In one exercise using the matched SIPP data, ORES researchers requested the CORSIM project team to generate a set of sixteen tables from a standard simulation. These tables examined the distribution of indexed monthly earnings for persons alive in 1991, classified by gender, race,

---

[18] Adapted from figure 5.21 in Favreault (1998).

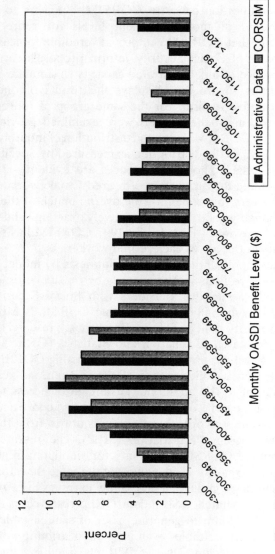

Figure 8.12. Percentage of Retired Female Workers by Monthly OASDI Benefit Level, 1997. *Source:* CORSIM and administrative data.

326

birth cohort, home owner status, and household net worth. Within groups specified by ORES, the value of indexed monthly earnings was calculated for persons located at exactly the 10th, 50th, and 90th percentile. The ORES researchers then compared the CORSIM tables to similar ones prepared within ORES, using the matched SIPP data. Figures 8.13 and 8.14 are drawn from a recent public presentation of these comparisons (Bailey, Cohen, and Iams, 1998). In Figure 8.13, mean indexed monthly earnings (MIME) are compared at the 10th, 50th, and 90th percentile for males living in a home-owning household across three successive birth cohorts. This comparison tests CORSIM's ability to simulate specific joint distributions relevant to Social Security outcomes. Figure 8.14 presents comparisons of the mean ratio of wife's MIME to husband's MIME for wives born in the 1931–1935 cohort, separately by race and household assets level. These ratios are important for the distribution of OASDI benefits across households. Both comparisons are reasonably successful. CORSIM seems able to simulate selected features of MIME levels and distributions for males, to capture trends by birth cohort, and to represent differences according to home ownership. CORSIM also accurately represents the mean ratios of wife's MIME to husband's MIME for wives in a specific birth cohort and classified by race and household assets level, although the ratio simulated for non-white wives is not as accurate as the ratio for white wives. Given the mass of comparisons possible across sixteen complex tables, the ORES researchers avoid simple summary evaluations. However, they cautiously suggest that CORSIM may be particularly strong in its projections for economically advantaged groups and its matching of husbands' and wives' earnings, but possibly less so for non-white females and persons with low assets.

Results from a second ORES validation exercise are not yet available for citation, but the study's author has given permission for a general description of the exercise. In this evaluation, individuals in both CORSIM and the matched SIPP file were classified by lifetime earnings pattern (low, middle, or high), earnings trend (declining, level, or rising), and earnings profile (sag, level, or humped). Comparing the CORSIM and SIPP lifetime earnings patterns as they are distributed across pattern, trend, and profile dimensions, the ORES study concluded that CORSIM succeeds generally in simulating a realistic variety of lifetime earnings patterns.[19]

A final validation issue involves the magnitude of the socioeconomic differentials in mortality in CORSIM, which in turn influence the socio-

---

[19] Personal communication from Lee Cohen, November 1998.

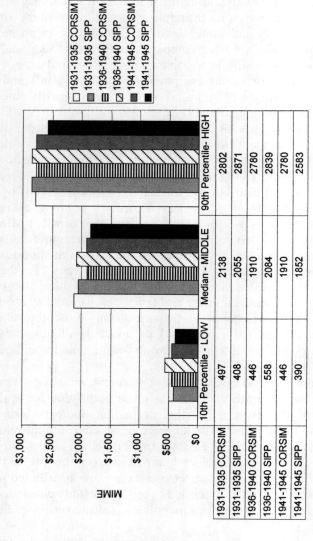

	10th Percentile - LOW	Median - MIDDLE	90th Percentile- HIGH
1931-1935 CORSIM	497	2138	2802
1931-1935 SIPP	408	2055	2871
1936-1940 CORSIM	446	1910	2780
1936-1940 SIPP	558	2084	2839
1941-1945 CORSIM	446	1910	2780
1941-1945 SIPP	390	1852	2583

Figure 8.13. Mean Indexed Monthly Earnings (MIME) for Male Home Owners by Rank and Cohort, 1931–45.
Source: CORSIM and SIPP administrative data.

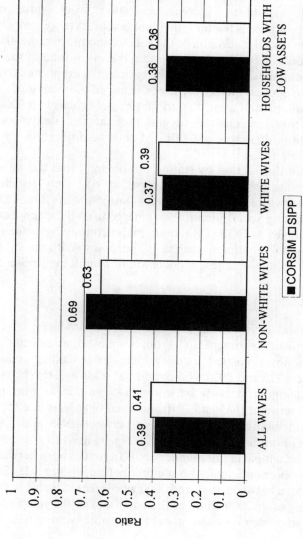

Figure 8.14. Mean Ratio of Wife's MIME to Husband's MIME for Wives Born 1931–35. *Source:* CORSIM and SIPP administrative data.

329

economic characteristics of Social Security beneficiaries. Socioeconomic differentials in mortality have been thoroughly documented (Caldwell and Diamond, 1979). Given previous research and the highly significant socioeconomic effects found by analyses of the National Longitudinal Mortality Survey, CORSIM's mortality module incorporates several socioeconomic variables – income, education, work status, marital status – as direct influences on individual-level mortality probabilities. However, from casual inspection of the socioeconomic parameters in the mortality module, it is difficult to estimate the magnitude of the cumulative socioeconomic differentials as the various effects play out over the life course.[20] To address this concern, we calculated the average CORSIM age at death distributed according to lifetime labor earnings. Displayed in Table 8.2, these calculations suggest that the cumulative socioeconomic mortality differences in CORSIM and the differences by sex lie within a credible range.[21]

We conclude this section by stating the obvious, that the handful of validation results presented above serve at best only to illustrate. Nothing remotely close to a definitive conclusion about CORSIM's adequacy for modeling Social Security can emerge from these few examples. Models as complex as CORSIM require major continuing evaluations to assess their suitability for a variety of purposes. Without substantial investment in validation, these models will not fulfill their potential.

Sample Selection

Our sample was drawn from a master sample produced by running CORSIM from 1960 through 2100. From this master, we selected the following: (a) all never-married males and females (including immigrants) born between 1945 and 2000 who lived to at least age 15; (b) all males (including immigrants) born between 1945 and 2000 who married women born between 1945 and 2010 and lived to at least age 15; and (c) all females (including immigrants) born between 1945 and 2000 who married males born between 1945 and 2000 who lived to at least age 15.

Selecting the sample in this manner omits (a) males born between 1945 and 2000 who married females born either before 1945 or after 2010 and (b) females born between 1945 and 2000 who married males born either before 1945 or after 2000. Thus, at the early end of the sample, we lose some males who married older women and some women who married

---

[20] The inability of casual inspection to predict outcomes as multiple effects play out over time is, of course, part of the rationale for complex simulation models such as CORSIM.

[21] Communications between Ron Lee and Larry Kotlikoff, November 19–20, 1998.

Table 8.2. *Average Age of Death by Lifetime Labor Earnings*

	Lifetime Labor Earnings (1997 dollars)										Sample Total
	0–120k	120k–240k	240k–360k	360k–480k	480k–600k	600k–720k	720k–840k	840k–960k	960k–1.08m	1.08m+	
Cohort 45	79.0	79.4	78.2	78.9	78.6	79.1	79.8	80.4	79.7	79.8	79.1
Cohort 50	79.2	78.7	78.2	78.4	79.2	78.8	79.3	78.7	79.4	80.3	78.9
Cohort 55	79.2	79.1	79.2	79.9	80.8	78.9	78.5	79.9	79.5	81.3	79.5
Cohort 60	79.6	79.4	80.0	78.3	80.5	81.6	80.4	79.8	80.2	82.3	79.9
Cohort 65	79.2	80.0	80.9	79.5	80.3	81.0	82.8	83.6	79.4	81.2	80.2
Cohort 70	80.0	80.5	81.3	80.8	80.7	81.7	81.7	79.1	80.9	81.7	80.7
Cohort 75	80.3	81.1	80.9	80.4	81.6	82.1	81.0	82.9	79.4	82.3	81.0
Cohort 80	80.9	80.9	80.4	80.8	81.2	81.4	83.8	80.8	81.0	82.1	81.1
Cohort 85	80.7	80.9	81.6	81.5	82.9	81.6	83.5	81.6	80.6	83.1	81.5
Cohort 90	80.8	80.5	81.3	80.7	81.2	81.0	81.4	82.7	80.9	82.8	81.2
Cohort 95	79.9	80.1	79.9	80.9	81.3	82.3	82.2	81.7	80.4	81.0	80.6
Men 45	70.2	74.5	74.4	76.8	77.0	77.8	78.7	78.5	78.3	78.8	75.8
Men 50	70.0	74.1	75.1	75.8	77.1	77.3	76.9	77.2	77.8	79.1	75.3
Men 55	71.2	74.0	76.2	77.3	79.2	77.0	75.8	77.8	78.9	80.0	76.0
Men 60	72.6	74.9	77.0	76.1	78.0	80.0	77.7	77.2	78.8	81.1	76.6
Men 65	72.1	75.7	77.1	77.2	77.3	78.7	82.1	82.3	78.3	79.6	76.9
Men 70	72.1	76.4	78.2	78.8	77.9	80.5	79.8	78.2	79.9	80.1	77.3
Men 75	73.2	76.8	77.8	78.2	80.1	78.8	78.4	78.7	77.3	80.7	77.6
Men 80	74.0	76.5	77.6	77.7	78.8	78.2	82.0	79.4	80.0	80.4	77.8
Men 85	73.4	76.7	77.9	79.2	80.3	79.9	80.3	79.4	77.5	81.9	78.3
Men 90	74.4	76.3	77.9	77.7	80.2	78.7	80.8	80.6	79.6	81.2	78.2
Men 95	74.3	75.7	76.9	79.2	78.8	80.9	80.1	80.9	79.6	79.5	78.0

(continued)

331

Table 8.2. (continued)

| | Lifetime Labor Earnings (1997 dollars) | | | | | | | | | | Sample |
	0–120k	120k–240k	240k–360k	360k–480k	480k–600k	600k–720k	720k–840k	840k–960k	960k–1.08m	1.08m+	Total
Women 45	81.4	82.4	83.0	83.0	82.6	84.7	84.2	86.1	84.0	83.8	82.2
Women 50	82.3	81.7	81.5	82.9	84.1	82.6	85.0	83.7	83.6	84.3	82.3
Women 55	82.4	82.6	82.6	83.7	83.5	83.0	84.7	83.0	81.0	84.7	82.8
Women 60	82.4	82.9	83.3	81.5	84.0	83.8	84.6	83.6	84.3	85.2	82.9
Women 65	82.2	83.4	85.0	82.6	84.7	85.4	83.9	85.6	82.2	85.8	83.4
Women 70	83.6	83.6	84.5	83.6	85.1	83.7	85.2	81.1	83.1	85.5	83.9
Women 75	83.1	84.4	83.8	83.6	84.3	87.1	84.8	88.2	84.7	86.2	84.1
Women 80	83.8	84.4	83.8	85.3	84.5	85.6	86.4	84.1	83.2	86.6	84.4
Women 85	83.6	84.1	84.6	84.2	86.3	84.3	88.5	85.4	87.6	86.0	84.4
Women 90	83.5	83.4	84.7	84.2	82.6	83.8	82.9	86.5	83.7	86.0	83.9
Women 95	82.2	83.2	83.1	83.0	84.6	84.8	85.5	83.8	81.7	84.3	83.2
White 45	79.6	79.5	78.8	78.9	79.0	78.6	79.7	80.8	80.5	79.5	79.3
White 50	79.7	78.9	78.4	78.3	79.3	78.9	79.1	78.5	79.1	80.4	79.1
White 55	79.6	79.4	79.5	79.9	81.2	78.8	78.8	80.7	79.8	81.2	79.8
White 60	80.1	79.6	80.4	78.6	80.3	81.7	80.3	80.2	80.0	82.4	80.2
White 65	79.8	80.4	80.6	79.4	80.0	81.6	83.0	83.4	78.3	81.1	80.4
White 70	80.5	81.0	81.6	80.9	81.0	82.0	81.4	78.2	81.6	81.3	81.0
White 75	80.8	81.7	80.6	80.7	81.9	81.8	81.7	83.4	80.2	82.0	81.3
White 80	82.0	81.1	80.4	80.8	81.0	81.3	83.4	81.3	80.4	82.3	81.4
White 85	81.3	81.3	82.1	81.7	82.9	81.5	83.8	81.5	81.2	83.0	81.9
White 90	81.4	80.9	81.7	80.9	80.8	81.0	81.4	82.7	81.7	83.1	81.5
White 95	80.5	80.6	80.4	81.4	81.8	82.5	82.0	81.6	80.7	81.5	81.0
Non-White 45	73.1	78.4	74.6	78.9	75.4	85.0	80.7	76.7	73.0	84.0	76.7
Non-White 50	74.7	77.6	76.9	79.0	78.9	78.2	79.9	80.3	81.2	79.2	77.4
Non-White 55	76.5	77.1	77.0	79.8	78.6	79.2	75.1	71.3	76.0	82.5	77.6

Non-White 60	76.6	77.6	78.0	76.7	81.7	80.9	81.2	75.8	82.2	82.1	78.2
Non-White 65	75.7	78.1	82.2	79.9	82.8	77.7	81.2	84.9	88.7	82.4	79.2
Non-White 70	76.8	78.3	80.0	79.7	79.4	79.6	83.4	86.1	77.2	84.3	79.2
Non-White 75	77.9	78.6	82.6	78.8	80.3	83.8	77.2	80.3	76.7	84.3	79.7
Non-White 80	76.1	80.1	80.1	80.8	82.3	81.9	85.4	78.9	82.9	81.3	79.6
Non-White 85	77.6	79.0	79.5	80.3	82.6	81.8	81.9	82.5	78.0	83.9	79.9
Non-White 90	78.3	79.0	80.1	80.0	82.7	80.8	81.5	83.0	76.7	80.9	79.8
Non-White 95	77.7	78.6	78.2	79.0	79.7	81.8	83.2	82.2	78.9	78.8	78.9
Non-College 45	78.4	78.4	77.8	78.0	78.2	79.3	79.9	80.6	78.4	80.1	78.5
Non-College 50	79.0	78.0	78.0	77.9	79.1	79.5	79.9	78.3	77.8	80.2	78.6
Non-College 55	78.5	78.9	79.0	80.0	81.3	77.3	77.5	79.9	77.8	80.8	79.1
Non-College 60	79.3	78.9	79.0	78.6	80.1	80.3	81.3	79.2	78.2	81.8	79.4
Non-College 65	78.9	79.7	80.2	78.4	80.9	81.2	82.2	82.2	78.5	81.0	79.8
Non-College 70	79.4	80.2	79.8	79.6	81.1	82.4	82.8	77.4	80.1	81.9	80.2
Non-College 75	79.6	80.0	80.1	80.6	80.8	80.3	80.5	82.3	80.1	80.7	80.1
Non-College 80	80.1	79.9	79.8	80.7	79.6	82.7	82.7	82.1	80.7	81.0	80.4
Non-College 85	80.0	79.8	80.7	81.2	82.3	81.5	83.3	82.9	81.2	82.5	80.8
Non-College 90	80.4	80.2	81.2	80.3	81.2	81.2	80.3	81.3	81.2	82.7	80.8
Non-College 95	79.3	80.0	79.8	79.9	79.8	82.3	80.8	81.4	79.9	80.2	80.0
College 45	80.7	82.1	79.6	80.9	79.3	78.9	79.6	80.1	81.6	79.4	80.4
College 50	79.6	80.3	78.6	79.4	79.4	77.7	78.5	79.1	81.3	80.4	79.5
College 55	81.0	79.4	79.5	79.6	79.9	80.8	80.0	79.8	82.1	81.7	80.3
College 60	80.2	80.1	82.1	77.9	80.9	83.2	78.9	80.5	82.9	82.8	80.8
College 65	80.0	80.4	82.0	81.0	79.6	80.8	83.5	86.0	80.7	81.4	80.9
College 70	80.9	81.0	83.4	82.0	80.3	81.1	80.7	80.4	81.8	81.5	81.4
College 75	81.5	82.7	81.9	80.1	82.6	83.5	81.5	83.5	78.7	83.6	82.1
College 80	82.1	82.2	81.1	80.9	82.9	79.8	84.9	79.7	81.2	82.9	82.0
College 85	81.7	82.4	82.9	81.8	83.4	81.7	83.6	80.8	80.1	83.6	82.4
College 90	81.4	80.9	81.5	81.2	81.2	80.8	82.4	84.3	80.6	82.8	81.6
College 95	81.0	80.3	80.1	81.8	83.0	82.4	83.7	81.9	80.8	81.5	81.3

older men. At the late end of the sample, we lose some males who married very much younger women and some females who married younger men.

SSBC

SSBC is a highly detailed OASI benefit calculator developed by Economic Security Planning, Inc., for use in its financial-planning software program, ESPlanner™. It also calculates retirement, spousal and child-dependent, and survivor benefits, using the Social Security earnings test, family benefit maxima, actuarial adjustments, benefit recomputation, eligibility rules, the ceiling on taxable earnings, and legislated changes in the normal retirement age.

Calculation of OASI benefits, the basics of which are described in the Appendix, is extremely complex. The *Social Security Handbook* describing the rules governing these benefits runs over 500 pages. Even so, on many key points, the *Handbook* is incomplete and misleading. This assessment is shared by Social Security's senior actuaries, who were consulted repeatedly in preparing SSBC. Their assistance, which proved invaluable, came in the form of both extensive discussions and the transmittal of numerous, highly detailed benefit calculations.

Comparing SSA and CORSIM-SSBC Aggregate Benefit and Tax Projections

In considering the differences between our own and SSA's projected aggregates of taxes and benefits, it's worth asking what microsimulation brings to the process of projecting aggregate taxes and benefits. The answer is twofold. First, the size of aggregate Social Security benefits and tax payments in future years depends on the distribution of lifetime earnings. Microsimulation can be used to explore how these distributions will evolve over time and the impact of the evolution of these distributions on aggregate taxes and benefits. Second, although it is not our focus here, microsimulation can also be used to project aggregates, such as aggregate covered labor earnings. SSA could, in principle, use these alternative aggregate forecasts in refining its own benefit and tax projection methodology.

Consider now Table 8.3, which reports our own and SSA's OASI aggregate benefit projections. One feature of this table that may at first seem counterintuitive is that both sets of projected aggregate benefits are lower under the high-cost assumptions than under the low-cost ones. The explanation here is that the high-cost assumptions, although they assume greater longevity, also assume lower real wage growth. Since absolute benefit levels are a function of absolute real wages, lower real wage

Table 8.3. *Total Benefits (millions of 1997 dollars)*

	Low-Cost Assumptions		Intermediate Assumptions		High-Cost Assumptions	
	CORSIM-SSBC	SSA	CORSIM-SSBC	SSA	CORSIM-SSBC	SSA
2000	958	329,555	907	329,188	953	321,807
2001	797	334,326	821	334,857	890	326,878
2002	949	339,696	992	340,706	1,021	337,536
2003	1,085	345,088	1,028	346,040	1,014	343,653
2004	1,120	350,698	990	351,788	975	349,637
2005	1,228	357,347	1,009	358,085	1,037	356,086
2006	1,425	363,617	1,089	364,632	1,133	362,468
2007	9,704	370,572	9,319	372,181	8,832	369,843
2008	20,040	379,910	19,040	380,855	17,962	376,784
2009	34,520	391,251	33,460	391,311	31,249	385,583
2010	55,244	403,980	54,518	402,956	49,239	395,419
2011	81,736	417,695	79,025	415,400	73,748	405,939
2012	109,836	432,906	104,842	429,118	96,395	417,510
2013	144,187	450,114	136,425	444,607	128,499	430,531
2014	174,787	469,082	165,600	461,662	151,327	444,966
2015	210,244	489,450	197,789	479,764	183,463	460,253
2016	243,098	511,104	227,260	498,735	208,113	476,140
2017	279,503	533,848	261,270	518,589	241,500	492,647
2018	310,487	556,357	287,581	538,520	263,045	509,682
2019	345,927	579,673	322,315	559,058	296,581	527,176
2020	380,607	603,323	354,339	579,820	320,580	544,732
2021	419,359	627,164	389,650	600,615	356,278	562,338
2022	453,682	648,078	420,604	618,598	380,027	577,481
2023	489,881	669,163	452,983	636,530	412,879	592,307
2024	523,765	692,214	481,150	656,010	436,972	608,409
2025	561,428	714,992	514,680	675,149	469,329	624,207
2026	584,068	737,297	535,478	693,747	483,878	639,479
2027	608,788	758,706	559,942	711,409	507,742	653,978
2028	629,954	779,710	579,375	728,787	522,975	668,339
2029	654,761	800,553	601,802	746,088	544,341	682,715
2030	674,837	820,573	621,009	762,567	556,907	696,311
2031	699,566	840,182	645,282	778,563	578,850	709,428
2032	719,319	859,273	661,224	793,872	592,746	721,875
2033	741,842	877,110	682,589	807,892	611,470	733,116
2034	753,320	893,209	692,703	820,203	618,913	742,827
2035	770,150	907,935	708,186	831,177	631,893	751,285

(continued)

Table 8.3. *(continued)*

	Low-Cost Assumptions		Intermediate Assumptions		High-Cost Assumptions	
	CORSIM-SSBC	SSA	CORSIM-SSBC	SSA	CORSIM-SSBC	SSA
2036	780,063	922,026	717,086	841,368	638,678	759,102
2037	793,007	935,733	730,055	851,115	651,076	766,485
2038	799,999	949,114	734,631	860,515	654,049	773,350
2039	811,561	961,996	745,572	869,276	663,494	779,579
2040	814,932	974,255	747,581	877,296	662,497	785,009
2041	827,598	986,624	754,335	885,038	672,855	789,979
2042	836,853	999,614	757,101	892,426	674,840	795,049
2043	850,575	1,013,263	768,768	901,378	684,490	800,216
2044	861,730	1,027,634	775,699	910,102	687,110	805,427
2045	876,427	1,042,566	787,229	919,138	693,310	810,811
2046	885,697	1,058,192	795,256	928,607	695,931	816,427
2047	900,933	1,074,885	805,963	938,798	704,811	822,456
2048	913,805	1,092,494	812,344	949,538	704,768	828,951
2049	935,929	1,110,803	826,074	960,764	713,922	835,639
2050	950,627	1,130,044	831,936	972,573	718,155	842,637
2051	970,013	1,150,514	845,966	985,207	728,889	850,234
2052	990,838	1,172,292	856,198	998,695	734,036	858,454
2053	1,012,679	1,195,051	869,567	1,012,871	747,380	867,018
2054	1,033,046	1,218,661	882,383	1,027,537	750,857	875,839
2055	1,056,564	1,242,885	898,325	1,042,525	763,501	884,955
2056	1,077,040	1,267,599	911,752	1,057,994	766,920	894,323
2057	1,103,248	1,292,924	926,183	1,073,853	781,201	903,997
2058	1,125,636	1,318,635	939,890	1,090,012	787,477	913,991
2059	1,144,622	1,344,501	953,767	1,106,286	797,834	923,943
2060	1,230,488	1,370,374	1,022,502	1,122,336	802,688	933,647
2061	1,296,186	1,396,148	1,074,913	1,138,147	857,945	943,131
2062	1,310,322	1,421,907	1,081,867	1,153,745	887,044	952,334
2063	1,302,490	1,447,842	1,072,638	1,169,143	883,289	961,305
2064	1,281,692	1,474,000	1,057,044	1,184,487	868,039	970,005
2065	1,262,763	1,500,473	1,041,212	1,199,769	856,721	978,465

growth will lower absolute real benefit outlays. As Table 8.4 indicates, it will also lower real tax revenue.

Turning to our findings, they suggest a potentially smaller imbalance between long-run benefits and payroll tax revenues than is being forecast by the actuaries. This is true for each of three alternative sets of actuarial assumptions entertained by the actuaries and arises with respect to taxes.

Consider first the benefit projections presented in Table 8.3. Recall that the period over which benefit comparisons are meaningful is 2050 and years close to 2050, since our sample ranges in age from 50 to 105 in 2050. In 2050, our projected benefits under the intermediate assumptions fall short of SSA's by almost 15 percent. Our high- and low-cost benefit projections for 2050 are also lower than those of SSA by about the same percentage. The underprediction of benefits by roughly 15 percent prevails for all years between 2045 and 2050 under all three sets of cost assumptions.

In thinking about the discrepancies between these two sets of benefit forecasts, it's important to bear in mind that the CORSIM data used in the SSBC are benchmarked, on an annual basis, to SSA's own forecast of aggregate employee wages plus proprietorship income, as well as to its coverage rate. In calibrating the lifetime and annual variances of the CORSIM weekly earnings module, which influence the division of earnings between covered and noncovered, we've also targeted and closely matched SSA's actual collection of OASI taxes over the period 1960 to 1998. This means that differences in the benefit projections should be arising for more microeconomic reasons, involving (a) the distribution of covered earnings within the workforce, (b) the distribution of completed lifetimes, (c) the distribution of completed work spans, (d) the eligibility of particular workers and their dependents for auxiliary survivor and other benefits, and (e) the extent to which benefits are earnings tested, actuarially reduced for early benefit receipt, limited by family maxima, subject to benefit recomputation, and affected by others of the highly detailed features of SSBC's benefit calculations. Since SSA's forecasting methodology does not attempt to consider these various factors, except in a highly aggregated manner, there might be some reason to favor our forecast over SSA's. But we would not advance this argument very far without substantial additional exploration.

On the other hand, since CORSIM's variances in lifetime and annual earnings have not, to date, been fully calibrated against the corresponding variances arising in the earnings records collected by SSA,[22] it could well be that the CORSIM micro earnings variance underlying the differences in projected aggregate benefits is off the mark. Another possibility is that there are some systematic differences in the calculation of benefits by the SSBC and by SSA. This possibility seems remote, however. SSBC

---

[22] However, recall the discussion in the validation section concerning validation tests of CORSIM lifetime earnings patterns carried out by ORES researchers in SSA.

has been tested against ANYPIA, SSA's published retirement benefit calculator. It has also undergone very extensive testing with respect to the calculation of ancillary benefits, earnings testing, benefit recomputation, etc. A third point is that the CORSIM data we are using constitute a random sample, not a population sample. To some extent, our underestimation of aggregate benefits might reflect sampling error. A final point is that 2050 is a long way off and that small differences in underlying distribution assumptions may translate into larger ones over time.

Table 8.4 shows a much closer match to SSA's projections when it comes to aggregate OASI taxes. The relevant comparison years in this case are 2010 through 2020. In 2010, our sample ranges in age from 10 to 65; in 2020, it ranges in age from 20 to 75. Consider 2018, when our sample ranges in age from 18 to 73 and presumably covers virtually the entire workforce. Under the intermediate assumptions, we project taxes that are 2.8 percent higher than those projected by SSA. Under the high-cost assumptions, our projected tax aggregate exceeds SSA's by 4.0 percent; and under the low-cost assumptions, we match SSA's projection within 1 percent.

Social Security's Treatment of Postwar Americans

Internal Rates of Return

Tables 8.5, 8.6, and 8.7 present, respectively, intermediate, high-cost, and low-cost calculations of internal rates of return on OASI contributions for postwar Americans distinguished by lifetime earnings amounts, cohort, sex, race, and education. For reference, Table 8.8 shows the numbers of observations in these cells. "Cohort 45" refers to those born from 1945 through 1949. Other cohorts are defined in the same manner, except for Cohort 95, which includes those born in 2000.

Consider first the total column in the top set of numbers (the cohort comparison) in Table 8.5. These figures suggest that postwar American cohorts will, under current law and under intermediate assumptions, earn less than a 2 percent real rate of return on their contributions, with the highest rate of return equal to 1.98 percent and the lowest equal to 1.73 percent. Other researchers, including Steuerle and Bakija (1994) and Coronado, Fullerton, and Glass (1999), have found similarly small rates of return.

Interestingly, there is no trend across the cohorts with respect to the rates of return they earn.[23] In other words, under current law, the deal

---

[23] The results in our recent NBER working paper (Caldwell et al., 1998) suggesting a lower internal rate of return for younger cohorts reflect a computer error and have been corrected in Caldwell et al. (1999).

Table 8.4. *Total Taxes (millions of 1997 dollars)*

	Low-Cost Assumptions		Intermediate Assumptions		High-Cost Assumptions	
	CORSIM-SSBC	SSA	CORSIM-SSBC	SSA	CORSIM-SSBC	SSA
2000	350,124	378,114	343,922	368,622	332,844	352,262
2001	362,195	385,753	354,369	373,417	341,037	353,825
2002	373,755	393,560	363,946	378,832	337,976	345,592
2003	386,543	401,545	374,207	383,609	350,068	351,126
2004	398,819	409,734	384,587	388,812	361,311	357,309
2005	411,882	419,469	395,110	394,996	369,909	363,302
2006	424,197	428,178	405,161	400,446	377,742	367,047
2007	437,912	438,838	414,994	407,913	385,005	371,485
2008	450,700	448,241	424,355	414,329	391,642	375,041
2009	464,949	458,581	435,142	421,144	399,419	378,991
2010	475,890	468,774	442,438	427,970	404,118	382,933
2011	485,463	478,813	449,246	434,542	407,372	386,439
2012	493,359	488,645	454,675	440,698	410,714	389,626
2013	500,948	497,810	459,534	446,389	411,848	392,442
2014	510,237	507,128	464,727	451,954	414,394	394,909
2015	517,142	516,073	469,264	457,322	414,890	397,325
2016	525,286	524,943	474,898	462,465	415,748	399,503
2017	533,322	533,709	480,214	467,400	416,486	401,530
2018	541,492	542,454	485,566	472,288	419,280	403,174
2019	549,642	551,255	487,977	477,089	420,087	404,770
2020	553,086	560,187	488,260	481,763	417,224	406,182
2021	553,370	569,195	486,610	486,423	412,569	407,526
2022	551,436	578,259	482,193	490,931	407,910	408,624
2023	547,609	587,318	476,492	495,266	400,848	409,577
2024	544,040	596,808	471,951	499,827	394,034	410,498
2025	541,446	606,541	465,873	504,438	386,443	411,409
2026	539,142	616,511	460,626	509,023	380,817	412,252
2027	532,151	627,071	452,446	513,900	371,408	413,278
2028	522,133	638,479	442,759	519,256	362,093	414,509
2029	512,419	650,292	432,335	524,797	351,728	415,785
2030	502,350	662,541	421,946	530,513	342,461	417,119
2031	492,831	675,246	411,442	536,411	331,554	418,534
2032	484,209	688,464	402,722	542,535	321,777	420,077
2033	475,038	702,094	392,210	548,825	310,306	421,574
2034	467,059	715,940	381,987	555,053	300,421	422,952
2035	455,493	729,982	369,432	561,193	289,049	424,124

(continued)

Table 8.4. *(continued)*

	Low-Cost Assumptions		Intermediate Assumptions		High-Cost Assumptions	
	CORSIM-SSBC	SSA	CORSIM-SSBC	SSA	CORSIM-SSBC	SSA
2036	444,784	744,326	358,671	567,395	279,651	425,214
2037	433,201	759,235	347,148	573,805	269,144	426,422
2038	423,161	774,673	337,579	580,431	259,712	427,643
2039	413,104	790,378	326,303	587,027	249,369	428,801
2040	402,390	806,132	317,279	593,549	240,242	429,680
2041	388,622	797,673	305,758	599,925	229,199	430,418
2042	376,085	838,325	294,964	606,253	220,172	431,075
2043	362,693	854,764	282,385	612,580	209,321	431,695
2044	349,079	871,521	270,990	619,000	201,029	432,212
2045	333,606	888,493	256,033	625,272	189,386	432,629
2046	319,094	905,713	243,085	631,556	181,143	432,985
2047	301,079	923,285	228,234	637,894	170,618	433,305
2048	286,945	941,240	216,656	644,291	161,251	433,582
2049	271,044	959,510	202,503	650,652	150,984	433,767
2050	257,437	978,022	190,750	656,976	141,657	433,856
2051	241,997	996,879	177,851	663,307	130,770	433,818
2052	223,970	1,016,259	166,411	669,740	121,946	433,783
2053	206,430	1,036,228	153,899	676,281	109,934	433,775
2054	190,130	1,056,465	141,831	682,809	101,844	433,658
2055	173,140	1,077,200	127,952	689,321	90,796	433,463
2056	156,143	1,098,234	114,803	695,881	82,138	433,227
2057	136,363	1,119,871	99,587	702,527	69,046	432,981
2058	117,090	1,142,113	86,539	709,396	60,591	432,747
2059	98,819	1,164,989	72,074	716,342	49,753	432,526
2060	82,893	1,188,341	59,808	723,364	41,044	432,261
2061	64,206	1,212,211	44,805	730,475	30,246	431,986
2062	49,525	1,236,656	34,334	737,655	24,356	431,697
2063	33,293	1,261,586	23,078	744,934	14,741	431,420
2064	20,878	1,287,085	13,749	752,289	9,444	431,104
2065	5,948	1,313,143	3,191	759,746	2,111	430,826

Table 8.5. *Internal Rates of Return under Intermediate Assumptions*

	Lifetime Labor Earnings (1997 dollars)										
	0–120k	120k–240k	240k–360k	360k–480k	480k–600k	600k–720k	720k–840k	840k–960k	960k–1.08m	1.08m+	Total
Cohort 45	4.91	3.00	1.99	1.53	1.21	0.88	0.78	0.92	0.52	0.53	1.84
Cohort 50	5.63	3.27	2.27	1.73	1.46	0.97	0.79	0.54	0.56	0.70	1.98
Cohort 55	5.25	3.17	2.21	1.81	1.49	0.93	0.62	0.52	0.47	0.54	1.81
Cohort 60	5.03	3.03	2.19	1.54	1.47	1.19	0.63	0.46	0.29	0.57	1.73
Cohort 65	4.97	3.10	2.38	1.64	1.53	1.27	1.07	0.97	0.34	0.39	1.74
Cohort 70	4.98	3.29	2.44	1.92	1.57	1.40	1.06	0.40	0.57	0.43	1.80
Cohort 75	5.09	3.38	2.48	1.95	1.73	1.61	1.20	1.12	0.47	0.52	1.87
Cohort 80	5.24	3.42	2.61	2.09	1.79	1.53	1.56	0.97	0.52	0.52	1.85
Cohort 85	5.31	3.57	2.79	2.36	2.00	1.70	1.65	1.14	0.75	0.66	1.99
Cohort 90	5.31	3.63	2.83	2.29	1.94	1.68	1.47	1.42	0.96	0.69	1.97
Cohort 95	5.45	3.73	2.89	2.39	2.10	2.03	1.78	1.33	0.93	0.41	1.87
Men 45	3.35	2.07	1.29	1.11	0.92	0.62	0.55	0.65	0.07	0.26	0.88
Men 50	3.45	2.27	1.55	1.21	1.08	0.64	0.35	0.21	0.27	0.48	0.99
Men 55	3.40	2.19	1.60	1.20	1.13	0.49	0.11	-0.01	0.17	0.35	0.91
Men 60	3.36	2.09	1.45	1.04	1.00	0.83	-0.09	-0.13	0.00	0.38	0.85
Men 65	3.41	2.26	1.62	1.14	0.92	0.83	0.89	0.74	0.09	0.11	0.90
Men 70	3.35	2.46	1.72	1.43	1.10	1.13	0.72	0.22	0.31	0.17	0.99
Men 75	3.50	2.64	1.85	1.50	1.40	1.07	0.68	0.51	0.06	0.27	1.07
Men 80	3.47	2.74	2.06	1.53	1.42	1.06	1.34	0.73	0.35	0.25	1.09
Men 85	3.82	2.96	2.17	1.88	1.63	1.47	1.10	0.74	0.17	0.47	1.25
Men 90	4.08	3.12	2.21	1.77	1.74	1.38	1.41	1.12	0.70	0.48	1.32
Men 95	4.37	3.23	2.44	2.16	1.62	1.87	1.54	1.20	0.81	0.25	1.29

(continued)

Table 8.5. *(continued)*

| | Lifetime Labor Earnings (1997 dollars) | | | | | | | | | | |
	0–120k	120k–240k	240k–360k	360k–480k	480k–600k	600k–720k	720k–840k	840k–960k	960k–1.08m	1.08m+	Total
Women 45	5.11	3.42	2.63	2.24	1.84	1.80	1.47	1.63	1.81	1.52	3.06
Women 50	6.06	3.77	2.89	2.45	2.15	1.61	1.65	1.41	1.16	1.31	3.15
Women 55	5.73	3.69	2.77	2.50	2.00	1.73	1.50	1.21	1.09	0.99	2.82
Women 60	5.47	3.57	2.80	2.12	2.04	1.63	1.50	1.15	0.97	0.96	2.65
Women 65	5.42	3.59	2.99	2.19	2.21	1.90	1.37	1.27	0.90	1.03	2.67
Women 70	5.48	3.77	2.97	2.48	2.17	1.83	1.57	0.79	1.14	0.95	2.71
Women 75	5.51	3.82	2.95	2.49	2.24	2.28	1.85	1.74	1.26	1.02	2.75
Women 80	5.72	3.82	3.15	2.70	2.23	2.02	1.83	1.46	0.87	1.11	2.75
Women 85	5.69	3.94	3.19	2.82	2.41	2.03	2.32	1.73	1.76	1.05	2.80
Women 90	5.65	3.92	3.29	2.76	2.20	2.01	1.59	1.88	1.47	1.10	2.72
Women 95	5.74	4.02	3.27	2.64	2.59	2.28	2.09	1.65	1.11	0.76	2.59
White 45	4.94	3.02	2.06	1.51	1.24	0.81	0.78	0.97	0.63	0.48	1.84
White 50	5.69	3.33	2.33	1.71	1.46	0.93	0.77	0.52	0.52	0.72	2.00
White 55	5.29	3.22	2.25	1.79	1.55	0.93	0.62	0.62	0.50	0.50	1.82
White 60	5.08	3.09	2.26	1.56	1.45	1.19	0.58	0.49	0.24	0.56	1.74
White 65	5.05	3.18	2.34	1.65	1.51	1.30	1.10	0.93	0.17	0.37	1.73
White 70	5.06	3.36	2.50	1.95	1.56	1.42	1.01	0.26	0.65	0.37	1.80
White 75	5.07	3.43	2.50	1.98	1.78	1.61	1.25	1.19	0.51	0.47	1.87
White 80	5.33	3.47	2.64	2.10	1.80	1.56	1.54	1.03	0.44	0.53	1.86
White 85	5.37	3.68	2.88	2.42	2.01	1.72	1.67	1.09	0.79	0.62	2.00
White 90	5.47	3.75	2.92	2.34	1.90	1.72	1.51	1.39	0.99	0.72	1.99
White 95	5.52	3.89	3.02	2.48	2.17	2.10	1.77	1.33	1.01	0.47	1.92
Non-White 45	4.64	2.91	1.47	1.69	0.93	1.60	0.67	0.48	−0.36	1.11	1.78
Non-White 50	5.11	2.88	1.91	1.82	1.44	1.27	0.90	0.69	0.80	0.51	1.83
Non-White 55	4.94	2.81	1.96	1.88	1.05	0.89	0.61	−0.90	0.05	0.91	1.78

Non-White 60	4.62	2.69	1.72	1.42	1.59	1.15	1.01	0.18	0.73	0.64	1.65
Non-White 65	4.43	2.69	2.55	1.61	1.66	1.07	0.85	1.18	1.61	0.51	1.81
Non-White 70	4.52	2.98	2.20	1.76	1.61	1.30	1.28	1.27	0.05	0.75	1.83
Non-White 75	5.17	3.18	2.37	1.80	1.53	1.65	0.91	0.69	0.33	0.76	1.86
Non-White 80	4.81	3.15	2.48	2.05	1.74	1.37	1.61	0.67	0.76	0.43	1.81
Non-White 85	5.02	3.08	2.38	2.07	1.96	1.61	1.54	1.44	0.51	0.86	1.94
Non-White 90	4.65	3.15	2.47	2.03	2.13	1.53	1.28	1.51	0.78	0.53	1.88
Non-White 95	5.13	3.20	2.41	2.00	1.86	1.71	1.81	1.32	0.45	0.16	1.67
Non-College 45	4.86	2.83	1.85	1.39	1.15	0.97	0.77	1.01	0.19	0.61	1.89
Non-College 50	5.57	3.12	2.18	1.59	1.38	1.04	0.78	0.46	0.33	0.62	2.04
Non-College 55	5.12	3.06	2.20	1.83	1.55	0.66	0.37	0.50	0.25	0.47	1.85
Non-College 60	4.91	2.90	1.97	1.53	1.39	1.00	0.77	0.28	-0.09	0.47	1.73
Non-College 65	4.87	3.02	2.27	1.44	1.56	1.19	0.98	0.79	0.12	0.29	1.74
Non-College 70	4.91	3.17	2.23	1.68	1.54	1.41	1.25	0.14	0.56	0.47	1.87
Non-College 75	4.92	3.23	2.36	1.97	1.61	1.33	1.14	0.96	0.48	0.21	1.86
Non-College 80	5.11	3.28	2.47	2.08	1.56	1.69	1.43	1.12	0.41	0.39	1.92
Non-College 85	5.22	3.39	2.60	2.30	1.86	1.65	1.58	1.11	0.94	0.59	2.04
Non-College 90	5.12	3.55	2.78	2.20	1.86	1.64	1.27	1.25	0.98	0.70	2.05
Non-College 95	5.23	3.65	2.84	2.20	1.83	1.86	1.56	1.22	0.76	0.30	1.92
College 45	5.04	3.44	2.36	1.81	1.33	0.79	0.78	0.81	0.97	0.46	1.75
College 50	5.78	3.60	2.45	1.99	1.57	0.83	0.80	0.63	0.78	0.77	1.88
College 55	5.55	3.38	2.25	1.77	1.37	1.24	0.95	0.55	0.78	0.61	1.75
College 60	5.25	3.24	2.57	1.57	1.57	1.40	0.34	0.69	0.73	0.65	1.72
College 65	5.16	3.22	2.54	1.90	1.50	1.38	1.19	1.27	0.62	0.47	1.73
College 70	5.07	3.46	2.70	2.18	1.61	1.40	0.87	0.59	0.57	0.39	1.74
College 75	5.34	3.57	2.61	1.92	1.87	1.81	1.24	1.26	0.46	0.73	1.88
College 80	5.40	3.59	2.76	2.09	2.01	1.32	1.67	0.82	0.62	0.60	1.79
College 85	5.43	3.79	3.02	2.44	2.13	1.74	1.69	1.17	0.55	0.71	1.93
College 90	5.58	3.74	2.90	2.38	2.04	1.72	1.62	1.59	0.94	0.68	1.89
College 95	5.77	3.85	2.95	2.56	2.36	2.21	1.98	1.41	1.10	0.49	1.83

Table 8.6. *Internal Rates of Return under High-Cost Assumptions*

	Lifetime Labor Earnings (1997 dollars)										
	0–120k	120k–240k	240k–360k	360k–480k	480k–600k	600k–720k	720k–840k	840k–960k	960k–1.08m	1.08m+	Total
Cohort 45	4.87	2.91	1.90	1.54	1.11	0.77	0.75	0.76	0.37	0.61	1.79
Cohort 50	5.47	3.11	2.22	1.69	1.30	1.02	0.87	0.46	0.64	0.64	1.93
Cohort 55	5.03	2.94	2.10	1.73	1.32	0.91	0.56	0.54	0.79	0.51	1.74
Cohort 60	4.78	2.86	2.08	1.46	1.43	0.92	0.65	0.71	0.25	0.42	1.65
Cohort 65	4.68	2.84	2.09	1.59	1.38	1.07	0.92	0.69	0.36	0.30	1.62
Cohort 70	4.63	2.98	2.23	1.86	1.57	1.19	0.70	0.69	0.65	0.38	1.76
Cohort 75	4.76	3.05	2.35	1.90	1.53	1.46	1.08	0.84	0.59	0.45	1.82
Cohort 80	4.75	3.15	2.37	1.91	1.63	1.37	1.23	0.81	0.80	0.60	1.87
Cohort 85	4.76	3.22	2.56	1.97	1.73	1.35	1.28	1.10	0.67	0.54	1.90
Cohort 90	4.82	3.26	2.52	2.02	1.84	1.30	1.37	0.87	1.00	0.52	1.92
Cohort 95	4.88	3.26	2.49	1.99	1.74	1.44	1.13	0.80	0.72	0.41	1.82
Men 45	3.42	2.08	1.27	1.13	0.82	0.64	0.48	0.46	0.09	0.30	0.87
Men 50	3.41	2.04	1.61	1.20	0.97	0.61	0.59	0.05	0.45	0.48	0.98
Men 55	3.26	2.12	1.57	1.20	1.00	0.41	0.21	0.23	0.45	0.29	0.91
Men 60	3.30	2.05	1.46	0.96	1.00	0.58	0.10	0.09	0.17	0.19	0.82
Men 65	3.26	2.05	1.51	1.05	1.12	0.70	0.87	0.32	0.11	0.03	0.87
Men 70	3.19	2.30	1.69	1.39	1.19	0.76	0.24	0.39	0.31	0.12	0.99
Men 75	3.47	2.44	1.85	1.44	1.19	1.11	0.96	0.30	0.14	0.24	1.13
Men 80	3.65	2.56	1.95	1.66	1.30	1.16	0.95	0.23	0.62	0.45	1.26
Men 85	3.73	2.77	2.07	1.66	1.48	0.99	1.01	0.85	0.50	0.41	1.27
Men 90	3.86	2.82	2.18	1.68	1.54	1.16	1.16	0.67	0.77	0.44	1.37
Men 95	3.83	3.06	2.27	1.73	1.57	1.27	0.90	0.69	0.46	0.28	1.32
Women 45	5.06	3.29	2.50	2.19	1.76	1.40	1.63	1.58	1.29	1.64	2.98
Women 50	5.90	3.65	2.75	2.39	1.91	1.67	1.55	1.60	1.00	1.11	3.04
Women 55	5.52	3.40	2.61	2.35	1.82	1.77	1.20	1.01	1.30	1.02	2.68

Women 60	5.19	3.36	2.59	2.02	2.03	1.38	1.37	1.53	0.41	0.87	2.51
Women 65	5.14	3.32	2.62	2.15	1.81	1.57	1.01	1.16	0.86	0.92	2.47
Women 70	5.10	3.41	2.70	2.40	2.04	1.87	1.30	1.26	1.18	0.90	2.60
Women 75	5.18	3.46	2.79	2.34	1.96	1.93	1.25	1.42	1.46	0.82	2.55
Women 80	5.13	3.54	2.76	2.26	2.13	1.74	1.59	1.64	1.16	0.92	2.60
Women 85	5.09	3.49	2.91	2.34	2.04	1.84	1.76	1.51	0.97	0.86	2.62
Women 90	5.17	3.52	2.87	2.40	2.16	1.54	1.69	1.22	1.26	0.71	2.55
Women 95	5.24	3.42	2.69	2.29	1.99	1.70	1.56	1.01	1.20	0.70	2.46
White 45	4.88	2.91	1.96	1.52	1.18	0.69	0.74	0.76	0.48	0.56	1.79
White 50	5.51	3.16	2.26	1.72	1.28	1.03	0.86	0.38	0.60	0.64	1.94
White 55	5.06	2.98	2.15	1.72	1.41	0.91	0.59	0.59	0.75	0.46	1.73
White 60	4.82	2.91	2.10	1.48	1.40	0.92	0.66	0.73	0.28	0.39	1.65
White 65	4.74	2.91	2.05	1.55	1.42	1.06	0.97	0.68	0.21	0.30	1.60
White 70	4.71	3.05	2.25	1.86	1.54	1.20	0.66	0.65	0.41	0.35	1.75
White 75	4.81	3.12	2.35	1.91	1.53	1.35	1.11	0.89	0.35	0.47	1.82
White 80	4.78	3.21	2.43	1.95	1.61	1.33	1.22	0.78	0.76	0.63	1.87
White 85	4.84	3.26	2.58	2.04	1.79	1.37	1.28	1.12	0.65	0.50	1.89
White 90	4.92	3.35	2.57	2.08	1.89	1.27	1.41	1.00	0.93	0.48	1.93
White 95	4.96	3.35	2.56	2.08	1.85	1.44	1.17	0.70	0.84	0.42	1.84
Non-White 45	4.76	2.92	1.52	1.60	0.54	1.59	0.86	0.83	-0.64	1.15	1.77
Non-White 50	5.07	2.81	1.97	1.53	1.40	0.83	0.91	1.13	1.03	0.60	1.80
Non-White 55	4.83	2.74	1.81	1.82	0.58	0.91	0.17	-0.01	1.11	0.97	1.78
Non-White 60	4.52	2.53	2.02	1.34	1.59	0.96	0.60	0.49	0.00	0.57	1.66
Non-White 65	4.32	2.45	2.28	1.82	1.10	1.18	0.53	0.84	1.41	0.32	1.73
Non-White 70	4.22	2.69	2.10	1.85	1.70	1.14	0.92	1.02	1.39	0.51	1.81
Non-White 75	4.49	2.75	2.33	1.86	1.52	1.85	0.94	0.51	1.50	0.34	1.80
Non-White 80	4.62	2.86	2.04	1.74	1.74	1.58	1.30	0.94	1.13	0.39	1.91
Non-White 85	4.42	3.05	2.45	1.66	1.37	1.20	1.28	0.95	0.81	0.82	1.95
Non-White 90	4.46	2.93	2.30	1.79	1.59	1.42	1.17	-0.03	1.33	0.73	1.90
Non-White 95	4.60	2.96	2.22	1.65	1.24	1.42	0.96	1.25	0.21	0.34	1.72

(continued)

Table 8.6. (continued)

	Lifetime Labor Earnings (1997 dollars)										
	0–120 k	120 k–240 k	240 k–360 k	360 k–480 k	480 k–600 k	600 k–720 k	720 k–840 k	840 k–960 k	960 k–1.08 m	1.08 m+	Total
Non-College 45	4.81	2.76	1.79	1.38	1.07	0.95	0.80	0.70	0.31	0.63	1.86
Non-College 50	5.40	2.96	2.11	1.54	1.22	0.89	0.72	0.47	0.34	0.63	1.96
Non-College 55	4.91	2.82	2.09	1.76	1.32	0.61	0.43	0.28	0.57	0.47	1.76
Non-College 60	4.72	2.74	1.94	1.38	1.39	0.75	0.60	0.64	0.03	0.34	1.68
Non-College 65	4.58	2.76	1.98	1.53	1.39	1.05	0.85	0.44	0.03	0.13	1.62
Non-College 70	4.50	2.91	2.00	1.62	1.41	1.38	0.55	0.56	0.71	0.37	1.79
Non-College 75	4.65	2.96	2.23	1.81	1.49	1.34	1.04	0.14	0.63	0.28	1.84
Non-College 80	4.71	2.97	2.32	1.95	1.46	1.38	1.30	1.04	0.78	0.49	1.94
Non-College 85	4.63	3.05	2.52	1.83	1.80	1.40	1.16	1.01	0.64	0.50	1.99
Non-College 90	4.69	3.19	2.49	1.89	1.68	1.28	1.33	0.68	0.91	0.45	1.95
Non-College 95	4.77	3.11	2.40	1.75	1.72	1.27	1.14	0.71	0.52	0.36	1.86
College 45	5.03	3.28	2.23	1.84	1.20	0.57	0.69	0.84	0.45	0.58	1.67
College 50	5.61	3.45	2.46	1.97	1.41	1.22	1.04	0.44	0.93	0.64	1.87
College 55	5.31	3.18	2.12	1.69	1.33	1.28	0.73	0.85	1.10	0.55	1.69
College 60	4.88	3.06	2.32	1.56	1.49	1.12	0.73	0.80	0.53	0.47	1.60
College 65	4.87	2.98	2.25	1.68	1.37	1.10	1.03	1.02	0.80	0.44	1.62
College 70	4.83	3.08	2.52	2.10	1.73	1.01	0.84	0.84	0.58	0.38	1.72
College 75	4.91	3.17	2.46	2.00	1.57	1.55	1.11	1.31	0.55	0.56	1.80
College 80	4.81	3.37	2.42	1.87	1.80	1.37	1.16	0.60	0.82	0.67	1.81
College 85	4.96	3.42	2.60	2.14	1.64	1.30	1.39	1.16	0.72	0.56	1.81
College 90	5.01	3.34	2.54	2.18	2.01	1.32	1.41	1.05	1.09	0.57	1.89
College 95	5.01	3.46	2.57	2.21	1.78	1.58	1.13	0.88	0.94	0.44	1.78

Table 8.7. *Internal Rates of Return under Low-Cost Assumptions*

				Lifetime Labor Earnings (1997 dollars)							
	0–120k	120k–240k	240k–360k	360k–480k	480k–600k	600k–720k	720k–840k	840k–960k	960k–1.08m	1.08m+	Total
Cohort 45	5.06	2.97	1.97	1.53	1.05	0.95	0.74	0.94	0.39	0.40	1.82
Cohort 50	5.79	3.29	2.35	1.67	1.47	1.07	0.74	0.68	0.65	0.68	2.01
Cohort 55	5.42	3.28	2.42	1.81	1.60	0.97	0.78	0.66	0.58	0.56	1.90
Cohort 60	5.31	3.16	2.30	1.65	1.51	1.12	0.77	0.47	0.27	0.46	1.77
Cohort 65	5.46	3.27	2.42	1.89	1.59	1.31	1.03	0.65	0.83	0.37	1.82
Cohort 70	5.35	3.53	2.59	2.12	1.64	1.46	1.20	0.71	0.46	0.41	1.88
Cohort 75	5.51	3.59	2.78	2.14	1.84	1.52	1.36	1.18	1.02	0.48	1.94
Cohort 80	5.61	3.80	2.72	2.39	1.99	1.70	1.31	1.11	0.93	0.57	1.95
Cohort 85	5.71	3.89	3.04	2.62	2.14	2.03	1.61	1.38	1.25	0.74	2.05
Cohort 90	5.86	4.09	3.26	2.62	2.12	2.09	1.70	1.46	1.45	0.67	2.04
Cohort 95	6.18	4.22	3.35	2.67	2.35	2.04	1.89	1.63	1.56	0.65	2.04
Men 45	3.60	1.99	1.30	0.98	0.69	0.75	0.41	0.66	0.22	0.13	0.81
Men 50	3.65	2.12	1.61	1.13	1.07	0.73	0.38	0.27	0.42	0.36	0.97
Men 55	3.52	2.27	1.70	1.23	1.08	0.56	0.26	0.27	0.06	0.35	0.95
Men 60	3.54	2.18	1.54	1.04	0.99	0.65	0.11	-0.35	-0.11	0.26	0.81
Men 65	3.61	2.34	1.58	1.34	0.94	0.78	0.87	0.36	0.38	0.03	0.88
Men 70	3.50	2.60	1.90	1.46	1.14	1.05	0.66	0.27	0.13	0.12	0.96
Men 75	3.73	2.82	1.90	1.72	1.21	0.97	0.83	0.67	0.60	0.12	1.04
Men 80	3.99	2.92	1.95	1.82	1.40	1.26	0.68	0.83	0.71	0.35	1.10
Men 85	3.75	2.91	2.36	2.07	1.59	1.63	1.29	0.96	0.85	0.44	1.21
Men 90	4.18	3.55	2.65	2.12	1.57	1.57	1.30	0.91	0.99	0.42	1.26
Men 95	4.34	3.65	2.86	2.18	1.89	1.76	1.52	1.19	1.34	0.41	1.31

(continued)

Table 8.7. (continued)

| | Lifetime Labor Earnings (1997 dollars) | | | | | | | | | | |
	0–120k	120k–240k	240k–360k	360k–480k	480k–600k	600k–720k	720k–840k	840k–960k	960k–1.08m	1.08m+	Total
Women 45	5.26	3.40	2.61	2.33	1.86	1.66	1.71	1.66	1.08	1.40	3.09
Women 50	6.21	3.85	2.96	2.40	2.20	1.67	1.54	1.70	1.15	1.51	3.22
Women 55	5.90	3.78	3.05	2.49	2.29	1.73	1.69	1.25	1.34	1.05	2.94
Women 60	5.76	3.70	2.88	2.37	2.15	1.74	1.59	1.30	1.04	0.87	2.75
Women 65	5.95	3.78	3.12	2.48	2.32	2.04	1.34	1.03	1.48	1.14	2.86
Women 70	5.88	4.02	3.10	2.84	2.24	2.06	2.10	1.30	0.98	0.98	2.86
Women 75	6.01	4.06	3.39	2.56	2.54	2.09	2.11	1.85	1.44	1.11	2.86
Women 80	6.05	4.27	3.29	2.99	2.67	2.35	1.92	1.60	1.40	1.09	2.95
Women 85	6.23	4.31	3.50	3.06	2.76	2.50	2.11	2.00	1.95	1.32	2.97
Women 90	6.26	4.36	3.72	3.13	2.65	2.66	2.22	2.12	2.00	1.15	2.90
Women 95	6.67	4.49	3.74	3.16	2.82	2.45	2.40	2.14	1.90	1.18	2.93
White 45	5.07	2.98	2.04	1.55	1.09	0.87	0.75	0.95	0.47	0.41	1.83
White 50	5.85	3.36	2.39	1.66	1.45	1.08	0.77	0.59	0.69	0.68	2.04
White 55	5.47	3.33	2.45	1.77	1.63	0.97	0.85	0.78	0.59	0.51	1.90
White 60	5.37	3.23	2.35	1.72	1.53	1.14	0.81	0.46	0.29	0.45	1.79
White 65	5.56	3.35	2.39	1.90	1.63	1.37	1.06	0.75	0.69	0.35	1.82
White 70	5.44	3.61	2.69	2.13	1.65	1.53	1.22	0.58	0.51	0.34	1.89
White 75	5.57	3.67	2.79	2.27	1.88	1.44	1.41	1.31	1.16	0.48	1.99
White 80	5.71	3.89	2.79	2.46	2.05	1.72	1.31	1.19	0.79	0.59	1.99
White 85	5.81	4.03	3.12	2.70	2.17	1.98	1.66	1.39	1.25	0.73	2.07
White 90	6.06	4.20	3.32	2.69	2.15	2.10	1.81	1.44	1.56	0.71	2.09
White 95	6.36	4.35	3.47	2.79	2.52	2.17	1.97	1.69	1.53	0.68	2.11
Non-White 45	4.99	2.91	1.46	1.40	0.76	1.75	0.68	0.87	-0.34	0.25	1.71
Non-White 50	5.18	2.83	2.09	1.68	1.59	1.02	0.58	1.57	0.27	0.63	1.83

Non-White 55	4.96	2.92	2.22	2.07	1.43	1.01	-0.05	-1.36	0.51	1.00	1.89
Non-White 60	4.87	2.63	1.98	1.25	1.34	0.96	0.29	0.54	0.02	0.57	1.58
Non-White 65	4.73	2.89	2.57	1.82	1.31	0.92	0.84	-0.36	1.62	0.53	1.80
Non-White 70	4.88	3.13	2.05	2.12	1.54	0.93	1.11	1.25	0.03	0.75	1.82
Non-White 75	5.21	3.23	2.71	1.53	1.62	1.81	1.11	0.21	0.06	0.45	1.72
Non-White 80	5.07	3.31	2.42	2.03	1.65	1.61	1.30	0.65	1.41	0.49	1.73
Non-White 85	5.17	3.25	2.57	2.33	1.97	2.27	1.34	1.35	1.30	0.82	1.94
Non-White 90	4.82	3.52	3.05	2.29	2.02	2.06	1.28	1.51	0.87	0.46	1.81
Non-White 95	5.26	3.71	2.91	2.23	1.74	1.57	1.55	1.48	1.73	0.48	1.76
Non-College 45	5.01	2.81	1.85	1.43	0.95	0.98	0.86	0.90	0.25	0.45	1.88
Non-College 50	5.70	3.13	2.25	1.49	1.37	0.92	0.78	0.63	0.73	0.56	2.05
Non-College 55	5.26	3.22	2.38	1.85	1.56	0.68	0.53	0.46	0.35	0.55	1.93
Non-College 60	5.30	3.02	2.13	1.56	1.35	0.88	0.75	0.21	0.07	0.27	1.78
Non-College 65	5.27	3.18	2.28	1.80	1.52	1.22	0.96	0.59	0.61	0.35	1.82
Non-College 70	5.24	3.45	2.33	1.82	1.44	1.36	1.49	0.20	0.06	0.49	1.92
Non-College 75	5.40	3.45	2.61	1.93	1.66	1.37	1.38	1.26	1.03	0.24	1.94
Non-College 80	5.61	3.57	2.51	2.22	1.92	1.71	1.42	0.90	0.32	0.55	1.99
Non-College 85	5.54	3.74	2.94	2.49	1.90	1.86	1.39	1.39	0.94	0.85	2.12
Non-College 90	5.72	3.98	3.02	2.42	2.14	1.99	1.60	1.27	1.32	0.55	2.06
Non-College 95	6.08	4.07	3.25	2.45	2.16	1.77	1.75	1.41	1.25	0.60	2.07
College 45	5.20	3.38	2.31	1.75	1.25	0.90	0.60	1.01	0.58	0.36	1.71
College 50	6.00	3.63	2.58	2.00	1.63	1.29	0.67	0.74	0.55	0.79	1.95
College 55	5.76	3.39	2.49	1.74	1.67	1.32	1.13	0.88	0.95	0.57	1.84
College 60	5.34	3.38	2.59	1.79	1.71	1.40	0.80	0.77	0.54	0.61	1.75
College 65	5.78	3.42	2.63	2.00	1.68	1.42	1.12	0.77	1.10	0.39	1.82
College 70	5.53	3.62	2.91	2.48	1.85	1.57	0.92	1.09	0.81	0.34	1.83
College 75	5.69	3.77	2.97	2.36	2.03	1.66	1.34	1.10	1.00	0.65	1.94
College 80	5.61	4.08	2.97	2.59	2.07	1.69	1.19	1.30	1.37	0.58	1.91
College 85	5.97	4.09	3.17	2.77	2.35	2.20	1.77	1.38	1.53	0.67	1.98
College 90	6.04	4.25	3.54	2.82	2.10	2.19	1.79	1.64	1.57	0.75	2.02
College 95	6.31	4.43	3.49	2.91	2.54	2.28	2.00	1.88	1.84	0.69	2.01

Table 8.8. *Number of Observations*

	Lifetime Labor Earnings (1997 dollars)										
	0–120k	120k–240k	240k–360k	360k–480k	480k–600k	600k–720k	720k–840k	840k–960k	960k–1.08m	1.08m+	Total
Cohort 45	1,406	1,030	721	514	375	240	165	120	87	343	5,001
Cohort 50	1,725	1,257	883	597	399	290	226	156	101	411	6,045
Cohort 55	1,980	1,465	1,043	689	441	300	223	182	123	630	7,076
Cohort 60	1,883	1,336	829	578	383	257	192	161	118	629	6,366
Cohort 65	1,664	1,196	792	509	362	293	200	153	117	571	5,857
Cohort 70	1,598	1,142	755	493	358	244	196	126	108	585	5,605
Cohort 75	1,516	1,121	753	493	375	242	209	141	111	584	5,545
Cohort 80	1,724	1,214	821	571	431	272	207	181	124	784	6,329
Cohort 85	1,665	1,309	874	617	452	318	235	176	127	825	6,598
Cohort 90	1,698	1,336	896	607	458	363	274	172	160	868	6,832
Cohort 95	1,632	1,418	973	710	527	372	290	229	196	1,087	7,434
Men 45	295	396	403	340	269	196	131	91	66	275	2,462
Men 50	433	498	459	382	279	205	160	120	74	315	2,925
Men 55	560	603	556	408	275	209	155	109	86	457	3,418
Men 60	535	589	430	338	228	151	116	97	87	442	3,013
Men 65	493	529	413	298	215	190	126	92	84	419	2,859
Men 70	500	496	378	290	218	153	126	87	74	413	2,735
Men 75	436	488	365	293	241	146	126	79	80	407	2,661
Men 80	502	543	453	337	250	155	121	127	88	563	3,139
Men 85	475	563	389	329	260	198	143	110	88	575	3,130
Men 90	508	547	445	323	268	204	187	110	109	593	3,294
Men 95	471	586	498	400	295	236	174	163	123	753	3,699
Women 45	1,111	634	318	174	106	44	34	29	21	68	2,539
Women 50	1,292	759	424	215	120	85	66	36	27	96	3,120
Women 55	1,420	862	487	281	166	91	68	73	37	173	3,658

Women 60	1,348	747	399	240	155	106	76	64	31	187	3,353
Women 65	1,171	667	379	211	147	103	74	61	33	152	2,998
Women 70	1,098	646	377	203	140	91	70	39	34	172	2,870
Women 75	1,080	633	388	200	134	96	83	62	31	177	2,884
Women 80	1,222	671	368	234	181	117	86	54	36	221	3,190
Women 85	1,190	746	485	288	192	120	92	66	39	250	3,468
Women 90	1,190	789	451	284	190	159	87	62	51	275	3,538
Women 95	1,161	832	475	310	232	136	116	66	73	334	3,735
White 45	1,279	902	623	434	331	220	153	108	77	321	4,448
White 50	1,539	1,080	749	508	348	261	191	141	89	373	5,279
White 55	1,737	1,267	901	602	377	268	205	166	114	571	6,208
White 60	1,626	1,150	711	492	334	225	170	144	107	548	5,507
White 65	1,428	980	650	434	318	251	177	133	105	504	4,980
White 70	1,352	921	613	422	287	215	164	112	90	500	4,676
White 75	1,263	891	639	407	300	205	176	117	86	498	4,582
White 80	1,419	991	672	472	364	225	167	146	97	679	5,232
White 85	1,367	1,058	715	519	367	256	194	151	106	701	5,434
White 90	1,345	1,060	707	499	374	275	221	132	134	742	5,489
White 95	1,288	1,072	751	556	401	301	229	194	163	893	5,848
Non-White 45	127	128	98	80	44	20	12	12	10	22	553
Non-White 50	186	177	134	89	51	29	35	15	12	38	766
Non-White 55	243	198	142	87	64	32	18	16	9	59	868
Non-White 60	257	186	118	86	49	32	22	17	11	81	859
Non-White 65	236	216	142	75	44	42	23	20	12	67	877
Non-White 70	246	221	142	71	71	29	32	14	18	85	929
Non-White 75	253	230	114	86	75	37	33	24	25	86	963
Non-White 80	305	223	149	99	67	47	40	35	27	105	1,097
Non-White 85	298	251	159	98	85	62	41	25	21	124	1,164
Non-White 90	353	276	189	108	84	88	53	40	26	126	1,343
Non-White 95	344	346	222	154	126	71	61	35	33	194	1,586

(continued)

Table 8.8. (continued)

	Lifetime Labor Earnings (1997 dollars)										
	0–120k	120k–240k	240k–360k	360k–480k	480k–600k	600k–720k	720k–840k	840k–960k	960k–1.08m	1.08m+	Total
Non-College 45	1,050	758	540	352	258	129	97	67	52	168	3,471
Non-College 50	1,233	887	601	401	242	179	124	86	55	201	4,009
Non-College 55	1,402	994	688	442	281	168	134	110	73	325	4,617
Non-College 60	1,297	843	549	356	224	144	121	91	67	288	3,980
Non-College 65	1,104	758	492	297	202	168	111	97	68	268	3,565
Non-College 70	1,006	679	430	264	202	117	95	57	58	247	3,155
Non-College 75	941	661	407	268	205	104	101	71	55	255	3,068
Non-College 80	1,034	695	444	310	227	147	103	87	60	310	3,417
Non-College 85	1,037	746	498	335	229	153	102	70	63	351	3,584
Non-College 90	1,039	775	514	321	237	180	126	90	78	364	3,724
Non-College 95	1,013	835	562	355	276	187	143	99	105	439	4,014
College 45	356	272	181	162	117	111	68	53	35	175	1,530
College 50	492	370	282	196	157	111	102	70	46	210	2,036
College 55	578	471	355	247	160	132	89	72	50	305	2,459
College 60	586	493	280	222	159	113	71	70	51	341	2,386
College 65	560	438	300	212	160	125	89	56	49	303	2,292
College 70	592	463	325	229	156	127	101	69	50	338	2,450
College 75	575	460	346	225	170	138	108	70	56	329	2,477
College 80	690	519	377	261	204	125	104	94	64	474	2,912
College 85	628	563	376	282	223	165	133	106	64	474	3,014
College 90	659	561	382	286	221	183	148	82	82	504	3,108
College 95	619	583	411	355	251	185	147	130	91	648	3,420

Social Security is offering current middle-aged Americans is not any better than the one it is offering younger Americans. On the one hand, earlier cohorts experienced lower OASI tax rates over the early parts of their working lives than is the case for later cohorts. On the other hand, later cohorts have greater longevity, reflecting the trends incorporated in CORSIM's mortality module. In evaluating these figures, one should also bear in mind that the observed differences might reflect sampling variability.

Interestingly, there is also not much difference across the three tables with respect to different cohorts' internal rates of return. On first thought, one might expect to observe, on average, a higher rate of return in the high-cost sample because its greater longevity means retirees collect their benefits for a longer period of time. On the other hand, greater longevity means that more of the sample will work for longer periods and pay more in taxes. In addition, the high-cost estimate assumes a 4.5 percent rate of inflation, whereas the low-cost estimate assumes a 2.5 percent rate of inflation. Since the OASI system is not fully indexed to benefits and since, *ceteris paribus*, real benefits are lower the higher the rate of inflation, the fact that rates of return are not higher under the high-cost assumptions may reflect this factor.

In contrast to the cross-cohort and cross-assumption comparisons, there are very marked differences in real rates of return across lifetime income levels. Across all cohorts, those in the lowest earnings group earn on average a 5.19 percent return, whereas those in the highest earnings group average a 0.54 percent return. On this metric, at least, the OASI system appears to be highly progressive.

There is also a systematic and significant difference in rates of return earned by women compared to men. Across all cohorts and under the intermediate assumptions, women earn, on average, 2.79 percent on their contributions whereas men earn only 1.05 percent. This difference reflects three things. First, women live longer than men do. Second, women are lower lifetime earners than are men and thus benefit compared to men from Social Security's progressive OASI benefit formula. Third, we are allocating dependent, mother and father, child, and survivor benefits to the recipients of these benefits even though these benefits are based on the earnings record of one's spouse.

Under the intermediate assumptions, non-whites average a rate of return about 15 basis points lower than that of whites, reflecting their shorter life span. Non-white/white differences are somewhat greater among low lifetime earners, where mortality differences are greatest. The differences between non-white and white internal rates of return are largest under the low-cost assumptions and smallest under the high-cost

353

assumptions. This reflects the fact that under the low-cost assumption of relatively short life spans, a relatively larger fraction of non-whites die before receiving benefits.

Table 8.5 also indicates a slightly higher internal rate of return for non–college-educated compared with college-educated postwar Americans. This is expected given the fact that those with less than a college education are lower lifetime earners and thus benefit, relatively speaking, from Social Security's progressive benefit formula.

Lifetime Net Tax Rates

Tables 8.9, 8.10, and 8.11 present lifetime net tax rates under the intermediate, high-cost, and low-cost assumptions. These lifetime net tax rates were computed by using a 5 percent real discount rate. On average, Social Security represents about a 5 percent lifetime net tax; that is for example, for every dollar that postwar Americans either have earned or will earn, five cents will be paid to Social Security in taxes above and beyond benefits received. The average lifetime net tax rate is somewhat higher under the high-cost assumptions and somewhat lower under the low-cost assumptions.

Lifetime net tax rates show no significant trend across cohorts. But there is also a very clear pattern with respect to income level. Specifically, the middle-income classes face the highest net tax rates. Consider, for example, postwar Americans with lifetime earnings of $600,000 to $720,000. On average, they face a 7.0 percent lifetime net tax rate, compared with an average negative net tax rate of 0.7 percent for those with lifetime earnings below $120,000 and a average net tax rate of 4.3 percent for those with lifetime earnings above $1.08 million. Table 8.9 also shows higher lifetime net tax rates for men compared with women, for the non–college-educated compared with the college-educated and for non-whites compared with whites.

The Impact of Raising Taxes or Cutting Benefits to Achieve Long-Run Solvency

Our final two tables, 8.12 and 8.13, consider the tax hike or benefit cut needed under the intermediate assumptions to achieve an equality between (a) the sum of the Social Security system's projected revenues (untruncated and measured in present value) and the trust fund and (b) the system's projected benefit payments (untruncated and measured in present value). The immediate and permanent tax hike needed is 38 percent, while the immediate and permanent benefit cut needed is 25 percent.

Table 8.9. *Lifetime Net Tax Rate under Intermediate Assumptions*

	Lifetime Labor Earnings (1997 dollars)										
	0–120k	120k–240k	240k–360k	360k–480k	480k–600k	600k–720k	720k–840k	840k–960k	960k–1.08m	1.08m+	Total
Cohort 45	0.4	5.5	6.7	6.8	7.1	7.1	6.8	5.9	6.0	3.7	5.5
Cohort 50	−2.3	4.1	5.5	6.0	6.4	6.7	6.6	6.3	6.2	3.6	4.9
Cohort 55	−0.9	4.6	6.0	6.4	6.6	7.2	7.4	7.3	6.7	3.9	5.2
Cohort 60	−0.1	5.1	6.4	7.0	7.1	7.3	7.6	7.4	7.5	3.9	5.2
Cohort 65	0.1	5.1	6.3	7.2	7.0	7.1	7.6	7.5	7.3	4.4	5.5
Cohort 70	0.1	4.8	6.2	6.7	7.2	7.2	7.7	7.8	7.5	4.3	5.4
Cohort 75	−0.3	4.6	6.1	6.7	6.9	7.0	7.2	7.4	7.8	4.5	5.4
Cohort 80	−1.0	4.5	5.8	6.6	6.8	7.2	7.0	7.6	7.5	4.6	5.4
Cohort 85	−1.2	4.1	5.7	6.3	6.7	6.8	7.0	7.4	7.6	4.4	5.1
Cohort 90	−1.2	4.0	5.5	6.3	6.7	6.8	7.0	6.9	7.6	4.7	5.3
Cohort 95	−1.8	3.8	5.3	6.1	6.4	6.4	6.7	7.3	7.3	4.9	5.3
Men 45	4.7	6.3	7.2	7.3	7.5	7.3	6.9	6.1	6.6	3.9	5.9
Men 50	3.6	5.4	6.3	6.5	6.7	6.8	7.0	6.5	6.2	3.7	5.5
Men 55	4.0	5.9	6.5	6.9	6.9	7.5	7.7	7.9	7.0	4.0	5.6
Men 60	4.2	6.2	7.2	7.3	7.6	7.6	8.2	7.7	7.7	3.9	5.6
Men 65	4.4	6.1	6.9	7.5	7.4	7.3	7.7	7.5	7.4	4.6	5.9
Men 70	4.4	6.0	6.9	7.0	7.5	7.3	8.0	8.0	7.9	4.6	5.9
Men 75	4.0	5.8	6.7	7.1	7.2	7.5	7.6	8.0	8.1	4.6	5.9
Men 80	4.3	5.3	6.5	7.1	7.1	7.4	7.2	7.8	7.6	5.0	5.8
Men 85	3.4	5.1	6.4	6.8	6.9	6.9	7.4	7.8	8.1	4.4	5.4
Men 90	2.8	4.9	6.1	6.8	6.8	7.1	7.0	7.2	7.9	4.9	5.7
Men 95	1.9	4.6	5.8	6.2	6.8	6.4	6.9	7.5	7.3	5.0	5.6

(continued)

Table 8.9. (continued)

	Lifetime Labor Earnings (1997 dollars)										
	0–120k	120k–240k	240k–360k	360k–480k	480k–600k	600k–720k	720k–840k	840k–960k	960k–1.08m	1.08m+	Total
Women 45	−0.6	4.9	6.0	5.9	6.1	6.1	6.5	5.2	4.1	2.7	4.4
Women 50	−4.3	3.3	4.7	5.3	5.7	6.4	5.6	5.7	6.0	3.3	3.8
Women 55	−3.0	3.6	5.3	5.6	6.1	6.4	6.7	6.4	5.8	3.7	4.3
Women 60	−2.0	4.2	5.7	6.5	6.5	6.9	6.6	7.0	6.9	3.8	4.7
Women 65	−1.8	4.3	5.5	6.7	6.5	6.7	7.3	7.4	7.0	3.9	4.9
Women 70	−2.0	3.9	5.6	6.3	6.6	6.9	7.3	7.3	6.5	3.7	4.6
Women 75	−2.3	3.7	5.5	6.1	6.5	6.1	6.5	6.7	7.2	4.2	4.7
Women 80	−3.3	3.8	5.1	5.9	6.3	6.8	6.8	7.2	7.3	3.9	4.5
Women 85	−3.1	3.4	5.1	5.8	6.3	6.7	6.3	6.7	6.3	4.2	4.6
Women 90	−2.9	3.5	4.9	5.8	6.5	6.6	7.0	6.3	6.9	4.5	4.7
Women 95	−3.3	3.2	4.8	6.0	5.9	6.4	6.5	6.8	7.4	4.7	4.8
White 45	0.3	5.5	6.6	6.9	7.1	7.1	6.9	5.8	5.9	3.7	5.4
White 50	−2.6	4.0	5.5	6.0	6.3	6.7	6.6	6.3	6.2	3.6	4.8
White 55	−1.1	4.5	5.9	6.4	6.5	7.2	7.4	7.3	6.6	3.9	5.1
White 60	−0.3	5.0	6.3	7.0	7.1	7.3	7.7	7.4	7.6	3.9	5.2
White 65	−0.2	5.0	6.3	7.1	7.0	7.0	7.5	7.5	7.5	4.3	5.5
White 70	−0.2	4.6	6.1	6.7	7.2	7.1	7.7	7.9	7.5	4.4	5.4
White 75	−0.3	4.5	6.0	6.7	6.8	6.9	7.1	7.4	7.8	4.4	5.3
White 80	−1.4	4.3	5.8	6.6	6.8	7.1	7.0	7.7	7.5	4.5	5.2
White 85	−1.5	3.9	5.5	6.2	6.7	6.9	6.9	7.4	7.4	4.3	5.0
White 90	−2.0	3.8	5.3	6.3	6.8	6.8	7.0	7.1	7.6	4.7	5.3
White 95	−2.2	3.4	5.1	6.0	6.3	6.3	6.6	7.2	7.3	4.8	5.2
Non-White 45	1.3	5.3	7.0	6.4	7.4	6.4	6.2	6.6	7.0	3.8	5.8
Non-White 50	−0.3	4.8	5.9	6.0	6.9	7.0	6.4	6.5	6.3	4.1	5.4
Non-White 55	0.2	5.3	6.5	6.2	7.1	7.2	7.7	7.6	7.9	4.3	5.6

356

Non-White 60	1.3	5.8	7.0	7.0	7.4	7.5	6.5	8.1	6.9	3.5	5.1
Non-White 65	1.9	5.7	6.1	7.2	7.4	7.3	8.1	7.4	5.3	4.8	5.8
Non-White 70	1.7	5.4	6.6	6.7	7.1	7.4	7.8	7.4	7.4	4.0	5.4
Non-White 75	-0.7	5.1	6.5	6.9	7.3	7.2	7.8	7.7	8.0	4.9	5.9
Non-White 80	0.7	5.1	5.9	6.7	6.7	7.4	7.3	7.3	7.9	5.5	6.0
Non-White 85	-0.1	5.1	6.3	6.8	6.5	6.6	7.3	7.1	8.3	4.7	5.5
Non-White 90	1.3	5.1	6.0	6.4	6.2	6.9	7.3	6.1	7.6	4.7	5.5
Non-White 95	-0.5	5.0	6.0	6.5	6.9	6.9	7.0	7.6	7.6	5.5	5.9
Non-College 45	0.6	5.7	6.9	7.0	7.2	6.8	6.8	5.7	6.4	3.8	5.7
Non-College 50	-2.0	4.4	5.7	6.2	6.5	6.8	6.5	6.5	6.1	4.0	5.1
Non-College 55	-0.4	4.7	6.0	6.4	6.5	7.4	7.6	7.3	7.0	4.2	5.4
Non-College 60	0.3	5.3	6.6	6.8	7.2	7.5	7.6	7.8	7.9	4.2	5.6
Non-College 65	0.5	5.2	6.4	7.3	7.0	7.2	7.7	7.8	7.6	4.7	5.8
Non-College 70	0.3	5.0	6.5	6.9	7.2	7.2	7.5	8.0	7.4	4.7	5.7
Non-College 75	0.3	4.8	6.2	6.5	7.0	7.3	7.2	7.7	8.0	4.8	5.7
Non-College 80	-0.4	4.8	6.0	6.4	7.0	7.0	6.9	7.6	7.9	5.0	5.6
Non-College 85	-0.9	4.5	5.9	6.3	6.8	6.9	7.0	7.5	7.4	4.6	5.3
Non-College 90	-0.5	4.2	5.5	6.4	6.9	6.9	7.1	6.9	7.8	5.2	5.6
Non-College 95	-0.9	3.9	5.4	6.2	6.7	6.8	7.1	7.6	7.3	5.6	5.7
College 45	-0.2	4.7	6.1	6.5	7.1	7.4	6.9	6.1	5.5	3.6	5.1
College 50	-3.0	3.5	5.2	5.6	6.3	6.6	6.7	6.2	6.3	3.3	4.6
College 55	-2.2	4.2	5.9	6.4	6.7	6.8	7.1	7.3	6.2	3.6	4.8
College 60	-1.0	4.8	6.1	7.2	7.1	7.1	7.6	7.0	7.1	3.6	4.8
College 65	-0.6	5.0	6.1	6.9	7.0	6.9	7.4	6.8	6.9	4.1	5.2
College 70	-0.3	4.5	5.9	6.4	7.1	7.1	7.9	7.7	7.6	4.1	5.1
College 75	-1.4	4.3	6.0	6.9	6.8	6.8	7.2	7.2	7.7	4.3	5.2
College 80	-1.8	4.1	5.7	6.9	6.6	7.3	7.1	7.6	7.2	4.4	5.1
College 85	-1.8	3.6	5.4	6.3	6.5	6.8	7.0	7.3	7.8	4.2	5.0
College 90	-2.6	3.8	5.5	6.2	6.5	6.8	7.0	6.8	7.4	4.4	5.1
College 95	-3.4	3.5	5.3	5.9	6.1	6.0	6.4	7.0	7.4	4.6	5.0

Table 8.10. *Lifetime Net Tax Rate under High-Cost Assumptions*

	Lifetime Labor Earnings (1997 dollars)										
	0–120k	120k–240k	240k–360k	360k–480k	480k–600k	600k–720k	720k–840k	840k–960k	960k–1.08m	1.08m+	Total
Cohort 45	0.6	5.7	6.8	6.9	7.3	7.3	6.8	6.0	6.3	3.7	5.6
Cohort 50	-1.7	4.4	5.7	6.1	6.6	6.8	6.5	6.4	6.2	3.7	5.0
Cohort 55	-0.1	5.0	6.2	6.5	6.9	7.2	7.7	7.3	6.5	4.0	5.3
Cohort 60	0.8	5.5	6.8	7.2	7.3	7.5	7.8	7.5	7.4	3.9	5.4
Cohort 65	1.2	5.8	6.8	7.4	7.1	7.7	7.6	7.8	7.4	4.4	5.8
Cohort 70	1.4	5.5	6.7	6.9	7.4	7.6	8.1	7.9	7.1	4.4	5.8
Cohort 75	0.9	5.3	6.5	7.1	7.4	7.4	7.4	7.6	7.8	4.2	5.6
Cohort 80	1.0	5.2	6.4	7.0	7.3	7.4	7.4	7.8	7.4	4.1	5.4
Cohort 85	0.9	5.1	6.1	6.8	7.2	7.3	7.4	7.2	7.4	4.3	5.4
Cohort 90	0.7	4.9	6.1	6.7	6.9	7.3	7.3	7.6	7.1	4.6	5.6
Cohort 95	0.5	4.8	6.1	6.8	7.0	7.4	7.5	7.6	7.7	4.6	5.6
Men 45	4.8	6.3	7.3	7.3	7.7	7.4	6.9	6.3	6.7	3.9	6.0
Men 50	3.7	5.7	6.4	6.5	6.8	7.0	6.8	6.7	6.3	3.7	5.5
Men 55	4.3	6.1	6.7	7.1	7.2	7.5	7.9	7.8	6.9	4.1	5.8
Men 60	4.5	6.4	7.3	7.5	7.6	7.9	8.2	7.7	7.4	4.0	5.7
Men 65	4.8	6.6	7.2	7.6	7.4	7.8	7.6	7.9	7.6	4.6	6.0
Men 70	4.8	6.3	7.2	7.3	7.6	7.9	8.2	8.1	7.5	4.6	6.1
Men 75	4.3	6.0	6.9	7.3	7.6	7.6	7.6	8.2	8.2	4.4	5.9
Men 80	4.1	5.9	6.8	7.1	7.6	7.5	7.4	8.3	7.7	4.2	5.7
Men 85	3.8	5.7	6.5	7.1	7.3	7.5	7.7	7.4	7.6	4.3	5.7
Men 90	3.5	5.4	6.4	7.1	7.0	7.3	7.5	7.6	7.2	4.7	5.8
Men 95	3.4	4.9	6.2	6.9	7.1	7.4	7.7	7.6	8.1	4.7	5.8
Women 45	-0.3	5.3	6.3	6.0	6.3	6.7	6.3	5.0	4.7	2.7	4.6
Women 50	-3.6	3.5	5.0	5.5	6.0	6.5	5.7	5.4	6.1	3.4	4.1
Women 55	-2.1	4.2	5.6	5.8	6.4	6.5	7.2	6.6	5.7	3.8	4.6

Women 60	-0.8	4.7	6.2	6.8	6.6	7.0	7.2	7.0	7.5	3.8	5.0
Women 65	-0.6	5.1	6.3	7.0	6.7	7.5	7.7	7.6	6.7	3.9	5.3
Women 70	-0.4	4.8	6.1	6.3	7.1	6.9	7.8	7.3	6.4	4.1	5.1
Women 75	-0.7	4.6	6.0	6.7	7.0	7.0	7.2	6.8	6.7	4.0	5.1
Women 80	-0.6	4.5	6.0	6.7	6.8	7.1	7.3	6.9	6.9	3.9	4.9
Women 85	-0.4	4.6	5.7	6.5	6.9	7.0	6.9	6.6	7.0	4.1	5.1
Women 90	-0.7	4.5	5.7	6.3	6.7	7.3	7.0	7.5	6.9	4.5	5.3
Women 95	-1.0	4.7	5.9	6.6	6.8	7.4	7.2	7.7	7.1	4.3	5.2
White 45	0.6	5.7	6.8	6.9	7.2	7.3	6.8	6.0	6.1	3.7	5.5
White 50	-1.9	4.4	5.7	6.1	6.5	6.8	6.5	6.4	6.2	3.6	5.0
White 55	-0.2	5.0	6.1	6.5	6.8	7.2	7.6	7.3	6.4	4.0	5.3
White 60	0.7	5.4	6.7	7.2	7.2	7.6	7.9	7.4	7.4	4.0	5.5
White 65	1.0	5.7	6.8	7.4	7.0	7.7	7.5	7.9	7.5	4.3	5.7
White 70	1.1	5.4	6.7	7.0	7.4	7.5	8.1	7.9	7.2	4.4	5.7
White 75	0.7	5.1	6.5	7.0	7.3	7.4	7.2	7.5	7.9	4.1	5.5
White 80	0.8	5.0	6.4	6.9	7.3	7.4	7.3	7.8	7.5	4.1	5.4
White 85	0.6	5.0	6.1	6.7	7.1	7.3	7.4	7.1	7.4	4.3	5.4
White 90	0.3	4.7	6.0	6.7	6.8	7.4	7.4	7.6	7.1	4.6	5.6
White 95	0.2	4.6	6.0	6.6	6.9	7.3	7.6	7.8	7.6	4.6	5.5
Non-White 45	0.9	5.4	7.1	6.5	8.1	6.5	6.6	6.3	7.2	3.8	6.0
Non-White 50	-0.2	4.9	6.0	6.3	7.0	7.5	6.5	6.2	6.2	4.1	5.5
Non-White 55	0.5	5.5	6.8	6.5	7.4	7.2	8.0	7.3	7.2	4.3	5.8
Non-White 60	1.6	6.1	6.9	7.2	7.4	7.1	7.2	8.1	7.6	3.5	5.3
Non-White 65	2.2	6.3	6.7	7.3	7.8	7.5	8.5	7.0	6.3	4.9	6.1
Non-White 70	2.7	6.0	6.7	6.8	7.3	8.1	7.9	7.7	6.7	4.7	6.0
Non-White 75	1.9	6.0	6.6	7.2	7.5	7.3	8.0	8.2	7.3	4.8	6.1
Non-White 80	1.4	5.7	6.7	7.2	7.1	7.2	8.0	8.3	7.4	4.0	5.6
Non-White 85	2.0	5.4	6.1	7.3	7.4	7.5	7.6	7.4	7.3	3.9	5.6
Non-White 90	1.9	5.5	6.4	7.0	7.2	7.0	7.1	7.8	7.1	4.8	5.9
Non-White 95	1.4	5.4	6.4	7.3	7.3	7.5	7.3	6.9	8.2	4.7	5.8

(continued)

Table 8.10. (continued)

	Lifetime Labor Earnings (1997 dollars)										
	0–120k	120k–240k	240k–360k	360k–480k	480k–600k	600k–720k	720k–840k	840k–960k	960k–1.08m	1.08m+	Total
Non-College 45	0.8	5.9	7.0	7.0	7.4	6.9	6.8	5.9	6.3	3.9	5.8
Non-College 50	−1.4	4.7	5.9	6.3	6.6	7.0	6.6	6.5	6.2	4.0	5.3
Non-College 55	0.3	5.2	6.2	6.5	7.0	7.5	7.7	7.5	6.9	4.3	5.6
Non-College 60	1.0	5.6	6.9	7.2	7.2	7.6	8.1	7.6	7.7	4.4	5.9
Non-College 65	1.5	5.9	6.9	7.3	7.2	7.7	7.8	8.0	7.9	4.6	6.1
Non-College 70	1.8	5.6	6.9	7.3	7.5	7.5	8.1	8.2	6.6	4.9	6.1
Non-College 75	1.3	5.4	6.6	7.2	7.4	7.6	7.3	8.1	7.7	4.6	5.8
Non-College 80	1.1	5.4	6.4	7.0	7.3	7.3	7.4	7.5	7.7	4.5	5.7
Non-College 85	1.4	5.3	6.2	7.1	7.0	7.1	7.5	7.4	7.3	4.4	5.7
Non-College 90	1.2	5.0	6.0	7.0	7.1	7.3	7.5	8.2	7.1	4.9	5.8
Non-College 95	0.8	5.1	6.2	7.0	7.0	7.5	7.5	7.9	8.1	4.9	5.9
College 45	−0.2	5.1	6.3	6.6	7.2	7.7	6.8	6.1	6.1	3.6	5.2
College 50	−2.3	3.8	5.3	5.8	6.4	6.6	6.5	6.3	6.2	3.4	4.7
College 55	−1.2	4.7	6.2	6.6	6.7	6.8	7.6	7.2	5.9	3.8	5.0
College 60	0.4	5.3	6.6	7.3	7.3	7.5	7.5	7.3	7.0	3.6	5.0
College 65	0.5	5.6	6.7	7.4	7.0	7.7	7.4	7.4	6.6	4.2	5.4
College 70	0.7	5.4	6.4	6.5	7.2	7.7	8.1	7.6	7.8	4.2	5.5
College 75	0.3	5.1	6.4	6.9	7.3	7.2	7.5	7.1	7.9	4.0	5.3
College 80	0.8	4.8	6.5	7.0	7.3	7.4	7.4	8.1	7.2	3.8	5.1
College 85	0.2	4.7	6.1	6.5	7.4	7.5	7.4	7.0	7.5	4.2	5.3
College 90	0.0	4.7	6.2	6.5	6.6	7.4	7.2	7.0	7.0	4.5	5.4
College 95	0.0	4.4	6.0	6.5	6.9	7.3	7.6	7.4	7.3	4.4	5.3

Table 8.11. *Lifetime Net Tax Rate under Low-Cost Assumptions*

	Lifetime Labor Earnings (1997 dollars)										
	0–120k	120k–240k	240k–360k	360k–480k	480k–600k	600k–720k	720k–840k	840k–960k	960k–1.08m	1.08m+	Total
Cohort 45	−0.3	5.5	6.6	6.8	7.3	7.0	6.8	5.6	6.5	3.7	5.4
Cohort 50	−2.9	4.0	5.4	6.1	6.3	6.5	6.7	6.1	6.0	3.6	4.8
Cohort 55	−1.5	4.3	5.7	6.3	6.4	7.0	7.1	7.3	6.6	3.9	5.0
Cohort 60	−1.2	4.8	6.2	6.8	6.9	7.2	7.4	7.3	7.5	3.9	5.1
Cohort 65	−1.9	4.7	6.0	6.7	6.8	7.0	7.2	7.6	7.1	4.3	5.3
Cohort 70	−1.4	4.2	5.8	6.3	6.9	7.1	7.1	7.8	7.8	4.3	5.2
Cohort 75	−2.1	3.9	5.5	6.4	6.7	7.1	7.1	7.3	7.3	4.3	5.1
Cohort 80	−2.6	3.5	5.6	6.1	6.5	6.6	7.1	7.3	7.5	4.5	5.1
Cohort 85	−2.9	3.3	5.0	5.6	6.3	6.5	6.8	7.2	7.1	4.5	5.0
Cohort 90	−3.8	2.8	4.6	5.7	6.3	6.3	6.7	6.8	7.0	4.8	5.0
Cohort 95	−5.4	2.4	4.3	5.6	6.0	6.3	6.5	6.8	6.8	4.9	5.0
Men 45	4.2	6.4	7.1	7.3	7.6	7.2	7.0	6.0	6.7	3.9	5.9
Men 50	3.2	5.5	6.1	6.4	6.6	6.6	6.9	6.4	6.1	3.7	5.4
Men 55	3.7	5.8	6.4	6.8	6.8	7.3	7.5	7.6	7.1	4.0	5.5
Men 60	3.8	6.0	6.9	7.2	7.3	7.6	7.9	7.8	7.9	3.9	5.5
Men 65	3.8	5.9	6.8	7.1	7.2	7.2	7.3	7.7	7.2	4.5	5.7
Men 70	3.9	5.5	6.5	6.9	7.3	7.4	7.6	8.0	8.0	4.6	5.8
Men 75	3.6	5.1	6.5	6.6	7.2	7.4	7.5	7.8	7.4	4.5	5.5
Men 80	3.0	5.0	6.4	6.7	7.0	6.9	7.4	7.6	7.6	4.6	5.5
Men 85	3.5	5.0	5.9	6.2	6.7	6.7	7.0	7.5	7.3	4.6	5.4
Men 90	2.5	3.8	5.5	6.2	6.7	6.7	7.0	7.2	7.2	4.9	5.4
Men 95	2.1	3.6	5.0	6.1	6.5	6.5	6.8	7.0	6.8	5.1	5.5

(*continued*)

Table 8.11. *(continued)*

	Lifetime Labor Earnings (1997 dollars)										
	0–120k	120k–240k	240k–360k	360k–480k	480k–600k	600k–720k	720k–840k	840k–960k	960k–1.08m	1.08m+	Total
Women 45	−1.3	5.0	5.9	5.8	6.3	6.1	5.8	4.5	5.6	2.7	4.4
Women 50	−5.0	3.0	4.6	5.4	5.6	6.3	5.8	5.2	5.7	3.2	3.7
Women 55	−3.7	3.4	4.8	5.5	5.7	6.3	6.2	6.6	5.7	3.6	4.1
Women 60	−3.3	3.8	5.5	6.0	6.3	6.5	6.8	6.7	6.6	3.9	4.5
Women 65	−4.4	3.8	5.1	6.1	6.2	6.6	7.1	7.4	6.7	3.7	4.5
Women 70	−3.9	3.2	5.2	5.4	6.4	6.7	6.1	7.5	7.4	3.7	4.3
Women 75	−4.6	2.9	4.5	6.1	5.9	6.8	6.3	6.6	7.1	3.8	4.3
Women 80	−4.9	2.4	4.8	5.3	5.7	6.2	6.8	6.7	7.2	4.3	4.4
Women 85	−5.7	2.3	4.3	5.1	5.7	6.1	6.3	6.7	6.4	4.3	4.3
Women 90	−6.1	2.2	3.7	5.0	5.9	5.7	6.1	6.3	6.6	4.5	4.4
Women 95	−8.6	1.8	3.7	4.9	5.4	6.0	6.0	6.5	6.7	4.4	4.3
White 45	−0.3	5.6	6.5	6.8	7.2	7.0	6.8	5.6	6.4	3.7	5.4
White 50	−3.2	3.9	5.3	6.0	6.3	6.5	6.6	6.2	5.9	3.6	4.7
White 55	−1.8	4.2	5.6	6.3	6.3	7.0	7.0	7.2	6.5	3.9	5.0
White 60	−1.4	4.7	6.1	6.7	6.9	7.1	7.5	7.3	7.5	3.9	5.1
White 65	−2.3	4.6	6.1	6.6	6.7	6.9	7.2	7.5	7.2	4.3	5.2
White 70	−1.7	4.0	5.7	6.3	6.9	7.0	7.1	7.8	7.7	4.3	5.2
White 75	−2.3	3.7	5.4	6.2	6.6	7.2	6.9	7.2	7.1	4.2	4.9
White 80	−3.0	3.3	5.5	6.0	6.4	6.6	7.1	7.2	7.6	4.5	5.0
White 85	−3.4	3.0	4.9	5.5	6.3	6.4	6.8	7.2	7.2	4.5	4.9
White 90	−4.8	2.5	4.5	5.6	6.3	6.4	6.6	6.8	6.8	4.7	4.9
White 95	−6.4	2.1	4.1	5.4	5.7	6.2	6.4	6.6	6.8	4.8	4.9
Non-White 45	0.0	5.3	7.0	6.7	7.7	6.3	6.8	5.5	7.0	4.0	5.9
Non-White 50	−0.6	4.8	5.7	6.1	6.6	7.1	6.9	5.3	6.5	4.0	5.3
Non-White 55	0.1	5.0	6.1	6.0	6.9	6.7	8.0	8.2	6.8	4.2	5.5

Non-White 60	0.5	5.7	6.7	7.0	7.2	7.7	7.2	7.5	7.6	3.6	5.1
Non-White 65	0.9	5.3	5.9	6.8	7.5	7.5	7.7	8.0	6.3	4.7	5.8
Non-White 70	0.5	5.0	6.7	6.2	7.0	7.8	7.5	7.4	8.1	4.5	5.5
Non-White 75	-0.8	4.8	5.6	7.3	7.2	6.9	7.8	8.3	8.2	5.0	5.8
Non-White 80	-0.3	4.6	6.0	6.5	6.9	6.7	7.5	7.9	7.0	4.9	5.5
Non-White 85	-0.6	4.7	5.6	6.4	6.4	6.6	7.0	7.2	6.6	4.8	5.3
Non-White 90	0.7	4.2	4.9	6.2	6.4	5.9	6.9	7.0	7.5	5.2	5.5
Non-White 95	-1.0	3.7	5.1	6.3	7.0	6.9	7.0	7.3	6.8	5.3	5.7
Non-College 45	-0.1	5.7	6.8	6.9	7.4	6.8	6.6	5.5	6.7	3.9	5.7
Non-College 50	-2.5	4.3	5.6	6.2	6.4	6.8	6.7	6.1	5.9	3.9	5.0
Non-College 55	-0.9	4.4	5.7	6.2	6.4	7.4	7.2	7.6	6.8	4.2	5.2
Non-College 60	-1.1	5.0	6.4	6.7	6.9	7.4	7.6	7.8	7.8	4.4	5.5
Non-College 65	-1.1	4.9	6.1	6.7	6.9	7.2	7.5	7.7	7.4	4.6	5.6
Non-College 70	-0.9	4.3	6.2	6.7	7.2	7.2	6.8	8.2	8.1	4.8	5.6
Non-College 75	-1.6	4.2	5.6	6.6	7.0	7.2	7.1	7.3	7.3	4.6	5.3
Non-College 80	-2.4	4.0	5.9	6.3	6.5	6.6	7.0	7.4	7.9	5.1	5.5
Non-College 85	-2.1	3.6	5.2	5.8	6.6	6.6	6.8	7.2	7.3	4.8	5.2
Non-College 90	-3.0	3.1	5.1	5.9	6.3	6.4	6.7	6.9	7.3	5.4	5.4
Non-College 95	-4.8	2.8	4.6	5.9	6.3	6.7	6.5	7.0	7.3	5.7	5.5
College 45	-1.0	4.9	6.0	6.6	7.0	7.3	6.9	5.8	6.1	3.5	5.1
College 50	-3.9	3.4	5.0	5.6	6.2	6.1	6.6	6.1	6.1	3.3	4.5
College 55	-3.0	4.2	5.6	6.3	6.3	6.5	7.1	6.9	6.2	3.6	4.7
College 60	-1.3	4.4	6.0	6.8	6.9	6.9	7.1	6.8	7.1	3.6	4.6
College 65	-3.4	4.6	5.9	6.6	6.7	6.8	6.9	7.4	6.6	4.0	5.0
College 70	-2.2	4.0	5.4	5.8	6.6	7.0	7.4	7.4	7.4	4.0	4.9
College 75	-2.9	3.5	5.3	6.1	6.4	7.0	7.0	7.4	7.3	4.0	4.8
College 80	-2.7	2.9	5.3	5.8	6.5	6.6	7.2	7.1	7.0	4.2	4.8
College 85	-4.2	2.9	4.8	5.5	6.1	6.3	6.8	7.1	6.8	4.3	4.7
College 90	-4.9	2.4	4.0	5.4	6.3	6.1	6.7	6.8	6.6	4.4	4.7
College 95	-6.3	1.9	4.0	5.2	5.7	6.0	6.4	6.5	6.3	4.5	4.7

Table 8.12. *Internal Rates of Return under Intermediate Assumptions: A 38% Tax Increase Beginning in 1999*

	Lifetime Labor Earnings (1997 dollars)										
	0–120k	120k–240k	240k–360k	360k–480k	480k–600k	600k–720k	720k–840k	840k–960k	960k–1.08m	1.08m+	Total
Cohort 45	4.85	2.88	1.82	1.31	0.97	0.60	0.49	0.61	0.18	0.18	1.62
Cohort 50	5.48	3.05	1.98	1.40	1.10	0.57	0.37	0.08	0.12	0.25	1.65
Cohort 55	5.01	2.84	1.82	1.37	1.02	0.42	0.09	-0.04	-0.10	-0.03	1.36
Cohort 60	4.71	2.61	1.70	0.99	0.92	0.59	-0.03	-0.20	-0.40	-0.08	1.18
Cohort 65	4.55	2.56	1.77	0.98	0.86	0.57	0.35	0.24	-0.44	-0.37	1.08
Cohort 70	4.41	2.62	1.71	1.15	0.78	0.59	0.24	-0.49	-0.31	-0.42	1.03
Cohort 75	4.38	2.58	1.65	1.08	0.85	0.73	0.29	0.22	-0.47	-0.39	1.00
Cohort 80	4.40	2.55	1.72	1.19	0.86	0.60	0.63	0.02	-0.47	-0.42	0.94
Cohort 85	4.45	2.69	1.91	1.47	1.09	0.77	0.73	0.21	-0.21	-0.28	1.07
Cohort 90	4.46	2.76	1.94	1.38	1.03	0.73	0.52	0.48	0.00	-0.28	1.04
Cohort 95	4.58	2.84	1.97	1.44	1.17	1.08	0.83	0.36	-0.06	-0.59	0.92
Men 45	3.15	1.90	1.09	0.87	0.69	0.33	0.25	0.33	-0.31	-0.11	0.60
Men 50	3.13	1.96	1.19	0.83	0.69	0.21	-0.10	-0.28	-0.22	0.01	0.57
Men 55	3.02	1.73	1.13	0.68	0.60	-0.07	-0.49	-0.62	-0.44	-0.24	0.36
Men 60	2.84	1.53	0.82	0.40	0.37	0.18	-0.85	-0.87	-0.74	-0.29	0.20
Men 65	2.83	1.55	0.89	0.40	0.15	0.05	0.12	-0.04	-0.72	-0.68	0.14
Men 70	2.61	1.66	0.86	0.56	0.24	0.26	-0.14	-0.68	-0.60	-0.70	0.12
Men 75	2.64	1.74	0.95	0.58	0.48	0.13	-0.28	-0.44	-0.93	-0.66	0.14
Men 80	2.57	1.78	1.11	0.58	0.46	0.08	0.39	-0.25	-0.66	-0.72	0.12
Men 85	2.88	2.01	1.22	0.94	0.68	0.51	0.13	-0.24	-0.85	-0.49	0.29
Men 90	3.16	2.17	1.23	0.81	0.78	0.40	0.44	0.16	-0.29	-0.52	0.34
Men 95	3.42	2.25	1.46	1.15	0.63	0.87	0.54	0.20	-0.21	-0.77	0.28
Women 45	5.06	3.32	2.49	2.03	1.59	1.55	1.21	1.33	1.55	1.22	2.90
Women 50	5.94	3.59	2.67	2.19	1.84	1.27	1.26	1.03	0.82	0.89	2.91
Women 55	5.53	3.43	2.43	2.16	1.62	1.32	1.07	0.73	0.60	0.47	2.47

Women 60	5.21	3.24	2.42	1.67	1.59	1.12	0.96	0.59	0.41	0.36	2.21
Women 65	5.04	3.14	2.50	1.63	1.64	1.32	0.74	0.61	0.19	0.34	2.12
Women 70	4.97	3.19	2.34	1.82	1.48	1.11	0.84	-0.08	0.33	0.17	2.04
Women 75	4.85	3.09	2.17	1.69	1.41	1.46	1.01	0.90	0.41	0.16	1.95
Women 80	4.90	3.00	2.31	1.87	1.34	1.15	0.95	0.56	-0.07	0.22	1.89
Women 85	4.86	3.10	2.35	1.98	1.55	1.14	1.47	0.86	0.90	0.14	1.94
Women 90	4.83	3.08	2.46	1.90	1.34	1.11	0.68	0.98	0.58	0.19	1.85
Women 95	4.89	3.18	2.41	1.77	1.72	1.39	1.20	0.74	0.17	-0.20	1.70
White 45	4.87	2.90	1.89	1.28	1.00	0.52	0.50	0.65	0.28	0.12	1.62
White 50	5.53	3.10	2.05	1.38	1.10	0.52	0.34	0.06	0.08	0.26	1.67
White 55	5.05	2.89	1.85	1.36	1.09	0.43	0.08	0.07	-0.07	-0.07	1.36
White 60	4.77	2.67	1.77	1.01	0.90	0.60	-0.09	-0.17	-0.45	-0.10	1.19
White 65	4.63	2.65	1.73	0.99	0.84	0.59	0.38	0.20	-0.62	-0.39	1.06
White 70	4.49	2.70	1.77	1.17	0.77	0.60	0.20	-0.65	-0.22	-0.48	1.02
White 75	4.37	2.63	1.67	1.12	0.90	0.72	0.34	0.30	-0.44	-0.43	1.00
White 80	4.49	2.60	1.74	1.20	0.87	0.64	0.62	0.08	-0.56	-0.41	0.95
White 85	4.51	2.80	1.99	1.53	1.10	0.79	0.75	0.15	-0.16	-0.32	1.08
White 90	4.63	2.88	2.03	1.43	0.98	0.77	0.56	0.46	0.03	-0.25	1.06
White 95	4.66	3.00	2.10	1.54	1.24	1.16	0.81	0.36	0.03	-0.53	0.96
Non-White 45	4.60	2.80	1.30	1.50	0.71	1.36	0.32	0.21	-0.71	0.86	1.59
Non-White 50	5.00	2.68	1.60	1.50	1.09	0.94	0.51	0.24	0.41	0.09	1.51
Non-White 55	4.71	2.49	1.58	1.45	0.56	0.36	0.10	-1.58	-0.49	0.38	1.35
Non-White 60	4.28	2.27	1.20	0.87	1.05	0.53	0.42	-0.45	0.05	0.04	1.11
Non-White 65	3.96	2.11	1.97	0.93	0.99	0.40	0.10	0.51	0.87	-0.22	1.16
Non-White 70	3.95	2.28	1.45	1.01	0.84	0.53	0.48	0.47	-0.87	-0.05	1.07
Non-White 75	4.41	2.37	1.55	0.91	0.65	0.78	0.04	-0.26	-0.59	-0.14	0.99
Non-White 80	3.97	2.28	1.59	1.18	0.81	0.39	0.70	-0.30	-0.22	-0.52	0.90
Non-White 85	4.18	2.18	1.48	1.18	1.05	0.67	0.63	0.54	-0.43	-0.07	1.03
Non-White 90	3.81	2.27	1.56	1.12	1.21	0.60	0.34	0.57	-0.15	-0.43	0.96
Non-White 95	4.28	2.31	1.49	1.05	0.94	0.75	0.90	0.37	-0.55	-0.84	0.73

(continued)

Table 8.12. *(continued)*

	Lifetime Labor Earnings (1997 dollars)										
	0–120k	120k–240k	240k–360k	360k–480k	480k–600k	600k–720k	720k–840k	840k–960k	960k–1.08m	1.08m+	Total
Non-College 45	4.79	2.70	1.68	1.17	0.90	0.70	0.46	0.70	-0.18	0.25	1.67
Non-College 50	5.41	2.88	1.89	1.24	1.02	0.65	0.34	0.00	-0.14	0.17	1.71
Non-College 55	4.86	2.72	1.79	1.39	1.08	0.12	-0.21	-0.07	-0.34	-0.10	1.40
Non-College 60	4.56	2.47	1.45	0.97	0.84	0.36	0.12	-0.39	-0.79	-0.19	1.17
Non-College 65	4.43	2.44	1.63	0.74	0.88	0.47	0.25	0.07	-0.68	-0.47	1.07
Non-College 70	4.33	2.47	1.47	0.87	0.75	0.60	0.43	-0.76	-0.31	-0.36	1.09
Non-College 75	4.18	2.41	1.50	1.09	0.71	0.42	0.23	0.04	-0.45	-0.72	0.98
Non-College 80	4.26	2.40	1.57	1.18	0.62	0.77	0.50	0.18	-0.58	-0.57	1.00
Non-College 85	4.35	2.50	1.69	1.40	0.94	0.71	0.65	0.17	-0.01	-0.36	1.13
Non-College 90	4.27	2.66	1.86	1.28	0.92	0.69	0.32	0.32	0.02	-0.27	1.12
Non-College 95	4.34	2.76	1.91	1.25	0.89	0.91	0.61	0.24	-0.24	-0.70	0.96
College 45	4.98	3.33	2.20	1.59	1.12	0.50	0.52	0.50	0.65	0.11	1.52
College 50	5.65	3.42	2.18	1.69	1.20	0.42	0.40	0.17	0.37	0.33	1.55
College 55	5.36	3.07	1.86	1.34	0.90	0.77	0.47	0.02	0.23	0.05	1.30
College 60	5.00	2.85	2.12	1.02	1.02	0.86	-0.34	0.03	0.07	0.01	1.18
College 65	4.77	2.74	1.98	1.29	0.84	0.70	0.48	0.54	-0.14	-0.28	1.08
College 70	4.53	2.82	1.99	1.44	0.82	0.58	0.06	-0.29	-0.31	-0.46	0.96
College 75	4.67	2.80	1.81	1.07	1.00	0.95	0.35	0.40	-0.49	-0.16	1.02
College 80	4.59	2.73	1.88	1.21	1.10	0.38	0.75	-0.16	-0.37	-0.33	0.88
College 85	4.59	2.93	2.15	1.56	1.24	0.82	0.78	0.24	-0.41	-0.23	1.03
College 90	4.75	2.88	2.03	1.48	1.14	0.78	0.67	0.65	-0.02	-0.28	0.97
College 95	4.93	2.97	2.05	1.62	1.44	1.25	1.03	0.46	0.12	-0.51	0.88

Table 8.13. *Internal Rates of Return under Intermediate Assumptions: A 25% Benefit Cut Beginning in 1999*

| | Lifetime Labor Earnings (1997 dollars) | | | | | | | | | | |
	0–120k	120k–240k	240k–360k	360k–480k	480k–600k	600k–720k	720k–840k	840k–960k	960k–1.08m	1.08m+	Total
Cohort 45	4.21	2.23	1.16	0.66	0.34	−0.01	−0.10	0.04	−0.39	−0.39	0.99
Cohort 50	4.86	2.46	1.40	0.85	0.59	0.08	−0.09	−0.38	−0.32	−0.20	1.12
Cohort 55	4.48	2.36	1.36	0.95	0.62	0.05	−0.26	−0.37	−0.42	−0.34	0.96
Cohort 60	4.25	2.23	1.36	0.69	0.63	0.33	−0.26	−0.42	−0.59	−0.29	0.89
Cohort 65	4.20	2.30	1.55	0.80	0.70	0.42	0.22	0.12	−0.54	−0.47	0.90
Cohort 70	4.20	2.50	1.62	1.08	0.74	0.56	0.22	−0.49	−0.31	−0.43	0.97
Cohort 75	4.33	2.59	1.66	1.11	0.89	0.78	0.35	0.27	−0.40	−0.32	1.04
Cohort 80	4.48	2.63	1.79	1.26	0.94	0.69	0.72	0.11	−0.38	−0.33	1.02
Cohort 85	4.53	2.78	1.98	1.55	1.17	0.86	0.82	0.30	−0.12	−0.19	1.16
Cohort 90	4.55	2.84	2.01	1.45	1.11	0.82	0.61	0.58	0.10	−0.18	1.13
Cohort 95	4.67	2.93	2.05	1.51	1.24	1.17	0.91	0.46	0.04	−0.48	1.01
Men 45	2.52	1.22	0.41	0.22	0.05	−0.29	−0.33	−0.24	−0.89	−0.69	−0.02
Men 50	2.55	1.38	0.62	0.29	0.18	−0.27	−0.56	−0.72	−0.66	−0.44	0.07
Men 55	2.54	1.29	0.68	0.29	0.24	−0.43	−0.80	−0.94	−0.76	−0.55	0.00
Men 60	2.49	1.21	0.53	0.13	0.12	−0.05	−1.03	−1.06	−0.91	−0.49	−0.04
Men 65	2.58	1.36	0.72	0.26	0.04	−0.06	0.01	−0.14	−0.81	−0.77	0.02
Men 70	2.51	1.60	0.81	0.54	0.23	0.26	−0.14	−0.66	−0.58	−0.71	0.11
Men 75	2.66	1.78	0.98	0.62	0.54	0.20	−0.21	−0.37	−0.85	−0.59	0.20
Men 80	2.66	1.87	1.18	0.65	0.55	0.17	0.48	−0.15	−0.56	−0.62	0.22
Men 85	2.98	2.10	1.29	1.01	0.77	0.61	0.22	−0.14	−0.75	−0.39	0.38
Men 90	3.25	2.27	1.30	0.89	0.87	0.50	0.53	0.25	−0.19	−0.42	0.43
Men 95	3.51	2.35	1.54	1.22	0.71	0.96	0.64	0.30	−0.11	−0.67	0.38

(continued)

Table 8.13. (continued)

	Lifetime Labor Earnings (1997 dollars)										
	0–120k	120k–240k	240k–360k	360k–480k	480k–600k	600k–720k	720k–840k	840k–960k	960k–1.08m	1.08m+	Total
Women 45	4.43	2.68	1.85	1.38	0.98	0.97	0.63	0.78	0.98	0.65	2.27
Women 50	5.32	2.99	2.08	1.62	1.32	0.76	0.82	0.53	0.35	0.43	2.34
Women 55	4.98	2.92	1.96	1.69	1.18	0.91	0.68	0.36	0.27	0.14	2.02
Women 60	4.73	2.81	2.03	1.32	1.25	0.81	0.68	0.32	0.16	0.13	1.86
Women 65	4.66	2.83	2.22	1.39	1.43	1.11	0.56	0.46	0.05	0.21	1.88
Women 70	4.72	3.02	2.22	1.70	1.39	1.03	0.78	-0.10	0.30	0.13	1.94
Women 75	4.77	3.07	2.17	1.71	1.44	1.49	1.04	0.94	0.46	0.21	1.96
Women 80	4.98	3.08	2.38	1.93	1.41	1.22	1.03	0.64	0.02	0.31	1.97
Women 85	4.94	3.19	2.43	2.05	1.63	1.22	1.55	0.94	0.98	0.24	2.02
Women 90	4.91	3.16	2.53	1.97	1.41	1.18	0.77	1.07	0.66	0.28	1.93
Women 95	4.98	3.27	2.49	1.84	1.79	1.47	1.28	0.82	0.27	-0.10	1.79
White 45	4.24	2.25	1.23	0.63	0.38	-0.09	-0.09	0.09	-0.29	-0.45	1.00
White 50	4.91	2.52	1.47	0.83	0.59	0.03	-0.12	-0.40	-0.36	-0.19	1.14
White 55	4.52	2.41	1.40	0.93	0.69	0.05	-0.26	-0.27	-0.39	-0.38	0.96
White 60	4.32	2.28	1.43	0.71	0.61	0.35	-0.31	-0.39	-0.64	-0.31	0.90
White 65	4.28	2.38	1.51	0.81	0.68	0.45	0.25	0.08	-0.72	-0.49	0.89
White 70	4.28	2.57	1.68	1.11	0.72	0.57	0.18	-0.64	-0.22	-0.49	0.97
White 75	4.31	2.64	1.68	1.15	0.94	0.77	0.39	0.36	-0.36	-0.37	1.04
White 80	4.57	2.69	1.81	1.27	0.95	0.73	0.70	0.17	-0.46	-0.31	1.03
White 85	4.59	2.89	2.07	1.60	1.18	0.88	0.84	0.24	-0.07	-0.23	1.17
White 90	4.71	2.96	2.11	1.51	1.06	0.86	0.65	0.55	0.12	-0.15	1.15
White 95	4.74	3.09	2.18	1.61	1.31	1.24	0.90	0.45	0.12	-0.43	1.05
Non-White 45	3.94	2.14	0.64	0.84	0.06	0.75	-0.23	-0.40	-1.29	0.29	0.95
Non-White 50	4.36	2.08	1.02	0.96	0.61	0.45	0.07	-0.22	-0.07	-0.38	0.98
Non-White 55	4.16	2.01	1.12	1.03	0.15	0.03	-0.22	-1.84	-0.79	0.05	0.94

Non-White 60	3.81	1.90	0.88	0.56	0.76	0.25	0.19	-0.67	-0.14	-0.17	0.82
Non-White 65	3.64	1.88	1.75	0.75	0.83	0.25	-0.01	0.38	0.77	-0.33	0.99
Non-White 70	3.77	2.19	1.37	0.93	0.81	0.49	0.45	0.44	-0.86	-0.08	1.01
Non-White 75	4.40	2.40	1.57	0.96	0.70	0.84	0.09	-0.19	-0.52	-0.07	1.04
Non-White 80	4.05	2.36	1.66	1.25	0.88	0.49	0.79	-0.20	-0.12	-0.42	0.98
Non-White 85	4.27	2.27	1.55	1.26	1.13	0.76	0.73	0.63	-0.34	0.03	1.12
Non-White 90	3.90	2.36	1.64	1.19	1.30	0.68	0.44	0.66	-0.06	-0.33	1.05
Non-White 95	4.36	2.40	1.57	1.13	1.02	0.83	0.98	0.47	-0.45	-0.73	0.82
Non-College 45	4.16	2.04	1.01	0.51	0.27	0.08	-0.12	0.13	-0.75	-0.32	1.04
Non-College 50	4.79	2.29	1.31	0.70	0.51	0.16	-0.12	-0.47	-0.59	-0.28	1.17
Non-College 55	4.33	2.24	1.34	0.96	0.68	-0.25	-0.54	-0.41	-0.65	-0.41	0.99
Non-College 60	4.12	2.09	1.12	0.66	0.55	0.11	-0.10	-0.61	-0.97	-0.40	0.88
Non-College 65	4.10	2.20	1.42	0.57	0.72	0.32	0.12	-0.05	-0.78	-0.57	0.90
Non-College 70	4.13	2.36	1.39	0.81	0.71	0.57	0.41	-0.76	-0.31	-0.38	1.04
Non-College 75	4.15	2.42	1.51	1.13	0.76	0.47	0.28	0.09	-0.38	-0.66	1.02
Non-College 80	4.34	2.48	1.64	1.25	0.70	0.86	0.58	0.27	-0.49	-0.47	1.09
Non-College 85	4.44	2.59	1.77	1.47	1.02	0.79	0.74	0.25	0.09	-0.26	1.21
Non-College 90	4.36	2.75	1.94	1.36	1.00	0.78	0.41	0.41	0.12	-0.17	1.21
Non-College 95	4.43	2.85	1.99	1.32	0.97	1.00	0.70	0.33	-0.14	-0.60	1.05
College 45	4.36	2.70	1.56	0.96	0.49	-0.10	-0.07	-0.07	0.08	-0.46	0.91
College 50	5.04	2.82	1.60	1.14	0.70	-0.07	-0.06	-0.28	-0.07	-0.13	1.03
College 55	4.81	2.59	1.41	0.91	0.51	0.38	0.12	-0.32	-0.11	-0.27	0.91
College 60	4.51	2.46	1.76	0.73	0.73	0.58	-0.55	-0.19	-0.15	-0.20	0.89
College 65	4.39	2.45	1.75	1.09	0.68	0.55	0.34	0.42	-0.24	-0.38	0.91
College 70	4.31	2.69	1.90	1.37	0.78	0.56	0.04	-0.29	-0.30	-0.47	0.91
College 75	4.60	2.81	1.83	1.10	1.04	0.99	0.40	0.45	-0.42	-0.10	1.06
College 80	4.67	2.81	1.95	1.28	1.18	0.46	0.84	-0.06	-0.27	-0.24	0.96
College 85	4.68	3.02	2.23	1.64	1.32	0.91	0.87	0.33	-0.32	-0.14	1.12
College 90	4.83	2.97	2.11	1.56	1.23	0.86	0.76	0.74	0.07	-0.18	1.06
College 95	5.02	3.06	2.13	1.69	1.51	1.34	1.12	0.55	0.22	-0.41	0.97

Both tables show dramatically lower internal rates of return, particularly for younger cohorts. Those in the 1995 cohort, for example, can expect a 0.92 percent rate of return under the tax hike and a 1.01 percent rate of return under the benefit cut. The benefit cut leaves men, on average, earning a 0.4 percent real return. In the case of the tax hike, the smaller percentage reduction in the rate of return received by early cohorts reflects the fact that for these cohorts many of their taxpaying years are already behind them when the tax is raised.

Summary and Conclusion

This chapter used CORSIM – a dynamic microsimulation model – and SSBC – a detailed Social Security benefit calculator – to project aggregate OASI benefits and taxes and to evaluate Social Security's treatment of different types of postwar Americans. Our forecast entails essentially identical tax revenues, but roughly 15 percent less in long-term benefit payments. The precise reason for the differences in long-term projected benefits, although difficult to determine, is an important area for future research.

Our internal rate of return calculations indicate that postwar Americans can expect, on average, to earn a very low real return – roughly 2 percent – on their Social Security contributions. Moreover, measured as a percentage of their lifetime incomes, postwar Americans can expect, on average, to pay a fairly high net tax – 5 percent of their lifetime labor earnings – to the system. These lifetime net tax rate calculations show that it is the middle classes who face the highest lifetime net tax rates; in other words, the system is not progressive when you discount benefits and taxes at 5 percent real.

Social Security's bad deal for postwar Americans will end up substantially worse if taxes are raised or benefits cut by the amount needed to produce true long-term solvency. If taxes are raised or benefits cut to eliminate the OASI system's long-term fiscal imbalance, Americans born this year will receive (after inflation) roughly 1 percent on their contributions.

Appendix
Specification Details for CORSIM and SSBC

CORSIM Processes Used in This Study

Table 8.1 lists the subset of CORSIM processes used in this study, the data used in their estimation, and the aggregate statistics used in their alignment. We briefly discuss each of the processes.

Fertility

This process is the probability that a female sample member will give birth in a given year. As indicated in the second column, separate logistic functions are used to calculate this probability – one for each of thirty different groups of women. These groups are distinguished by their martial status, race, work status, and whether they already have children. Each logistic function was estimated from NLS data, with some or all of the variables listed in column 3 used as regressors. These regressors include age, past births, duration of current marriage, current marital status, and labor earnings. Alignment of the logistic probabilities is done first on an age-, race-, and marital-status–specific basis using Vital Statistics and then on an overall basis using the Social Security Administration's annual total fertility rate.

Mortality

The logistics for the probability of dying in a given year are calculated separately for fifty-one groups distinguished by age, sex, race, and marital status. Note that the regressors for these logistics include two economic variables – employment status and family income – and education, which is highly correlated with income. This is important. The intragenerational progressivity of Social Security depends critically on whether poor members of particular generations live long enough to receive their benefits. Fortunately, the National Longitudinal Mortality Study used to estimate these logistics contains these key variables. As an individual is "aged" in CORSIM, CORSIM updates the values of these three variables and uses them in calculating the individual's current probability of dying. The Vital Statistics series is used to align predicted mortality rates for each of eighty-eight distinct age-race-sex groups, and then the Social Security Administration's age- and sex-adjusted annual death rate is used as a final global alignment.

Enter Marriage Market for First Time

This logistic function was estimated separately for twenty groups differing by age, race, sex, schooling, marital status, and weeks worked. The estimation was done on NLS data on individuals who changed their marital status between one year and the next from never-married to married. Since Social Security spousal benefits are available to dependent spouses and Social Security survivor benefits are available to widows and widowers, having marriage depend on earnings and education, as CORSIM does, is another prerequisite for understanding Social Security's intragenerational redistribution. Census data are used to align the logistic-imputed probabilities to produce the correct national totals of first-time marriages across sixteen age-sex groups.

Assortative Mating

CORSIM also must decide who marries whom. It does so through an assortative mating process. Specifically, it considers all pairings of unmarried males with unmarried females. Each pairing is assigned a marriage probability, and then those pairs with the highest probability are selected as actual marriages. The probability of marriage, which is estimated on the basis of Census data, depends on the differences between and levels of the male's and female's ages, the differences in their incomes, race, state of residence, labor force participation, and other factors. Males and females who are closer in age and whose educational levels are closer have higher probabilities of marrying. Given Social Security's provision of spousal and survivor benefits, how marriages are formed will matter to the system's redistribution, both across and within generations.

Marital Dissolution

The determinants of this logistic process are the difference in spouses' ages, the duration of the marriage, the husband's wages, race, and the differences in wage rates between the husband and wife. The process is estimated with PSID data separately for four different groups of married couples. The four groups are distinguished by the earning status of the wife and the presence of children under 18. National data on divorce are used to align the probabilities, which are derived from the predicted values of the logistics, for fourteen groups defined by duration of marriage.

Reentry into the Marriage Market

CORSIM keeps track of individuals who have become divorced or widowed and gives them the opportunity to reenter the marriage market and, potentially, remarry. There are seven different logistics for reentry into this market, which are distinguished by the individual's race, age, sex, and other characteristics. The actual determinants of these functions, which were estimated on PSID data, include education, income, whether one is divorced or widowed, and whether one has children. National Center for Health Statistics data were used to align predicted logistics for twenty-six groups defined by age, sex, and the reason for dissolution of the prior marriage (divorce versus widowhood).

Education

The education processes (one for each of thirty-three separate groups) are also logistics. These logistics, which were estimated with High School

& Beyond (HSB) and NLS data, determine whether an individual with a certain number of years of education chooses to continue his or her education for at least one more year. A variety of factors, including age, whether you have a child, whether you're living on your own, and your parents' education, influence schooling outcomes. High school graduation rates are then aligned by sex, and a global alignment of college enrollment rates is also imposed.

Work Status and Weeks Worked

CORSIM's earnings module starts with group-specific probits determining (a) whether sample members work zero or a positive number of weeks during the year, and (b) given that weeks worked is positive, whether weeks worked exceeds forty-seven weeks per year (i.e., whether the worker works full-year or part-year). The 174 groups for which these probits are estimated differ by age, sex, race, whether the sample member has a child, and whether he or she worked part-year or full-year in the past year. The explanatory variables in the probits, which were estimated on PSID data, include age, education, presence of children, youngest child's age, and marital status. Benchmarking of work status (full-year, part-year, none at all) is done separately for thirty-five age-race-sex subgroups based on Census and CPS data and is then aligned to coincide with Social Security's aggregate proportion of the population in covered work.

These probits are then followed by regression equations, again estimated on PSID data, which predict the actual number of weeks that an individual works. The prediction is distinct for each of fifty-eight groups differentiated first by full- or part-year work status and then by age, race, sex, marital status, living with parents, and the presence of children. The regressors in this equation include education and marital status.

Weekly Earnings

To calculate annual earnings, CORSIM multiplies weeks worked by weekly earnings. Weekly earnings is imputed by means of a regression on age, lagged earnings, education, education times earnings, marital status, number of children, and the youngest child's age. Separate imputation regressions were estimated for 116 groups broken down by age, the presence of children, marital status, race, and sex. Total weekly earnings are aligned separately for seventy groups (based on age, sex, full-year vs. part-year status, and, for women, marital status and presence of children) using CPS data, and then each of these groups is subjected to the same global alignment to ensure that predicted aggregate earnings coincide with the National Income and Product Account (NIPA) aggregates.

Age of Receipt of Social Security Retirement Benefits

This is a key variable used by SSBC in assigning Social Security retirement, spousal, and dependent benefits to CORSIM sample members. It is key because Social Security reduces retirement benefits for early retirees and increases them for late retirees. Social Security also subjects benefits to an earnings tests once individuals start receiving them. Finally, Social Security's provision of spousal benefits to current spouses and dependent benefits to children on a worker's earnings record is contingent on whether or not the worker is entitled to collect retirement benefits. For workers who are eligible to become entitled for retirement benefits, CORSIM uses logistic functions, estimated on PSID data, to determine the probability of entitlement. The logistic's regressors include age, lagged change in weeks worked, the level of earnings, education, home ownership, living arrangement, asset income, lagged income, marital status, race, and sex. Social Security Administration data on total numbers of workers applying for retirement benefits are used to align the data for twelve age-sex groups.

CORSIM Post-1996 Alignments

For each year between 1960 and 1996, CORSIM's alignments are based on actual historical aggregates or aggregates that are interpolated between actual historical data. Take, as an example, the proportions of individuals who elect to receive their Social Security retirement benefits at various ages (e.g., 62 and 65). CORSIM calculates the historical proportions for these variables by dividing aggregate data on new awards from the *Annual Statistical Supplement to the Social Security Bulletin* by the total population in the age group. Likewise, historical alignment data for birth probabilities come from live birth registration data that are collected annually by each of the fifty states.

CORSIM's annual alignment totals for years beyond 1996 incorporate many of the intermediate assumptions pertaining to aggregate fertility, mortality, and migration developed by the Office of the Actuary of the Social Security Administration and reported in the 1997 *Trustees' Report* (U.S. Board of Trustees, 1997). Neufeld (1996a) details this procedure. CORSIM uses the Trustees' assumptions for the total fertility rate (assumed to reach its ultimate level of 1.9 in the year 2020) and the age- and sex-adjusted death rate[24] (assumed to decline from 832.0 per thou-

---

[24] This is defined as the crude rate that would occur in the enumerated total population as of April 1, 1990, if that population were to experience the death rates by age and sex observed in or assumed for the selected years (Board of Trustees, 1997, 64).

sand in 1996 to 529.8 in 2075). It does not include the Trustees' estimates of life expectancy, although it is fairly close to their estimates.[25]

CORSIM further incorporates several of the 1997 Trustees' intermediate assumptions about anticipated economic changes, including the expected growth of wages and prices. The Trustees currently assume that the future value of increase in the consumer price index (CPI) will vary between 3.2 and 3.5 percent over the projection period. Average wages in CORSIM grow as the Trustees anticipate, at a rate of CPI plus a real differential, which, in the long term, equals 0.9 percent per year. Again, this is implemented as a part of CORSIM alignment, specifically, the aggregate alignment of workers' wages to the NIPA totals. The Trustees' intermediate projected changes in the size of the labor force suggest continual growth over time, ranging up to an annual increase of 1 percent. Concerning the composition of the labor force, the SSA actuaries anticipate that there will be further declines in work effort among men and eventual plateauing of increases among women in the future. CORSIM ensures that this outcome is replicated by adjusting the probability that an individual's number of weeks worked is nonzero, using the Trustees' sex-specific coverage rate, defined as the proportion of the population age 16 and over that has Social Security–covered employment in that year.[26]

CORSIM's Shortcomings

The beauty of the dynamic microsimulation model – its great capacity for incorporating complex behavioral and administrative rules, interactions, and feedbacks – is also a potential weakness. If one is modeling dozens of interacting processes, then there are many places at which one could make errors, errors that could cumulate over the simulation process if undetected and/or left unchecked. Caldwell and Morrison (1999) list seven potential sources of error in the outcomes generated in dynamic microsimulation analyses: programming mistakes; imperfect micromodules, that it is, to the errors that one might make in representing the underlying behavioral processes one is modeling, and this includes specification and estimation issues; inaccurate inputs to a social or demographic process simulated in the model; random variation in the initial sample of a model; pure random variation, or Monte Carlo

---

[25] Life expectancy can be defined at birth or at any other age; the SSA uses estimates from birth and from age 65.

[26] These data are not available in published Office of the Actuary reports but were provided by Nettie J. Barrick and Robert Baldwin (personal correspondence, 1997).

variability; differences between micro- and aggregate-level processes; and inaccurate aggregate data. In this chapter, we concentrate on specification and estimation issues in CORSIM, though a more general discussion is available in Favreault (1998).

One particular area of concern for estimation is that the time frames of data used in the estimation of the social and demographic processes don't cover the entire post-1960 period (e.g., mortality logistics are estimated on the basis of 1980–89 data). In the particular case of the mortality functions, we believe that these data are the best available, and using the most current data for projection purposes is standard practice in demographic modeling. Keeping CORSIM functions updated to the best available data is a never-ending process. Especially troublesome is the fact that the set of equations that generate earnings for individuals in the model are now ten years old. One's concerns about stale data should be attenuated by the alignment procedures, which are in fact year-specific.

One should also consider that data from the PSID and other sources are subject to measurement error, which affects the size of the standard errors used in the calculation of earnings. Many of the data from which parameters for CORSIM functions are estimated are based upon self-reports, and errors in self-reports are known to vary in important ways. Measurement error in self-reported earnings, for example, has been shown to vary inversely with true earnings (see, e.g., Pischke, 1995). This could lead to biased parameter estimates for these critical model functions.

One important and appealing feature of the CORSIM specification is the multiple equations and alignment groups, but there are hazards to this modeling approach. When one moves from one regression to another as one "ages" and moves from one alignment group to another, there can be rather dramatic variability in predicted outcomes. Patterns in fertility and mortality probabilities illustrate this well. When one examines a distribution of fertility probabilities for women in their child-bearing years that are based on Vital Statistics and Census data, for example, one sees a smooth curve that is skewed to the left and peaks in the late 20s. If one plots these same probabilities for CORSIM women, one sees the same overall pattern, but one also sees a few dramatic discontinuities between distinct ages.

In the CORSIM model, benchmarking is done on an annual basis rather than a lifetime basis. As already noted, this ensures annual consistency but not necessarily realistic life paths. Perhaps the most profound challenge that microsimulation modelers now face is to meet annual group-level targets and effectively replicate life paths simultaneously.[27] Through experimentation with CORSIM, we frequently find that in order to generate more realistic life paths, we need to relax some cross-sectional constraints. For example, one of the most unrelenting problems we face is the effective replication of individual earnings histories. Under CORSIM's original specification, many workers in the simulated population had extremely variable careers, with earnings jumping and falling dramatically, indeed, implausibly, across just a few years. Our current representation of workers' earnings has eliminated a good deal of this variability, but at a certain cost: specifically, relaxation of the constraint that mean earnings for part-time workers in various groups not be less than annual national means (though earnings totals do continue to meet an overall wage target). We believe that this trade-off is worthwhile, but will continue to develop strategies to see that the demands of both realistic life paths and historical cross-sectional totals are satisfied. For example, more-complicated lag structures in work and wage rate equations, among others, are likely to improve the realism of workers' trajectories.

SSBC's Benefit Calculations

Allocation of Benefits

The taxes and benefits used in forming lifetime OASI taxes and benefits are those nominally paid by the taxpayer and his or her employer and received by the beneficiary. Thus, a dependent benefit paid to a husband is counted as his benefit notwithstanding the fact that the benefit is based on his wife's earnings record.

Retirement Benefits

Eligibility. Individuals must be *fully insured* to receive retirement benefits based on their earnings records. Becoming fully insured requires sufficient contributions at a job (including self-employment) covered by Social Security. For those born after 1929, acquiring 40 *credits* prior to

---

[27] One major complication that modelers face is a dearth of reliable data for validating simulated life paths. Access to the comprehensive earnings data files held by the Social Security Administration is restricted, and these records lack links between spouses. One of the richest publicly available sources of longitudinal data on individuals in the United States, the Panel Study of Income Dynamics, began in 1968, which means that the maximum period for which one can currently validate trajectories using the PSID is less than thirty years. While some retrospective surveys cover longer time frames, data of this sort have numerous limitations. Even if researchers had unrestricted access to ideal validating data, conceptual issues about how to best employ these data would arise. A particularly important issue is the time frame for validation. Validating outcomes in pairs of years or in sets of three years can be quite fruitful, but, again, meeting two- or three-year validation targets won't necessarily ensure realism over a longer time frame.

retirement suffices for fully insured status. Earnings between 1937 and 1951 are aggregated and divided by $400, and the results (rounded down to an integer number) are the pre-1952 credits, which are added to the credits earned after 1950 in determining insured status. After 1951, workers earn one credit for each quarter of the year they work in Social Security–covered employment and earn above a specified minimum amount. The year of *first eligibility* for retirement benefits is the year in which the individual becomes age 62. The individual is *entitled* to retirement benefits after an application for benefits is submitted, but never before age 62.

Determination of Primary Insurance Amount (PIA). The PIA is the basis for all benefit payments made on a worker's earnings record. There are several steps in computing the PIA.

Base years are computed as the years after 1950 up to the first month of entitlement to retirement benefits. For survivor benefits, base years include the year of the worker's death.

Elapsed years are computed as those years after 1950 (or after attainment of age 21, whichever occurs later) up to (but not including) the year of first eligibility. The maximum number of elapsed years for an earnings record is forty (it could be shorter, for purposes of calculating survivor benefits if the person dies prior to age 62).

Computation years are calculated as the number of elapsed years less five or two, whichever is greater. Earnings in base years (up to the maximum taxable limit in each year and through age 60 or two years prior to death, whichever occurs earlier) are wage indexed according to economy-wide average wages. Of these, the highest earnings in years equaling the number of computation years are added together, and the sum is divided by the number of months in computation years to yield *Average Indexed Monthly Earnings (AIME)*.

Bend points are used to convert the AIME into a PIA by means of a formula with *bend points*. The bend point formula is specified as 90 percent of the first X dollars of AIME plus 32 percent of the next Y dollars of AIME plus 15 percent of the AIME in excess of Y dollars. The dollar amounts X and Y are also wage indexed and are different for different eligibility years. The dollar amounts pertaining to the year of attaining age 60 (or, for survivor benefits, the second year before death, whichever is earlier) are applied in computing the PIA.

Benefits. A person who begins to collect benefits at his or her *normal retirement age* (currently age 65) receives the PIA as the monthly retirement benefit. In subsequent years, the monthly benefit is adjusted according to the CPI to maintain its purchasing power.

Increases in the Normal Retirement Ages. After 2003, the normal retirement age is scheduled to increase by two months for every year from 2003 to the year of a person's 65th birthday. This progressive increase in the normal retirement age for those born later than 1938 ceases between the years 2008 through 2020; those attaining age 65 in these years have a normal retirement age of 66. The postponement in retirement ages resumes after 2020, with those born after 2025 having a normal retirement age of 67. All cohorts attaining age 65 after that year have a normal retirement age of 67.

Reductions for Age. A person who begins to collect retirement benefits earlier than the normal retirement age receives a *reduction for age.* The reduction factor is 5/9 of 1 percent for each month of entitlement prior to the normal retirement age. The reduced benefit payment (except for the inflation adjustment) continues even after the person reaches or surpasses the normal retirement age. If the number of months of reduction exceeds thirty-six months (e.g., in case of entitlement at age 62 when the normal retirement age is 67), then the reduction factor is 5/12 of 1 percent for every additional month of early entitlement.

Delayed Retirement Credits. Those who begin to collect benefits after the normal retirement age (up to age 70) receive *delayed retirement credits.* The amount of the delayed retirement credit for each month of delayed entitlement depends on the year in which a person attains the normal retirement age. For example, those attaining age 65 in 1997 receive an additional 5 percent in monthly benefits for each year of delay in entitlement. However, those attaining age 65 in the year 2008 will receive an additional 8 percent in benefits for each year of delayed entitlement.

Earnings Test. If a person continues to work and earn after the month of entitlement, benefits are reduced because of an *earnings test.* Beneficiaries under the normal retirement age, lose $1 for each $2 earned above an earnings limit. Those older than the normal retirement age, lose $1 for each $3 earned above a higher earnings limit. The earnings limits have already been specified through the year 2000 and are scheduled to grow with average wages in subsequent years. All benefits payable on a worker's earnings record, including the worker's own retirement benefits and spousal and child-dependent benefits, are proportionally reduced by the testing of the worker's earnings.

Recomputation of Benefits. Earnings in any year after entitlement to benefits are automatically taken into account in a recomputation of the PIA for determining the subsequent year's benefit amount. However, these earnings are not indexed before they are included in the AIME calculation. If such earnings are higher than some prior year's earnings (indexed earnings through age 60 or unindexed earnings after age 60), they result in an increase in the PIA and benefit payable. If they are lower than all previous year's earnings, they will not lower the PIA or benefits, since only the highest earnings in base years are included in the calculations.

Spousal and Child Dependent Benefits
Eligibility. Wives and husbands of insured workers (including divorced spouses) are entitled to *spousal benefits* if the couple was married for at least ten years at the time of application for spousal benefits, the spouse is over age 62 or has in care a child under age 16 entitled to benefits under the insured worker's record, and the insured worker is collecting retirement benefits. Children of insured workers under age 16 are entitled to *child-dependent benefits* if the child is unmarried and the worker is collecting retirement benefits.

Benefits. Spousal and child benefits equal 50 percent of the insured worker's PIA (each). Child-dependent benefits may be lower only if the *family maximum* applies. Spousal benefits may be lower because of the family maximum, a reduction for age, the application of the earnings test, or the spouse's receipt of retirement benefits based on her or his own earnings record.

Family Maximum. All benefits paid under a worker's record (except retirement benefits and spousal benefits of a divorced spouse) are reduced proportionately to bring them within the family maximum benefit level. The maximum benefits payable on a worker's earnings record is determined by applying a bend point formula to the PIA similar to that applied to the AIME in calculating the PIA. For example, the family maximum equals 150 percent of the first X of PIA plus 272 percent of the next Y of the PIA plus 134 percent of the next Z of the PIA plus 175 percent of the PIA greater than $X + Y + Z$. The values X, Y, and Z are adjusted for each year of the calculation according to the growth in economy-wide average wages. In case the spousal benefit is eliminated for any reason, the benefits payable on the insured worker's record are subjected to the family maximum test again, with the spouse treated as though he/she were not eligible for spousal benefits. This may result in higher benefits for children, who may be eligible for dependent benefits under the worker's record.

Reduction of Spousal Benefits for Age. Spouses eligible for the spousal benefit may elect to receive (i.e., may become entitled to) their benefits before the normal retirement age. In this case, the spousal benefit is reduced by 25/36 of 1 percent for each month of entitlement prior to the normal retirement age. If the number of months of reduction exceeds thirty-six months (e.g., in the case of entitlement at age 62 when the normal retirement age is 67), then the reduction factor is 5/12 of 1 percent for every additional month of early entitlement.

Earnings Testing of Spousal Benefits. If a spouse is earning above the amount allowed by the earnings test, the spousal benefits he or she is eligible to receive will be earnings tested according to the pre– and post–normal retirement schedule described above.

Redefinition of Spousal Benefits. If a spouse is already collecting retirement benefits, the spousal benefit is redefined as the greater of the excess of the spousal benefit over the spouse's own retirement benefit or zero.

Survivor Benefits (Widow/Widower, Father/Mother, and Children) Eligibility. The surviving spouse of a deceased worker is eligible for *widow(er) benefits* if the widow(er) is at least age 60, the widow(er) is entitled to (and has applied for) the benefits, the worker died fully insured, and the widow(er) was married to the deceased worker for at least nine months. The widow(er) of a deceased worker is eligible for *father/mother benefits* if the widow(er) is entitled to benefits (and has applied for them), the worker died fully insured, and the widow(er) has in care a child of the worker. A surviving child is eligible for *child survivor benefits* on the deceased worker's record if the child is under age 18, the child is entitled (and an application has been filed), and the worker was fully insured.

Survivor Benefits. Monthly benefits equal 100 percent of the worker's PIA for a widow(er); they equal 75 percent of the PIA for father/mother and child survivor benefits. Widow(er) and child survivor benefits may be lower only if the family maximum applies. Widow(er)s may become entitled to (i.e., elect to receive) survivor benefits earlier than the normal retirement age, but not earlier than age 60. In this case, the reduction is 19/40 of 1 percent for each month of entitlement prior to the normal retirement age. After the widow(er) is 62, he or she may become entitled to (i.e., elect to receive) retirement benefits based on his or her own past covered-earnings record. In this case, the widow(er) benefits are redefined as the excess over own retirement benefit or zero, whichever is greater. Finally, widow(er) survivor and own retirement benefits are also subject to the earnings test. If the deceased worker was already collecting a reduced retirement insurance benefit, the widow(er)'s benefit cannot be greater than the reduced widow(er) benefit or the greater of 82.5 percent of the worker's PIA or the worker's own retirement benefit. If the deceased worker was already collecting a retirement insurance benefit greater than the PIA because of delayed retirement, the widow(er) is granted the full dollar amount of the delayed retirement credit over and above the (reduced) widow(er) benefit. Father/mother benefits are not similarly augmented by delayed retirement credits that the deceased worker may have been receiving.

Father/Mother Benefits. These benefits may be reduced if the family maximum applies or if the father or mother is entitled to the own retirement benefit. In this case, the father/mother benefit is redefined as the excess over the father or mother's own retirement benefit or zero, whichever is greater. Father/mother benefits are also subject to the earnings test. On the other hand, they are not reduced for age. For those eligible to receive both widow(er) and father/mother benefits, the program calculates both and awards the larger benefit.

Calculation of a Deceased Worker's PIA. The calculation of survivor benefits in the case of a widow(er) uses the larger of two alternative calculations of the deceased worker's PIA. These are the *wage-indexing method* and the *reindexing method*. Moreover, the year up to which the worker's wages are indexed may differ, depending upon whether the deceased worker would have become age 62 before or after the widow(er) attains age 60.

Under the *wage-indexing method*, the last year for indexing earnings is the earlier of (a) the year the worker dies minus two years or (b) the year the worker would have attained age 60. Bend point formula dollar amounts are taken from the year the worker dies or the year the worker would have attained age 62, whichever is earlier. The PIA thus calculated is inflated by the CPI up to the year the widow(er) turns age 60 (or later if widowhood begins after age 60) to obtain the PIA value on which widow(er) benefits are based. Where applicable, these benefits are then adjusted for the family maximum, reduction for age, delayed retirement credits, and the earnings test.

Under the *reindexing method*, the worker's original earnings are indexed up to the earlier of (a) the year the widow(er) attains age 58 or (b) the year the worker attains age 60. The elapsed years are computed as the number of years from 1951 (or the year the worker attained age 22 if later) through the year the widow(er) attains age 60. The computation years equal elapsed years minus five years (the number of computation years cannot be less than two). Bend point formula dollar values are applied from the year the widow(er) attains age 60. There is no subsequent indexing of the PIA for inflation.

Sequencing of Widow(er) Benefit Calculations. Widow(er) benefit reductions proceed in a particular sequence. First, the widow(er), benefit plus children's benefits are subjected to the family maximum. Second, the widow(er) benefit is reduced for early entitlement, that is, entitlement of the widow(er) prior to normal retirement age. Third, the widow(er) benefit is compared to the widow(er)'s own retirement benefit if the widow(er) is entitled to the latter. Fourth, the widow(er) benefit is redefined as the excess over the widow(er)'s own benefit if the latter is positive. Finally, the earnings test is applied, first to the widow(er)'s own benefit and then to the widow(er) benefit that is in excess of the widower's own benefit. If the widow(er) benefit is eliminated as a result of these tests, the benefits payable on the insured worker's record are subjected to the family maximum test again, with the widow(er) treated as though he/she were not eligible for the widow(er) benefit. This procedure can potentially increase children's benefits if the family maximum limit was binding the first time through.

References

Anderson, Joseph M. "Retirement Policy Analysis: Models, Data and Requirements for the Future." Report prepared for the American Society of Actuaries. Chevy Chase, MD: Capital Research Associates, 1998.

Bailey, Deborah, Lee Cohen, and Howard Iams. "Comparison of MIME's between CORSIM and SIPP-DPE." Paper presented at the annual meeting of the Association for Public Policy and Management, New York City, 1998.

Bongaarts, John, T. Burch, and K.W. Wachter, eds. *Family Demography, Methods and Their Applications.* Oxford: Clarendon Press, 1987.

Caldwell, Steven B. "Recognizing Heterogeneous Responses to Policy." *Sociological Methods* and Research. 1985;13(3):387–406.

"Health, Wealth, Pensions and Life Paths: The CORSIM Dynamic

Microsimulation Model." In Ann Harding, ed., *Microsimulation and Public Policy*. Amsterdam: North Holland, 1996.

and Ted Diamond. "Income Differentials in Mortality: Preliminary Results Based on IRS-SSA Linked Data." *Proceedings of the American Statistical Association*, 1979.

et al. "CORSIM 3.0 Technical and User Documentation." Unpublished manuscript, Department of Sociology, Cornell University, 1996.

Melissa Faverault, Alla Gantman, Jagadeesh Gokhale, Thomas Johnson, and Laurence J. Kotlikoff. "Social Security's Treatment of Postwar Americans." NBER Working Paper Series, 1998.

Melissa Faverault, Alla Gantman, Jagadeesh Gokhale, Thomas Johnson, and Laurence J. Kotlikoff. "Social Security's Treatment of Postwar Americans." In James Poterba, ed., *Tax Policy and the Economy*. Cambridge, MA: MIT Press, 1999.

Melissa Favreault, and Neil Swan. "Work and Earnings over the Life Course: Validation Using Dynamic Microsimulation." Unpublished paper, Cornell University, 1996.

and Richard J. Morrison. "Validation of Longitudinal Dynamic Microsimulation Models: Experience with CORSIM and DYNACAN." In Holly Sutherland, ed., *Microsimulation in the New Millenium: Challenges and Innovations*. New York: Cambridge University Press, 1999.

Citro, Constance, and E. Hanushek, eds. *Improving Information for Social Policy Decisions: The Uses of Microsimulation Modeling*. 2 vols. Washington, DC: National Academy Press, 1991.

Coronado, Julia Lynn, Don Fullerton, and Thomas Glass. "Distributional Impacts of Proposed Changes to the Social Security System." In James M. Porterba, ed., *Tax Policy and the Economy*. Vol. 13. Cambridge, MA: MIT Press, 1999.

DeVos, Susan, and A. Palloni. "Formal Models and Methods for the Analysis of Kinship and Household Organization." *Population Index* 55(1989):174–98.

Favreault, Melissa. "Whose Safety Net? Social Security, Life-Course Processes, and Inequality in the United States." Doctoral dissertation, Department of Sociology, Cornell University, 1998.

and Steven B. Caldwell. "Whose Social Safety Net? Differential Life Course Patterns and the Progressivity of the OASDI System." Paper presented at meeting of American Sociological Association, Toronto, 1997.

"Assessing Distributional Impacts of Social Security by Cohort, Gender, Family Status, Lifetime Earnings and Race using Dynamic Microsimulation." Paper presented at annual meeting of the Association for Public Policy and Management, New York City, 1998.

Hammel, Eugene A., D. Hutchinson, K. Wachter, R. Lundy, and R. Deuel, *The SOCSIM Demographic-Sociological Microsimulation Program Operating Manual*. Institute of International Studies Research Monograph no. 27, University of California, Berkeley, 1976.

Harding, Ann, ed. *Microsimulation and Public Policy*. Amsterdam: North Holland Press, 1996.

Johnson, Thomas. "On Methods for Alignment in CORSIM/DYNACAN." Unpublished paper, Cornell University, 1996.

Kennell, D. L., and J. F. Sheils. "PRISM: Dynamic Simulation of Pension and Retirement Income." In *Microsimulation Techniques for Tax and Transfer Analysis*, edited by G. H. Lewis and R. C. Michel. Washington, DC: Urban Institute Press, 1990.

Morris, Pamela A., and S. B. Caldwell. "The Dynamics of Female-Headed Families: Changes in Children's Life Course." Draft, Cornell University, 1999.

Morrison, Richard J. "DYNACAN: A Canadian Microsimulation Model for Public Pension Analysis." Office of the Superintendent of Financial Institutions, Ottawa, Canada, 1998.

Neufeld, Christopher. "Aligning Sub-groups and Aggregates Simultaneously in Two Passes." Unpublished paper, Office of the Superintendent of Financial Institutions, Ottawa, Canada, 1996a.

"Final Report on a New Variance Reduction Method for CORSIM and DYNACAN." Unpublished paper, Office of the Superintendent of Financial Institutions, Ottawa, Canada, 1996b.

Orcutt, Guy. "A New Type of Socio-Economic System." *Review of Economics and Statistics* 58(1957):773–97.

Steven B. Caldwell, and Richard Wertheimer, *Policy Exploration through Microanalytic Simulation*. Washington, DC: Urban Institute, 1976.

Martin Greenberger, John Korbel, and Alice M. Rivlin. *Microanalysis of Socioeconomic Systems: A Simulation Study*. New York: Harper and Row, 1961.

Pischke, Jörn-Steffen. "Measurement Error and Earnings Dynamics: Some Estimates from the PSID Validation Study." *Journal of Business and Economic Statistics* 13, no. 3(1995):305–14.

Ross, C. M. "DYNASIM2 and PRISM. Examples of Dynamic Modeling." In *Improving Information for Social Policy Decisions: The Uses of Microsimulation Modeling*, Vol. II, *Technical Papers*, edited by C. F. Citro and E. A. Hanushek. Washington, DC: National Academy of Sciences Press, 1991.

Smith, James E. "The Computer Simulation of Kin Sets and Kin Counts." In *Family Demography*, edited by J. Bongaarts, T. Buch, and K. Wachter. Oxford: Clarendon Press, 1987.

Steuerle, C. Eugene, and Jon M. Bakija. *Retooling Social Security for the 21st Century*, Washington, DC: Urban Institute Press, 1994.

Swan, Neil. "Problems in Dynamic Modeling of Individual Incomes." Paper delivered to Swedish Conference on Microsimulation, Stockholm, 1997.

U.S. Board of Trustees of the Federal Old-Age and Survivors Insurance and Disability Insurance Trust Fund. *1997 Annual Report*. Washington, DC: U.S. Government Printing Office, 1997.

Zedlewski, S. R. 1989. "The Development of the Dynamic Simulation of Income Model (DYNASIM)." In *Microsimulation Techniques for Tax and Transfer Analysis,* edited by G. H. Lewis and R. C. Michel. Washington, DC: Urban Institute Press.

Comment

NADA EISSA

Introduction

More than six decades after its introduction, the Social Security system faces a funding crisis. By most accounts, Social Security benefits paid out to recipients will exceed Social Security contributions in just over a decade, and the trust fund will fail to meet its entire obligation in just over thirty years. More uncertainty surrounds the magnitude of the adjustments required to maintain the solvency of the system, however. As the authors argue, the potential size of the required payroll tax hike (40 to 60 percent) and/or benefit reductions merits an evaluation of the methods used to generate the figures. Additionally, less discussed are the distributional implications of the adjustments required to maintain the financial solvency of the system.

The chapter by Caldwell and his colleagues has two broad objectives. The first part of the chapter is primarily methodological, providing an overview of the Social Security Administration's (SSA) forecasting methods and contrasting those methods to microsimulation methods using a specific model, CORSIM. In the second part of the chapter, output from the microsimulation model is used to project aggregate contributions and revenues and to estimate internal rates of return for different lifetime-income groups of postwar Americans differentiated by birth cohort, sex, race, and educational attainment. The authors' findings suggest that postwar Americans can expect a low rate of return from Social Security (roughly 2 percent) and that the required adjustment (to taxes or benefits) will reduce that rate to about 1 percent.

A potentially important contribution of microsimulation is its capacity to model both changing distributions of outcomes and the impact of changes in the distributions on the projected Social Security benefits and contributions. For example, married women's labor force participation rose from 23 percent in 1964 to 65 percent by 1994. Over the same period, both the educational attainment of women and their pay have increased. Because they interact with the spousal benefit, these changes in the earnings of married women are important for the projected contributions and possibly benefits. In principle, microsimulation models, such as CORSIM, are well suited to evaluate such changes in the distribution of educational attainment, employment, and earnings.

Previous work evaluating the distributional impact of Social Security has generally assumed defined lifetime-income groups. An additional advantage of the approach used here over previous analyses of the distributional impact of Social Security is the attempt to capture individual heterogeneity. Individuals within lifetime-income groupings are not homogeneous and can have different earnings profiles, for example. The cost, however, is the added complexity in the model. As a result, problems can arise in multiple places. My comments focus largely on empirical issues related to the data and to identification. Most of the concerns are basic and well known but worth discussing in the context of this model because of its complexity.

Empirical Issues

Data

CORSIM starts with the 1960 Census data and then "ages" the sample, using estimated "transition" probabilities. Synthetic lives are generated from several data sources, including the *Current Population Survey* (CPS) and the *Panel Study of Income Dynamics* (PSID). The point I want to raise here is a general one about survey data, including the CPS, and concerns coverage in the survey and sample size. At a basic level, sample size is important because of the associated sampling variability. In this chapter, the authors report the number of observations in each cohort, sex, education, and race cell. For some groups, very small sample sizes can have noticeable implications, for example, thin data at the top of the income distribution. Consider, for example, average age of death (Table 8.2). The table shows a sharp jump of six to eleven years from one lifetime-income cell to the next. Sharp drops in life expectancy also help explain the negative internal rate of return estimates for the 1945 (1955) cohort of non-whites in the $960K ($840K) income group. A second concern is coverage. Household surveys undercount certain populations. The 1984 CPS, for example, covered 92 percent of all males but only 84 percent of black males (Citro, 1991). Given that these populations are at different points in the income distribution, there is potential to distort both the projections and the distributional analysis (see discussion below). It is not clear that any alternative exists, since administrative data (say, SSA data) typically lack information on required individual characteristics. Nonetheless, the quality of the data interacts with the complexity of the model in potentially important ways that are not explored in the analysis.

Identification

While data issues are important, the primary concern with the use of microsimulation models such as CORSIM must be identification. An important advantage of CORSIM over other methods used is its ability to capture within-group (e.g., lifetime income, sex, and race) heterogeneity in behavior. By necessity, then, CORSIM must model multiple outcomes, including fertility, mortality, family formation and dissolution, human capital investment, earnings, and labor supply (including age of retirement) to measure eligibility for benefits. These outcomes are not modeled independently, but rather depend on one another in ways that are not always transparent. For example, marital status depends on the number of weeks worked (education), while weeks worked (educational attainment) depends on marital status. Ultimately, what generates identification is functional form assumptions (that is, using lagged variables and/or interactions of variables). Given these dependencies, it is difficult to assess what factors ultimately drive the results. Additionally, the authors choose to estimate separate equations for different groups, so that the employment status is estimated for 174 separate groups differing by age, sex, last year's employment status, and the presence of a child. Thus, CORSIM is based on several hundred equations. The argument used here is that any particular variable need not have the same effect on different groups. For example, the impact of children on employment varies for men and women. It is not clear, however, that 174 groups is in any way an optimal number; the trade-off here is to estimate a smaller number of regressions and use interaction terms to test whether specific variables have differential effects.

To ensure that model predictions match observed group outcomes, CORSIM aligns the group predicted mean to the actual group mean from various data sources on an annual basis. The alignment procedures seem to vary by the outcome, but they effectively scale the estimated parameters by an adjustment factor that depends on the discrepancy between the group predicted mean and the actual group mean. An issue that may arise in this context concerns coverage in survey data. Consider that we observe only part of the bottom of the income distribution because such individuals are difficult to trace and/or to interview. CPS data, which undercount blacks relative to whites, are used to align both educational attainment and work status. Using this information to align the observed group mean may, then, bias parameters that are then used for successive cohorts. A second issue, raised in the chapter, is the fact that these alignments are done on an annual basis, which does not guarantee that the synthetic lives are realistic. Here, PSID data, which currently allow for up to twenty-eight years of data, could be used to test the generated income streams for a subset of the sample. Also, it would be useful to contrast the approach used here to that of Coronado, Fullerton, and Glass (1999), who use twenty-two years of data from the PSID to create earnings histories.

Projections

Projecting Social Security benefits and taxes using demographic and economic outcomes, the authors find that CORSIM closely matches the SSA-generated Social Security contributions but that the benefit calculator underestimates benefits. A main difference between the tax and benefit projections is timing. Because this model "ages" the 1960 Census sample, CORSIM projections are not uniformly comparable to SSA projections. Taxes are compared to benefits in 2010–2020 (when the sample is 10–75 years old), and benefits are compared around 2050 (when sample members are between 50 and 105 years old). Therefore small errors compound over time, and this may explain the divergent projections of benefits because benefit projections occur later than projections of taxes. Another consideration is that taxes are a function of only the level and distribution of earnings, whereas benefits depend on family structure as well. Not only do spousal and dependent benefits matter for the projections, but also the treatment of divorce under Social Security is fairly complicated. The authors suggest a number of explanations, but the divergent benefit projections remain unexplained. While they suggest (although not too strongly) that their projected benefits should be preferred to SSA's because they model the distribution of outcomes (lifetimes, work spans, etc.), it is necessary to evaluate the sensitivity of projected benefits to the distributions of relevant outcomes. Ultimately, the advantage of microsimulation is in the modeling of various outcomes and their distributions, so such sensitivity analyses should be of high priority.

References

Citro, Constance. "Databases for Microsimulation: A Comparison of the March CPS and SIPP." In *Improving Information for Social Policy Decisions: The Uses of Microsimulation Modeling*, edited by Constance Citro and E. Hanuschek. Washington, DC: National Academy Press, 1991.

Coronado, Julia L., Don Fullerton, and Thomas Glass. "Distributional Impacts of Proposed Changes to the Social Security System." NBER Working Paper no. 6989, 1999.

CHAPTER 9

Demographic Change and Public Assistance Expenditures

ROBERT A. MOFFITT

A notable feature of most developed economies in the postwar period has been a seemingly inexorable growth in expenditures on entitlements. Although most nations have made attempts to restrain that growth through legislation, administrative action, and other policy mechanisms, for the most part these attempts have not met with success. While there are good and obvious political reasons for this failure – sometimes the programs have strong constituencies, for example – the causes of this growth are still not completely understood.

The role of demographic forces in contributing to the growth of social welfare expenditures in the United States is the subject of this chapter. This issue has been a topic of considerable interest in policy discussions surrounding welfare but little formal analysis. There is a perception among the public and in some policy and research circles that the growth of the main cash program in the United States, formerly called Aid to Families with Dependent Children (AFDC), has been the result of an increase in the number of female-headed families, most commonly (in the public eye) because of increases in the rate of out-of-wedlock child-bearing. Yet this has not been shown, and economic research on the determinants of participation in welfare programs has concentrated instead on other factors – for example, the influence of the level of the welfare benefit relative to private labor market opportunities. Indeed, most of the economic research literature on the determinants of AFDC participation examines the determinants of participation in welfare conditional on demographic status, rather than the impact of demographic influences per se.

The author would like to thank Xue Song and Zhong Zhao for research assistance and Rebecca Blank, David Card, George Cave, and Philip Morgan for comments.

The specific contribution of this chapter is to decompose the growth in welfare expenditures per capita over the last thirty or so years into three parts: growth in welfare benefits, growth in the recipiency rate for different demographic groups, and growth in the relative sizes of those demographic groups. The first represents the influence of direct expansions in program services and benefits, while the second represents the influence of the participation rate of the population in the program. The third component represents the contribution of demographic forces and is the main object of interest.

The major programs examined are AFDC, Food Stamps, and Medicaid. We find that over the last thirty years demographic influences – in particular, growth in female headship rates – have been by far the most important contributor to trends in real AFDC expenditures per capita, greatly outweighing changes in benefits and in participation rates. However, in the short run – over four-year periods – fluctuations in participation rates have been equally important. Over the long run, these participation rates have risen and fallen, fluctuating around a fairly unchanging average level, whereas demographic influences have trended steadily in the direction of greater caseloads and expenditures. The analysis also shows that increases in Food Stamps and Medicaid expenditures, on the other hand, have been more influenced by increases in benefit levels and participation rates and less by demographic forces, compared to AFDC.

At least for AFDC, the short-run and long-run demographic influences have been largely unanticipated by the public sector. These influences have led to spurts of unanticipated expenditure growth, which appear to have led in each historical instance to a political reaction and subsequent retrenchment in the welfare system. A cycle of short-run booms in expenditures, followed by cutbacks and retrenchment, is revealed in the history of expenditures and benefits over the last thirty years. Neither the federal nor the state public sector in the United States has done a very good job of dealing with these unanticipated fluctuations.

Looking to the future, a natural question is whether demographic forces will continue to exert a major effect on public assistance caseloads and therefore expenditures. One immediate problem with any forecast of public assistance expenditures arises because a major change in the structure of the welfare system has recently (1996) occurred, which makes forecasting of both benefits and participation rates hazardous. In addition to this problem, however, population projections of the Census Bureau and the Social Security Administration do not attempt to project demographic composition at the level of female headship, but only by age, race, and sex (and occasionally marital status). Projections of female headship would be, in any case, difficult given the unsettled state of research on the causes of its secular upward trend. Nevertheless, because age-race-sex population projections are available, projections of how public assistance expenditures would change on this basis alone can be conducted. Such projections are also provided in this chapter.

The outline of the chapter is as follows. The next section provides a discussion of trends in social welfare expenditures in the United States over the last thirty years and examines whether there is a prima facie link to trends in demographic composition. The subsequent section presents the results of a formal decomposition of the growth in per capita welfare expenditures from 1968 to 1996 in AFDC, Food Stamps, and Medicaid and shows the importance of demographic change, particularly for AFDC. Next is a discussion of demographic feedback loops, followed by projections of real welfare expenditures arising from future changes in the age, race, and sex composition of the United States. A summary and conclusions end the paper.

Trends in Public Assistance Expenditures and Demographic Structure

Expenditures

There are a large number of programs in the United States that can be, and have been, termed "welfare" programs. One of the most authoritative accounts lists over eighty programs that have some means-tested component and are nontrivial in size, excluding social insurance programs, such as Medicare and Social Security, but including tax-based programs, such as the Earned Income Tax Credit (EITC) (Burke, 1995). This makes an accounting for trends in expenditures among the programs difficult because of the diversity of groups eligible for the programs and the complex eligibility and benefit rules of most of the smaller ones.

Nevertheless, clear patterns in expenditure growth emerge when the programs are taken as a whole and when the major programs are considered. Figure 9.1 shows trends in the per capita real expenditure on the top eighty means-tested benefit programs in the United States from 1968 to 1994, both in absolute terms and as a share of GDP.[1] The most important single point to note in Figure 9.1 is that real per capita expenditure

---

[1] The set of programs in the expenditure totals excludes unemployment and workers' compensation, Social Security, and Medicare and includes only one tax transfer program (the EITC). For the EITC, only the direct credit portion is counted as an expenditure, not the reduction in tax liability.

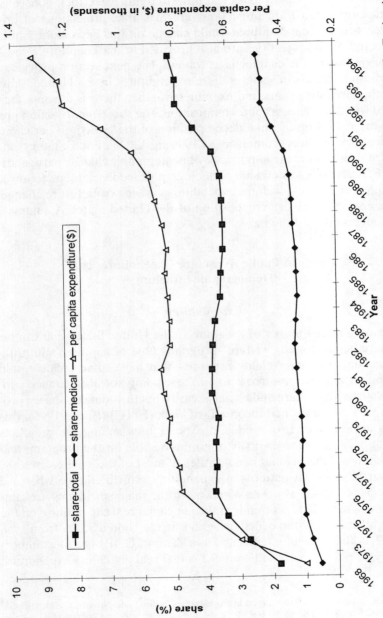

Figure 9.1. Real per Capita Expenditures on Income-Tested Benefits and Share of GDP Used for Need-Tested Benefits, Total and Medical, 1968–94. *Sources:* Burke, 1995, tables 3 and 7; U.S. Department of Commerce, 1996, p. 8.

on these programs is higher today than it ever has been and that there has never been a serious decline in expenditure since 1968. Therefore, despite periodic perceptions of retrenchment and cutbacks in means-tested programs, they have grown secularly. This is also true of such expenditures as share of GDP, which rose from 1.8 percent in 1968 to 5.4 percent in 1994. A large fraction of that share growth has occurred in expenditures on medical programs, primarily Medicaid.[2]

The second major feature of Figure 9.1 to note is the uneven growth of expenditures. During the last thirty years, there have been two major spurts of growth. There was an explosion of welfare spending in the late 1960s and early 1970s and another in the late 1980s and early 1990s; over the period 1975–1988, however, there was no growth. This same pattern will appear for many of the major individual programs as well, such as AFDC, Food Stamps, and Medicaid, although the magnitudes will differ.

The influence of demographic forces and alternative explanations for these two periods of expenditure growth is the subject of the analysis below and will be discussed in detail. However, it is worth noting at this point that each of the booms in expenditure was followed by a significant political retrenchment in the system. Following the explosion of expenditures in the late 1960s and early 1970s, state legislatures let their real AFDC benefits decline steadily, for example. Following the explosion of expenditures in the late 1980s and early 1990s, states began reforms attempting to control caseload growth in the AFDC program, and Congress eventually followed with the most significant contractionary piece of legislation in the history of the program, the 1996 Personal Responsibility and Work Opportunity Reconciliation Act. A prima facie case can be made that this pattern of boom and retrenchment can be explained with relatively simple political models.[3]

By 1994, six individual programs constituted 74 percent of total means-tested expenditure, as shown in Table 9.1. The analysis in the subsequent parts of this chapter will concentrate on three of these pro-

---

[2] Federal expenditures on welfare programs accounted for 11.0 percent of the federal budget in 1973 and for 16.9 percent in 1994 (U.S. House of Representatives, 1996, p. 1321).

[3] See Moffitt (1999) for a discussion of the 1996 Act and its political origins and Moffitt et al. (1998) for a discussion of the causes of the real benefit decline. These papers argue that something more than simple rises in expenditures is needed to explain the political retrenchment and that the growth of inequality and reduction in the real incomes and wages at the bottom of the distribution has played an additional role. See also Burtless (1994, pp. 53–63) for a discussion of the time-series pattern of real means-tested expenditures and trends in welfare generosity, and see Blank (1997a, pp. 85–8) for another discussion.

Table 9.1. *Expenditures in the Six Largest Welfare Programs in the United States, 1994 (millions of dollars)*

	Total	Federal	State-Local
Medicaid	143,593	82,147	61,446
Food stamps	27,396	25,599	1,797
SSI	27,310	23,544	3,766
AFDC	25,920	14,141	11,779
EITC	16,549	16,549	0
Section 8 low-income housing	14,576	14,576	0

Source: Burke (1995, table 2).

grams – Medicaid, Food Stamps, and AFDC.[4] Supplemental Security Income (SSI) receipt is concentrated among the elderly and disabled, and demographic effects on its expenditures are largely driven by increases in the size of the aged and disabled population, which is covered by other chapters in this book and could not be considered without also considering Social Security and other programs for the aged and disabled. The EITC is relatively new, at least at its current scale, and has not yet developed much of a history with which demographic effects can be assessed, though this may well change in the future. Section 8 housing assistance, like other forms of housing assistance, is rationed and hence represents the only nonentitlement program in the table. But the consequence of this feature is that expenditures in housing assistance programs are driven largely by the cost of housing and by programmatic developments, of which there have been few major ones in the last twenty years. Thus the influence of demographic forces is less important for it than for most of the other programs.[5]

The three programs to be analyzed here – AFDC, Medicaid, and Food Stamps – also are responsible for almost all of the growth in expenditures in the late 1980s and early 1990s. Total real expenditures on the entire set of over 80 programs identified by the Congressional Research Service were $213 billion in FY 1988 and $344 billion in FY 1994, imply-

---

[4] The Medicaid expenditure total in Table 9.1 includes a large component for the elderly. This portion will be subtracted out below.

[5] Many of the programs of great analytic interest to the policy evaluation and research communities are considerably smaller in terms of expenditure. These include, in descending order, General Assistance ($9.0 billion including the medical component), Head Start ($4.1 billion), the Special Supplemental Nutrition Program for Women, Infants and Children, also known as WIC ($3.3 billion), job training programs including the Job Corps ($2.6 billion), and energy assistance ($1.7 billion).

ing an increase of $131 billion, or a 62 percent growth rate. Increased spending on medical programs constituted approximately $80 billion of this increment, while increases in cash welfare expenditures contributed $23 billion of new spending and food benefit programs contributed $13 billion, thereby accounting for almost all of the recent increase in expenditures (Burke, 1995, table 6).

Expenditure trends in these three programs are illustrated in Figure 9.2, and the relative contributions of caseload and benefit growth are shown in Figures 9.3 and 9.4, respectively. As shown in Figure 9.2, real per capita AFDC expenditures grew rapidly in the late 1960s and early 1970s, declined significantly from 1975 to 1983, declined slightly more through 1989, and then rose somewhat in the late 1980s and early 1990s before turning down again. Thus there have been no major increases in expenditures in this cash assistance program since the mid-1970s. Expenditures in the Food Stamps program, on the other hand, grew all the way until 1980, at which point they declined for a few years, but then rose suddenly in the late 1980s and early 1990s (although, like AFDC expenditures, they have recently turned around). Per capita Medicaid expenditures rose from 1972 to 1978, as the program was still being extended and formed, maintained relative constancy from the late 1970s to the mid-1980s, then skyrocketed upward in the late 1980s and early 1990s, and have only recently peaked. In fact, Medicaid expenditures now exceed those of AFDC or Food Stamps.[6]

Thus the two periods of aggregate welfare expenditure growth are reflected fairly well by these three programs. Particularly in the late 1960s and early 1970s, expenditures in all three programs grew rapidly. For the Food Stamps and Medicaid programs, this was partly a result of their newness, for both were still in a formative period.[7] In the late 1980s and early 1990s, growth in Medicaid expenditures was very strong, as was that in Food Stamps, albeit growth was only very slight for AFDC.

The long-term trends in expenditure in these three programs also clearly demonstrate once again the replacement of cash benefits by in-kind transfers in the U.S. social welfare mix. Working somewhat against this trend has been the growth in SSI benefits and in the EITC, which are also cash programs. The growth of the latter suggests that it is not cash per se that the voters and legislators do not prefer, but rather it is

---

[6] The Medicaid expenditures in Figure 9.2, unlike those in Table 9.1, pertain only to dependent children and their adult caretakers. The elderly and disabled are excluded.

[7] The Food Stamps program was created by federal legislation in 1964, and the Medicaid program was created by federal legislation in 1965, but over the subsequent ten years both programs were only gradually extended to all parts of the country, and benefits and services were only gradually made nationally uniform.

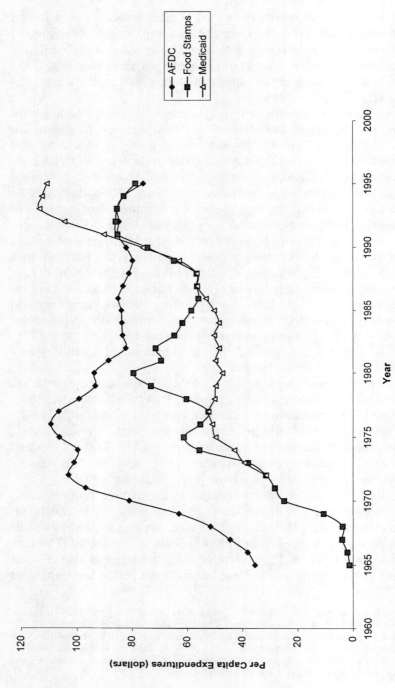

Figure 9.2. Real Welfare Expenditures per Capita, 1965–95. *Sources:* U.S. Social Security Administration, 1991, table 7.E; 1997, tables 9.G1, 9.H1, and 8.E2; U.S. Department of Commerce, 1996, p. 8.

the purpose to which the funds are directed and their underlying ratio-nale that matters (aged, blind, and disabled for SSI and low-income earners for EITC).

Figures 9.3 and 9.4 decompose these expenditure trends into trends in numbers of recipients (i.e., the caseload) per capita and real expendi-tures per recipient, the latter of which is a proxy for average benefit levels. The figures show clearly that caseload growth is the primary factor responsible for expenditure growth, although growth in benefit levels has played some role in the Medicaid program. Figure 9.3 shows that case-load growth patterns in the three programs show the same pattern of two periods of expansion (late 1960s/early 1970s and late 1980s/early 1990s) as aggregate welfare expenditure, for example. Even caseloads in the AFDC program grew in the latter boom period, and the fact that AFDC expenditures did not exhibit the same growth is a result of con-tinued declines in real AFDC benefits. Figure 9.4 shows that benefit trends have not followed any of those patterns, except for a growth in per-recipient Medicaid expenditures in the late 1980s and early 1990s. Real AFDC benefits have, in fact, declined over the period, as state leg-islatures have failed to raise nominal benefit levels enough to keep up with inflation. Real Food Stamps benefits have been roughly constant, for those benefits are indexed to inflation by law.[8]

Demographic Influences

That the major force behind trends in expenditures has been the growth in the numbers of recipients rather than expenditures per recipient warrants an examination of the possible role of demographic influences, the main subject of this chapter. In considering demographic influences, it is natural to begin by noting that the most important single criterion for welfare eligibility historically has been the combination of marital status and childbearing that leads to female headship, or single mother-hood. The Temporary Assistance to Needy Families (TANF)–AFDC program has been almost exclusively composed of female-headed fami-lies or children in such families, defined as families in which there are

---

[8] The rise of in-kind transfers and decline of cash transfers is again reflected in the case-load figures, for AFDC has been the smallest of these programs since 1972. It is also inter-esting to note that most of the policy developments in AFDC in the last 30 years – the 1967 Social Security Amendments, which increased work incentives; the 1981 Omnibus Budget Reconciliation Act, which decreased them and made eligibility more restrictive; the 1988 Family Support Act, which mandated participation in training programs; and a wide variety of state-level initiatives – appear to have had no major impact on the case-load trends, and therefore no major impact on expenditure trends.

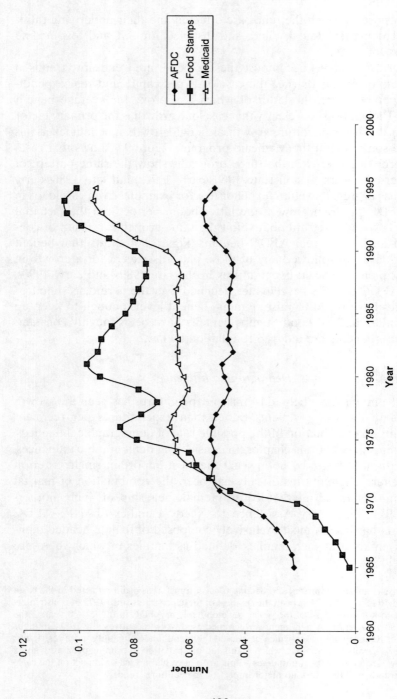

Figure 9.3. Numbr of Welfare Recipients per Capita, 1965–95. *Sources*: U.S. Social Security Administration, 1991, table 7.E; 1997, tables 9.G1, 9.H1, and 8.E2; U.S. Department of Commerce, 1996, p. 8.

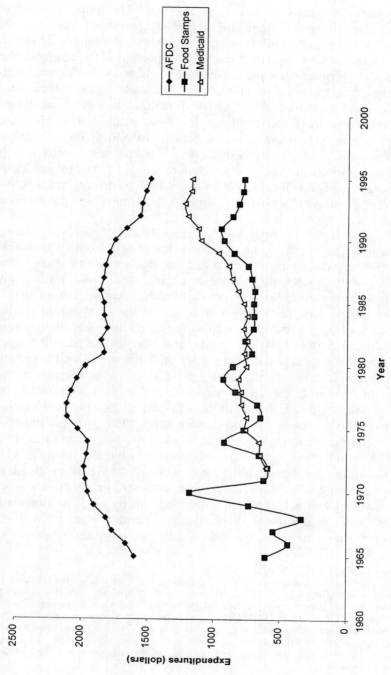

Figure 9.4. Real Welfare Expenditures per Recipient, 1965–95. *Source:* Derived from Figures 9.2 and 9.3.

children under age 18 but there is no able-bodied father of the children present.[9] A program called the AFDC–Unemployed Parent (UP) program, which makes children eligible when both mother and father are present, has never represented more than 7 percent of the caseload. The Food Stamps program, while universally available to low-income families regardless of family structure, has nevertheless always been disproportionately composed of AFDC-TANF families, because food stamps are automatically made available to those families. The Medicaid program also has always provided benefits to AFDC-TANF families automatically, but eligibility has been broadened recently to include children, albeit rarely the adults, in nonwelfare families.[10] Welfare participation rates among female heads of household will be demonstrated below to still be far above those of other demographic groups, even for the Food Stamps program.

The main trends in the growth of female-headed families are shown in Figures 9.5 and 9.6. Figure 9.5 shows that growth from 1940 to 1994 and demonstrates the now-familiar fact that it accelerated starting in the 1960s and has continued to grow at a fairly steady pace all the way through the present. What is somewhat less well known, but important for an examination of welfare trends, is that the composition of this growth has changed over time. As also shown in Figure 9.5, divorce rates rose dramatically at about the same time that female headship rates began increasing, but peaked and leveled off in the late 1970s. The growth of female-headed households since that time has instead been generated by an increase in birthrates among unmarried women, who tend to be younger and to have higher welfare participation rates. Figure 9.6 shows trends in those rates by age and shows a strong increase in the rates for women in the age range 15–29. Not only has this latter trend therefore kept the number of female-headed families growing at a steady pace; it has also induced a change in the composition of the AFDC caseload, as shown in Figure 9.7. In 1942, the program consisted primarily of widows and wives of men who had been disabled, but by 1973 the dominant group in the program was divorced and separated women. By 1992, however, never-married women accounted for the majority of

---

[9] There are many important details in this definition, which we will not take the time to dwell on here. The presence of a stepfather does not automatically disqualify the family for AFDC, nor does the presence of a cohabiting male who is not the natural father of any of the children. The AFDC-UP program, on the other hand, makes eligible for benefits children whose father is present but unmarried to the mother. See Moffitt, Reville, and Winkler (1994, 1998).

[10] See Blank (1997a) for a more detailed discussion of the rules governing eligibility for these programs.

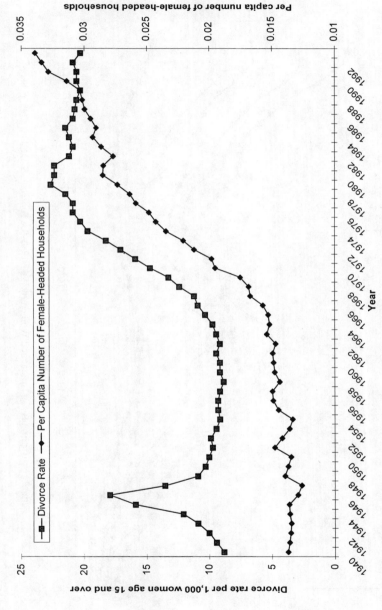

Figure 9.5. Divorce Rate and per Capita Number of Female-Headed Households, 1940–94. *Sources:* U.S. DHHS, 1995, pp. 26, 62; U.S. Department of Commerce, 1996, p. 8.

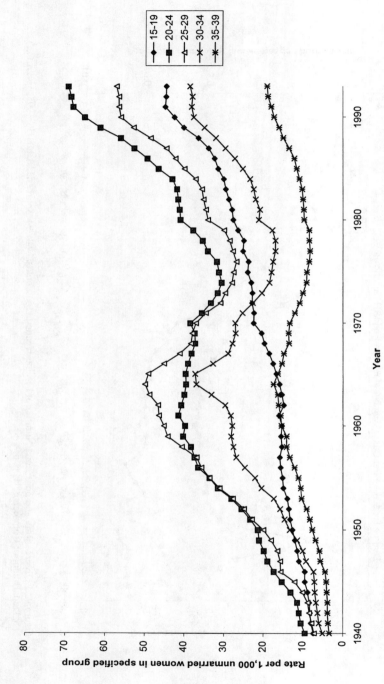

Figure 9.6. Birthrates for Unmarried Women by Age, 1940–93. *Source:* U.S. DHHS, 1995, p. 88.

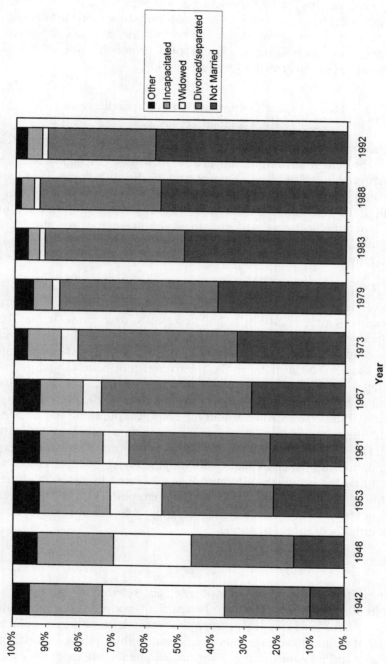

Figure 9.7. Basis of AFDC Eligibility, 1942–94. *Source:* U.S. DHHS, 1995, p. 63.

405

participants, and the fraction consisting of widowed and divorced women had declined. These observations lead naturally to a more formal consideration of the role of demographic factors in caseload trends. Together, these figures are suggestive of a prominent role of demographic forces in the growth of welfare caseloads.

A Demographic Decomposition of Expenditure and
Caseload Trends

The goal of this section is to use *Current Population Survey* (CPS) data to present a decomposition of the growth of per capita welfare expenditures in AFDC, Food Stamps, and Medicaid between 1968 and 1996 into growth of the relative fractions of different demographic groups in the population, growth in the welfare participation rate within each demographic group, and growth in the average expenditure per recipient. Our main interest is in the first of these in explaining expenditure growth, but the role and relative weight of other two are also of interest.

Issues of endogeneity of demographic change arise here more than in some of the other chapters in this volume. While age, race, and sex are exogenous, female headship is not necessarily so because it may be affected by the level of welfare benefits. This issue will be discussed later in the chapter. Changes in participation rates are certainly not exogenous, however, and respond to the relative level of benefits and potential wages in the labor market. The conventional model of welfare participation in the economics literature supposes participation to be a function of these two variables, and the empirical literature has demonstrated their importance in welfare participation decisions (Moffitt, 1992). However, if demographic forces have been more important than participation-rate changes in explaining caseload growth, it could be argued that the economics literature has misplaced its research efforts because participation, conditional on demographic eligbility, has been the major area of that research. Demographic growth has received relatively little theoretical attention.

Past Work

Although formal decompositions of caseload growth into growth of the eligible population and growth in the participation rate conditional on eligibility have been relatively rare in the research literature on welfare, dozens of studies have calculated participation rates per se in different programs and how they change over time. Sometimes demographic and other eligibility factors are examined, and sometimes these are tied in with growth of the aggregate caseload in informal ways. For example, the explosion of the AFDC rolls in the late 1960s and early 1970s received considerable attention, starting with a seminal study by Boland (1973) and a follow-up and extension conducted by Michel (1980), both of whom found that that explosion was primarily the result of an increase in participation rates among eligibles, where eligibility was defined as not only having the right family structure (female-headed family) but also having income below the AFDC eligibility levels.

This conclusion has been generally accepted by subsequent analysts, and Boland's and Michel's studies also sought to explain the rise in participation rates using the conventional economic model viewing participation in welfare as resulting from a trade-off between the attraction of benefits from the program, on the one hand, and potential wages off the program, on the other (the stigma of welfare receipt is also used to explain the failure of some eligibles to participate in the program; see Moffitt, [1983]). It was initially thought that the welfare caseload explosion in the late 1960s and early 1970s could not be explained by the conventional economic model because AFDC benefits did not rise nor did wages fall over the period. The increase in the participation rate was generally ascribed to a reduction in stigma and to Supreme Court decisions outlawing the man-in-the-house rule and residency requirements (Michel, 1980). However, the importance of Food Stamps and Medicaid, both of which are heavily tied to AFDC receipt, was only later recognized. When the growth of those benefits was considered, a much stronger argument could be made that it was the attraction of benefits from welfare that played a role in the increase in the participation rate (Moffitt, 1992, pp. 7–8).

Participation rates subsequent to the welfare explosion reached over 90 percent in the mid-1970s. Rates have been shown to have subsequently declined over the late 1970s and 1980s, and it has been noted that the growth of the female-head population offset that decline over that period, keeping the caseload growing (Moffitt, 1992, pp. 8, 11). These declines in participation are more easily explainable by declines in both AFDC benefits and the benefit "sum" obtained by adding together AFDC, Food Stamps, and Medicaid benefits (Moffitt, 1986, 1992). Analyses of the growth in the AFDC caseload over the late 1980s and early 1990s indicate a major role for demographic factors. Gabe (1992) concluded that the participation rate remained unchanged from 1987 to 1991 and that all the increase in the AFDC caseload resulted from an increase in the numbers of female heads of household, while the U.S. Congressional Budget Office (1993, p. 3) concluded that one-half the increase from 1989 to 1992 was the result of increases in female headship. Blank (1997b) decomposed the AFDC caseload from 1984 to 1995 in twelve large states and also concluded that all of the caseload increase was a result of increases in eligibility, although changes in income were not separated from demographic changes leading to eligibility.[11] On the other hand, the increase in participation rates in this period has not been successfully explained. Blank (1997b) concludes that the growth in the caseload is entirely unexplained by benefits, wages, and related factors, for example. Gabe (1992) and the U.S. Congressional Budget Office (1993), on the other hand, find some role for economic factors in the growth of the caseload and for programmatic changes such as the expansion of Medicaid (which could be thought to draw recipients onto welfare in general).

Studies of the Food Stamps program have also been conducted, where the major interest has been in calculating participation rates conditional on eligibility to determine how much of the target population is being served. In the very early years of the program, the late 1960s and early 1970s, essentially all growth was necessarily the result of increases in participation because the program was still being put in place and expanded to cover all parts of the country (Ohls and Beebout, 1993, pp. 15–16). Participation rates among eligibles have grown from 33 percent of households in 1976 to 67 percent in 1995 (Cody and Trippe, 1997, table 1). This growth dominates the growth of eligibles. The increase in participation rates occurred mainly in the late 1970s and in the late 1980s and early 1990s; rates were more or less stable in between.[12] These studies have generally ascribed the growth in participation in the late 1970s to the elimination of the purchase requirement.[13] Growth in participation in the late 1980s and early 1990s has been ascribed to the economy, as well as to Medicaid expansions, which were thought to bring families onto the welfare rolls in all programs, and to increased access to food stamp offices (Cody and Trippe, 1997, pp. 9–10).

As for Medicaid, the dominant factor in most discussions has been increases in participation. This is somewhat unusual because prior to

[11] Blank, like many other authors in this literature, also discusses the AFDC-UP program. All statements in this section refer only to the regular AFDC program for female-headed households. The AFDC-UP program is ignored because it is such a small portion of the total caseload.

[12] Once again, as in most of these studies, income eligibility and demographic eligibility are not, however, separated.

[13] The purchase requirement was a provision that required recipients to buy Food Stamps; after its elimination, the stamps were provided free of charge. The "bonus" value was unchanged because the value of the stamps after the change equaled the difference between the value of the stamps and the purchase amount prior to the change.

1984, Medicaid receipt, at least among women and poor children, was mostly tied to AFDC receipt, and demographic growth has been thought to have been a significant contributor to the latter. But subsequent to 1984, eligibility for Medicaid has been expanded tremendously and decoupled to a significant degree from AFDC, now covering most poor children and some poor adults (Gruber, 1997). Participation rates are quite low, however, around 25–33 percent. Still, most of the growth of the program in the late 1980s and early 1990s, which has been so important to overall growth of expenditures, has clearly not been the result of a change in the demographics of the U.S. population. The Medicaid program is also the one program among the three examined here that has seen significant increases in expenditure per recipient, which are traceable to increases in medical care prices, the quality of care, and the use of medical technology (see Chapter 7, by Cutler and Sheiner, for discussion of these issues).

New Decompositions

The analysis presented in this chapter uses March CPS data from 1968 to 1996 to provide a more systematic and comprehensive examination of the relative contributions of demographic factors and participation rate influences to the caseload and the contribution of expenditures per recipient to total expenditures. The AFDC program is examined over the entire period, but the Food Stamps program is examined only after 1980 and Medicaid only after 1989, as a result of limitations on when CPS questions on receipt of those benefit types began.[14] We use answers to CPS questions about receipt of benefits, along with information on the demographic and economic structure of each household, to conduct the decomposition.

We write expenditures per capita in the population as the sum over population subgroups $k = 1, \ldots K$ of the product of the fraction of the population in that subgroup (w_k), the welfare recipiency rate, or participation rate, in that subgroup (p_k), and the average expenditure per recipient in that subgroup (b_k). Adding year subscripts t, we have

$$y_t = \sum_k w_{kt} p_{kt} b_{kt}, \tag{1}$$

where y_t is mean expenditure per capita in the population at time t. Differencing across periods t and t^*, we have

---

[14] Medicaid questions were asked prior to 1989, but the questions were changed in a major way at that time, to such an extent that many analysts feel the participation rates before and after the change in questions are noncomparable.

$$y_t - y_{t^*} = \sum_k a_{kt}(w_{kt} - w_{kt}*) + \sum_k b_{kt}(p_{kt} - p_{kt}*) + \sum_k c_{kt}(b_{kt} - b_{kt}*), \quad (2)$$

where a_{kt}, b_{kt}, and c_{kt} are weights. The decomposition in (2) can be constructed by using six different sets of weights, which differ according to whether the sums are evaluated at the period t or t^* values of the other variables, yielding six different estimates of the relative importance of the three factors. This is a necessary consequence of the nonlinearity of the relationship. Rather than seek a unique decomposition that relies on an assignment of joint explanatory power to each of the three factors, here we simply compute and present all six to show the sensitivity of the weighting to the conclusions.[15]

The most important demographic criteria we use to construct groups are those that separate households by whether they are female-headed or not and by whether children under 18 reside in the household, both of which are key eligibility criteria for all three programs we consider. However, none of the programs excludes other demographic groups entirely from possible receipt of benefits, especially the Food Stamps program, so we use a relatively comprehensive definition of eight household types. These are defined according to whether the family head is (1) married, (2) female and never married, (3) female and divorced, widowed, or separated, or (4) male and unmarried, and, secondarily, whether children under age 18 are present in the household. All four headship types are combined with the two presence-of-children types to yield the eight household categories. We also test age of the head as an additional criterion, and we stratify by race.[16]

Along with household structure, we also stratify the population by income. The growth in individual earnings inequality and family income inequality, and the decline of real wage rates among less skilled workers in the United States in the 1970s and 1980s, make it necessary to control for changes in income distribution because those changes should also contribute to changes in participation rates within demographic strata and hence to caseload and expenditure changes. We define six economic strata of real nonwelfare income (total family income minus welfare income) of the primary family. The strata are defined as absolute numbers, which are held fixed from 1968 to 1996, as follows: (stratum 1)

---

[15] It is worth emphasizing that decompositions of this type are purely mechanical and cannot be given any simple causal interpretation by themselves. For example, the third component, the level of the benefit (b), could be one cause of both participation (p) and demographics (w). We will discuss the influence of b on w later in the paper.

[16] Only heads less than 60 years of age are included. Thus all calculations below exclude the elderly.

$0; (stratum 2) $1–5,000; (stratum 3) $5,001–10,000; (stratum 4) $10,001–20,000; (stratum 5) $20,001–50,000; and (stratum 6) $50,001 and over. These brackets were chosen after inspecting welfare participation rates for different intervals and ascertaining how quickly those rates fall to zero when moving up the income distribution. Crossing the eight demographic cells with the six income strata yields a total of forty-eight population cells.

In contrast to much of the past literature, our goal here is to isolate demographic influences from those of income, so we will ascertain the contribution of income influences alone by conducting the decomposition solely with income. This assigns all joint influence entirely to economic factors and hence will represent an upper bound on the influence of income distribution on the change in expenditures per capita.[17]

Table 9.2 shows participation rates of U.S. households in the AFDC, Food Stamps, and Medicaid programs in the mid-1990s by household type. The table shows clearly the heavy participation in all three programs among households with children headed by women who have never been married. Almost 50 percent of such households received AFDC income and around 60 percent received food stamps and Medicaid benefits.[18] Note that no conditioning on income is made in the calculation of these participation rates, so it is the entire U.S. population of households headed by never-married females, at all income levels, that exhibits these high participation rates; their high levels are an indirect indication of the extremely low income levels of such families.

While households headed by divorced, widowed, and separated women also participate in AFDC at fairly high rates, other demographic groups have much lower participation rates. But those other groups are more likely to receive food stamps and, sometimes, Medicaid. Almost 20 percent of households headed by unmarried males with children

---

[17] An alternative procedure would be to hold the income distribution fixed while conducting the decomposition for demographic influences. But one would have to pick a particular income distribution at which to evaluate the demographic effects in that case. We should also stress that the participation rates we calculate on the basis of these demographic-economic groups are not comparable to those calculated in the past literature, which attempt to define eligibility more narrowly by using the actual benefit formulas and rules in each program together with household economic and other characteristics. Our participation rates represent a combination of eligibility and take-up rates conditional on eligibility.

[18] The definition of Medicaid "participation" is somewhat ambiguous in the CPS because the question asks whether families are "covered" by the program. In all likelihood, families are answering the question by interpreting the question not to mean eligibility, but rather to mean having used Medicaid services. Nevertheless, some families may be answering it the other way.

Table 9.2. *Welfare Participation Rates by Demographic Group, 1994–96 (percent)*

Household Type	AFDC	Food Stamps	Medicaid
With children			
Married	3.8	7.6	5.2
Female, never married	49.2	60.0	58.0
Female, divorced-widowed-separated	23.7	35.1	29.8
Male, unmarried	9.8	18.7	10.4
Without children			
Married	0.6	1.9	2.0
Female, never married	5.0	11.3	9.9
Female, divorced-widowed-separated	4.2	10.2	9.1
Male, unmarried	2.5	6.8	5.9

Note: Participation rate is percentage of all U.S. households in each subgroup receiving income in prior year from program in question.

Source: Author's tabulations from pooled 1994, 1995, and 1996 March CPS files.

received food stamps, for example, and many households without children did so as well. Medicaid receipt is also high among several groups for whom AFDC participation is considerably lower.[19]

Table 9.3 shows changes in population shares and AFDC participation rates for selected population subgroups between the late 1960s and mid-1990s. Among households headed by never-married women with children, for example, AFDC participation rates were either unchanged over the period or rose slightly, as did the participation rates of households headed by divorced, widowed, or separated women with children. Their shares in the population rose tremendously, however, particularly for households headed by never-married women, whose population shares rose by factors of 6, 7, or 8. The table also shows the trends in popula-

[19] Some of the entries in Table 9.2 with positive participation rates, for example, those for households without children receiving AFDC, may seem unusual, but it is possible that someone else in the household other than the head is eligible for benefits. Note also that cohabiting couples are not classified as married in the CPS and may also be eligible for benefits.

Table 9.3. *Changes in Population Shares and AFDC Participation Rates,*
Selected Groups and Income Levels, 1968–70 to 1994–96

Household Type and Nonwelfare Income, 1994–96 (dollars)	Share of U.S. Population (%)		AFDC Participation Rate (%)	
	1968–70	1994–96	1968–70	1994–96
Never-married women with children				
0	0.15	0.95	88.8	88.0
1–5,000	0.13	1.08	68.9	75.3
5,001–10,000	0.08	0.76	36.2	47.5
Divorced, widowed, and separated women with children				
0	0.68	0.73	80.5	83.8
1–5,000	0.99	1.30	57.4	63.4
5,001–10,000	0.90	1.35	26.2	34.7
Unmarried men with children				
0	0.02	0.09	50.0	60.3
1–5,000	0.04	0.20	16.7	35.8
5,001–10,000	0.05	0.26	17.1	21.6

Notes: Nonwelfare income is annual average for period. Participation rate is percentage of subgroup.

Source: Author's tabulations from CPS files.

tion shares of a much smaller group, unmarried men with children, whose sizes also rose, but by smaller amounts. The rise in population shares of the male-headed households is a rough indicator of the decline of wage rates at the lower part of the skill distribution.

Table 9.4 shows decompositions of the change in real AFDC expenditure per capita between the late 1960s and mid-1990s and demonstrates the contribution of demographic influences to that growth, the main goal of the analysis. Decompositions are shown for different types of weighting, which essentially represent different allocations of the influence of joint contributions of the three factors to the different components. In all cases, it is clear that the rise of $14.50 in real expenditure per capita (refer back to Figure 9.2) over the period was the result of an increase in the caseload, which outweighed a decline in expenditures per recipient, a rough proxy for benefits.[20] Moreover, it is also clear that regard-

---

[20] We use the same real expenditure per recipient in all cells, which we calibrate to national expenditures per capita; that is, the average expenditure amount is calculated by dividing the participation rate into per capita national expenditure. There is no attempt to differentiate benefit levels for different types of recipients.

Table 9.4. *Decomposition of Change in Real AFDC Expenditures per Capita, 1968–70 to 1994–96*

	Weighting Type					
	(1)	(2)	(3)	(4)	(5)	(6)
Change in real AFDC expenditures per capita	$14.50	$14.50	$14.50	$14.50	$14.50	$14.50
Components (% change)						
Change in population share	27.05	27.05	26.76	39.18	38.76	38.76
Change in participation rate	7.65	11.09	7.95	11.09	11.51	7.95
Change in expenditures per recipient	−20.20	−23.63	−20.20	−35.76	−35.76	−32.19
Change in population share, income strata only (% change)	18.75	18.74	15.81	27.14	22.90	22.90
Change in population share, demographic strata only (% change)	29.92	29.92	35.57	43.33	51.51	51.51

Source: Author's tabulations from CPS files.

less of the weighting method, the change in population share was of far greater importance than the change in the participation rate. Thus a prima facie case for the importance of demographic influences in the long-run growth of expenditures is strongly established by these results.

The last two rows of the table furnish evidence on the degree to which the influence of population shares reflects changes in the inequality of nonwelfare income rather than changes in the distribution of household types. A decomposition that ignores family type altogether allocates a considerably smaller portion of the total change in expenditure to population shares, although certainly a nonzero and strongly positive portion. Decompositions based upon the change in household type alone are a much more powerful factor in explaining expenditure, up to twice as important for some forms of weighting. Thus it is clear that, while downward shifts in income were an important contributor to the rise in expenditure, they were less important than the influence of shifts in the distribution of household types.

Although the primacy of the influence of demographic shifts – mainly the rise in the percentage of unmarried women with children in the

414

population – relative to changes in the participation rate in AFDC is thus established for the long run, the relative importance of participation rate changes is considerably more important in the short run. This is illustrated in Figure 9.8, which shows the relative contributions of population shares (the lighter bars) and participation rate changes (the black bars) to growth in per capita AFDC expenditure over four-year periods.[21] That both bars are positive in both the early and late periods reflects the positive growth of the caseload in the late 1960s and early 1970s, on the one hand, and the late 1980s and early 1990s, on the other. That the two bars sum to a much smaller total in the years in between reflects the relative stability of caseload growth then. More important, the figure demonstrates that participation rates have gone through a long-term cycle of strong growth in the early years, followed by negative growth in the middle period, followed by positive growth again in the later period. The net result is participation rates that are somewhat higher in the mid-1990s than they were in the late 1960s, but not by a large amount. The influence of population shares, on the other hand, has been more consistently strong and positive throughout the entire period of almost thirty years. It was the growth of female-headed households in the 1970s and early 1980s that kept the caseload from falling in the face of declining participation rates, for example. But it is also true that in the two major welfare growth periods, the late 1960s and the late 1980s, growth of participation rates was essentially equal in importance to that of demographic and other population share influences (including declines in income). Thus in the relatively short run, participation rate changes are much more important relative to population share influences than in the long run. No doubt this is largely a result of short-run fluctuations in welfare policy, as well as short-run fluctuations in the economy and in potential wage rates off welfare relative to benefits available on welfare, which tend to drive eligibles onto and off the rolls.

Table 9.5 shows long-run decompositions for AFDC expenditure by race, as well as decompositions for Food Stamps and Medicaid. Interestingly, major black-white differences appear in the change in real expenditure per capita. While real AFDC expenditure per capita has grown by a moderately large amount for the white population, such expenditures have fallen drastically for the black population. The sharp decline of expenditures on the black population is a result of the greater

---

[21] Each year denoted in the figure represents the midpoint of a four-year interval. Thus "1971" represents the pooled years 1969–1972, "1975" represents the pooled years 1973–1976, and so on.

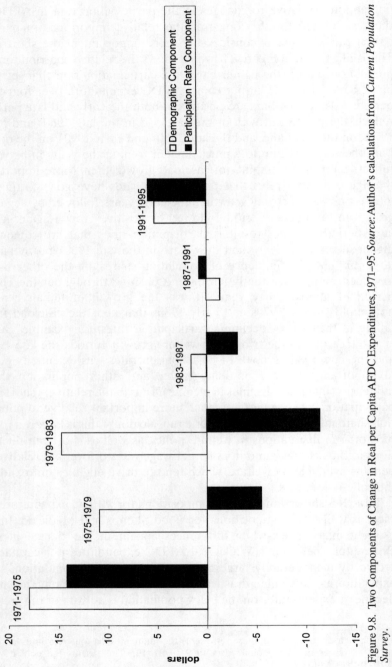

Figure 9.8. Two Components of Change in Real per Capita AFDC Expenditures, 1971–95. *Source:* Author's calculations from *Current Population Survey.*

Table 9.5. *Decomposition of Change in AFDC Expenditures by Race, Food Stamps Expenditures, and Medicaid Expenditures*

	AFDC, 1968–70 to 1994–96		Food Stamps, 1981–84 to 1993–96	Medicaid, 1889–92 to 1993–96
	White	Black		
Change in real benefits per capita	$16.9	–$51.8	$15.5	$29.0
Components (% change)				
Change in population share	20.9	48.3	2.6	5.7
Change in participation rate	9.3	–15.8	7.3	15.8
Change in expenditures per recipient	–13.3	–84.2	5.7	7.5
Change in population share, income strata only	14.4	19.6	0.3	6.5
Change in population share, demographic strata only	20.7	87.8	9.5	4.6

Note: Weighting method (1) used.

Source: Author's tabulations from CPS files.

participation rates and population shares of welfare-eligible groups in the black population: a greater participation rate (which implies a greater weight in the decomposition) means that any given decline in benefit levels has a much larger impact on aggregate expenditure on the group in question and hence on national expenditure per capita. Compounding the influence of this force has been a decline in participation rates among the black population, as compared to a increase in participation rates among whites over the period.

In any case, however, the influence of demographic factors is vastly stronger for the black than for the white population. When demographic factors alone are considered (last row of the table), black demographic shifts exerted a strong positive influence on caseloads and hence on expenditures. The influence of income inequality growth, while positive, was much less important. For the white population, on the other hand, changes in population shares were, as for the total population, more important than changes in participation rates in contributing to expenditure growth, but not nearly so much as for the black population. These

417

relative comparisons are consistent with the greater growth of female-headed households over the period in question in the black population as compared to the white.[22]

The last two columns of Table 9.5 show decompositions for the Food Stamps and Medicaid programs for the periods for which CPS data provide consistently defined measures of household receipt. In both cases, the results show a much stronger contribution to growth by participation rate influences and a smaller contribution by population share and demographic influences than for AFDC. For the Food Stamps program, for example, growth in expenditures per capita from the early 1980s to the mid-1990s was primarily a result of increases in participation rates and secondarily of growth in expenditures per recipient; population share influences were third in importance. The secular growth of participation rates in the Food Stamps program, referred to earlier, is consistent with this finding; participation rates for this program have not shown the major, long-run cyclical pattern of those for AFDC. This, in turn, may be a simple result of the fact that real Food Stamps benefits have not declined, unlike the AFDC benefits.[23] The broader population base and coverage of the Food Stamps program may, in turn, be responsible for the lesser importance of demographic factors in contributing to caseload and expenditure growth.

A decomposition for the Medicaid program can be conducted only for the most recent period, from the late 1980s to the early 1990s. Expenditures per capita grew strongly during this period, and the table shows that increases in participation rates among the population groups was by far the most important contributor to that growth. This growth largely reflects the expansions of program eligibility over the period, which brought many new non-AFDC population groups into the program. Growth in expenditures per recipient is second in importance, and changes in the population share distribution is the least important factor, as in the Food Stamps program. This is somewhat more surprising for Medicaid, which is not so universal in eligibility as the Food Stamps

[22] In addition to race, the AFDC decompositions were broken out by the age of the household head. Adding age strata to the demographic and income strata changed the relative importance of population share and participation rate influences very little. This result is largely a consequence of the strong age correlation of the demographic categories, particularly for never-married and divorced-widowed-separated, which already capture the major influences of changes in the age structure over the 1970s and 1980s. Once these trends are captured, additional age-related compositional shifts have little additional role to play.

[23] As noted earlier, the elimination of the purchase requirement (EPR) also exerted upward pressure on Food Stamps participation rates, but the periods shown in the table are largely after the influence of the EPR had worked itself out.

program, and may be partly the result of examining only a relatively short time frame, over which demographic factors did not have a chance to change in a major way.

Demographic Feedback Loops

Given the strong long-run influence of demographic factors on expenditure growth, at least for the AFDC program, it is natural to ask whether there is likely to have been any feedback from the caseloads, benefit levels, or expenditures of the program to the growth of female-headed households in the United States in the first place.[24] The major source of research evidence on the strength of the association between AFDC and female-headed households is the rather old but sizable research literature on this issue. It is fair to say that the research findings from the literature are quite dispersed (see Moffitt [1992, 1998] and Hoynes [1997] for reviews). There is quite noticeable evidence of welfare effects in cross-sectional data: female headship rates, out-of-wedlock birthrates, and other outcomes of relevance are significantly correlated with welfare benefits in cross-section, and do not appear to go away when other differences (at least at the individual level) are controlled for. Models with state "fixed effects" – that is, a set of state-specific dummy variables – which compare changes in female headship rates across states with different growth rates of benefits, generally find smaller correlations, although there are exceptions to this generalization as well. The evidence that is available is consistent with the existence of a true but weak effect, which is difficult to detect amid the myriad other factors that are affecting demographic behavior of the low-income population – such as the growth of female wages, the decline of male incomes, and the decline of the male-female sex ratio in some low-income populations – and which is not robust to changes in specification. Nevertheless, there is a rough consensus in the literature that welfare benefits do indeed have a significant effect on family structure, but that its magnitude is not large, or at least has not been shown convincingly to be so thus far.

What is less in dispute is that, regardless of the cross-sectional effect of welfare on family structure, it is difficult to explain the time series increase in female headship and out-of-wedlock birthrates with welfare

---

[24] Feedback loops could also exist in earnings, which are affected by benefit levels working through labor supply, and in benefit levels themselves, which respond through the political process to changes in caseloads and expenditures. Note that if benefit levels respond to changes in demographics – for example, changes in the number of female-headed households – through the political process, then the role of demographics is even larger than what the decompositions in the last section imply.

benefits. Figures 9.5 and 9.6 showed female headship rates to have grown steadily, divorce rates to have risen and then flattened out, and out-of-wedlock birthrates to have jumped in the 1980s. None of these patterns even roughly coincides with the time series pattern of AFDC benefits, which have declined secularly at a steady pace. Of course, other things have been going on, one of which is a decline in real wage rates at the bottom of the skill distribution, and this has attenuated the importance of the decline in welfare benefits; nevertheless, wage rates have not fallen as much as the benefit, and the benefit-wage ratio has consequently still declined, so it is difficult to make the argument that welfare has become an even more attractive option over the last ten or twenty years because of the wage decline. To say that female headship rates have been forced upward by other factors, which have been occurring simultaneously with the benefit decline, is not to say that benefits have had no effect, but is only to say that female headship rates might have increased even faster in the absence of the benefit decline. However, it does imply that the source of the increase in headship rates has to be sought elsewhere.

Another body of relevant evidence is the demographic literature, which seeks to determine whether the increase in female headship is more a result of a decline in marriage rates, rather than an increase in fertility rates (outside of marriage). That the major force behind the growth of nonmarital childbearing might be a decline in marriage, and might have little or nothing to do with fertility, is suggested by the time series trends in fertility, which show secularly declining childbearing rates for the whole population, including women with less education, for many years. It is quite possible that the rise of nonmarital childbearing is not the result, therefore, of any increase in overall fertility, but rather that an increasing share of a declining volume of births is occurring outside of marriage because marriage rates themselves have declined.

Trends in nonmarital fertility can be decomposed into components due to declines in marriage and rises in nonmarital fertility (Smith et al., 1996). Such a decomposition demonstrates that a decline in marriage rates is indeed the most important single component overall, at least for the period since 1975, and especially for the black population. An increase in the birthrates of unmarried women, especially for the white population, has played an important secondary role, however. These decompositions were not conducted for the low-income population per se and hence are not as directly relevant to the issues of concern of this chapter as they could be. Nevertheless, they do suggest that a decline in the return, or gains, to marriage, particularly in the low-income population, may be an alternative explanation for the rise in female headship, rather than the welfare system or other policy forces.

Projections to 2050

For the purposes of this volume, it is useful to ask whether demographic influences in the future will continue to exert their strong, dominant influence on AFDC expenditures as they have in the past and whether those influences will continue to be weak or will grow stronger for the Food Stamps and Medicaid programs. Unfortunately, any exercise of this kind must be heavily qualified because it requires conditioning on fixed participation rates and benefit levels, and there is considerable reason to think these may differ considerably in the future from what they are now. The recent 1996 federal legislation replacing the AFDC program with the TANF program changed the program in fundamental ways, which will, in the short run, reduce expenditures per recipient and expenditures per capita by a large amount. Whether these reductions will be reversed in the future or will be permanent is impossible to reliably forecast at the present time. The provisions of the legislation also have led to significant reductions in participation rates in TANF, abetted by a strong economy, introducing further uncertainty into the future course of participation rates.

A further problematic factor in projections of the influence of demographic factors is the lack of reliable forecasts of the future course of female-headed households. Such forecasts would require a joint forecast of marital status and fertility trends, which would be extremely tentative given our rather rudimentary understanding of the structural causes of past trends in female headship. Yet because female headship is such a critical element in establishing eligibility for AFDC TANF, as well as Food Stamps and Medicaid, projections that assume headship rates to be fixed are especially subject to uncertainty.

With these caveats, however, population projections for the age, race, and sex composition of the U.S. population furnish a basis for projecting the changes in welfare expenditures that would result from these basic demographic forces, if nothing else changed. Using the CPS to construct population shares for thirty-two age-race-sex demographic groups (five-year age categories, starting at 15–19 and ending at 50–54, plus blacks and whites and men and women) and AFDC, Food Stamps, and Medicaid participation rates and expenditures per recipient for each group in the mid-1990s, we can compute mean expenditures per capita in those years on an individual, rather than household, basis. Holding the participation rates and benefit levels constant, but changing the population shares to match those in Census Bureau forecasts to 2050 (U.S. Department of Commerce, 1997), yields a projection of the change in real expenditures per capita.

Table 9.6. *Projections of Real per Capita Expenditures to 2050 (dollars)*

	AFDC	Food Stamps	Medicaid
1993–96	82.48	83.48	110.46
2050	93.22	93.23	122.83

Sources: Author's calculations from CPS files and Bureau of the Census population projections.

The results of this exercise for the three transfer programs are shown in Table 9.6. As the table shows, the population share changes forecast by the Census Bureau imply positive – but relatively small by historical standards – increases in real expenditure. Inspection of the changes in population shares from 1995 to 2050 reveals that this growth is almost entirely the result of the projection of considerably faster growth of the black population than of the white population. While the age distribution of both populations changes slightly – shares at the younger ages grow somewhat, and shares at the later ages decline (recall that an upper cutoff of age 54 is used, so the growth in the elderly does not influence these projections) – shares of the black population at all ages, young and old, increase, and those of the white population decline. Given the much higher participation rates of the black population than of the white population, even though the gap is narrowing, the increase in the black population share results in the increases in expenditure shown in Table 9.6. However, as noted previously and as can be seen in Figure 9.2, the magnitudes of the changes are quite modest compared to the magnitudes of expenditure changes in the programs experienced over the past thirty years. Thus it is fair to characterize these projections as showing that basic age-race-sex demographic forces will have, at best, only a modest influence on future welfare expenditures (holding constant the factors previously noted).[25]

[25] It is important to note that these basic age-race-sex demographic forces have not had an influence in the past thirty years either. When only age, race, and sex are used to represent demographic influences in a decomposition of real AFDC expenditures per capita from the late 1960s to the mid-1990s, the influence of demographics is, in fact, negative. This is because the aging of the baby boom cohorts has shifted the age distribution toward middle ages and away from young ages, where welfare participation rates are the highest. Thus, just as in the past, it has been the trend in female headship that has been the demographic influence of importance, so it will be in the future, if demographic influences continue to be important.

Summary and Conclusions

The analysis in this chapter has suggested that trends in real per capita AFDC expenditures over the last thirty years have been, on net, primarily a result of shifts in demographic influences rather than of shifts in participation rates conditional on population shares or of average expenditures per recipient. While prior work on the welfare growth of the late 1960s and early 1970s suggested that it was increases in the conditional participation rate that was primarily responsible for AFDC caseload growth, the analysis here shows that the long-term rise in expenditures is instead primarily demographic in nature. These conclusions do not apply to the Food Stamps and Medicaid programs, however, where eligibility is more broadly based among different demographic groups and where programmatic changes, as well as changes in participation rates, have dominated demographic influences.

The two periods of growth of U.S. real per capita welfare expenditures illustrate the nature of the problem facing the government. Expenditure growth occurred in the late 1960s and early 1970s and then again in the late 1980s and early 1990s. The period in between was a stable period in which per capita expenditures grew very little. Both growth periods were a surprise to policy makers. The welfare explosion of the late 1960s and early 1970s was a major event in welfare policy, which had significant political repercussions, and can be plausibly argued to have led to the reaction of the 1970s, in which retrenchment was the norm. The jump in both rolls and expenditures in the late 1980s and early 1990s was also unexpected and once again led to a reaction, which can also be plausibly argued to have contributed to the retrenchment that has recently occurred. Whether better forecasting of demographic trends, or other allowances for uncertainty, can be used in a way that will reduce the amplitude of the surprise-reaction-retrenchment cycle in welfare policy remains to be seen but should be a major policy goal.

References

Blank, Rebecca. 1997a. *It Takes a Nation.* New York: Russell Sage Foundation.
   1997b. What Causes Public Assistance Caseloads to Grow? Mimeographed. Evanston, IL: Northwestern University.
Boland, Barbara. 1973. Participation in the Aid to Families with Dependent Children Program. In *Studies in Public Welfare – The Family, Poverty, and Welfare Programs.* Paper No. 12, Part 1. U.S. Congress, Joint Economic Committee, Subcommittee on Fiscal Policy. Washington, DC: U.S. Government Printing Office.

Burke, Vee. 1995. *Cash and Noncash Benefits for Persons with Limited Income: Eligibility Rules, Recipient and Expenditure Data, FYs 1992–1994.* Washington, DC: Congressional Research Service.

Burtless, Gary. 1994. Public Spending on the Poor: Historical Trends and Economic Limits. In *Confronting Poverty*, ed. Sheldon Danziger, Gary Sandefur, and Daniel Weinberg. Cambridge, MA: Harvard University Press.

Cody, Scott, and Carole Trippe. 1997. Trends in FSP Participation Rates: Focus on August 1995. Mathematica Policy Research and USDA Food and Consumer Services, Washington, DC.

Gabe, Thomas. 1992. Demographic Trends Affecting AFDC Caseload Growth. Mimeographed, Congressional Research Service, Washington, DC.

Gruber, Jon. 1997. Policy Watch: Medicaid and Uninsured Women and Children. *Journal of Economic Perspectives* 11:199–208.

Hoynes, Hilary. 1997. Work, Welfare, and Family Structure: What Have We Learned? In *Fiscal Policy: Lessons from Economic Research*, ed. Alan Auerbach. Cambridge, MA: MIT Press.

Michel, Richard. 1980. *Participation Rates in the Aid to Families with Dependent Children Program*, Part I, *National Trends from 1967 to 1977*. Washington, DC: Urban Institute.

Moffitt, Robert. 1986. Trends in AFDC Participation over Time: Evidence on Structural Change. Special Report No. 41, Institute for Research on Poverty, Madison, WI.

———. 1992. Incentive Effects of the U.S. Welfare System: A Review. *Journal of Economic Literature* 30:1–61.

———. 1993. An Economic Model of Welfare Stigma. *American Economic Review* 73:1023–35.

———. 1998. The Effect of Welfare on Marriage and Fertility. In *Welfare, the Family, and Reproductive Behavior*, ed. Robert Moffitt. Washington, DC: National Academy Press.

———. 1999. Explaining Welfare Reform: Public Choice and the Labor Market. *International Tax and Public Finance* 6:289–315.

Moffitt, Robert, Robert Reville, and Anne Winkler. 1994. State AFDC Rules Regarding the Treatment of Cohabitors: 1993. *Social Security Bulletin* 57:26–33.

———. 1998. Beyond Single Mothers: Cohabitation and Marriage in the AFDC Program. *Demography* 35:259–78.

Moffitt, Robert, David Ribar, and Mark Wilhelm. 1998. The Decline of Welfare Benefits in the U.S.: The Role of Wage Inequality. *Journal of Public Economics* 68:421–52.

Ohls, James, and Harold Beebout. 1993. *The Food Stamp Program: Design Tradeoffs, Policy, and Impacts*. Washington, DC: Urban Institute.

Smith, Herbert, S. Phillip Morgan, and T. Koropeckyj-Cox. 1996. A Decomposition of Trends in the Nonmarital Fertility Ratios of Blacks and Whites in the United States, 1960–1992. *Demography* 33:141–51.

U.S. Congressional Budget Office. 1993. *Forecasting AFDC Caseloads, with an*

Emphasis on Economic Factors. Washington, DC: U.S. Government Printing Office.

U.S. Department of Commerce, Bureau of the Census. 1996. *Statistical Abstract of the United States: 1996.* Washington, DC: U.S. Government Printing Office.

——— 1997. *Population Projections of the United States by Age, Sex, and Hispanic Origin: 1995 to 2050.* Current Population Report P25-1130. Washington, DC: U.S. Government Printing Office.

U.S. Department of Health and Human Services. 1995. *Report to Congress on Out-of-Wedlock Childbearing.* Washington, DC: U.S. Government Printing Office.

U.S. House of Representatives. 1996. *Background Material and Data on Programs within the Jurisdiction of the Committee on Ways and Means.* Washington, DC: U.S. Government Printing Office.

U.S. Social Security Administration. 1991. *Annual Statistical Supplement to the Social Security Bulletin, 1991.* Washington, DC: U.S. Government Printing Office.

——— 1997. *Annual Statistical Supplement to the Social Security Bulletin, 1997.* Washington, DC: U.S. Government Printing Office.

Comment

DAVID CARD

Robert Moffitt argues that trends in U.S. public assistance expenditures from the late 1960s to the mid-1990s have been driven by "demographic" factors, particularly the rise in the fraction of households headed by single women. The evidence for this conclusion derives from a simple accounting identity that expresses mean welfare benefits per capita for a demographic group as the product of an annual welfare participation rate and a conditional mean level of benefits among participants. For the country as a whole, mean welfare benefits per capita are a weighted average of per capita benefits among each group, leading to Moffitt's equation (1). Over time, one can therefore decompose the change in per capita benefits into a component due to shifting weights, another due to shifting participation rates, and a third due to changes in the mean levels of benefits received by participants. As is well known from the wage discrimination literature (e.g., Oaxaca, 1974), there is no unique way to perform such a decomposition. Moffitt presents six variants, which give similar answers with respect to the trend in AFDC/TANF spending per capita (Table 9.4). Had benefit levels per participant remained constant, the changing shares of different household types (married, female never-married head, female divorced/separated head, male head) would have led to a substantially larger increase in benefits than actually occurred. This rise was offset by reductions in average benefits per participant, presumably driven by the secular decline in AFDC/TANF benefit rates.[1] Thus, demographic changes "explain" *well over 100 percent* of the trend rise in AFDC/TANF benefits per capita over the past thirty years.

---

[1] Annual benefits per participant will also change if there is some change in the distribution of months of benefit receipt among those who receive at least some benefits in a year.

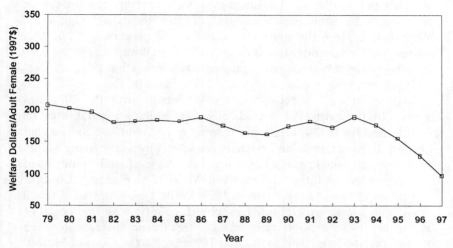

Figure 9-1.1. Average Welfare Expenditures per Adult Female, United States.

In this comment, I expand on Moffitt's provocative analysis in two directions. First, I use a slightly different data set to examine very recent trends in welfare expenditures. Welfare participation rates have plummeted in the past four years, leading to a rather different impression than does Moffitt's analysis, which stops in 1995. Second, I pick up on a very interesting finding in Moffitt's paper regarding differential trends in welfare expenditures by race.

Recent Trends in Welfare Expenditure

In the early 1990s, many states began experimenting with welfare reforms under waivers granted through the Aid to Families with Dependent Children (AFDC) program (see Blank, 1997, for a discussion of these reforms). The pace of welfare reform accelerated across the country with the passage of the Personal Responsibility and Work Opportunity Reconciliation Act of 1996, which replaced AFDC with the new TANF (Temporary Assistance to Needy Families) grant system and removed many constraints on state welfare policy design (see Gais and Nathan, 1998). Welfare reforms, coupled with the extraordinarily strong economic climate of the late 1990s, have led to dramatic declines in welfare caseloads. This trend is illustrated in Figure 9-1.1, which shows mean annual AFDC/TANF benefits received per capita by all adult women in the United States.[2] This series is not exactly comparable to

427

Moffitt's, because he also considers male welfare recipients and divides his receipts by total population (rather than the adult population). Nevertheless, given the small fraction of single male fathers and their modest welfare participation rates, trends in welfare receipts by adult women presumably track per capita expenditures rather closely.

Consistent with Moffitt's Figure 9.4, the data in Figure 9-1.1 show little trend in welfare receipts per adult female over the 1979–1994 period. In the post-1994 period, however, welfare expenditures fell sharply, and by 1997 receipts per woman were about one-half of their 1994 level. These trends have been driven in part by a drop in the welfare participation of single mothers: the fraction of single female family heads with dependent children who received AFDC/TANF dropped from 31 percent in 1993 to 19.2 percent in 1997. While I have not tried to calculate per capita expenditures exactly, I believe that the post-1993 decline in welfare receipts more or less offset the net increase in expenditure from the late 1960s to the mid-1990s that is the focus of Moffitt's chapter.[3] Thus, if his analysis had run to 1997, there would have been little or no trend in national AFDC/TANF expenditures per capita to decompose.[4]

National trends in welfare spending mask important differences at the state or regional level that could be used to examine the relative importance of demographic versus other factors in explaining trends in welfare expenditure. Figure 9-1.2 presents data on welfare expenditures per adult female in four of the nine regions of the country.[5] In the late 1970s three of these regions – the Middle Atlantic (New York, New Jersey, Pennsylvania), East North Central (Michigan, Wisconsin, Ohio, Indiana, Illinois), and Pacific (Washington, Oregon, California, Alaska, Hawaii) regions – had roughly similar expenditure levels, while expenditures per female were only about one-third as high in the South Atlantic region (Delaware, Maryland, D.C., Virginia, West Virginia, North and South

[2] These are derived from the March *Current Population Survey* (CPS). Comparisons of national totals of benefit amounts suggest that the CPS questionnaire undercounts welfare income by as much as 20–30 percent; this should be kept in mind in interpreting CPS welfare data.

[3] From 1979–1981 to 1997, real AFDC/TANF expenditures per adult female fell by about 50 percent (from $202 in 1997 dollars per adult female in 1979–1981 to $97 in 1997). A similar proportional decline in expenditures per capita would imply a 1997 level about equal to the level in the mid-1960s (see Moffitt's Figure 9.2).

[4] Expenditures on food stamps have not declined nearly as rapidly as those on AFDC/TANF. In 1979–1981, 9 percent of adult women lived in households that received Food Stamps. In 1997, this fraction was 8 percent.

[5] The regions not shown in the figure are New England, West North Central, East South Central, West South Central, and Mountain. Levels and trends for the East South Central and West South Central regions are very similar to those in the South Atlantic region.

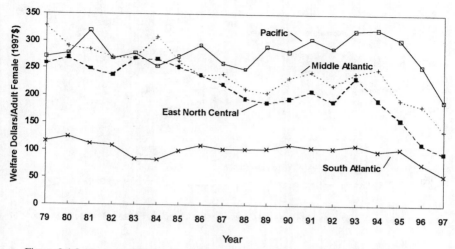

Figure 9-1.2. Average Welfare Expenditures per Adult Female, Four Selected Regions.

Carolina, Georgia, Florida). During the 1980s and early 1990s, expenditure trends in the four regions were quite different, with relative stability in the South Atlantic region, modest growth in the Pacific region, and declines in the Mid-Atlantic and East North Central regions. Since the mid-1990s, expenditures have fallen dramatically in all regions, but at different rates.[6] The variation in spending trends at the regional level (and the even greater variability at the state level) suggest that future research could profitably focus on the subnational level and attempt a more structurally oriented decomposition of the sources of these trends.

Trends by Race

One of the most interesting results that emerges from Moffitt's analysis of national data is the difference in trends in welfare expenditure between whites and blacks (see Table 9.5). Moffitt reports that over the 1968–1970 to 1994–1996 period welfare expenditures for whites rose, while those for blacks declined substantially. Figure 9-1.3 and Table 9-1.1 provide more information on the differential racial trends in welfare receipts per adult female. I have broken the population into three groups: white non-Hispanics, nonwhite non-Hispanics, and Hispanics.

---

[6] The change from 1992–1994 to 1997 was –47 percent nationally, –43 percent in the Mid-Atlantic region, –54 percent in the East North Central region, –48 percent in the South Atlantic region, and –39 percent in the Pacific region.

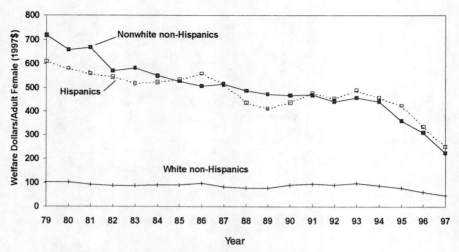

Figure 9-1.3. Average Welfare Expenditures per Adult Female By Race.

For simplicity, I will refer to these groups as "whites," "nonwhites," and "Hispanics."

Figure 9-1.3 shows trends in expenditures per adult woman in the three groups. In the late 1970s and early 1980s, expenditures per woman were about six to seven times higher for nonwhites than for whites and slightly lower for Hispanics than for nonwhites. During the 1980s and early 1990s, expenditures for whites were stable, while those for nonwhites and Hispanics trended downward. From the early 1990s to 1997, welfare receipts of all three groups have declined by roughly the same percentage.[7] In terms of *dollars* of spending, however, it is clear that a disproportionate share of the reductions in welfare expenditures have come from reductions in welfare receipt by nonwhites and Hispanics.

This is illustrated by the decompositions in Table 9-1.1, which reports some descriptive data for adult women in 1979–1981 and 1997, along with changes in average welfare benefits received per capita, changes in the welfare participation rate, and changes in average benefits received per participant. In the bottom rows of the table, I report a decomposition of

[7] Average AFDC receipts per woman in 1979–1981 were $100, $682, and $583 (in 1997 dollars) for whites, nonwhites, and Hispanics, respectively. The respective averages in 1992–1994 were $92 (a decline of 8 percent), $447 (a decline of 35 percent), and $467 (a decline of 20 percent). Receipts per adult women in 1997 were $47 for whites (a decline of 49 percent from 1992–1994), $224 for blacks (a decline of 50 percent), and $253 for Hispanics (a decline of 46 percent from 1992–1994).

Comment

Table 9-1.1. *Decomposition of Change in per Capita Welfare Benefits Received by Adult Women, 1979–81 versus 1997*

	All	Non-Hispanics White	Non-Hispanics Nonwhite	Hispanics
1979–81 data				
Percent of adult females	100.0	81.7	13.2	5.1
Percent with children	46.8	43.1	61.3	67.7
Percent dual heads	55.3	58.5	37.2	52.0
Percent single heads	11.4	8.6	25.9	17.0
Percent live alone	16.7	17.6	14.5	8.9
Average welfare (1997$)	201.6	100.2	681.2	581.1
Percent received welfare	3.4	1.7	11.5	8.1
Average benefit among recipients (1997$)	6,014.3	5,748.7	5,942.1	7,191.8
Percent received Food Stamps	8.9	5.3	27.1	19.4
Mean weeks of work	23.4	23.7	22.7	20.6
1997 data				
Percent of adult females	100.0	73.7	16.7	9.6
Percent with children	42.8	38.0	52.8	61.4
Percent dual heads	51.1	55.2	35.1	48.2
Percent single heads	13.9	10.1	27.7	19.4
Percent live alone	20.5	22.2	18.2	11.9
Average welfare (1997$)	96.6	47.1	224.3	253.0
Percent received welfare	2.4	1.3	5.6	5.7
Average benefit among recipients (1997$)	3,996.7	3,705.7	4,020.4	4,443.3
Percent received Food Stamps	7.9	4.8	16.6	16.5
Mean weeks of work	28.3	28.7	28.6	24.7
Change in average welfare (1997$)	−105.0	−53.1	−456.9	−328.1
Change in participation rate (Percent)	−0.9	−0.5	−5.9	−2.4
Change in average benefit among recipients (1997$)	−2,017.6	−2,043.0	−1,921.6	−2,748.6
Percent of total change explained by:[a]				
Change in participation	53.1	15.1	32.1	5.9
Change in benefits received by participants	46.8	20.8	17.9	8.0
Total of both components	100.0	36.0	50.0	13.9

Note: Based on females age 16 and older in March CPS.

[a] Decomposition uses 1979–81 population shares and average weighting method; see text.

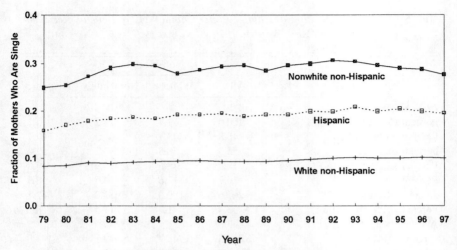

Figure 9-1.4. Female Headship Rates By Race.

the net $105 change in real welfare spending per woman across the three groups into changes in participation and changes in benefits per recipient.[8] This decomposition uses the 1979–1981 population shares of the three race groups (shown in the first row of the table), which will tend to understate the contributions of nonwhites and blacks, who are a growing share of the population. Even with this method, however, 50 percent of the reduction in welfare spending is attributable to black women and 14 percent to Hispanic women, compared to their population shares of 13 and 5 percent, respectively. Across all women, about one-half of the reduction in welfare benefits per capita is attributable to a reduction in welfare participation and one-half to a reduction in benefit levels per welfare participant. Within the race groups, however, the participation effect is greater for nonwhites, while the benefit level effect is greater for whites and Hispanics. In fact, the declining welfare participation of black women accounts for 32.1 percent of the *overall* decline in welfare receipts per woman between 1979–1981 and 1997.

One possible explanation for the relatively greater decline in welfare participation rates of nonwhite women is that female headship rates have grown less for nonwhite women than for other race groups. As shown by the data in Figure 9-1.4, however, this does not seem to be true. The

<hr />

[8] The change in benefits per woman in each race group is decomposed by using an average of participation rates to weight the change in conditional benefits received per welfare participant and the average of benefit levels to weight the change in participation rates. Each of the two components is then adjusted proportionally to sum to 100 percent.

fraction of all black women who are single heads of a family with dependent children rose from 26 percent in 1979–1981 to 28 percent in 1997, versus a change from 9 to 10 percent for white women and 17 to 19 percent for Hispanic women. Another possible explanation is the geographic concentration of black women in Southern states. Welfare reductions have been as big or even bigger (in absolute and percentage terms) in Northern states as in Southern states (see, e.g., Figure 9-1.4), so this explanation also seems unlikely. A third possibility is that black women are disproportionately likely to have left welfare and entered the labor force in response to the incentives of welfare reform efforts. There is some evidence for this hypothesis: as shown in Table 9-1.1, mean weeks of work have risen more for black women than for white women between 1979–1981 and 1997. All of this relative rise is concentrated in the late 1990s.[9] Moreover, the relative rise in work activity is especially pronounced for black single mothers, whose mean weeks of work rose from 26.2 weeks in 1992–1994 to 31.2 weeks in 1997, versus a rise from 30.9 to 32.2 weeks for white single mothers and from 23.3 to 27.6 weeks among Hispanic single mothers.

Conclusions

Moffitt argues that long-run trends in welfare benefit expenditures are attributable mainly to demographic change. His conclusion is based on trends from the late 1960s to the mid-1990s. Recent changes in AFDC/TANF receipts, driven by welfare reform and the strong labor market, have been much faster than those observed in earlier periods and have reversed the net growth observed over the previous three decades. Thus, while the proportion of female-headed families has risen substantially, real welfare expenditures per capita have changed little from the late 1960s to today. The recent evidence shows that programmatic changes matter and suggests that any assessment of the relative importance of demographic factors will be different when post-1995 welfare reforms are taken into account.

References

Blank, Rebecca M. 1997. *It Takes a Nation: A New Agenda for Welfare Reform.* Princeton, NJ: Princeton University Press.

---

[9] From 1992–1994 to 1997, white women's mean weeks rose from 27.8 to 28.7, black women's mean weeks rose from 26.1 to 28.6, and Hispanic women's mean weeks rose from 22.9 to 24.7.

Gais, Thomas L., and Richard P. Nathan. 1998. *Overview Report: Implementation of the Personal Responsibility Act of 1996.* Albany, NY: Nelson A. Rockefeller Institute of Government.

Oaxaca, Ronald. 1974. Male-Female Wage Differentials in an Urban Labor Market, *International Economic Review*, 14:693–709.

CHAPTER 9-2

Comment

S. PHILIP MORGAN

My comments on Moffitt's useful chapter include a narrow technical issue, elaborations on the explanation for increases in female-headed households, and discussion of the interrelatedness of demographic problems.

A Narrow Technical Issue

Many outcomes, such as the aggregate incidence of AFDC recipiency, can be viewed as the product of two components. Typically, one component is the number or population share of the subpopulation at risk (called "composition"), and the other is the rate at which those at risk experience some event, such as receipt of AFDC. Decomposition analysis attempts to allocate responsibility for overall change between changes in composition and changes in rates. While there is much that is intuitive about decomposition, there are also inherent complexities. Given two components (here, composition and rates) and two time points (before and after the change), there will be an effect of changes in the first (with the second held constant) and a comparable effect for changes in the second. The influence of both changes simultaneously adds a residual, interaction effect. More components and more years make these interaction effects numerous, and their magnitude will vary by the year chosen as the baseline and the order in which components are introduced. Moffitt (in Table 9.4) chooses the earliest and latest time period (only two time periods) and to include six "weighting types" that allow for all possible orderings of the three components. Thus the Moffitt approach is to assign these "interaction" effects to factors in all possible ways to see if such assignments make a substantive difference. In this case, they do not; and if they did, one would be hard pressed to provide

435

a substantive explanation. Das Gupta (1993; see Smith et al. [1996] for an application) provides a method for *averaging* these different calculations, producing a single decomposition for two time periods (e.g., in Table 9.4). Equally important, the Das Gupta approach allows for year-by-year decompositions that are internally consistent. Thus the Das Gupta approach would allow construction of a time series of the *net effects* of *each* of the three components across *each* year. Such calculations make fuller use of the available data and reduce the complexity of results presented.

The Importance of Increasing Female Headship

Moffitt's chapter offers a classic demographic decomposition. Does the "inexorable growth in expenditures on entitlements" result from shifts in population composition, changed uptake rates, or increased costs per capita? As Ryder (1980, 15) has characterized methodologically similar work, "the sole justification for such a pedestrian exercise" is to describe more precisely what has changed. Perhaps "pedestrian," but careful description is crucial because it allows one to identify the dynamic components of change and to seek an explanation of them from relevant substantive domains. Demographic decomposition gives answers in terms of more proximate variables but begs additional questions.

Moffitt's descriptive task is not simple; his interest lies in the growth of spending on welfare programs. There are more than eighty such programs. Spending on each program could provide a focus; Moffitt wisely chooses to examine three major programs: AFDC, Food Stamps, and Medicaid. Potential complexity is realized since the role of demographic factors (i.e., changing population composition) varies across these programs. Moffitt focuses most attention on AFDC, and so do I.

The AFDC decomposition attributes increased costs to changes in population composition (or share), with increased participation (or uptake) rates playing a secondary role. Expenditures per recipient actually *declined*, reducing the costs of the program net of other changes. This is the "decomposition answer," but it raises three other questions: Why did family and living arrangements shift so that many more persons were eligible for AFDC? Why were there modest increases in uptake rates? Why did costs per recipient decline?

Each of these questions could provide the focus for an essay, and Moffitt only sketches the outline of possible answers. The key compositional, or demographic, shift is an increase in female-headed households. Prior work (see Wojtkiewcz, McLanahan, and Garfinkel, 1990) provides a decomposition of increasing female headship (over the period

1950–1980) into marriage, marital disruption, and childbearing decisions. Marital disruption was more important (than nonmarriage) in earlier decades compared to later ones and among whites compared to African Americans. How can this pattern of change be explained? Welfare payments themselves could be a cause (i.e., AFDC has produced an incentive for nonmariage and nonmarital childbearing). Moffitt points out that decline in AFDC benefits with time run counter to increased divorce and nonmarital-childbearing trends. Further, the best micro-level evidence suggests "a true but weak effect" of AFDC on marriage and childbearing decisions. A more promising explanation focuses on a general weakening of the institution of marriage. Increases in delayed marriage and marital disruption are not confined to lower socioeconomic groups; these changes have been pervasive. Moreover, increasing divorce for marriage cohorts shows a secular increase beginning in the nineteenth century (Preston and McDonald, 1978). Declining economic incentives to marry and to remain married are likely the fundamental causes of these pervasive shifts, but subsequent increased acceptance of nonmarriage and divorce have certainly contributed. Racial differences reflect different contemporary experiences but are also likely affected by cultural and historical continuity. Contemporary racial differences are likely "rooted in long-standing differences in family and household processes, differences that are nurtured by enduring traditions of racial separation and exclusion" (Morgan et al., 1993, 824; see also Pagnini and Morgan, 1996).

Table 9.3 shows that the increase in never-married women with children has been substantial over the study period (1968–1970 to 1994–1996). As Moffitt notes, there are demographic decompositions of changes in the nonmarital ratio, too. These studies point to declines in the proportion married, not increased fertility rates among the unmarried or declining marital fertility, as the key component of change (e.g., Smith et al., 1997). Such findings are important because much popular and policy discussion of nonmarital childbearing has a moralistic and individualistic tenor; today, people are perceived as behaving in "unacceptable ways" or "making the wrong choices," at least in comparison with previous time periods. By and large, unmarried women are not making different choices. There are just many more of them. The most relevant question for policy makers is thus why marriage is not feasible or desirable for so many.

The Interrelatedness of Demographic Problems

Demographers believe that population size and composition matter, i.e., that they impact on individual well-being and contribute to many social problems. Focusing on one aspect of population at a time might lead one to imagine the "perfect population": where people lived a long time, where individuals had all the children they wanted, where population size did not increase, and where the dependency ratio remained low. Choosing such attractive characteristics from a *smorgasbord* of options is not possible, because these demographic changes are interrelated. We are faced with choosing clusters of demographic characteristics, a *basket*. The central concern of this conference, the aging of the population, provides an example. Twenty-five years ago, the mention of a demographic crisis was synonymous with concerns about overpopulation. Very rapid population growth in many newly industrializing countries coupled with moderate growth in industrialized countries raised anew the Malthusian scenario – greater populations leading to widespread impoverishment and serious environmental deterioration. Ironically, the solution to this overpopulation crisis, rapid fertility declines in much of the world, has generated another, fiscal exigencies resulting from a rapidly aging population. Falling fertility rates are the major factors producing an older population. Moreover, population aging is intensified by dramatic declines in old-age mortality. For the first time in recorded history, larger declines in mortality have occurred at older, as opposed to younger, ages. Thus this mortality decline, unlike those of the past, is contributing to an older age structure. Note that few would choose to reverse these demographic trends. Our rapidly aging population is the kind of problem one wants – it is the inevitable result of achievements desperately sought.

In the area of family/household change, the inevitability of "baskets" of characteristics is less certain, but current associations are noteworthy. Moffitt has shown that growth in AFDC expenditures can be traced to greater female headship, which in turn can be traced most directly to marital disruption and nonmarriage. The stronger substantive arguments implicate declining incentives to marry and to stay married as the key causal factors. Both sociologists and economists argue that the declining incentives for traditional marriage are inexorably connected to greater gender equality. For instance, Durkheim ([1983] 1933, 56) argued that the "sexual division of labor is the source of conjugal solidarity"; Becker (1981) agrees that traditional gender arrangements create specializations that, in turn, encourage marriage. Thus again, change on one front, i.e., greater gender equality, produces nontrivial consequences in related domains.

Substantial nonmarital fertility versus very low fertility may provide another example of linked demographic options. The United States has one of the higher fertility rates among industrialized countries. Corrected for timing shifts, the total fertility rate has hovered near the replacement level for fifteen years (Bongaarts and Feeney, 1998). Future projections of Social Security solvency depend upon this level of fertility. Elsewhere (i.e., Italy or Spain), very low fertility is a major concern, linked to future provision of care for the elderly. While it is too early to fully understand the determinants of very low fertility, a crucial contrast in the fertility of the United States and Italy/Spain is the level of nonmarital childbearing. If unmarried women in the United States bore children at the rate of unmarried Italian/Spanish women, the U.S. fertility rate would be substantially reduced, and the aging of the population would be sharply accentuated.

Lee and Miller (1990; also see Smith and Edmonston, 1997, chap. 7) provide estimates of the net contributions to public finances that individuals make over their lifetimes. These externalities of an added child are substantial and are especially large if these persons are highly educated. From this perspective, nonmarital births may represent a substantial economic asset, especially if these children can be provided with substantial human capital. Public expenditures directed at children, including AFDC, could be viewed as investments in future productivity (as opposed to consumption). If AFDC encourages higher fertility, then this could be viewed as another advantageous feature.

Thus, given increased gender equality, one might most logically consider the alternatives of low overall fertility (and little nonmarital fertility) or moderate levels of fertility (including substantial nonmarital fertility). If the later is preferred, then public expenditure on children born to unmarried women is a wise investment and not a welfare policy.

References

Becker, Gary S. 1981. *A Treatise on the Family*. Cambridge, MA: Harvard University Press.

Bongaarts, John, and Griffith Feeney. 1998. "On the Quantum and Tempo of Fertility." *Population and Development Review* 24:271–92.

Das Gupta, P. 1993. *Standardization and Decomposition of Rates: A User's Manual*. Washington, DC: U.S. Government Printing Office.

Durkheim, Emile [1893] 1933. *The Division of Labor in Society*. Reprint, London: Macmillan.

Lee, Ronald, and Tim Miller. 1990. "Population Policy and Externalities to Childbearing." *The Annals* 510:17–32.

Morgan, S. Philip, Antonio McDaniel, Andrew Miller, and Samuel Preston. 1993. "Racial Differences in Family Structure at the Turn of the Century." *American Journal of Sociology* 98:798–828.

Pagnini, Deanna, and S. Philip Morgan. 1996. "Racial Differences in Marriage and Childbearing: Oral History Evidence from the Early Twentieth Century South." *American Journal of Sociology* 101:1694–718.

Ryder, Norman B. 1980. "Components of Temporal Variations in American Fertility." In R. W. Hiorns, ed., *Demographic Patterns in Developed Societies.* London: Taylor and Francis.

Smith, Herbert L., S. Philip Morgan, and Tanya Koropeckyj-Cox. 1996. "A Decomposition of Trends in the Nonmarital Fertility Ratios of Blacks and Whites in the United States, 1960–92." *Demography* 33:141–51.

Smith, James P., and Barry Edmonston. 1997. *The New Americans: Economic, Demographic and Fiscal Effects of Immigration.* Washington, DC: National Academy Press.

Wojtkiewcz, Roger A., Sara S. McLanahan, and Irwin Garfinkel. 1990. "The Growth of Families Headed by Women." *Demography* 27:19–30.

Index

accounting, generational: as analysis of well-being, 249; limitation in dealing with, 248; to measure intergenerational distribution, 213–19; sensitivity to demographic projections, 251–2; traditional method, 217. *See also* redistribution, intergenerational

accounts, generational: before and after reform in EU member states, 232t, 233–5; calculation of, 243–4; concept of, 242–3; generational contracts in Germany, 235–7; minima, maxima, and scaled accounts of selected EU countries, 222–4; for present and future birth cohorts, 243–4; for selected EU member countries, 219–29, 249–50

activities of daily living (ADLs), 269–70, 276–7, 281–4. *See also* instrumental activities of daily living (IADLs)

age profiles: for Social Security, 42–3; of tax payments, 42

Aid to Families with Dependent Children (AFDC): case load and benefit growth (1965–95), 397, 399–401, 407; decompositions of factors contributing to change in spending, 413–15, 417–18; demographic factors, participation rates, and spending per recipient, 407–19; effect of demographic influences, 392; growth in spending for (1965–95), 396–8; trends in real per capita spending, 423; waivers for welfare reform experiments, 427. *See also* Temporary Assistance for Needy Families (TANF)

Altonji, J., 65

Auerbach, Alan, 202, 213–19

Bayo, Francisco R., 48

Becker, Gary S., 157, 438

Bell, William, 25n3

benefits: availability of U.S. Social Security, 168–9, 171–2; early eligibility for retirement benefits, 173–4; under EITC, 397, 399; under Supplemental Security Income, 397; to TANF-AFDC families under Medicaid, 402

Bergstrom, T., 103

Blank, Rebecca, 408

Boe, Carl, 31

Bohn, Henning, 78

Boland, Barbara, 407

Börsch-Supan, Axel, 188

Bureau of the Census (BC): baseline fertility projection, 69–70; fertility projections: actual, high, and low, 16; forecasts of total fertility rate (1940–2005), 14–15; range of uncertainty for OADR and TDR, 22–3

Butcher, K., 65

Caldwell, Steven B., 375

Card, D., 65

Carter, Lawrence, 25, 27–30

Congressional Budget Office (CBO), 41, 407–8; probabilistic forecasts of federal budget, 41–3

contracts, generational: in Germany, 235–7

CORSIM microsimulation model, 298; CORSIM-SSBC model, 311–38; identification and projections, 388–9; processes used in Social Security projections, 370–4; shortcomings, 375–7

Cutler, David M., 40, 103, 274, 275, 280, 288

441